David W. Folsom

Assets Unknown

HOW TO FIND MONEY YOU DIDN'T KNOW YOU HAD!

SECOND EDITION

TWO DOT PRESS
BILLINGS, MONTANA

Editor: John T. Lowry
Managing Editor: Alana L. Folsom
Research Staff: Liza Folsom and many others
Cover: Lester Zaiontz

ISBN 0-9641164-3-X

Printed in the United States of America

Second edition

To order ***Assets Unknown: How To Find Money You Didn't Know You Had*** call 1-800-286-5669.
E-mail: *assetsunknown@mcn.net*
Internet address: *http://www.mcn.net/~assetsunknown*

Dedication

This book is dedicated to my father, Willard K. Folsom, whose example I have tried to live by, whose courage I have tried to emulate.

Dad only had an 8th grade education because, while he was an eager learner, he contracted tuberculosis of the spine at the age of 11. He spent the next seven years of his life in a body cast, told by his doctor that he would never walk again, that he probably wouldn't live past 30. When he was 44, Dad went to his doctor's funeral — and then lived on until the age of 89.

During most of his life, he owned and operated Folsom's Lobster Mart in Boston. I worked there as a child. The Mart was Dad's "ministry," where he put his deep religious faith into practice by serving all comers with diligence and dedication. Among his customers he numbered the rich and famous, people like conductor Arthur Fiedler, who demanded special treatment — and got it. But Dad also extended the same courtesies to all who entered his place of business, regardless of station. For example, because there was a large immigrant population in Boston, he learned the native languages of his regulars—so he could greet them in Italian or German or French and carry on a simple conversation.

Although it was late in his life that Dad settled issues involving eternity, he spoke to me often about the way God intends us to live — serving others as we would serve Him. But mostly, Dad taught by example. Dressed in his white apron and soft felt hat, moving from day to day among his customers, smiling and cordial even when he was in pain, he made me understand that I—blessed with good health—had the responsibility to persist and to accomplish great things in my own life, not just for myself but for others as well.

I hope this book will prove useful and profitable to many, many people. If it helps those I've never met it will surely please my father.

Table of Contents

Preface

Unless you are *extremely* wealthy, I venture to guess you'd be quite pleased to open tomorrow's mail and come across a surprise check made out to you for a few hundred (or several thousand!) dollars. Am I right?

Very few people strike it rich, or even get a big boost in that direction, by playing their state lottery—Lotto, PowerBall, and all that—or by entering various sweepstakes "contests." How often has the Publisher's Clearing House van pulled up to an address in *your* neighborhood? Not many have that sort of good luck. But *everyone* has deceased or disabled relatives.

This book shows you, in great detail, how to find money which was laid aside by your forebears (or, in some cases, by you yourself) *which legally belongs to you* and which they would want you, and their other legitimate heirs, to enjoy. At the present time in this country there are **billions of dollars** available (possibly even as much as a trillion dollars), in cash, which older and deceased Americans should have kept better track of. You have every expectation of finding some of this family windfall and putting it to whatever useful purpose you want. This book tells you how.

My intention was to make this volume useful and understandable to any interested reader. While I had some years of business experience when I began looking into the hidden assets left by my own relative (cousin Rand; our story is in Chapter 1), you won't need that kind of head start to be successful in your own assets search. Whatever you require in the way of knowledge about pension plans or stocks, or of any complicated financial dealings, appears in this self-contained book. The only background you need is a *family* background; and we all have that.

Many misconceptions surround the existence of unknown assets. One is that they have mostly evaporated due to legal time limits, "statutes of limitations." Another is that the state simply and quietly absorbs them, permanently. A third is that finding and reclaiming this money that is rightfully yours is very complicated, requiring the services of an attorney. None of that "conventional wisdom" is true. Chances are overwhelming that the vast majority of your relative's unpaid insurance claims, overpaid taxes, abandoned utility deposits, forgotten pension contributions, etc., etc., are still there, waiting for you, the lawful heir, to claim. Often that money has been growing at compound interest over the years. It only takes a little work to find the funds and this book furnishes you a map for doing just that.

I have divided the book into two parts. Part One, the four chapters of text, contains both narrative accounts of actual searches and explanations showing you how to go about your own search. These two aspects work together. The case histories and anecdotes highlighting problems faced by actual persons looking for lost assets, and how they solved them, put flesh on the bare bones of informative charts, lists, and tables. Part One gives you general information on:

- How to plan your search for information about undiscovered assets;
- Which documents you need to support your search; and
- Where the money is.

Part One gives you necessary preparation and I urge you to read it before attempting to use the detailed material in Part Two.

Part Two—the more than thirty Appendices containing sample letters and forms, lists of places to seek information, and thousands of focused and cataloged names, addresses, and phone and fax numbers to contact—makes up the real nitty-gritty of the book. Each Appendix is introduced by a brief explanation of its contents. Many of the Appendices contain forms you'll need to photocopy and fill in once your assets search gets underway.

Even in the four chapters of text we have deliberately left wide margins—to accommodate your handwritten notes. Yes, this is a "workbook." But the work is not hard and the rewards, both personal and financial, are likely to be great. Have fun.

As your author, there is one more thing I ask of you besides that you use this book to successfully recover assets your relatives left behind. And that is to let me know of your experiences—both positive and negative. If you've found what you were looking for, I'd like to share in your excitement. If you've encountered a problem, perhaps I can help.

Currently, I am amassing a database even more extensive than the one I have placed in your hands—an electronic resource containing so much information that I couldn't possibly include all of it in one book.

In addition, I am fully aware that some of you may encounter special problems in dealing with state bureaucracies and large financial institutions—problems that may seem insurmountable to you. While this book, together with a lot of perseverance, should answer most questions, there may be times when special cases require extra help.

I conceived of this book as a way of reawakening the old frontier virtue of helping your neighbor, particularly in time of stress or need. I believe that if, as a people, we return to our Judeo-Christian values, we can learn to be as good to each other as we once were. In the final analysis, my success in writing this book will depend on your success in using it. May we both be successful!

David W. Folsom
Billings, Montana
July 1996

Acknowledgments

This book proved to be an arduous undertaking. I could never have completed it without the attentive and persistent efforts of my family. They spent many long days and sleepless nights gathering information and proofing the many drafts of my manuscript. This is their book as well as mine.

I am also indebted to a number of friends who helped me in a variety of ways, from giving me helpful information and critical commentary to remembering me in their prayers. In consideration of their privacy, I won't mention their names with one exception: Alana Folsom, my wife, who has stuck with me despite all my frailties and stubbornness—for 35 years.

Finally, I am grateful to the kind and often anonymous people working in government agencies and private offices who came up with the right answers to my questions.

Introduction

What you hold in your hands looks like a book. But treat it like a door—the door to your life and to your family's life—because that is what this book has been for me. Not much in it is original. There are few secrets to tell. The information you need to discover unknown assets has long been available to anyone for the asking. But few asked. I myself simply stumbled upon it, stepped through the door, and found not only unclaimed assets but something better—a story of myself, my family. And that is what I hope you'll find.

We live in a cynical age. Some persons have approached me, with smirks on their faces, saying I've hit two of the big three: sex, secrets, and money. Though some will see it that way, writing just to push "hot buttons" was not my intent. If I may change the metaphor, I've been on a journey and have simply drawn a map. This map, once you've personalized it with your family's story, can be the map to their life. You may find money. *You may also find riches that money can't buy.* In your search for hidden assets, you may come upon stories of dads and moms, uncles and aunts, who in a private moment planned for the lives of their children and their children's children. You, too, may find that *someone long ago was thinking of you.*

Solomon, the wise, said long ago: *A good man leaves an inheritance for his children's children* (Proverbs 13:22). In your search you'll find that a dad or mom took time to prepare for the future—your future. For whatever reason, their story remains hidden. You are invited to find it, enjoy it, and pass it down to your children. It is my hope that this book will **bring families closer together**. The search for hidden assets can be a family affair. For this reason I have tried to keep the book as simple as possible. Like hiking up a good mountain trail, it will require effort, but when you place one foot in front of the other it is pretty straightforward. And when you do, you will find treasures—be they money or precious memories.

While I have provided much information for you in this book, don't think it takes a genius to use it. I'm just not that smart. I often tell people that this book was more given *to* me than written *by* me. That's true. God gave it to me. I wasn't looking for it. He opened the door for me and I simply stepped through it. Now I'm inviting you to follow.

Chapter 1

From Innocence to Information

This book would never have been written had it not been for my first cousin Rand. Every family can claim at least one Rand, and some have several. The son of my father's sister, he led a sad and solitary life, traveling from place to place, settling for a while in one city, and then abruptly moving on to another. He lived in eight different states, never married—and if he made any close friends, we never heard of them. About his private life, he was deliberately vague and uncommunicative.

Sometimes we would lose touch for years. Then one day he would show up at the front door, an awkward smile on his face, his eyes signaling a desperate and unfulfilled need. He would hang around town for a few days, perhaps a week, and then—reassured by the love and attention of the family —he would strike out again and lose himself for another two or three years among the anonymous hoards of transient Americans.

My brother, who ran a restaurant in Boston, also reported periodic visits from Rand. The last time Rand showed up he was so emotionally disoriented he barely knew who he was. My brother fed him and tried to straighten him out, but Rand disappeared as abruptly and mysteriously as he had arrived.

So we were saddened but not really surprised when, in 1987, we got the news that Rand had died, at the age of 65, alone and apparently unattended, near Sacramento. My sister had been contacted by an official of North San Juan, California — located in Nevada County — who had brought up her name on a computer while conducting a search to discover if Rand had any survivors. This search had eventually led the official to records in Boston, where a Social Security number match had linked Rand's mother to our father, both of whom were deceased. "There'll be a little money for us," my sister said, "maybe a thousand apiece." But then, like so many people, we let the matter slide. Four and a half years later, Rand's name came up in a casual conversation, and I remembered the unresolved business in California.

But it wasn't really the money that made me initiate an inquiry. It was curiosity. I wanted to find out about Rand's last days. Did he really die alone as the caller had indicated? Was he living on the streets? Did he have proper hospital care? Where and by whom was he buried? I knew some of the answers might be painful, but I felt his family should know the truth.

First I called an attorney in North San Juan, a woman whose name had been mentioned by the official who first contacted my sister. This woman was cool and businesslike. The estate no longer interested her, she said, because it had so little money left in it. She told me that if I wanted to pursue the matter, I would have to do it on my own. At that point I learned the first important lesson in searching for assets: **you can get along just fine without a lawyer.**

My next call was to the County Attorney. He told me I should try the Nevada County Administrator. I ended up talking to the Assistant County Administrator and he turned out to be just the right man; he told me some of what I needed to know. First he gave me the details of Rand's end—how he had died, who had found him, what had become of his remains. It was a troubling narrative, but I wanted to hear it all.

Then I asked about Rand's assets.

"It's a good thing you called me," he said. "I'd come to the conclusion that this man's heirs weren't going to come forward. I was about to write the state of California a check for the amount of his estate and close the case."

"How much is the estate?" I asked.

"Not a lot," he said. There was a pause. "But if you scratch around, you might find some assets we've missed. Happens all the time."

Those words — spoken by one of the few thoughtful and concerned government officials I've ever talked to — started me on my quest. By the time I had investigated Rand's tangled past in California, his estate amounted to a little over $16,000. And we still hope to find three more accounts of value in his estate.

That was the second lesson I learned. **Don't ever assume assets are too small to be worth pursuing.** When we finally settled the estate, we got many times the amount we had originally expected.

Of course, Nevada County didn't just accept my claim that my sister, my brother, and I were Rand's legal heirs. The Assistant Administrator said the court would demand proof.

"What do we need?" I asked.

"Based on what I know about the relationship," he said, "I'll draw up a genealogical chart and fax it to you. What I'll need is evidence that this chart is factual. In other words, you'll have to prove that your father was your cousin's mother's brother — that they had the same parents. That means you'll also have to prove that your grandparents were married. We already know that your aunt is dead, but you'll have to prove that you father is also deceased. That means a marriage license for your grandparents, birth certificates for their children and grandchildren, and a death certificate for your father. *All certified copies*."

It sounded as though I might be collecting all these vital statistics for years. I also figured it would cost me a small fortune. (I would soon discover that tracking down assets is something a lay person can do, though I had to start from scratch and accumulate the necessary information.)

"You mentioned that you were about to write a check to the state of California," I said. "Will I have time to do all this?"

He promised that he would not close out my cousin's estate until he'd heard from me. *It didn't take nearly as long as I thought it would.* My sister, my brother, and I already had our birth certificates. And within a few weeks I had located my grandparents' marriage license in Revere, Massachusetts; a certified copy of my father's birth certificate; a certified copy of my aunt's birth certificate; and a certified copy of my cousin's birth certificate. **The total cost — $27.50.**

The County Administrator, after looking over the evidence, concluded that the three of us were in fact sole heirs to Rand's estate. In about four months we each received a check for $4300. And that was just the beginning. As a matter of fact, I'm still searching for more of Rand's assets.

The whole experience left me with the realization that most people are unprepared to do what I had done. In addition to being driven by insatiable curiosity, I had been the beneficiary of *undeserved Grace:* the Assistant County Administrator had been unusually sympathetic and helpful. Had he been unresponsive or preoccupied, I would not have known how to begin such an obscure and complicated legal process, much less to obtain results in such a short time.

Early in my search I went to the local library to find a how-to-do-it book on the subject of locating inheritances. I was shocked to find that *none existed.* Sure, the librarian gave me a long list of books on the settling of estates, but they all began with the assumption that the estate inventory was already complete.

And none of these guides had a comprehensive inventory of possible assets — a complete list of what to look for in an inheritance. The more research I conducted, the more I concluded that even lawyers and other professionals don't know all the possibilities. In many cases they don't have incentive to learn; states like California limit the amount a professional may charge for handling a small estate (i.e., under $600,000). Now I understood why the attorney had said my cousin's estate wasn't worth her time.

At this point, I decided that I would compile a list of potential assets — a list as complete as possible. Originally I was thinking only in terms of the most obvious resources: bank accounts, stocks and bonds, life insurance policies. *I soon realized, however, that assets came in all sizes and descriptions, many of them substantial.* There was unclaimed property held by the state. There were government pension funds and private pension funds, some of which had residual balances. There were IRAs and Keogh plans. There was life insurance. There were other kinds of insurance policies, including: unclaimed health insurance, homeowner's insurance (if the house of the deceased had been recently damaged or repaired), and automobile insurance (if the deceased had died or been recently injured in an accident). There were money market accounts and antiques, rental property and utility deposits, profit sharing plans and stored goods. **There were literally dozens of assets that most people never think of when they begin to settle an estate.**

By this stage in my investigation I no longer thought merely of my own private quest. I was thinking in terms of a much larger constituency, and I knew I wanted to write and publish a book instructing others on how to go about locating lost inheritances. Initially I planned to concentrate on the needs of blue-collar workers, people who weren't earning enough to hire a lawyer to conduct this kind of legal research. But the more I looked into the matter, the more I realized that I had a much wider potential audience:

- needy college students who could find money for tuition in their own families;
- widows, divorcees, and children of divorcees;
- families of sufferers from Alzheimer's disease whose loved ones might well forget where their own assets were located;
- victims of natural disasters, whose records were burned or swept away in flood waters or buried beneath tons of wreckage; and
- children of parents who moved to retirement villages and then died without making an inventory of assets and their locations.

The more I probed, the more I realized how many families needed guidance in locating assets and benefits—not just tens of thousands, as I had originally suspected, but literally millions.

For example, I was shocked to learn that **over five million people suffer from Alzheimer's disease**, and many of them experience significant lapses of memory before they come under the complete care of family members or professionals.

I also found out something else: the nation's financial institutions keep a very poor accounting of some of these assets—if they keep any records at all.

(In part, this slovenliness is the result of a general breakdown in the old-fashioned concept of service, the idea that we are all on the same team.) For example I discovered that my cousin had maintained a savings account with a small bank in Pennsylvania. It was one of many throughout the nation that had collapsed in recent years and subsequently merged with a larger institution — in this case, the Mellon Bank. When I called the chief cashier at Mellon, however, he gave me some grim news.

"We have no record of that bank's savings accounts. All we acquired were the assets. These accounts were liabilities, money invested that had to be paid back. Since the FDIC had insured these investors up to $100,000, that agency took all of the records. You'll have to call Washington."

I wasn't too happy. It was bad enough dealing with an institution the size of Mellon. Now I had to deal with the Federal Government.

But I did call. After being switched from office to office, I ended up talking to a middle manager in the agency.

"I'm sorry," he said, "but we don't keep records like that either."

"You mean you don't have a list of the people whose accounts you owe money?" I asked in disbelief.

"Not in any form that would be useful for your purposes," he told me.

I knew I had to get information on my cousin's assets. Eventually I figured a way, but I'm certain that people with less determination would have given up and simply left that portion of their inheritance in Uncle Sam's deep pockets.

In addition to the government, many highly respected private institutions also keep poor records. I tried to find out whether my cousin had owned an insurance policy and was told by the insurance industry that no comprehensive database with that information existed. If I didn't know his policy number and insurance company, I was out of luck. Again, I muddled my way through.

I soon found I was not alone in this regard. All too often, such records are lost or destroyed. People stick them in books or in cardboard boxes where they languish unremembered or are thrown out by mistake. And even when care is taken, uncontrollable and unforeseen forces sometimes intervene.

After great natural disasters—earthquakes, hurricanes, floods—65 percent of the people most directly affected lose 100 percent of their vital papers. **During hurricane Hugo, over 90,000 people lost their financial and family records** as rains poured down on exposed documents and clean-up crews bulldozed the shells of houses. Many of these victims undoubtedly gave up in the wake of such destruction and despaired of ever recovering the assets and benefits they could no longer document. And, once again, in more than a few cases the nation's great financial institutions were of no help.

I also discovered, in the course of compiling the material for this book, that hundreds of thousands of Americans who had worked for the government at various levels were unaware that they were "vested" and therefore eligible for pensions. In fact, fully 10 percent of these government workers — city employees, state employees, policemen, firemen, teachers, building inspectors — are eligible for benefits, **yet never contact their pension plan offices to claim this earned income.**

The same is true of people who are eligible for private pension plans. In many cases, those who administer pension programs make little or no effort to keep accurate, up-to-date records on eligibility.

By the time I had been tracking Rand's assets for several years and had begun to look into the way America's financial institutions operated, I had come to a depressing conclusion: **people in positions of responsibility just don't care.** Instead of trying to help people with their problems, bureaucrats were intent on wasting as little time as possible on the legitimate concerns of those they were supposed to serve. In business, if the matter didn't affect the bottom lines of their balance sheets, corporate officials couldn't care less.

Frankly, I was bewildered by this cold lack of interest. This wasn't the country I had known as a child. These weren't the people I had grown up among. They were a new breed, caught up in the machinery of enterprises so vast and complicated that, somewhere along the way, individuals like Rand and I were refined out of the picture.

Except for that Assistant County Administrator in Nevada County, California, and a few others along the way, bureaucrats I talked with were sleepy and resistant. I was taking up their time, upsetting the orderly operation of their systems. A New York City official looked up at me with a contemptuous smile and said, "Look, Buddy, you come from a little town in the middle of nowhere, so you don't know how big things are around here. *We have five different pension plans for city employees.* If you want to check all of them, fine. But I have other things to do. So get lost!"

When I came to full realization of their hostility, I was doubly determined to write this book. **If the current system was the enemy of families trying to claim their inheritance, then I would be their friend**, and it is in the spirit of friendship and a desire to restore old-fashioned American teamwork that I offer the materials that follow.

Chapter 2

You Can Find Hidden Assets

Let's Check The $$ Landscape

Look out your window. Unless you happen to be a captive in one of the concrete canyons making up America's largest cities, it's likely that green trees dot your visible landscape. But there are also green trees dotting the invisible *financial* landscape—**Money Trees**. Some of those bonanza bushes have your name (or that of one of your relatives) on them, but the labels are small and perhaps a bit faded with time. To find them and decipher them, you'll have to do some serious looking. First you must decide, quite firmly, to do just that. Next, you should consider the level of effort you are willing to undergo to find that money. The chances are great that you have been left money by one or another out-of-touch relative or loved one, but **it is up to you to find it**.

I don't want to be termed a "nattering nabob of negativity," but for a moment I'm going to sound off about a number of misconceptions many people have about inheriting lost assets. I want you to get rid of those bad vibrations right off. Some of these negative thoughts are quite reasonably based on so-called "common sense." Other self-imposed roadblocks grow out of the tendency of ordinary citizens to expect too much of government bureacracy or of business and financial institutions. We may have gotten too passive, figuring "if it were really my money, they would have located me and given it to me." Not so.

Here are some of the major misconceptions we need to let go of:

Once a person dies, assets are no longer carried in his or her name. Or, there is a statute of limitations on inheritances.

Until those assets are claimed, almost all private property is *held forever* under the name and Social Security number of the deceased owner. And often these assets earn interest and appreciate in value. Even when there are limits, those are liberal. Don't "assume away" your inheritance.

Estates must be handled by costly attorneys. Or at least by someone with a high IQ and advanced academic degrees.

A particularly knotty legal problem may require an attorney, granted. But even so nothing in law or custom requires an attorney in your search for hidden assets. It's your perfect right to look for what's yours. In addition, you will probably do better in the search than would your legal representative. Your motivation is stronger, for one thing; for another, your time is probably not as costly. Certainly the advice and information given in this book is the least expensive way to get started looking!

Estate taxes gobble up everything so there's no use looking.

Laws governing taxation of estates differ from state to state, but most small estates are not taxed at all. And the federal government doesn't tax estates worth less than $600,000.

Everything you hear from the county clerk (or other government functionary you may have contacted) is "the gospel truth."

They are fallible, as all human beings are, and they certainly don't have the personal interest in your search which you do. So they may very well give incomplete or incorrect answers to your inqueries and questions. Persevere!

Lawyers, bankers, accountants—solid professional and business persons—are *never* motivated by greed.

In my more cynical moments (and certainly when I read reports of the recent savings and loan bailouts) I believe just the very opposite. The truth lies in between; some are greedy, some are not.

Only men (or millionaires, or those engaged in big business) leave substantial assets. And those titans keep such accurate records that nothing lies undiscovered.

You'd be surprised how much money a frugal old-maid aunt, or a financially venturesome grandfather, can amass over a lifetime. Women control the bulk of the wealth in the U.S.; women outlive men and 90% of the wealth is held by persons over 60. While you would think people who have been in business would carefully plan their estates and leave good records, many do not. On the other hand, I've run across quite a few blue-collar workers who did an excellent job of making their assets accessible to their heirs.

Searching for recoverable hidden assets is too big and complicated a job for the ordinary person (like me!) to tackle.

Don't just throw yourself at this job. Calm planning, good simple records (what was said with whom about which matter, and when), and stick-to-it-ivity will win the day. Finding the money trees hidden away in the bureaucratic byways *will* take some time. But time is on your side.

This book shows you how to get the job done. It is intended to help ordinary families like yours find money they should have and, along with the money, to find out something inspiring about their forebears and their roots. The book has helped thousands of everyday people discover money and other assets that are rightfully theirs. They have simply used the book, their telephone, some stationery, and a little common sense. **I have never collected a "finder's fee" and never will. I'm not a finder; I'm a consumer advocate.**

Imagine yourself spending a few minutes on the telephone and coming up with (say) $250. Unexpectedly! I'll bet that would get your attention. Those finds have been experienced countless times by earlier readers of this book. Their success is a large part of the reward I've enjoyed by writing it. Let's now look at a few of their stories.

Success Stories

Overlooked Retirement

My own situation illustrates this point. I taught at a private liberal arts college from 1967 to 1974. When I left, the business office gave me a check for the amount of my contributions to the retirement plan. I was only 34 years old at the time and unconcerned about any further details.

I took this nice-sized check, went on about my career, and never gave another thought to that retirement program. Until 1983, that is, when I received a letter from that retirement system. My then-current address was handwritten on the envelope.

I found to my surprise that *the college's contributions* towards my retirement had not only remained in my name but had grown substantially. When I called the toll-free number given in the letter, they confirmed that I would be able to draw on that account at age 65. Even though I had lived in the same county as the college for 18 years, they had lost me!

Unclaimed Property Office

While doing research for this book, I called the Montana Unclaimed Property Office to see whether anyone in my immediate family had any money on account there. Nothing large, but, to my daughter's surprise, there was a check for $59.18. That was the "holdback" amount our car insurance company had held while waiting for her to bring in the repaired car to be photographed. One phone call and five minutes of my time had paid off.

Forgotten Retirement Account — Unions

Nadine, age 39, had worked as a grocery store clerk for nine years and seven months during her twenties. To have become vested in the grocery clerk's union retirement fund, unfortunately, a worker needed to have 10 years of service. But after reading my book she called the union anyway. She discovered that her overtime put in during the 9½ years made up for the four-month vesting shortfall. She will be entitled to a pension of $275 a month once she reaches age 65.

Teacher Retirement Account — Pensions

A nursing home administrator read my book and came to hear me speak at an association meeting. After the talk, she ran back to her office and made a phone call to the administrator of the State Teacher Retirement System. Nineteen years earlier she had worked as a school nurse for four years. Now that wasn't long enough to be vested in the Teacher Retirement plan, but she had contributed 5% of her income to it during those four years and had not withdrawn it when she left. Her contributions had matured nicely. She instantly became $5,000 richer.

A few pages back we disposed of seven very negative barriers. Now let's turn to some ***positive* statements** you may find interesting. And, more to the point, ideas you will find useful in your search.

THINGS YOU SHOULD KNOW

- Estate records are *always public information,* with or without a will. Trusts are accessible only to beneficiaries.

- But beneficiaries become obsolete. Most people list a beneficiary only when they enter a program, join a union, begin employment or purchase insurance. They seldom update that list.

- Most Americans—62% of us—die without a will! And it's safe to assume a like percentage didn't do much in the way of estate planning or even letting their heirs know where their wealth is located.

- **90% of all unclaimed assets remain in the owner's name forever.** On the other hand, insurance companies, pension plan administrators—even Uncle Sam—have to do no more than mail one letter to one address, or advertise once, to notify you of this money.

- Relatives who **pass away between the ages of 40 and 65 seldom do detailed estate planning.** Odds are very good for finding money in such cases.

- Most group life insurance policies are forgotten over time because the employer pays the premium, and no reminders are issued to policyholders. Listed beneficiaries may be obsolete due to death, marriage (name change), divorce, or changes of address.

- 60% of all health insurance policies have a death benefit life insurance rider. Hurried final arrangements and the normal processes of grieving interfere with the heirs' good business judgment. Few read the fine print on the policy. But **those benefits don't disappear.**

- 50% of Americans divorce—at least once—and this makes it more difficult for ex-spouses and children to trace inheritance. But it can be done.

- With life expectancy increasing, our aging loved ones are more likely to suffer memory loss. The earlier in life we make a detailed list of our assets the better for our heirs. **You may use this book for your planning–prevention.**

- We have become more mobile and therefore harder to find when the system is looking to distribute benefits. *The average family lives in one place for less than 6 years.*

- When you call to ask a difficult question about your possible inheritance the first answer you receive may not be final and correct. Make sure you talk to someone with experience and authority. The telephone receptionist is probably the newest and therefore least knowledgeable person in the office.

THINGS YOU SHOULD KNOW *continued*

- Persistence and patience are musts as you begin your search. You are likely to be asking unexpected questions of employees whose workload is heavy. It is important to find someone who is willing to help you and go the extra mile for you.

- There are many reasons why the U.S. Postal System cannot be relied on to properly forward mail.

- When you have good reason to believe your relative invested in stocks, bonds, or other securities, try to find the local broker or brokerage office he or she bought the stocks from. Canceled checks may lead you to them. When you find the broker, he may have valuable financial information, in addition to stocks and bonds, for you to pursue.

- There is also money you yourself might have forgotten. Perhaps a small amount in an old bank account, or a Christmas Club fund; maybe a security deposit when you rented that first apartment. That money remains in your name **forever.**

Now I want to say something serious and personal to you about two kinds of *motives*: Motives of your forebears whose assets might be lying in wait, and your own motives in finding those assets.

People leave money to loved ones in the hope that somewhere down the line that money will help those heirs. **It's a gift of love.** Many assume—and many of those, incorrectly—that their families know where they left it. There are many reasons heirs don't know where to look or how much is to be found. *But that doesn't mean your forebear wouldn't want you to find those assets.* They just slipped through the cracks. You need to get out the whisk brooms in this book's Appendices and start dusting. It troubles me to realize how many people out there really need and deserve this money—not for a new car or TV—but for medicine, tuition, even food. The idea of this money being held up, lying fallow, was simply not acceptable to me. My father once gave me some advice I try to heed: **"Justice can be your legacy."** Your relative would want his estate disposed of in a just and proper manner.

Next is the matter of your own motivation. Soon after the death of a beloved relative, it's hard to get going. There have already been too many nagging details to settle, too many final affairs to straighten out.

Bereavement and Its Consequences

In addition to these common misconceptions about inheritance, many survivors put off dealing with practical problems and details following the death of a loved one. When someone you love is suddenly taken from you, you find yourself in a state of shock and depression, preoccupied with your loss.

Material matters seem inconsequential, perhaps even irreverent. Certainly an aggressive search for hidden assets—an activity which requires concentration and organization—is about the last thing the recent survivor wants to tackle. Reluctance to undertake a search is a very natural consequence of bereavement.

I recently spoke with a woman whose sister had lost her husband. His death had been sudden; he had been only 46 years old and had suffered a massive stroke. The issue we were discussing revolved about the mortgage debt on the couple's home. The husband had told his wife, on a number of occasions, that in the event he died their home mortgage would be paid off by the insurance company.

"Has she filed a claim?" I asked.

The sister shook her head. "No. Since Bob died she's refused to look at the papers in their safe deposit box. She says doing so would remind her of Bob—the good times they had or the bad times. She says she'll get around to the insurance eventually."

This widow's grief was so heartfelt and so recent it had paralyzed her will, her ability to act. Fortunately she had a good job and enough income; she could afford to drift a while. But many surviving spouses don't have that luxury.

Some in this situation even feel guilty at the thought of concerning themselves with mundane monetary matters. To help counter this understandable but overly–passive attitude, I offer three pieces of advice.

First, if you are so devastated that you cannot think about business matters, then find a close friend or family member—someone you trust—to act in your behalf. Their service should only last until you feel ready to reassume full responsibility. Substitute management of financial affairs is not a risk–free solution. You never know how any person—particularly a family member who may feel he or she is owed "a slice of the pie"—is going to behave while exercising fiduciary responsibility. Still most of us do have a relative or friend to whom we can entrust this all–important task. If he or she is an attorney, so much the better. Don't overlook your clergyman. Besides being able to offer you wise counsel on a variety of personal matters, he may have the necessary experience to give you good advice on your choice of temporary assistant in settling your relative's estate.

Second, don't wait too long to make your move. Some benefits are easier claimed immediately than later. My cousin's estate would have been turned over to the unclaimed property office if I had delayed acting much longer. For Social Security death benefits and IRS refunds you must apply within three years.

Third, reviewing your relative's papers and documents can be an enlightening and even healing experience, a contact which helps you feel closer to him or her. A man told me recently about going through his recently–deceased uncle's papers. He made the surprising discovery that the old man had spent hours in prayer every day. This deeply religious aspect of his uncle's personality was one the family had never suspected.

"I must say," the man told me, "this discovery gave me a fresh perspective both on my uncle's life and on my own lack of faith. I realized that he had been ready to die; and that I was not. He was a better man than I had ever guessed from my casual contacts with him. And all this came out because I had the opportunity to go through his papers."

My own aunt left behind lists of people in our family for whom she had prayed on various occasions. I'm sure that God in His mercy responded fairly often to her prayers in my particular direction.

While a period of bereavement is a natural and necessary part of getting over one's loss, it is important to begin the search for assets as soon as possible. Relatives, close friends, and clergy might be able to help at first; but the surviving heir must fairly soon take responsibility for conducting the search. A death often entails large expenses and can pose unforeseen financial and legal problems. At precisely the moment when you least want to conduct a search for assets, you need to do just that. ***The story of Walter is a case in point.***

And that's just one reason why it's so important to keep track of accrued benefits and to search for assets. No reason to leave that task to your survivors. You might as well take advantage of the financial premiums that you, yourself, have earned. Indeed, people can make good use of this book while they are still living, not only to prepare for the distribution of their assets at the time of death, but also to find additional income they can enjoy right now.

In addition, the book can be extremely helpful to those whose relatives are terminally ill with Alzheimer's disease, cancer, and other long-term ailments. The location of assets and benefits may well mean the difference between being able to afford only minimal health care and having the best that money can buy.

Roadblocks and Speedbumps

Grief is by far the biggest single obstacle to finding hidden assets. While it occasionally helps to motivate the assets search, death more often makes survivors resist the very idea of digging through the deceased's records.

Others are held back by cultural constraints. For instance, a stockbroker acquaintance began reading the first edition

Walter's Story

Walter arrived in Billings, Montana, eager to make a new start. He had recently incurred two losses. First, through no fault of his own, he had lost his job. Second, he had lost his father, who died at the age of 81 after spending his last five years living with Walter. The two were very close, and Walter was still coming to terms with his grief when he arrived in Billings.

At the same time, he was facing a financial crisis. With no job, he was counting every penny; and he had taken on the additional burden of paying off his father's one outstanding debt—an $1800 Visa bill. He'd paid off $600 before he lost his job; but he was still facing another $1200, which he was slowly reducing at the rate of $50 a month. The trouble was, he couldn't afford the $50—not until he'd gotten on his feet again.

He mentioned his predicament to a woman who processed insurance claims for me and who knew about my work on this book. She immediately sent Walter to my office. I suspect he came to my office with little hope of finding a solution to his financial problems. After all, he and his father had talked about such matters and Walter was certain his father would have told him had there been any unclaimed assets.

We spent two and a half hours on his problem. I asked him questions about his father's life and career. Fortunately, he knew most of the answers. At the end of this session we had determined the following:

First, since Walter's father had been drawing Social Security, Walter was immediately eligible for a $255 death benefit—enough to make five payments on the Visa bill.

Next, Walter told me that his father had once worked for the State of Montana, which meant that he might have earned benefits. It all depended on how long he'd been employed. I immediately called Helena and discovered that Walter's father had been on the state payroll for five years and two months. He was "vested"—which meant that he'd served the state long enough to be eligible for retirement pay. ***As a matter of fact, the amount due him when he reached retirement age was $7500!***

- *But that was only half the good news from the State of Montana. The $7500 had been sitting there since 1965—* ***drawing interest****. I calculated that in the intervening years the principal had probably tripled. So Walter, as his father's heir, was going to receive* ***over $21,000 from that retirement plan alone!***

continued on next page

Walter's Story *continued*

- *But we'd only begun to find assets. Walter told me his father had also worked in Arizona as a guard in a defense plant. In order to hold down that job, he'd joined the union. Later he moved to California where he obtained similar work as a member of the same union. I called the union's national headquarters and found out what I already suspected:* ***members automatically receive a permanent group life insurance policy of $3000.*** *As his father's heir, Walter would receive that amount simply by filling out the proper papers.*

- *Walter couldn't believe what he was hearing, but we weren't through yet. At that point, I tackled the problem of the Visa bill. I already knew that 60 percent of all card holders had "credit life insurance" — that is, insurance which paid the bill in full in case of death. It took only one call to verify the fact that Walter's father's Visa had indeed included this provision. Walter didn't owe Visa $1200.* ***Visa owed him a $600 refund for the amount he'd already paid!***

- *As I write this book, Walter and I are still searching for unclaimed assets. His father once worked for Hewlett Packard, and it's entirely possible that he was employed long enough to be eligible for benefits. Meanwhile, Walter no longer stays awake nights worrying about the Visa bill, and his financial future seems reasonably secure.*

Ironically, the man who earned these benefits by honest work, Walter's father, never knew they existed. Like most people, he was unsophisticated in the ways of huge financial institutions—state governments, major corporations, trade unions—and so he lived his retirement years in meager circumstances when he might have been able to afford a few more of life's simple pleasures. How many retired people are in the same boat? Who knows? Probably hundreds of thousands. Possibly millions.

of this book, but stopped after about thirty pages, saying, "This is morbid." Then on further reflection he said to himself, "No, my relatives would want me to have what money they had left."

How did these lost assets get that way? How did we get in this pickle? Well, nothing manages itself automatically. People move away and addresses get lost or forgotten. The longer we live, the greater the risk of Alzheimer's disease, arteriosclerosis, and other memory-robbing illnesses. Then there's the fact that **over 60% of Americans die without a will**. I recently heard a European say that the most characteristic thing about Americans is that none of us believes he is ever going to die. With this head-in-the-sand attitude it's not hard to see why so few of us plan our estates properly and let our next of kin know, in writing, what the worth of our assets is and where those assets are located.

The older generation by no means deserves all the fault here. Many prospective heirs simply make the unwarranted assumption that Grandma didn't own anything. You've probably heard stories proving how wrong this "reasonable" assumption can be. I recently read a newspaper article about a woman who passed away leaving $2 million to a university which didn't even know she existed. Her neighbors thought they knew her fairly well but had no idea she was rich. In her later years she had lived the simple but somewhat eccentric life of a pauper.

My message is simple. It is worth anyone's time to look for hidden family assets. **The odds are better than Lotto**. And it's not that difficult. Just follow the step-by-step instructions in this book. And please let me know what you discover. Finally, if you discover money and don't really need it, you can certainly pass what you found along to a friend or relative who does. Or you can give it to a charity. Giving has long been the American way.

Chapter 3

Sources of Information in Your Assets Search

Our current era is often termed The Age of Information. Yes, knowledge is power. But where do we get it? The information we need in our assets search is spread all over the financial/social/legal/governmental landscape. That needn't discourage us, but it should make us realize that we're going to have to get organized.

This chapter focuses on information **resources** you can use to speed up and deepen and broaden your search for unclaimed assets. Our first items of information will be the names of relatives (or other possible benefactors) whose assets may be awaiting discovery. Next comes the gathering of information about those persons. This is of two types: (1) general information such as birth and death dates, Social Security numbers, places and dates of residence and employment, names of friends and advisers they had and organizations they joined, etc.; and (2) specific information on assets those relatives may have lost track of (insurance policies, security deposits, retirement benefits, real estate, etc.).

Searching Smart I: Search Target Names

The first thing you need to do is make a list of all of your immediate relatives and loved ones—aunts, uncles, brothers, sisters—and other possible benefactors (see the sidebar "Splitting Heirs").

Split those names into the "A List"—no more than fifteen, which you'll investigate first—and the "B List," the not–such–good bets which you'll set aside for now. Future information may lead you to move a name from one List to the other, but you have to start somewhere. The object of the A/B categorization is simply to keep focused, to not get distracted.

Many of those names you already know; though perhaps not completely. 'Uncle Joe,' say, needs to be recorded in your list correctly as 'Francis Joseph Willoby, Jr.' Other important names may be unknown to you. Keep your ears open at family gatherings and reunions. The name of a deceased relative who was frugal and hard–working may come up. Don't be shy about asking for details on when and where they worked, what kind of work they did, and what happened to their money or investments or property. What you ultimately recover will go to all the proper heirs; you're doing those family members a service in pursuing your assets search.

Two wrinkles to keep in mind while you're collecting names. First, don't forget yourself! (See the sidebar "What Have We Ourselves Overlooked?")

Second, broaden your name search to include names of your relatives' surviving close friends, trusted advisers, doctors, lawyers, and accountants. It may take a little digging to find their whereabouts, but once contacted they might furnish valuable information. Ask them what they remember about your relative's business interests. And they very well might know of his or her

Splitting Heirs

Direct bloodlines —"Next of Kin"— this is how we think about wills and estates. Blood is thicker than..., you know.

Don't dismiss the idea of an inheritance from anyone other than a blood relative.

It could be that the elderly neighbor you befriended years ago who, due to illness, moved into a nursing home, remembered you in her will before she passed away. Include her on your list. Perhaps that sounds greedy, but you know that she would want you to have your inheritance rather than have it repose with the government or private industry.

Lightning strikes! *If you know where the death occurred, ask for a copy of her will in that county. It is public information and may be obtained quite easily in most cases.*

financial holdings and investments. *Perhaps your relative "crowed" to a few of his friends about his investment successes.* And everybody needs a shoulder to cry on when the stock market takes a hit. Your relative's friends may enjoy being helpful. They probably realize that your relative would prefer his or her heirs to have any unclaimed assets.

Once you have your A List, regroup those names by the more important states they lived in between childhood and death or disability. We're a mobile society; quite a few of the names will be duplicated under the headings of several states. Psychologists tell us we learn better from success than through failure. The purpose of this state–by–state breakdown (even though it's a bit out of order) is to achieve some quick successes in your search.

Next, call each state's Unclaimed Property Office (see Unclaimed Property Offices Appendix R1 and the corresponding section in the next chapter) and ask if they hold any assets in the names of any of your relatives who once lived in that state. Most offices will do a complete computer search for you at no cost and while you wait on the telephone. It only takes a phone call; at most a few calls.

Some offices may enforce a policy of only looking up say three names on any one call. Still, the state Unclaimed Property Offices are good bets for a good return. Be polite and well organized, but persistent and assertive, when dealing with these public servants. It is their job to furnish you this **public information**; it is information to which you are entitled.

What Have We Ourselves Overlooked?

Over 30 percent of my readers have found assets that were not left by relatives but forgotten by themselves. I was speaking to a group of senior citizens one afternoon when an elderly man in the audience stood and spoke:

*"Dave, I know exactly what you mean. When I turned 65 I sat down and wrote a list of every employer that I had ever worked for, then I called them up. I asked one simple question: 'Are there any benefits in my name?' **There were.** To my complete surprise, I received a check from a former employer, Travelodge, where I had worked almost forty years ago. It was for **$4,000.**"*

The company had held the man's contribution to his retirement plan, and his long forgotten $350 investment blossomed into a nice little check. He had moved without leaving a forwarding address. Who is thinking about retirement at age twenty–five?

Searching Smart II: Information About Search Targets

Your next job is to fill in the blanks on each of the target relatives on your A List. This information ranges from items pertaining to almost everyone—Social Security numbers and dates and places of employment—to items only a minority will have—airline frequent flier accounts and corporation records. Here are the six major information sources you'll want to consider:

1. Social Security Number

The first piece of the puzzle is your loved one's Social Security number because most unclaimed assets and forgotten properties are indexed under SSNs. So this is a "must have" item.

Listed below are the simplest ways to find a Social Security number.

- **State Income Tax Returns.** In all, 43 states and the District of Columbia (all but Alaska, Florida, Nevada, South Dakota, Texas, Washington, and Wyoming) have state income tax.

- **Death Certificates.** Death certificates have Social Security numbers on them if the death occurred after 1956.

- **Bank Accounts.** The law requires that every savings, checking, and IRA account have an associated Social Security number.

- **Credit Reports.** Credit reports should be obtained if your relative died less than 10 years ago. All are indexed by the Social Security number.

- **Hospital Records.** Most hospitals keep records forever because of the potential for malpractice suits. At admission the Social Security number is listed.

- **Driving Record.** If you have a "friend" who supplies your auto insurance, ask him to "add" your relative to your auto insurance. 70% of all U.S. drivers are listed in a national driver's record database.

- **The Social Security Administration**, itself, will tell you they are the office of last resort in finding a Social Security number. But if all else fails, do go to your local Social Security office. They will require proof of your relationship to your target relative before they will provide his or her number.

2. Your Relative's Will

Most people think that ***only an attorney*** *can obtain estate probate files—****not so.*** *Unless the deceased established a trust, all probate information is public.* ***Anyone can get copies of the county probate records just for the cost of photocopies.***

When a person passes away, a record of his or her assets (even if there is no recorded will) becomes part of the public county records in the county where the death occurred. If there is a will and the will is registered elsewhere, the county of death will list access. If you know the state where your relative died, you can find the county by contacting the state. The records are collected by the county and then sent to the state. Within 12 months of the date of death, the state office will have recorded the county where the person died. Remember that the county where the death occurred (see Counties Appendix S4 for listings) is where you start looking for assets.

When you contact the county where your loved one died, first request a copy of the **Estate Inventory**—a list of all known assets. This list may increase during the first year or two beyond the date of death. Be aware that this inventory is related to assets held in the name of the deceased in the county where death occurred. Over time, assets may flow to that county from other counties and other states. Be sure to register your interest with the Clerk of the County Court handling the probate. If no family member is aware of the death, only by pure chance would assets be sent from other states or counties to the county where the person died. *There is no adequate network of information.* You may have knowledge of assets of which public officials are unaware and thus you have the right to make an inquiry and request that they add these assets to the inventory. Don't disregard the fact that **you and your family have the greatest motivation** to construct an accurate estate inventory. It pays off. Remember this list will appear even if there is a recorded will and many times it will tell you about other interested parties.

The majority of *improved real estate* sold for taxes will generate money after the tax bill is paid. The county will then forward that money to the Unclaimed Property Office (in the state where the property is located) in the name of the original owner(s).

Only trusts are private. Individuals conducting a search need to determine if there is a will. All filed wills are public information, so you can request a copy of one if you discover where it is filed. They are generally filed in the Clerk of Court's office in the county of longest or most recent residence, where the loved one did the majority of his business. There may be exceptions, so be diligent.

3. Employment History

To get the hang of it, start with yourself. List every company where you worked, your job title or capacity, and the inclusive dates. There might be money in the form of **IRAs, 401K** plans, or your contributions to various retirement programs. If you worked there long enough to be vested, you need to know what program benefits you will receive (e.g., retirement income, paid health insurance) when you retire and how much each is worth. Build a file. When you've finished with your own case, go on to get the same kind of information on your A–List relatives.

Be especially alert for employment-related benefits for any relative who died between the ages of forty and sixty-five. Their employer at the time of their death often owes their estate a lump-sum pension settlement or group life insurance death benefit; most times that asset simply stays there until someone claims it.

4. Life Insurance Agents

Look for a general agent or a specific insurance company, such as Metropolitan Life Insurance, where your relative did his business locally. They will have life and health insurance policy numbers for you. Request replacements for any missing policies and a copy of your relative's file. Insurance files often contain other significant information such as the banks he used, charities to which he contributed, insurance information involving other carriers and, most importantly, investments. Read casualty insurance accounts carefully because those often reveal real estate holdings and other personal financial information. Local insurance agencies are often sold "lock, stock, and barrel." This means all their business files are transferred to the new owners. Even many years later, these successor agencies can be an excellent search information source for you.

One day while doing research for the first edition I was talking to an insurance librarian. When I brought up the topic of door–to–door insurance salesmen she suddenly remembered an old paid up 50 cents per week policy of her own. A quick inquiry found her $8700; this windfall helped pay for her daughter's last year of college. Don't fail to check out insurance policies carefully.

It may happen that the local insurance agent with whom your relative did business has retired, or even that the insurance agency has been sold. Don't be deterred. Old policy records are part of the sale-of-agency package. Even if the agency has changed hands a dozen times, they still have a file on every one of the original insurer's clients—including a file you would like to review. For broader insurance policy searches across the country it is unfortunate that most life insurance policy numbers are not currently cross-indexed with their owner's Social Security number.

5. Banking Information

The bank where your loved one kept his account(s) is a resource of importance. Ask for his file and the name of his loan officer, the person who helped him process paperwork whenever he applied for a loan. Most loan applications will include a listing of all assets and/or a financial statement. This information is always vital, but especially if your loved one died suddenly or suffered a serious medical problem that might have impaired his memory — Alzheimer's disease, for instance, or a stroke.

If you can locate them, don't neglect such routine bank records as canceled checks. These may help you identify insurance agents or their companies, business contacts, investments, property on which taxes were paid, club affiliations, even airlines where your relative had a frequent flier account.

Special Note: If your relative was wealthy, perhaps he set up a trust for specific family members or a local charity. Trust officers are another excellent source of information. It could be that one might remember financial details not in the files. Trusts are usually handled by your relative's bank. Blue-collar workers may have business information at the local union office. Cover the entire money landscape!

6. Missing Person Information

If you start off not knowing much about the life and times of your relative, you'll need to play part-time detective. This is especially true when you suspect that relative is still alive. Then your search has the unexpected fringe benefit of helping to bring together long-separated branches of your family. Here are some simple straightforward ways to find a missing person.

Credit Reports

A man called me during a radio interview on the east coast. He said, "My mom told me my dad left us when I was six months old. I'm now twenty-nine, married, with two small children, and I've always wanted to find my dad. How would you suggest I do that?"

Without hesitating, I told him that if he had his father's Social Security number he could request a credit report. He later wrote to say he had found his father in an adjoining state and they had arranged a reunion. So grandfather got to meet his two grandchildren as well as his daughter-in-law. This could happen to you or to someone you know.

Anyone with good reason can order a credit report. You will need the subject's Social Security number to be sure you have the right account. The cost is about $8.00 for each report. Credit reports provide up to fifteen years of business history. They include addresses, phone numbers, buying practices, etc. I suggest you work through an established business that regularly requests credit reports. If you want to contact the credit reporting agencies directly, here is the contact information for the three major ones.

TRW Inc. Information Technology Services
P.O. Box 2350
Chatsworth, CA 91313-2350
(800) 862-7654

TransUnion
P.O. Box 390
Springfield, PA 19064
(800) 851-2674

Equifax
P.O. Box 740241
Atlanta, GA 30374
404) 885-8000

Hospital Records

Because of potential medical malpractice lawsuits, hospitals keep patient records forever. Even if the former hospital has been converted into a nursing home, files are often kept somewhere in a vault or other records storage depot. These files could reveal birth information, medical history, accidents, and even details about your relative's death.

Church Records

Most churches keep records of baptisms, confirmations, marriages, and funerals. The Catholic Church maintains birth and baptism records. The Lutheran Church keeps especially good confirmation records. The Church of Jesus Christ of Latter Day Saints (LDS) has the most thorough collection of genealogical records of any organization in the world and those records are not limited to LDS members. Local LDS churches can access records inexpensively. The family Bible, catechism manual, or prayer book may reveal family records along with inspirational notes on the faith of family members. In my own family religious records, I discovered touching entries telling of relatives praying for me when I was a tiny baby.

Death Records

Each state has a listing of deaths which took place within that state. However it takes up to twelve months beyond the time of death for the information to be transferred to the state records from the county where the death occurred. Once it has the death certificate of your relative, the State Vital Statistics Department will be able to tell you in which county the death occurred.

State Archives

Most records eventually go to the State Archives. For example, if your target relative worked for state or local government, his resume and personnel file eventually end up in the State Archives. Perhaps your relative was notorious in one way or another. Many State Archives retain newspaper accounts of historical events and personages. *National Archives* are even more extensive, keeping records dating back to the Revolutionary War.

Newspaper Records

If your relative had a high profile in the town or city where he resided, you might search at the local newspaper for articles mentioning him or her. Obituaries often reveal names of otherwise obscure relatives. Many newspapers have microfiche and computer search capability.

State Corporate Records

The Secretary of State (in most states) keeps a database of persons who are principal stockholders in closely-held corporations. ("Closely held" corporations are those businesses where stock or ownership is held by 20 or fewer investors.) You might also ask the Secretary of State whether your relative might have done business under a "dba" (doing business as) name or as a member of a partnership. If so, these records may reveal important assets which have so far failed to come to light.

City Directories

Most city libraries have city directories dating back in time to the 1930's. From these directories you might find your relative's former addresses and places of employment. Look for them at the local public library.

Insurance Agents

Automobile driving record databases are kept by 70% of the auto insurance companies. If you suspect the person you are searching for has a driver's license or owns a motor vehicle, you may be able to obtain his or her driving record or record of automobile title through your insurance agent. A Social Security number may speed up your search; in the opposite direction, a name search for your relative may bring up his or her long sought after Social Security number out of this database.

State Motor Vehicle Departments

This department should be contacted if you think there may be an abandoned vehicle belonging to your relative. This may also be the office holding records of recreational vehicles, or other types of motor vehicles, registered in your relative's name. Such records would reveal an address or lienholder; sometimes even a temporary address.

Especially if your relative may have had a motor or mobile home, don't neglect searching the motor vehicle departments of states other than that of his residence. There are hundreds, if not thousands, of motor and mobile homes abandoned in Arizona, Florida, Texas, and California every year. Their owners commonly rent spaces for rental periods of up to three years. Then death, Alzheimer's disease, or some other illness occurs and the rest of the family, usually living in another state, is totally unaware of that rolling asset. When the space rental period expires and the owner of that space wants to proceed with its income potential, those motor or mobile homes are typically sold at auction. Proceeds of the sale will (or should!) be sent to the Unclaimed Property Office of the state where the vehicle was licensed.

For obvious reasons, states with no sales tax are often selected for vehicle purchase and registration. An unusually large number of motor homes is licensed in Oregon because of that state's favorable tax rates. This should mean to you that Oregon is a place to look for this kind of asset even though your relative never lived there or kept a motor home there.

The Internet

There are Internet tools to help you locate long lost Uncle John's e-mail address, of course, but there are also online phone books that might pinpoint his street address and telephone number. Here are details, if you are "online," on how to use one of these free services, SWITCHBOARD, which has about 100 million U.S. residential and business address and phone number listings. (If you are not yet fluent in "computerese" this would be a good time to enlist the aid of a computer "nerd" in your family or among your acquaintances.)

SWITCHBOARD is accessed through the World Wide Web. To get started, feed your Web browser (e.g., Netscape, Mosaic) this address:

> http://www.SWITCHBOARD.com
>
> Once you're into SWITCHBOARD's home page you simply follow obvious prompts for Uncle John's first and last name and state of residence. If successful, you'll be given his name, address, and telephone number.

This same database can be accessed via the Yahoo! People Search at:

> http://www.YAHOO.com/search/people
>
> which also allows reverse searches, from phone number to the name of the listed party. Isn't technology wonderful?

Be sure to warn your relative's surviving spouse, especially if elderly, that there are unscrupulous people who prey on vulnerable persons. Ask them *not* to make any large or long term financial decisions without *first* discussing the matter with a **trusted family member, friend or professional.**

In addition, some criminals watch the obituary pages so they can burglarize a recently-deceased person's empty house. To guard against these sick minds, contact the local police department and ask them to place the property under "special watch" — they will. Should your relative's home be robbed or vandalized, his home owner's insurance should cover the loss. Most such policies are prepaid and generally cover the time period during which most loss occurs—up to six months beyond the death notice.

When a young person begins his career, say as a union member, he is given a large sheaf of papers to fill out. Included in these is space to list the person the employee wants to receive his group life insurance proceeds, as well as pension benefits, in the event of his death. If, as is often the case, the employee is unmarried, he lists his mother or a brother or sister as beneficiary. Some years later, his life circumstances change. But unless he is reminded to do so—a fairly seldom occurrence—**updates of beneficiaries never occur.** It can easily happen that those early beneficiaries precede the employee in death and then there is essentially no known beneficiary to whom those assets should go. This is where you should pay special attention; the money actually belongs to the next of kin.

Then there is the fact that over 50% of Americans get divorced at least once. But a much smaller percentage remember to change their policies' beneficiaries from ex-spouse to current spouse. Even someone plotting to hide assets from an ex-spouse seldom wants to leave his children out in the cold.

If you are a child whose parents divorced, you have an excellent chance of recovering money. Most parents want their children to benefit.

Further complications occur when a correct beneficiary moves, leaving only a stale address. This makes proper distribution of proceeds difficult. Perseverance will pay off.

I hope ALL my readers will take this opportunity to update ALL the designated beneficiaries mentioned in their own estate planning documents. Let this be a reminder we should all heed!

With this information (or at least this information on how to get information) at your fingertips, it's time to consider, in depth, the actual places, policies, and programs in which your relative's unclaimed assets may be hidden.

Chapter 4

Locations of the Money: Resources

By this time your head is reeling and your desk is a mess. You have stacks of notes and forms and affidavits holding dozens of names and hundreds of numbers—Social Security numbers, military service numbers, union card numbers, bank and credit union and savings and loan association account numbers, life insurance policy numbers, and so forth. Don't despair! Your phone calls and letters and personal interviews—all your interesting or saddening or frustrating leg work—is about to turn into the kind of numbers you deserve and most appreciate: dollar numbers. **This is just as your relative would wish!**

This chapter gives you general information you need about the kinds of places where hidden assets are tucked away. The Appendices, which form the latter sections of the book, contain specific details such as names and phone numbers you'll need to contact.

Your preparation is largely over. Now it's time for the main event. But please don't let your enthusiasm make you forget to keep accurate records on precisely where and how you uncovered the hidden assets you do eventually locate. And how much they turned out to be worth. At a minimum, I think you'll discover that your summarized search will turn out to be something like the flip side of paying household bills: perhaps no one of them is very big, but the aggregate is surprisingly large. I'd say finding $50 is a blood transfusion and an ego boost! The result of your search for hidden assets is that it's all money coming in, money you didn't even know you had.

State Unclaimed Property Offices

There is an Unclaimed Property Office, repository of the net cash value of any property abandoned within its borders, in **each and every state**. (See Appendix R1 for the phone numbers of each such office.) Each state has laws governing what banks (and all other agencies, both public and private) must do with unclaimed or abandoned property under their control: how long it is before the property passes to them, what they must do to try to find the rightful owners, etc.

Despite the fact that most of these offices are cooperative—even aggressive—in their attempts to return money to the rightful owner or estate, they continue to collect money twice as fast as they are able to return it. There is currently **25 to 30 billion dollars** held by unclaimed property offices nationwide. Even so, this staggering sum represents only about 5% of the total unclaimed money in this country.

States are not the only entities with unclaimed property. **The Federal Government is the largest single holder of unclaimed money**, but they do not comply with state laws. I am happy to report that a group of interstate corporations have formed an organization set up to send unclaimed money they control back to the appropriate State Unclaimed Property Office. This author hopes that laws and practices will change so that more organizations, public and private, will join in this effort. If this happens, each state's Unclaimed Property Office will see its cash totals increase very rapidly.

If you find the state Unclaimed Property Office is indeed holding an account in your relative's name, they may ask for his or her last known address, so be ready to supply that. This check is to confirm that you and they are talking about the same person. If the address matches up, you or your relative will be sent an affidavit, a form which, **once signed and notarized**, verifies rightful ownership. (Notaries are available to witness your signature, for a small fee, in most banks and in many other places of business.)

There are Unclaimed Property Offices in every state, and they hold, conservatively, more than $30 billion. Most of the money is being held in the names of persons who are still alive. Thirty billion dollars — and it stays there forever! Or until the owner or his or her heirs claim it. Most of these offices are eager to return money.

Most people have never called an Unclaimed Property Office even if they know those offices exist. And if they have, they've given up after a first fleeting contact. Be persistent. You should understand that most property is not turned over to the state until *three to five years after abandonment.* For example, a bank is not required to turn over money for three to five years (this varies from state to state) after the last bank account transaction. So if your deceased relative passed away only three years ago, his property may not show up for some time. But remember: if he died 20 years ago, his money should and probably will still be there—forever—waiting to be claimed!

Others assume that the state will advertise the property and that all property will be claimed; that is simply not true. Only 20% to 40% of those assets advertised, as required by state law, are claimed by the owner or the heirs. In the case of unclaimed property belonging to deceased persons, the small recovery rate is largely due to the length of time which goes by between the death and the property's passing to the control of the Unclaimed Property Office. As a rule you should check all relevant State Unclaimed Property Offices beginning 5 years after death. Certainly it pays to check more than just once. **To those readers who may feel "there is nothing out there for me" I suggest they survey the Unclaimed Property Offices as a very easy and efficient first step.**

Unclaimed Property Step-by-Step

I am happy to report most states' Unclaimed Property Offices are extremely cooperative and helpful.

Before you make your first call to an Unclaimed Property Office you should sit down and list as many as possible of your siblings, aunts, uncles, cousins and grandparents. List those who are living and those who are deceased. Then group them by the states where they lived.

Once you have this list, contact the Unclaimed Property Offices located in each state. Generally they will do a search for each person over the telephone. They will often limit the inquiries to three persons; if you have a long list for some state, you may have to make several calls. The odds of finding money this way are good—*much better than Lotto.* If you have ten or more

Dan's Story

I recently appeared as guest on a nationwide TV program. About an hour before the show went on the air I had my usual brief chat with Dan, the program host. To illustrate what my book was about and how it worked, I asked him a few questions about himself and his family.

Dan said he was raised in a small city in Michigan and that he went to college in Missouri. His father had recently retired and moved. Dan mentioned a stepbrother and a number of other family members.

It took me about 15 minutes and four quick telephone calls to Unclaimed Property Offices in Missouri and Michigan to find an account for Dan's stepbrother and an account his father had dating back to when he was a practicing dentist.

The total of the two accounts was over $700! Not bad findings for a few minutes work. Dan was amazed.

names you have a very good chance of finding unclaimed money. (See Unclaimed Property Offices Appendix R1.)

Reciprocity of Unclaimed Property

A group of forward–looking states have joined together in instituting **unclaimed property reciprocity agreements**. An example showing how these mutual agreements work is in the Unclaimed Property Office Appendix R1.

Social Clubs

Find out whether your loved one belonged to any service clubs (VFW, Knights of Columbus, Rotary, etc.). Many of these offer their members group life insurance. Also check volunteer groups, country clubs, alumni associations, hobby groups—any organization your loved one might have joined. Even though the group has no direct financial orientation it might still have offered these benefits. That is because by doing so the organization often gets a cut of any such business transacted.

Checking your relative's business and social organizations has the added benefit of putting you in contact with some of his or her close friends. Your relative may have told these friends about important financial information which can help you in your assets search. Ask them!

Automobile Insurance and Accident Records

If your loved one was once involved in a serious automobile or other transportation accident, there is often a dormant question of who was at fault and therefore liable for damages. We, as relatives, may have no idea, long after the fact, that an insurer is prepared to settle in our relative's favor. Even uncontested accident insurance settlements take from 7 to 10 years to settle. Your relative's insurance agent is the place to go for informaiton on this possibility.

Each state keeps a detailed record of **fatal accidents** which includes the names of insurers, of the party at fault, and a summary of the outcome. Call your local police department for the name of the agency that holds this information in your state. (See the Accident Reports Appendix S8 for further information.)

Tax Refunds

If your relative died while still employed he or she very likely overpaid withheld or estimated state and federal income tax. (See the State Income Tax Appendix S5 for a numerical example showing how this could happen.)

Obsolete or Lost Stock

You may find old stock certificates among your deceased or disabled relative's possessions (or among your own) and wonder if they are of any value. Old certificates are often for equity in smaller companies which have since merged with, or were bought out by, larger companies.

I have found the following two books to be extremely helpful resources in researching historical stocks. Though the books are now out of print, many libraries have them; if not, they should be available through Interlibrary Loan. Once you have these books in hand, you'll have the information you need to make proper inquiry on the value of the stock.

Obsolete Securities, Printed by Financial Information, Inc., *1993*

Obsolete American Securities, Published by R.M. Smyth, contains information from 1940-1945.

If you have reason to believe your relative owned stock in a major publicly–held company—a Fortune 500 company, say, or one listed on either the New York or American Stock Exchanges—you need to contact the "transfer agent" for that company's stock. For the most up–to–date information, call my office at 406–259–1699 and our staff will help you. Or e-mail us the details of what you know of the stock to: assetsunknown@mcn.net.

Here's a special case. Yours may be one of the many families who have been told that during the 1920's or 1930's members of your family bought AT&T stock. The best way to track down this particular possibility is to contact the Chicago Trust Company of New York at 800-348-8288. This is the transfer agent handling all AT&T stock. Initially they may tell you their records only go back ten years; my experience has been that, if pressured, they will search further. They will require that you send the first name, middle initial, last name of the stockholder, approximate number of shares purchased, last known address, and any other pertinent information about the relative or person who held the stock.

If on the other hand you believe you have stock certificates from a "closely held" corporation, contact the Secretary of State in the state where the corporation operated. As an heir, you are entitled to full disclosure of a deceased loved one's shares and all other similar information you are interested in. Again, it's public information.

IRAs, 401K and Keogh Plans

Congress has passed various pieces of legislation allowing taxpayers to defer taxes by setting aside part of their income for retirement. But just imagine how many of these tax-deferred set-aside retirement plan accounts go unclaimed because their owners change jobs or get divorced or, as they grow older, suffer from memory loss. This might be one of your *relative's larger hidden assets*, scattered in time and space over his or her work history.

If your relative was self–employed any time after 1974, he may have purchased an IRA, an Individual Retirement Account. This is a personal tax-deferred retirement plan which may be established by anyone, under

70½ years of age, who receives compensation or by anyone, of whatever age, seeking to defer taxes by rolling over eligible distributions from a qualified retirement plan. At the present time, the person may defer up to $2,000 per year. Eligible accounts may have been set up at a stock or mutual fund brokerage firm, by an insurance agent, or at a bank. In order to qualify for a reduced net taxable income, the owner must list this account on his Federal Income Tax form 1040, line 16 or 17. Tracking down this account may require a combination of canceled checks and contact with the bank or brokerage house who sold it to your relative. **Searching out this prospect may be very important.**

On the other hand, 401K plans are held by the employer and so that is where you should direct your search for this kind of asset. Does your relative's former employer hold a 401K account in his name? Remember, no one may have notified the employer of your relative's death or disability. Withdrawals from 401K plans may begin when the person is 59½ years old. Once they begin receiving money these distributions should be listed on your relative's federal income tax return.

Keogh Plans have been available since the 1970's. A Keogh Plan is a qualified retirement plan maintained for the benefit of employees of unincorporated businesses or for self-employed individuals.

To see whether your relative had such an account during a given year, look on line 16 or 17 of his 1040 Federal Income Tax form. There he must list this account in order to enjoy the tax deferral. Reminder: Copies of *state* income tax forms also have this information and these can be obtained more quickly than their federal counterparts.

Uncollected Life Insurance Benefits

Here is a truly astounding statistic: more than 25% of all life insurance policies go unpaid upon the death of the insured! This may be because the insurance company is unaware of the death, or because they cannot find the policy beneficiary. In any event, that amounts to a lot of unclaimed money. Although most insurance companies desire to do the right thing, **it is obviously in their best interest not to find the beneficiary**. Since insurance policies are not cross-indexed by the insured's Social Security number, it is hard to find a policy without the insurance company name and that policy number.

What do you do if your relative mentioned a life insurance policy but, following his death, none was found? Begin by going through canceled checks looking for an insurance company name. If that doesn't pan out, question family members. It is likely that that same insurance agent sold policies to several family members. Check with your relative's banker; perhaps the insurance policy was listed as collateral in a loan file or on a financial statement.

Despite the fact that many insurance companies recommend that you search for a policy by contacting the American Council of Life Insurance, in Washington D.C., their poor success rate makes this suggestion unacceptable. The Council typically finds less than 2% of lost policies they search for. They are restricted to no more than 4,000 inquiries per month, nationwide, so many inquiries never get processed. Finally, unless they do find the policy, they will not send you any notice of the result of their search. For most of us, a policy search utilizing the American Council of Life Insurance is a search "in name only."

If you do locate a policy you may be told that the policy has lapsed. **Be sure to check the date when the policy lapsed with the date on the death certificate. Remember, deceased persons are not obligated to continue paying life insurance premiums!**

Keep in mind that the Insurance Commissioner of the state where your relative lived and owned insurance may be able to assist you in learning what insurance laws apply to your particular situation.

Real Estate

At first glance, you might decide that real estate abandoned or forgotten by a now-deceased relative, and subsequently sold for delinquent taxes, might be worthless. Property in that category is sold at public, advertised auctions. **But the value (selling price) might well have exceeded what was owed for taxes.** The difference should have been sent, by the county treasurer of the county in which the property is located, to the state's Unclaimed Property Office fund.

Sometimes these orphaned parcels are "out in the country." While urban decay can of course adversely impact the value of property in the central city, the other side of this same coin is that urban sprawl and expansion can mean substantial increases in values of rural holdings.

Improved property—property with buildings, roads or utility connections on it—is very likely to have brought, even at forced auction sale, more than the taxes owed on it. This is even more likely to be the case when the property was, until recently, an active residence. If your relative lived on the property up to the time of his or her death, it may have retained significant value over and above the amount of the taxes owed.

For example, Uncle John bought a "ranchette" and planned to retire there. He bought this 40-acre tract in the 1950's with cash; there was never a loan on it or its improvements. During the sixties he built a garage and shop on the property; later he added a "cabin." Since 1960 the city limits moved steadily closer and closer to his ranchette; by 1985, city water and sewer hookups were available at the property line.

Uncle John died unexpectedly. No one in the family—most of them lived back east—knew much about any of his property and knew nothing about the ranchette. Three years went by with no one paying real estate taxes on the property; those taxes amounted to $17,300. As is customary, the county then advertised it in a delinquent tax sale. A real estate developer bought the ranchette at the auction, planning to put a housing subdivision on it; he paid $6,000 per acre, a total of $240,000. That meant $222,700 in equity; it was eventually sent to the State Unclaimed Property Office. Relatives had not been notified by county authorities of the property auction because they were unknown. By the same token, they had no way of knowing what awaited them in the Unclaimed Property Fund. The $222,7000 simply went to the Unclaimed Property Office. There it would sit until recovered. Forever!

When "exploring" real estate assets check first with the county assessor or property records department in the county where you suspect the property is located. Then check that state's Unclaimed Property Office. Be persistent!

Trudy's Story

Trudy is a member of the "Baby Boomer" generation. Mother of three, she was raised with her four siblings in California. Her father was a minister, but mostly in small congregations. So to better support his family, Dad often worked as a carpenter. In many of these commercial construction jobs he was required to be a member of the Carpenter's Union. His membership spanned a long period of time. In some instances he was placed on inactive status between jobs.

Last August, Trudy's dad told her that the doctors had told him that his heart condition had deteriorated to the point that another operation was impossible; his life expectancy was brief. He asked the family to travel to his home in California for a family gathering. Foremost on her dad's mind was the financial well-being of his wife after he passed away.

Trudy had read the earlier edition of this book, but when she read it she did not immediately see how it could benefit her or her family. Under these new circumstances, however, she decided to read the book more carefully, especially the section dealing with "Union Pensions." She had a lengthy conversation with me in which I encouraged her and her mother to contact the local Carpenter's Union and have them check their records on her father's account.

Dad was uncertain as to his eligibility for a Carpenter's Union pension at age 65. (He was by now 69.) When he began receiving Social Security benefits, he assumed that he was not eligible for the union pension. Perhaps he considered his calling as minister to be his main vocation. In any event, he had not been receiving a union pension.

A family reunion was planned and Trudy traveled to California. She and her mother called the union office; the secretary suggested they come in and fill out an application. They were told that the union would check into her father's file to determine whether or not he was eligible for benefits. They were told that her parents would not be eligible to receive any retroactive pension income, despite the fact that her dad was more than four years past retirement age. The application was completed and returned the following day.

continued on the next page

Union Benefits

Most longtime union members—those who have been in long enough, usually 3 to 5 years, to be vested—have established a pension and own a small life insurance policy which provides for a death benefit to their listed beneficiary. There's the rub: listed beneficiaries are very often obsolete. Death or divorce or any number of life changes may have made the listed beneficiary impossible to locate. Where vestment, or lack of it, is a question, do not overlook the fact that military service often contributes to the period of time required for vestment.

Shortly after the Social Security system came into existence (1935), most unions started pension programs. The employee and employer made equal contributions and the union kept track of the account. If you or any of your relatives belonged to a union for five or more years anytime after 1935, chances are excellent that there is a retirement account and a life insurance policy waiting for you or for the estate to claim. While many of these benefits are forgotten and go uncollected, they do not cease to exist.

To check the status of these accounts, contact the local union where your relative may have worked. If you do not know the whereabouts of the local union office, you can lean on the union's national or regional office for help. Depending on your relationship, you may be asked to provide a death certificate, birth certificate, or marriage license. Keep in mind that **certified copies** are the only documents recognized by unions, companies, banks, etc. In order to get information to fulfill your assets search, you may have to provide proof that you are indeed an heir, executor of the estate, or have power of attorney to act on behalf of an incapacitated relative.

Every union member (or an heir) is entitled to a copy of his or her record of retirement benefits. If you have ever been a union member—especially if you are an *inactive vested* member—it might be wise to request this record early in the process of getting your own affairs in order.

Pension Funds

Pension funds are among the most likely of all lost assets to yield high returns to the persistent searcher. It is surprising how many people are unaware that they are eligible for pensions. During their youth, retirement seems far in the future. Most hold several jobs during their lifetime and move from one position to another without realizing the pension benefits they are leaving behind. Nonetheless, those pensions remain in their name, growing in value. I have run across numerous cases in which a deceased relative leaves behind two or three pensions that heirs can claim.

Of course not all such cases pan out. I found that when my cousin Rand worked for the City of New York, where there are five different pension plans, he had earned benefits under two of them. But he had withdrawn both those funds when he left the job.

There are two basic kinds of pension funds, **public and private**. Many were established after the Great Depression of the 1930's. Their purpose was to provide older Americans with a better standard of living so they would not be a burden to younger family members or to society. At that time life expectancy was about 20 years shorter than it is today.

Pension plans use actuarial tables (statistical projections) to establish a formula forecasting how much money pensioners will receive starting at the retirement age—usually age 63 or 65—defined by their particular plan. The pension fund is usually financed by contributions from both employer and employee. Most plans designate a period—sometimes 5 years, sometimes 7 years, sometimes 10 years—of required time on the job in order for a worker to become "**vested**." Once the person becomes vested contributions of both the employer and employee are locked in place regardless of whether the employee continues in that job. His or her retirement account continues to gain value—even beyond the retirement age of 63 or 65—based on the successful investment strategy of the retirement fund managers. It is important to understand that each plan has its own rules. Each program has a board of directors that sets the overall policies of the retirement fund and oversees the prudent investment of all the contributions in the fund. For this reason there is wide variation in the interest earnings of investments from one pension plan to another. But almost all of them continue to increase in value.

In addition, you should know that **contributions by the employee can often be withdrawn** (but only if they have **not** become vested) when a worker leaves one employment for another. If the employee withdraws his or her contributions before being vested, the employee usually forfeits the employer's contributions. Lots of workers can't recall whether or not they withdrew their contributions when they changed jobs; it is certainly worth checking. When the employee leaves under stressful circumstances, such as being laid off due to company "down-sizing," their emotional state may preclude their planning and thinking clearly. It's at times like that that former employees tend to walk away from benefits.

Trudy's Story continued

After the application was duly processed, her parents were told they were eligible for $198 each month. During this conversation, her mother was told that the union had not yet received a copy of her birth certificate so the application could not be completed until that certificate was received. Mom assured the clerk that the certificate had been sent but that she would send another copy. While having this same conversation, she told the clerk that she had talked to an attorney and that she had been told they were most likely eligible for retroactive payments dating back to age 63 or 65, whichever was the union's recognized retirement age. The clerk seemed startled, perhaps because she had not seen the age of the applicant as being 69 or perhaps because there may have been an "informal policy" of non-disclosure.

In any event, Trudy's parents were soon informed that they would receive a lump sum check for ***$10,000 in retroactive payments in addition to the monthly check of $198*** *for the rest of her dad's life. That monthly payment would decrease by 50% upon his death. Both of these payments were received within a month.*

You won't believe it, but her parents received yet another call from the union a few weeks later telling them that a mistake had been made in the original calculations and that the monthly payment would actually be ***$249*** *per month. And that they would soon receive* ***an additional check for $2,000 in retroactive payments!***

This kind of story, and similar ones, come up over and over again. So dig in for your own family. Or consider helping someone else with his family's union benefits situation. When you hit "pay dirt," write and tell me what you found.

Sometimes an employee leaves a company, withdrawing all available pension funds, only to return to the same company a few years later. He is then often eligible to reactivate the original pension plan by "buying back" the lost equity. Be sure to check the status of any pension plan in which your relative participated over a lifetime. If the pensioner dies after retirement, the estate may be due a **lump sum benefit**. Also be aware that a designated beneficiary may have either died or is no longer eligible to inherit because of divorce and remarriage, or other factors. That may have cleared the way for your claim. While you may not be eligible for benefits, it may turn out that your children are or will be entitled to a variety of benefits or assets.

To locate all possible potential benefits, compile a complete employment history of your relative or the most complete record possible under the circumstances. (See the Life Pathway Form in Appendix S2.) Then contact each employer, establish yourself and your reason for inquiry, and ask whether or not your relative participated in his pension plan. If the answer is yes, ask about the current status of the account. In order to receive immediate and satisfactory answers to your questions, you should be prepared to furnish the full name of your relative, a Social Security number, and the approximate years of employment. If the Social Security number is unknown, see the section, early in Chapter 3, on finding it. Your relative's residential address during each period of employment is nice to have, but probably not essential. Many pension plans, particularly those offered by government (at every level), give an employee vestment credit for military service. For example, if your relative served in the military for three years and worked for a government agency or company for seven years, he or she could be vested in a plan that required ten years of employment. It's worth a look.

When looking into pension benefits, keep this in mind: a person who reaches retirement age and begins to draw monthly checks, then dies shortly thereafter, may not have used all of the money that he or she contributed to the plan or is entitled to. This means that the legitimate heir or beneficiary is entitled to the rest of the deceased relative's contribution in a lump sum. So if you discover that your relative had begun to draw benefits, ask for the ledger sheet on his or her retirement program and for the rules on the disposition of any residual lump sum. You may be pleasantly surprised.

Pension Benefit Guaranty Corporation

If your relative worked for a company that went out of business, then their retirement is gone forever, right? Not necessarily.

During the 1960's Congress created a **pension protection** plan that currently insures 52 million individual pensions, including those of former Eastern Airlines employees. If you or your relative was employed by a company having more than 25 employees, but is now out of business, you need to find out whether your pension survived.

To make an inquiry, simply call **800-400-7242**. You will need a full name, a Social Security number, and the name and address (at least city) of the company that provided employment.

This guarantee program can pay up to $2,900 per month in retirement benefits and will pay up to three years' back payments. So it could be very important to follow up on this suggestion.

Special note: If the "Life Pathway Form" (Target Outline Appendix S2) of your relative indicates that retirement began or would have begun during the 1980's, and that person passed away prior to 1990, then **the lump sum remainder of his retirement would be unusually large**. During the 1980's interest earnings on retirement annuities were much higher than had been predicted.

Teacher Retirement

Don't be surprised to learn that your deceased relative was a teacher at some time during his lifetime. If he or she did teach, contact the State Teachers Retirement system (see the State Public Employee and Teacher Retirement Programs Appendix R2 for contact information), or the local school system where your relative taught, to get his or her employment history. In some states the teacher retirement program is part of the larger Public Employee Retirement program (see the Appendix R2, mentioned above, for contact details).

These programs began in the mid-1930's under the supervision of state governments. Boards were established to oversee investments and the distribution of retirement benefits. Anyone who ever taught in a public school has invested a percentage of his gross salary into a retirement program. If they were vested, the school district has also contributed its portion. And in most cases, interest has accrued over the years. Several billion dollars are currently held in inactive accounts within teacher retirement programs in the United States.

Why so much? Teachers have historically moved from school to school, from district to district. Some suffer "burn out." Others move on to other professions. Young women often obtain their teaching certificates, teach for a few years, then marry and raise a family. Keep the teaching possibility in mind when searching for lost or forgotten pensions. For generations, teaching was one of the few professions readily open to women.

Vestment takes five years in most teacher retirement programs. Until that requirement is met, a teacher who leaves the system may withdraw his or her contribution. But once a teacher is vested, the contributions made by **both** the employee and employer are locked in. There they remain, in an annuity, until the teacher's retirement age is reached.

If your relative was a teacher, first find out whether he or she was vested and, if so, in which state retirement system. Check with that state's retirement system office. Remember that in almost all teacher retirement programs you can count military service towards vestment in the system. Some states will even give credit for time spent teaching in another state, allowing transfer of retirement funds across state borders.

Every teacher retirement program publishes an annual report. Nowhere in that report, however, must they identify the number and value of their inactive retirement accounts. This makes it very difficult to quantify the total dollar volume of such inactive accounts. Despite this, there are vague reports that 10% or more of these accounts are inactive. These assets go unclaimed unless people like you locate them. In California alone, more than $500 million is set aside for inactive accounts which might someday be claimed. Don't forget! **These accounts remain in the owner's name forever.**

Even should you discover that your relative was already drawing teacher's retirement benefits at the time of death, don't assume that no further assets are there for you to claim. He or she may have an undistributed balance left in the account. If so, this should be paid, in a **lump sum**, to a designated beneficiary or to the estate. It only takes one call to find out about such an account.

During the time I was doing research for the first edition, a couple visited my office and noticed my desk was piled high with research files. The husband asked, "What are you doing, Dave?"

"Writing a book," I replied. I explained that my current research was on teacher retirement. As I gave them some details about hidden assets in teacher retirement programs, I noticed the wife had become very interested.

"I taught in Ohio for seven years," she said. "Do you suppose I was in a retirement program?"

"Chances are good that you were," I told her. "We'll check on it tomorrow." I made a call, and sure enough, she had an account with $4,800 in it!

"But why didn't they tell me?" she asked.

"They may have tried. If the letter to you was returned, they can only assume you could not be located, and from that point on the responsibility rested with you. Remember, too, the retirement system benefits from the use of your money." This lady had moved at least five times since that period of teaching employment and had never returned to that profession.

Railroad Retirement

The Railroad Retirement System began in 1935 and is administered in conjunction with Social Security. As of 1992 there were about 286,000 persons enrolled in the Railroad Retirement Program. (Remember, the ten years of service needed for vestment can be accelerated by credit for military service.) Those enrolled and vested prior to 1974 have more liberal benefits, so it is important to determine when your relative first enrolled. There are Railroad Retirement Offices located in major cities throughout the country. Call them. See the U.S. Railroad Retirement Board Appendix R7 for contact details.

Lump sum payments made during 1992 averaged $4,800. This is *eighteen times more than* the $255 lump sum death and burial benefit paid by Social Security.

Vested railroad employees continue to have a **group life insurance policy valued between $1,500 and $50,000**. Consult Appendix R7, mentioned above, for toll free numbers you can call to check on this possibility. There are sixteen unions (now merged to fourteen) serving railroad workers. **Contact the union** (check the listing in Appendix R7) to find out what insurance coverage your loved one has and the name, address and phone number of the company. I've had many active railroad employees, as well as retired ones, tell me they had forgotten they had a policy.

In earlier days of railroad employment, a railroad employee's Social Security number began (the first three digits of the total of nine) with '700'. Between 1960 and 1975, many railroads were involved in mergers; many many employees accepted buyouts. That could have had a significant impact on their retirement benefits, but don't assume that early buyouts automatically cancel benefit potential. Check on it.

Keep in mind that railroad workers have a shorter life expectancy than the general population, and a higher incidence of disability. It's hazardous work. As in most other cases, the burden of claiming benefits from a railroad retirement fund rests with the retiree or the heirs. This retirement program is unique in its complexity, but it reaches across state borders. Except in one respect: when death occurs, that death is recorded only in the state where it occurred.

Death before retirement age means that the retirement file is not activated. So if your relative had not received retirement benefits before passing away, you can take steps to determine benefits owed to his widow, children or heirs. Personal contact with the Railroad Retirement Offices is best, but most of these offices are very cooperative in responding to written requests.

Public Employee Retirement

Each state has a Public Employee Retirement Program which covers police officers, firemen, elected officials, county and state employees, (sometimes) teachers and other school employees, judges, etc. Ordinarily, both the government and the employee make contributions, with the government matching some or all of what the employee contributes. In many cases, each contributes 5% of the employee's salary. (Check the State Public Employee and Teacher Retirement Programs Appendix R2 for contact information.)

A surprising number of these accounts are inactive. **One has to ask why**. By most estimates the value of these inactive accounts is more than a billion dollars, perhaps several billions. Public employees or their heirs have failed to claim their legitimate benefits.

When you investigate the employment history of your deceased relative, be sure to take special note of any short-term employment with a U.S. Government agency at any level. It usually takes very little time to become vested in one of these programs if the employee spent time in the military. If your relative was vested then, as usual, the contributions from both employee and the government are committed in the retiree's name until his retirement.

But remember that if the pensioner dies it becomes the responsibility of the heir to notify the pension office of that fact. Otherwise the money often remains unclaimed. **This is especially true when the pensioner dies in a state other than the one in which he or she earned the pension.** Be sure to contact the proper state pension office immediately upon the death of your relative, especially if he or she had moved recently to another state or had changed addresses frequently.

Mortgage Insurance Rebates

Over thirty million families and individuals have Federal Housing Administration (FHA) insured loans. There are about ten million mortgages insured privately by companies like General Electric and Westinghouse. And there are many others which provide mortgage insurance protection. This insurance should not be confused with property and casualty insurance associated with the property. **This is insurance covering the investment of the lender.**

When you take out a loan secured by a mortgage, you attend a "closing" at a title insurance company. The loan proceeds go to pay all expenses; one of these is a 30- to 40-year **prepaid** mortgage insurance premium. The cost of this insurance runs from 2% to 3½% of your total loan. If you borrowed $100,000, $2000 to $3500 of the closing costs would go to **prepay this mortgage insurance.**

The average American family lives in a home for about 5½ years. Very often, in settling the estates of our older family members, their home is sold and the mortgage paid off. If the loan is paid off **before the full term of the loan (30 to 40 years) expires** the home owner (or estate) is entitled to a **mortgage insurance premium rebate**. This can easily amount to several hundred dollars. Maybe thousands.

To inquire about such an account, first find the mortgage account number. Be persistent and you may get a pleasant surprise!

The bank where the mortgage payments were made usually acts as a loan servicing agency. You may need to get the address and phone number of the last owner of your mortgage (lender), so that you can obtain the FHA loan number. Once full mortgage assumption has taken place, then the named borrower is entitled to a rebate. More recently, most insured mortgages have become unassumable; when these properties are sold, then, rebates are always due.

See the Federal Home Loan Mortgage Guarantors Appendix R3 for a list of regional Housing and Urban Development (HUD) offices which may be of assistance in processing your claim for the unused portion of your prepaid mortgage insurance.

Frequent Flyer Credits

You probably know that most air travelers earn Frequent Flyer mileage credits. But you may not know that those credits may very well become part of the **deceased traveler's estate**. After all, these Frequent Flyer miles have monetary value. I recently came across a person whose mother-in-law received (or inherited) the Frequent Flyer mileage credits left by her late husband. An employee of United Airlines told me about a widow who had more than 500,000 miles transferred from her husband's account. United currently allows only the surviving spouse to inherit Frequent Flyer credits but that policy is coming under question.

We will continue to research the various laws regulating these credits and the policies that the various airlines use regarding them.

Most airlines have a method whereby an heir can claim these credits. Some have a three-year limitation on the transfer. If your relative often traveled by air, contact one of his or her most frequent carriers. Perhaps someone in the family has a record of the Frequent Flyer account number. Check credit card account statements; those often contain the Frequent Flyer account number. Or, try contacting your relative's travel agent; he or she may very likely have a record of the mileage account.

It only takes 25,000 to 35,000 flying miles to earn a domestic round-trip airline ticket. Thousands of travelers have this much, or more, to their credit. There's no reason for their families to ignore the value of these accounts. Because of the possible time limitation, they should inquire relatively soon.

To effect the transfer, you or the appropriate heir must have a Frequent Flyer account with the airline in question. If you don't, simply open one. Besides the actual mileage flown, there are some indirect ways the account may grow: credit card use, car rental, motel rooms, etc. There is every indication that mileage earnings will continue to grow as an airline industry incentive.

Some airlines will initially tell you that the Frequent Flyer mileage is non-transferable or that it has no monetary value. But if pressured, most airlines will "do the right thing." Be persistent in claiming what is rightfully yours!

For more mileage account information, call the following:

United Airlines
800-421-4655

American Airlines
800-433-7300

Delta Airlines
800-323-2323

Southwest Airlines
800-445-5764

Northwest Airlines
800-327-2881

U.S. Air
800-872-4738

Foreign Affairs and Others

Millions of Americans have worked overseas. Many of them overlook the fact that they may have retirement benefits due them from a foreign government or company. In most cases a person is eligible if he or she worked at least five years or more in a single European country. It may be worth checking.

In addition to the obvious assets we've detailed for you—property, life insurance, pensions, etc.—there are a number of other small assets our loved ones accumulate: security deposits for utilities, escrow accounts, and on and on. See how creative you can be in unearthing some of these. They are almost always worth the trouble it takes to recover them.

Closing Thought

My hope and prayer for all of you is that the information I have provided will provoke you to action. Action to benefit yourself, your family, or your friend.

Our entire staff is determined to "excavate" and identify what some knowledgeable people say could be a trillion dollars in "Unknown Assets." Please write and tell me your story.

Source Appendices

Appendix S1.	Family Trees
Appendix S2.	Target Outline
Appendix S3.	Vital Records
Appendix S4.	Counties
Appendix S5.	State Income Tax
Appendix S6.	Credit Reports
Appendix S7.	General Information Sources
Appendix S8.	Accident Reports
Appendix S9.	Motor Vehicle Departments
Appendix S10.	Credit Card Reports
Appendix S11.	State Bank Regulators
Appendix S12.	State Savings & Loan Regulators
Appendix S13.	National Credit Union Offices
Appendix S14.	State Insurance Regulators
Appendix S15.	Professional Licensing
Appendix S16.	Corporate Records
Appendix S17.	State Archives
Appendix S18.	Women's Commissions
Appendix S19.	Internal Revenue Service
Appendix S20.	Federal Archives
Appendix S21.	Passport Office
Appendix S22.	Freedom of Information Act Inquiries

APPENDIX S1

Family Trees

This Appendix consists of three blank genealogical charts in which you should record your target relative's ancestry. These forms enable you to visualize who the heirs are in your target search.

NOTES:

Who in your family can best help you fill in the blanks? (The "family genealogist" is the person to start with.)

Remember, "blood" relatives are the only ones in line to be heirs. For example, if your deceased cousin was from your mother's side of the family, then your father, who is not a blood relative, would not be an heir. This kind of consideration usually eliminates 50% of the people with whom you might have thought you would have to share the inheritance.

ANCESTRAL CHART
BLOODLINES – FAMILY TREE

Youngest Relative *Oldest Relative*

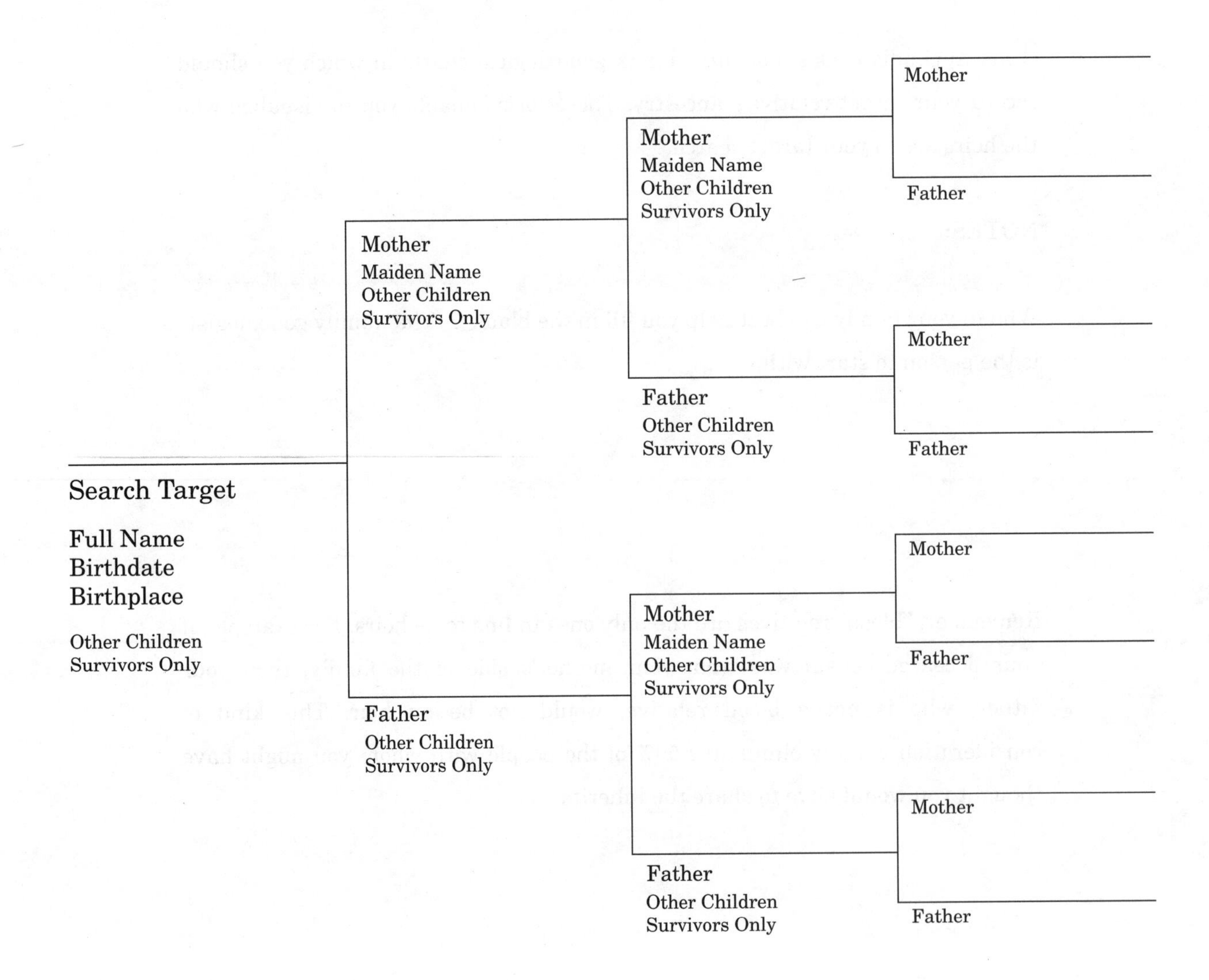

TARGET RELATIVE'S SIBLINGS
(And Their Children)

Target Relative

Brothers & Sisters | *First Cousins*

Brother or Sister
- Oldest Child
- 2nd Child
- 3rd Child

Brother or Sister
- Oldest Child
- 2nd Child
- 3rd Child

Brother or Sister
- Oldest Child
- 2nd Child
- 3rd Child

Brother or Sister
- Oldest Child
- 2nd Child
- 3rd Child

Brother or Sister
- Oldest Child
- 2nd Child
- 3rd Child

Brother or Sister
- Oldest Child
- 2nd Child
- 3rd Child

TARGET RELATIVE'S DESCENDANTS

Target Relative

1st Spouse

- Oldest Child
  - Oldest Grandchild
  - Next Grandchild
  - Next Grandchild
- 2nd Child
  - Oldest Grandchild
  - Next Grandchild
  - Next Grandchild
- 3rd Child
  - Oldest Grandchild
  - Next Grandchild
  - Next Grandchild
- 4th Child
  - Oldest Grandchild
  - Next Grandchild
  - Next Grandchild

2nd Spouse

- Oldest Child
  - Oldest Grandchild
  - Next Grandchild
  - Next Grandchild
- 2nd Child
  - Oldest Grandchild
  - Next Grandchild
  - Next Grandchild
- 3rd Child
  - Oldest Grandchild
  - Next Grandchild
  - Next Grandchild
- 4th Child
  - Oldest Grandchild
  - Next Grandchild
  - Next Grandchild

APPENDIX S2

Target Outline

This appendix of two forms is the heart of your plan for running the money–finding maze. Start by filling out the Life Pathway Form. The first time through, list all items that you can remember. There is a lot of detail in the form; if you fill in even half the blanks you'll have dramatically increased your chances of finding assets. Remember to be persistent, but always courteous, while conducting your search. Be sure to ask questions of the "family busybody"—you know, that person who knows the most details about every family member—and many others.

The Life Pathway Information Checklist can be your "perseverance prompter." Put a copy on your bulletin board or refrigerator as a running to–do list. Keep it up to date.

The "**Notes**" spaces provided in these Appendices are to hold your jotted comments. These remind you (and possibly remind future generations of asset–searchers) where to turn next. Today's blind alley may someday turn into an open road. Keep good records.

LIFE PATHWAY FORM

VITAL STATISTICS

Name

Address | City/State/Zip | Telephone

Social Security Number | Date of Birth | Place of Birth

Age at Death, years | Current Age, years (if alive)

Closest Living Relative(s) Address | Telephone

Closest Personal Friend(s) Address | Telephone

Personality Description: (check all that apply)

- [ ] Social/Outgoing
- [ ] Healthy
- [ ] Irresponsible
- [ ] Private/Reserved
- [ ] Sickly
- [ ] Risk Taker
- [ ] Conservative
- [ ] Personality Change
- [ ] Church Member
- [ ] Traveler
- [ ] Social Drinker
- [ ] Caring
- [ ] Selfish
- [ ] Other

MEDICAL HISTORY

If Deceased: Name(s) of Family Doctor/Specialist

Date of Death | Place of Death

Cause of Death | Doctor Name | Witness Name

Is there a will: ( ) YES ( ) NO If yes, location of document

Start Date of Last Injury or Disability | Date and type of last known Accident

Other Medical History

Was Death Anticipated: ( ) YES ( ) NO | Explain

Estate Executor Name: | Address | City/State/Zip

Why was this person chosen Executor?

LIFE PATHWAY FORM

EDUCATIONAL HISTORY

Grade School | Dates of Attendance | Address | Years Completed

High School | Dates of Attendance | Address | Years Completed

College | Dates of Attendance | Address | Years Completed

Special college scholastic achievements or awards | Alumni Activity

Graduate Education | Dates of Attendance | Address | Years Completed

Technical School | Dates of Attendance | Address | Years Completed

MILITARY HISTORY

Dates: Rank:

Other: (length of service, wounds, type of discharge, honors received, disability status, etc.)
List any special military recognition or achievements.

ACTIVITIES (list all memberships)

Professional Organizations

Hobbies/Social Groups

Service Clubs

LIFE PATHWAY FORM

WORK HISTORY

Area(s) of Employment: (check all that apply)

☐ Self Employed ☐ Management ☐ Small Company Employee

☐ Union Member ☐ Large Company Employee ☐ Licensed Professional

☐ Other ***Note:*** Look for 401k plans, IRA accounts, and group life insurance at each place of employment.

CHRONOLOGICAL WORK ACTIVITY

Company Name	Dates Employed	Address	Position Held	Income Level
Company Name	Dates Employed	Address	Position Held	Income Level
Company Name	Dates Employed	Address	Position Held	Income Level
Company Name	Dates Employed	Address	Position Held	Income Level
Company Name	Dates Employed	Address	Position Held	Income Level
Company Name	Dates Employed	Address	Position Held	Income Level

List in chronological order all states in which search target lived. (Include the number of years in each state.)

____

State Unclaimed Property Office phone number. ____________

(See Unclaimed Property Offices Appendix R1.)

After filling in the above, stop and call the state offices listed.

In most cases they will search for the information while you wait.

RETIREMENT HISTORY

____

Last Salary/Wage Earned: ( ) monthly ( ) annually Social Security Income: ( ) monthly ( ) annually

____

Other Income Business activity that deferred income tax Expense

If search target is or was of retirement age, what pensions did he or she receive (include policy/account numbers):

☐ Keogh Plans ☐ 401K ☐ Group Pensions

☐ Group Life Insurance ☐ IRA ☐ Annuities (individual or group)

☐ Other

LIFE PATHWAY FORM

BANKING ACTIVITY

(Indicate in "account type" whether checking, savings, outstanding loan or credit life.)

COMMERCIAL BANKS:

Name	Address	Account #	Account Type

SAVINGS AND LOANS:

Name	Address	Account #	Account Type

CREDIT UNIONS:

Name	Address	Account #	Account Type

Location(s) of any safe deposit boxes ______________________________

In any of the above, is there a loan file? ( ) YES ( ) NO
If yes:

Name of Loan Officers	Line of Established Credit	Maximum Actual Credit Utilized

Note: Be sure to ask each institution if they have a financial statement. If so, request a copy.

List checks of over $1000 paid to individuals or companies during the last three years:

Date	Name	Purpose	Amount

CREDIT HISTORY

Recent Credit Card Activity: (check all that apply)

☐ VISA ☐ MasterCard ☐ Discover ☐ American Express ☐ Department Store ☐ Other

Check to see if there is life insurance benefits in the name of the cardholder.

____
Credit Reports

Agency Name	Address	Telephone Number

LIFE PATHWAY FORM

FINANCIAL ASSETS

____
Personal Real Estate

____
Address | Legal Description | Estimated Value

____
Amount of Insurance | Name of Mortgage Company | Mortgage Balance

Is Real Estate covered by Credit Life, HUD, or FHA and is there equity interest? ____________________

Has any property recently been sold or liquidated? ( ) YES ( ) NO

____
Other Real Estate Properties (cabins, vacation homes, condos, time shares)

____
Vehicles (auto / truck / RV / trailer)

____
Make | Model | Title Holder | Estimated Value

Business Interest ____

____
Name of Partnerships | Type of Business | Estimated Value

____
Farming Interests (during lifetime)

____
Family Farm / Ranch | Address | Type | Dates

Co-operative Memberships (patronage accounts)

☐ Rural Electric ☐ Rural Telephone ☐ Fuel Co-op ☐ Grain Co-op ☐ Farm Implement Co-op

LIFE PATHWAY FORM

INSURANCE

Life Insurance	Insurance Agent(s)	Address	Policy Type	Policy Number

Beneficiary(ies)

Health Insurance	Insurance Agent(s)	Address	Policy Type	Policy Number

Beneficiary(ies)

Casualty Policy	Insurance Agent(s)	Address	Policy Type	Policy Number

Beneficiary(ies):

PERSONAL ADVISORS

Name	Address	Date of Last Contact
Doctor		
Accountant		
Lawyer		
Trust Officer		
Stockbroker		License #
Financial Planner		License #
Psychiatrist		
Psychologist		
Psychotherapist		

Other important confidential or intimate associations.

List any important information that you have been told to pursue or that you have always wondered about.

LIFE PATHWAY INFORMATION CHECKLIST

Place this list on your refrigerator door or other conspicuous location.

VITAL DOCUMENTS	Date Requested	Date Received	Contact Name / Address / Telephone
Genealogical Chart/Family Tree			
Certified Birth Certificates			
Certified Marriage Certificates			
Certified Divorce Records			
Death Certificate			
Will			
Passport			
State Motor Vehicle Department			
Law Enforcement Agencies			
Professional Licenses			
Veteran's Records			
PERSONAL RECORDS			
Canceled Checks			
Deposit Slips			
City Directories			
Telephone Directories			
Post Office Addresses			
TAX RETURNS			
Federal Income Tax Returns			
State Income Tax Returns			
REAL ESTATE			
HUD			
FHA			
GI Bill			
BANKING INSTITUTIONS			
Checking Accounts			
Savings Accounts			
Bank Loan Portfolio			
Bank Trust Documents			
Safe Deposit Box			
IRA			
Credit Unions			

LIFE PATHWAY INFORMATION CHECKLIST

Place this list on your refrigerator door or other conspicuous location.

EMPLOYERS	**Date Requested**	**Date Received**	**Contact Name / Address / Telephone**
Retirement Plans			
401K			
IRA			
Annuities			
Tax Free Bond Investments			
Public Pension Funds			
Private Pension Funds			
Professional Licenses			
Savings and Loan Agencies			
DBA (Doing Business As) Records			
INSURANCE			
State Insurance Regulators			
American Council of Life Insurance			
Social Security Administration			
Automobile Insurance			
Home Owner's Insurance			
COOPERATIVES			
Rural Electric Cooperatives			
Rural Telephone Cooperatives			
Rural Farmers Cooperatives			
OTHER RESOURCES			
State Unclaimed Property Offices			
Credit Reports			
Personal Contacts			
Credit Card Histories			
Unions			
Public Employee's Retirement			
Teacher's Retirement			
Railroad Retirement			

APPENDIX S3

Vital Records

Records of pertinent births, deaths, marriages, and divorces will be important in establishing legal heirship to your target relative's assets. These records are filed permanently either in: (a) a State Vital Statistics Office; or (b) in the offices of various local county offices. Your goal is to establish that you or the family member for whom you are searching are either the sole surviving next of kin or else that the searcher is one of several persons with equal claim to the estate. As vital statistic records become 12 months old they are transferred from the county to the State Vital Records department where they remain forever.

Most of these vital records concerning your target relative are not accessible to just anyone. To get them, you'll need your own records establishing your identity and, often, proof of your relationship to the target. Examples of acceptable personal ID (preferably with your picture) include:

- Driver's License (state, license number, or copy)
- Picture ID Card (state, number, or copy)
- Social Services ID (state and number)
- Employment ID (firm and number)
- Payroll Stub
- Social Security Card (SSN or copy)
- Voter Registration Card
- Credit Card (issuing company and number)
- Miliary ID (military serial or service number, or copy)

To obtain the records you need in your search, use the sample letters in this Appendix and include proof of your own identity or authority. A simple photocopy of a vital record is not legally acceptable in circumstances having to do with inheritance. **Always request a certified copy!**

You may not know the precise date, or even the exact year, of the birth, death, marriage, or divorce you are interested in. Most states have set time intervals for enlarging your search horizon. For example assume you have good reason to think someone of importance to your search died around 1942. If the state in which you are seeking their death certificate conducts searches in five–year intervals, you would request a search to cover the 1940–1944 period inclusively. If that search bore no fruit, you might then request 1935–1939 or possibly 1945–1949.

If the record you are requesting was filed before the State Vital Records Office began keeping records, you may need to request the record from the appropriate State Archives Office. Those are listed in Appendix S17.

SUGGESTED LETTER FOR BIRTH OR DEATH RECORDS

Date

Your Full Name
Address
City/State/Zip
Day Phone
Nights/Weekend Phone
Fax

Vital Records Office
Address (see Vital Records Appendix S17)

To whom it may concern:

I need to obtain a certified record (birth or death) for the person listed below:

1. Full name of person whose record is being requested.
2. Month, day, year of birth or death
3. Sex
4. Place of birth or death (city/town, county, state, and, if known, name of hospital)
5. Parents' names, including maiden name of mother
6. Purpose for which copy is needed
7. Your relationship to the person whose record is being requested

I have included the proper fees and documentation that will allow you to provide me with the copies of the information requested. (See Enclosure.)

Please contact me at the address/telephone number listed above if further information is needed in order to obtain the record(s).

Sincerely,

Signed

SUGGESTED LETTER FOR MARRIAGE RECORDS

Date

Your Full Name
Address
City/State/Zip
Day Phone
Nights/Weekend Phone
Fax

Vital Records Office
Address (see Vital Records Appendix S3)

To whom it may concern:

I need to obtain a certified marriage record from your office for the following people:

1. Full name of husband and wife
2. Month, day, and year of marriage (Give year and county if that is all you know.)
3. Place of marriage (city or town, county and state)
4. Purpose for which copy is needed
5. Your relationship to the persons whose record is being requested

I have included the proper fees and documentation that will allow you to provide me with the copies of the information requested. (See Enclosure)

Please contact me at the address/telephone number listed above if further information is needed in order to obtain the record(s).

Sincerely,

Signed

SUGGESTED LETTER FOR DIVORCE RECORDS

Date

Your Full Name
Address
City/State/Zip
Day Phone
Nights/Weekend Phone
Fax

Vital Records Office
Address (see Vital Records Appendix S3)

To whom it may concern:

I need to obtain a certified marriage record from your office for the following persons:

1. Full name of husband and wife
2. Date of divorce or annulment
3. Place of divorce or annulment (city or town, county and state)
4. Type of final decree
5. Purpose for which copy is needed
6. Your relationship to the persons whose record is being requested

As far as I know, I have included the proper fees and documentation that you need to provide me with the copies of the information requested. (See Enclosure.)

Please contact me at the address/telephone number listed above if further information is needed in order to obtain the record(s).

Sincerely,

Signed

VITAL RECORDS

ALABAMA

Agency:	Alabama Dept. of Public Health Center for Health Statistics P.O. Box 5625 Montgomery, AL 36103-5625
Telephone:	(334) 242-5033
Fax:	(334) 240-3315
Available Records:	Births in Alabama since 1908 Deaths in Alabama since 1908 Marriages in Alabama since August 1936 Divorces in Alabama since 1950 Marriage records prior to August 1936 are with the Probate Judge in the county where the license was issued. (See County Appendix S4.) Divorce records prior to 1950 are with the Clerk or Register of Court of Equity in the county where the divorce was granted. (See County Appendix S4.)
Fees:	Certified Birth/Death/Marriage/Divorce: $12.00 each $4.00 for a duplicate copy of the same record ordered at the same time (Search fee is included for the first copy of each record.) If the precise information is not known in order to find the record, a ten (10) year search will be made based on the information you provide. If the record is not found, all fees are retained for each record and a statement of search will be issued.
Method of Payment:	Money order payable to: State Board of Health Credit Card: VISA, Mastercard, Discover, or American Express For credit card orders call: (334) 242-5033 $27.00 by regular mail / $36.50 by Federal Express overnight / $4.00 for a duplicate copy of the same record ordered at the same time. If you wish to have a document expedited by regular mail, you must include $10.00 extra, and mail the request to them by an overnight express mail service. Call (334) 613-5418 for this service.
Accompanying Documentation:	The registrant, a member of his immediate family, his guardian, or their respective legal representatives shall be considered to have a direct and tangible interest. Others may demonstrate a direct and tangible interest when information is needed for determination or protection of a personal or property right. Proof of relationship to the registrant must accompany the record request.

NOTES:

VITAL RECORDS

ALASKA

Agency:	Bureau of Vital Statistics P.O. Box 110675 Juneau, AK 99811-0675
Telephone:	(907) 465-3392 (Direct) (907) 465-3391 (Recording)
Fax:	(907) 465-3618
Available Records:	Births in Alaska since 1913 Deaths in Alaska since 1913 Marriages in Alaska since 1913 Divorces in Alaska since 1950 Divorce records prior to 1950 are with the Clerk of Superior Court in the judicial district where the divorce was granted. (See County Appendix S4.)
Fees:	Certified Birth/Death/Marriage/Divorce: $10 each (Search fee is included for the first copy of each record.) If the precise information is not known in order to find the record, a three (3) year search will be made based on the information you provide. Add $1.00 for each additional year to be searched. If a record is not found, the $10.00 search fee will be retained and a statement of search will be issued.
Method of Payment:	Money order payable to: State of Alaska Credit Card: VISA, Mastercard, American Express, or Discover For credit card orders call: (907) 465-3038 or 465-3394 (Add a $10.00 service fee.)
Accompanying Documentation:	In accordance with Alaska Statute 18.50, in addition to having one's own record, a birth record can be furnished to the parents, guardian or respective representative. Proof of relationship to the registrant must accompany the record request. If you do not fall into one of the above categories, we will need written permission from one of the eligible persons above. The written consent must be sent with your request along with a valid reason such as being a blood relative.

NOTES:

VITAL RECORDS

ARIZONA

Agency:	Office of Vital Records Arizona Dept. of Health Services P.O. Box 3887 Phoenix, AZ 85030
Telephone:	(602) 255-3260 (press 0)
Fax:	No Fax Credit card: (602) 249-3040
Available Records:	Births in Arizona since July 1909 Deaths in Arizona since July 1909 Marriage records are with the Clerk of Superior Court in the county where the license was issued. (See County Appendix S4.) Divorce records are with the Clerk of Superior Court in the county where the divorce was granted. (See County Appendix S4.)
Fees:	Certified Birth: $9.00 each Certified Death: $6.00 each (Search fee is included for the first copy of each record.) Photo after 1950: $6.00 (computer generated) If the precise information is not known in order to find the record, a three (3) year search will be made based on the information you provide. Add $3.00 for each additional year to be searched. If a record is not found, the search fee will be retained and a statement of search will be issued.
Method of Payment:	Money order payable to: Office of Vital Records Credit Cards: VISA, Mastercard, Discover, or American Express $5.00 service fee, $12.50 for Federal Express
Accompanying Documentation:	For the protection of the individual, certificates of vital events are NOT open to the public inspection. Only an immediate family member may apply for the records or you must prove legal interest in the record with documentation to support your interest, such as, a copy of the will. If you will be utilizing the record for genealogy purposes, you must prove your relationship. Also include a genealogical chart, birth certificates, etc. You must also have a notarized signature and a valid I.D.

NOTES:

VITAL RECORDS

ARKANSAS

Agency: Arkansas Dept. of Health
Division of Vital Records
4815 W. Markham St. – Slot 44
Little Rock, AR 72205

Telephone: (501) 661-2134 (Direct)
(501) 661-2336 (Recording)

Fax: (501) 663-2832

Available Records: Births in Arkansas since February 1914
Deaths in Arkansas since February 1914
Marriages in Arkansas since 1917 (verifications only)
Divorces in Arkansas since 1923 (verifications only)
Certified copies of marriage records may be obtained from the County Clerk in the county where the license was issued. (See County Appendix S4.) Certified copies of divorce records may be obtained from the Circuit or Chancery Clerk in the county where divorce was granted. (See County Appendix S4.)

Fees: Certified Birth: $5.00 each
Certified Death: $4.00 each
$1.00 for a duplicate copy of the same death record ordered at the same time.
Marriage/Divorce: coupon verifications only – $5.00 each
(Search fee is included for the first copy of each record.)

If the precise information is not known in order to find the record, a three (3) year search will be made based on the information you provide. Of the total fee you send, $5.00 (birth, marriage, or divorce request form) and $4.00 (death record request) will be kept in this office to cover search charges if no record is found.

Method of Payment: Money order payable to: Arkansas Dept. of Health
Credit Card: VISA, Mastercard, American Express, or Discover
For credit card orders call: (501) 661-2726
(Add a $5.00 service fee.)

Accompanying Documentation: Arkansas state law limits the access to certified vital records to the person or blood relatives of that person whose records you are requesting. Proof of relationship to the registrant must accompany the record request. It does not need to be notarized.

NOTES:

VITAL RECORDS

CALIFORNIA

Agency: State Dept. of Health Services
Office of Vital Records
304 S. St.
P.O. Box 730241
Sacramento, CA 94244-0241

Telephone: (916) 445-1719 (Direct)
(916) 445-2684 (Recording)

Fax: (800) 858-5553

Available Records: Births in California since July 1905
Deaths in California since July 1905
Marriages in California from 1905-1986
Divorces in California from 1962-1984 (verifications only)

Certified divorce records can be obtained from the Clerk of Superior Court in the county where the divorce was granted.
(See County Appendix S4.)

Fees: Certified Birth / Marriage: $13.00 each
Certified Death: $9.00 each
Divorce: (verifications only)-$13.00 each
(Search fee is included for the first copy of each record.) If the precise information is not known in order to find the record, a ten (10) year search will be made based on the information you provide. If record is not found, the search fee will be retained and a statement of search will be issued.

Method of Payment: Money order payable to: Office of Vital Records
Credit Card: VISA, Mastercard, American Express, or Discover
For credit card orders call: (916) 445-1719
(Add a $5.00 service fee.)

Accompanying Documentation: Applicant must be able to identify the record by name and give an approximate date to search. Most records are therefore open to the public.

NOTES:

VITAL RECORDS

COLORADO

Agency:	Colorado Dept. of Health Vital Records Section 4300 Cherry Creek Dr. S. Denver, CO 80222-1530
Telephone:	(303) 692-2200
Fax:	(800) 423-1108
Available Records:	Births in Colorado since 1900 Deaths in Colorado since 1900 Marriage and divorce verifications in Colorado from 1900-1939 and 1975 to present Certified marriage records can be obtained from the County Clerk in the county where the license was issued. (See County Appendix S4.) Certified divorce records are with the Clerk of District Court in the county where the divorce was granted. (See County Appendix S4.)
Fees:	Certified Birth\Dealth: $15.00 each $6.00 for a duplicate copy of the same birth record ordered at the same time. Marriage\Divorce: verifications only-$15.00 each. (Search fee is included for the first copy of each record.) If the precise information is not known in order to obtain a record, send an additional $5.00 for each ten (10) year index to be searched. If the record is not found, the $15.00 search fee will be retained and a statement of search will be issued.
Method of Payment:	Money order payable to: Vital Records Section Credit Card: VISA, Mastercard, American Express, or Discover For credit card orders call: (303) 692-2200 (Add a $4.50 service fee.) Include appropriate additional fees if you wish your certificate returned certified mail, Express Mail, or Federal Express.
Accompanying Documentation:	Pursuant to Colorado Revised Statutes 1982, 25-2-118 and as defined by Colorado Board of Health Rules and Regulations, applicant must have a direct and tangible interest in the record requested. Only the registrant (person named on the certificate) parents, grandparents, stepparents, siblings, spouse, children, grandchildren, legal guardian, or legal representative of the registrant may obtain a certified vital record. Proof of relationship to the registrant must accompany the record request. You must also state the reason and relationship to the registrant.

NOTES:

VITAL RECORDS

CONNECTICUT

Agency: State of Connecticut
Dept. of Public Health
Vital Records Section
410 Capitol Ave.
P.O. Box 340308
Hartford, CT 06134

Telephone: (860) 509-7897 (Direct)
(860) 509-7899 (Recording)

Fax: (860) 509-7964

Available Records: Births in Connecticut since July 1897
Deaths in Connecticut since July 1897
Marriages in Connecticut since July 1897
Divorce records are kept with the Clerk of Superior Court in the township where the divorce was granted. Birth, death, and marriage records can also be found in the township where the certificate originated. (See County Appendix S4.)

Fees: Certified Birth: $15.00 each
Certified Death/Marriage: $5.00 each
(Search fee is included for the first copy of each record.)

This agency will search for a record until found or determined not to be on file in this office. If the record is not found, the search fee will be retained and a statement of search will be issued.

Method of Payment: Money order payable to: Connecticut Dept. of Public Health & Addiction Services.
Credit Card: not accepted

Accompanying Documentation: A full certified copy of a birth record can be obtained only by a registrant, who is 18 or older, parent, legal representative, or member of a legally incorporated genealogical society. Proof of relationship to the registrant must accompany the record request. Death records (with the exception of cause of death) and marriage records are open to the public.

NOTES:

VITAL RECORDS

DELAWARE

Agency:	Office of Vital Statistics P.O. Box 637 Dover, DE 19903
Telephone:	(302) 739-4721
Fax:	(302) 739-3008
Available Records:	Births in Delaware since 1924 Deaths in Delaware since 1956 Marriages in Delaware since 1956 Divorces in Delaware since 1935 (verifications only) To obtain a certified copy of a divorce decree, contact the Family Court in the county in which the divorce was granted. (See County Appendix S4.)
Fees:	Certified Birth/Death/Marriage: $6.00 each $4.00 for a duplicate copy of the same record ordered at the same time. Divorce: verifications only - $6.00 each (Search fee is included for the first copy of each record.) If the precise information is not known in order to find the record, a five (5) year search will be made based on the information you provide. If a search is unsuccessful, and has been paid by money order, a partial refund will be made.
Method of Payment:	Money order payable to: Office of Vital Statistics Credit Card: VISA, Mastercard, Discover, or American Express For credit card orders call: (302) 739-4721 (Add a $5.00 service fee.)
Accompanying Documentation:	The files of the Delaware Office of Vital Statistics are confidential and are not open for public inspection. An individual may obtain a copy of his or her own birth or marriage record or the death record of a family member. Proof of relationship to the registrant must accompany the record request. Certified copies of vital records are also issued to attorneys, the Court system, etc., or those who demonstrate the need to obtain said records. Documents may be obtained for genealogy or family tree purposes.

NOTES:

VITAL RECORDS

FLORIDA

Agency:	Dept. of Health & Rehabilitative Services Office of Vital Statistics P.O. Box 210 1217 Pearl St. Jacksonville, FL 32231-0042
Telephone:	(904) 359-6911 (Direct) (904) 359-6900 (Recording)
Fax:	(904) 359-6993
Available Records:	Births in Florida since 1865 Deaths in Florida since 1877 Marriages in Florida since June 6, 1927 Divorces in Florida since June 6, 1927
Fees:	Certified Birth: $9.00 each Certified Death/Marriage/Divorce: $5.00 each $4.00 for each additional copy of the same record ordered at the same time. (Search fee is included for the first copy of each record.) Only the year stated on the request will be searched if the precise information to obtain the record is not known. Add $2.00 for each additional year to be searched. If record is not found, the search fee will be retained and a "no record found" statement of search will be issued.
Method of Payment:	Money order payable to: Vital Statistics Credit Card: VISA, Mastercard, Discover, or American Express For credit card orders call: (904) 359-6911 $23.50 for a birth record / $19.50 for all other records by regular mail. Rush Service: Mark envelope RUSH and enclose $10.00 extra. Response will be mailed within 1 full workday of receipt providing that the vital record and the request are in agreement.
Accompanying Documentation:	With the exception of cause of death, information contained on the death record, marriage record and dissolution of marriage record are public records and available to any person requesting the record. Birth records are restricted pursuant to law and can only be issued to the registrant, his or her parents, guardian, other legal representative, or upon order of any court of competent jurisdiction. Proof of relationship to the registrant must accompany the record request.

NOTES:

VITAL RECORDS

GEORGIA

Agency:	Georgia Dept. of Human Resources Vital Records Service 47 Trinity Ave. S.W., Room 217-H Atlanta, GA 30334-5600
Telephone:	(404) 656-4750
Fax:	No Fax
Available Records:	Births in Georgia since 1919 Deaths in Georgia since 1919 Marriages in Georgia since June 9, 1952 Divorces in Georgia since June 9, 1952 (verifications only) Marriage records prior to June 9, 1952 are with the Probate Judge in the county where the license was issued. (See County Appendix S4.) Certified divorce records are with the Clerk of Superior Court in the county where the divorce was granted. (See County Appendix S4.)
Fees:	Certified Birth/Death/Marriage: $10.00 each $5.00 for a duplicate copy of the same record ordered at the same time. Divorce: verifications only - $2.00 each ($0.50 per page) (Search fee is included for the first copy of each record.) If the precise information is not known in order to find the record, a three (3) year search will be made based on the information you provide. If the record is not found, the $10.00 search fee will be retained and a statement of search will be issued.
Method of Payment:	Money order payable to: Georgia Dept. of Human Resources Credit Card: VISA, Mastercard, Discover, or American Express For credit card orders call: (404) 656-4750 Total $30.50. This fee includes $5.00 service fee, a certified record, and $15.50 for Federal Express.
Accompanying Documentation:	Georgia law provides for the issuance of certified copies of birth records only to: (1) the person whose birth is registered, (2) either parent whose name is listed on the certificate, (3) the legal representative of the person whose birth is registered, (4) the Superior Court upon its order, and (5) any governmental agency, provided such certificate shall be needed for official purposes with the proper identification. Relationship to the registrant MUST be stated. Proof of relationship to the registrant must accompany the record request and should be notarized. Death (with the exception of cause of death), marriage, and divorce certificates are public information.

NOTES:

VITAL RECORDS

HAWAII

Agency:	State of Hawaii Dept. of Health Research & Vital Statistics Office P.O. Box 3378 Honolulu, HI 96801
Telephone:	(808) 586-4539 (Direct) (808) 586-4533 (Recording)
Fax:	No Fax
Available Records:	Births in Hawaii since 1896 (Some since 1841) Deaths in Hawaii since 1896 (Some since 1841) Marriages in Hawaii since 1896 (Some since 1841) Divorces in Hawaii since July 1951 Marriage/Divorce records prior to July 1951 are kept at the Circuit Court in the county in which the event occurred. (See County Appendix S4.)
Fees:	Certified Birth/Death/Marriage/Divorce: $2.00 each (Search fee is included for the first copy of each record.) If the precise information is not known in order to find the record, a five (5) year search will be made based on the information you provide. If a record is not found, the $2.00 search fee will be retained and a statement of search will be issued.
Method of Payment:	Money orders payable to: State Dept. of Health Credit Card: not accepted
Accompanying Documentation:	The registrant, an immediate family member, or legal representative may obtain a certified vital record. Proof of relationship to the registrant and a reason must accompany the record request.

NOTES:

VITAL RECORDS

IDAHO

Agency:	Vital Statistics 450 W. State St. P.O. Box 83720 Boise, ID 83720-0036
Telephone:	(208) 334-5980 (Direct) (208) 334-5988 (Recording)
Fax:	(208) 389-9096 If faxing information, write "ATTN: Vital Records" on record requests. Written and fax requests are accepted. No phone requests are taken.
Available Records:	Births in Idaho since July 1911 Deaths in Idaho since July 1911 Marriages in Idaho since May 1947 Divorces in Idaho since May 1947 Marriage and divorce records prior to May 1947 are with the County Recorder in the county where the event occurred. (See County Appendix S4.)
Fees:	Certified Birth/Death/Marriage/Divorce: $8.00 each (Search fee is included for the first copy of each record.) Search will be made based on the information you provide, until the record is found or determined not on file in this office. If a record is not found, the $8.00 search fee will be retained and a statement of search will be issued.
Method of Payment:	Money order payable to: Idaho Vital Statistics Credit Card: VISA, Mastercard, Discover, or American Express For credit card orders call: (208) 334-5980 Total $28.50 for Federal Express, certified copy and $5.00 service fee for credit card service. (Fax requests only)
Accompanying Documentation:	Certified records can only be issued to immediate family members, their legal representatives, or a person that can prove a direct and tangible interest as defined by regulation. Proof of relationship to the registrant and identification must accompany the record request.

NOTES:

VITAL RECORDS

ILLINOIS

Agency:

Division of Vital Records
Illinois Dept. of Public Health
605 W. Jefferson St.
Springfield, IL 62702-5097

Telephone: (217) 782-6553 (Direct)

Fax: (217) 523-2648

Available Records:

Births in Illinois since 1916
Deaths in Illinois since 1916
Marriages in Illinois since 1962
Divorces in Illinois since 1962
(Marriages and Divorces, verifications only)
Certified marriage records are with the County Clerk in the county where the license was issued. (See County Appendix S4.) Certified divorce records are with the Clerk of Circuit Court in the county where the divorce was granted. (See County Appendix S4.)

Fees:

Certified Birth/Death: $15.00 each
$2.00 for a duplicate copy of the same birth or death record ordered at the same time.

Must have the exact date of birth.
Marriage/Divorce: verifications only – $5.00 each
(Search fee is included for the first copy of each record.)

If the precise information is not known, a search will be made based on the information you provide. If record is not found, a search fee will be retained and a statement of search will be issued.

Method of Payment:

Money order payable to: Illinois Dept. of Public Health
Credit Card: VISA, Mastercard, Discover, or American Express

For credit card orders call: (217) 782-6553
(Add a $5.00 service fee.)

Accompanying Documentation:

A certified record may be obtained upon the specific written request signed by the person, if of legal age, or by a parent or other legal representative of the person to whom the record of birth relates; or upon the specific written request for a certification or certified copy by a Dept. of the State or a Municipal Corporation or the Federal Government; or upon the order of a court of record. Death records (with the exception of cause of death) and marriage and divorce verifications are public information.

NOTES:

VITAL RECORDS

INDIANA

Agency:	Indiana State Dept. of Health Vital Records Section 1330 W. Michigan St. P.O. Box 7125 Indianapolis, IN 46206-7125
Telephone:	(317) 383-6274
Fax:	(317) 383-6210
Available Records:	Births in Indiana since October 1907 Deaths in Indiana since 1900 Marriage records are with the Clerk of Circuit Court or Clerk of Superior Court in the county in which the license was issued.(See County Appendix S4.) Divorce records are with the County Clerk in the county where the divorce was granted. (See County Appendix S4.)
Fees:	Certified Birth: $6.00 each Certified Death: $4.00 each $1.00 for a duplicate copy of the same birth or death record ordered at the same time. (Search fee is included for the first copy of each record.) If the precise information is not known in order to find the record, a five (5) year search will be made based on the information you provide. If the record is not found, a search fee will be retained and a statement of search will be issued.
Method of Payment:	Money order payable to: Indiana State Dept. of Health Credit Card: VISA, Mastercard, American Express, or Discover For credit card orders call: (317) 383-6274 (Add a $5.00 service fee.)
Accompanying Documentation:	The individual named on the certificate, his/her mother, father, grandparents, siblings, aunts, uncles, spouse, children, or legal guardian may obtain a unnotarized certified birth record. Proof of relationship to the registrant must accompany the record request. Death records (with the exception of cause of death) are public information. (Need not be notarized.)

NOTES:

VITAL RECORDS

IOWA

Agency: Iowa Dept. of Public Health
Vital Records Bureau
Lucas State Office Bldg.
321 E. 12th St.
Des Moines, IA 50319-0075

Telephone: (515) 281-5871 (Direct)
(515) 281-4944 (Recording)

Fax: (515) 281-4529

Available Records: Births in Iowa since July 1880
Deaths in Iowa since July 1880
Marriages in Iowa since July 1880
Divorces in Iowa since 1906 (statistics only)
Divorce inquiries will be forwarded to appropriate office.
Certified copies of divorce records are with the Clerk of District Court in the county where the divorce was granted. (See County Appendix S4.)

Fees: Certified Birth/Death/Marriage: $10.00 each
(Search fee is included for the first copy of each record.)

If the precise information is not known in order to find the record, a five (5) to ten (10) year search will be made based on the information you provide. If the record is not found, the $10.00 search fee will be retained and a statement search will be issued.

Method of Payment: Money orders payable to: Iowa Dept. of Public Health
Credit Card: VISA, Mastercard, American Express, or Discover

For credit card orders call: (515) 281-5871 or (515) 281-4944
(Add a $5.00 service fee.)

Accompanying Documentation: At the county level, all vital records (excluding fetal death, adoptive records, and out-of-wedlock births) are open to the public. Vital records maintained at the state level are not open to the public. Copies of these records are issued only to the registrant or the legal parents, grandparents, spouse, brothers or sisters, children, legal guardians or respective legal representatives. Proof of relationship to the registrant must accompany the record request.

NOTES:

VITAL RECORDS

KANSAS

Agency: Office of Vital Statistics
Landon State Office Bldg.
900 S.W. Jackson, 1st Floor, Room 151
Topeka, KS 66612-2221

Telephone: (913) 296-1400

Fax: No Fax

Available Records: Births in Kansas since July 1911
Deaths in Kansas since July 1911
Marriages in Kansas since May 1913
Divorces in Kansas since July 1951
Divorce records prior to July 1951 are with the Clerk of District Court in the county where the divorce was granted. (See County Appendix S4.)

Fees: Certified Birth/Death/Marriage/Divorce: $10.00 each
$5.00 for a duplicate copy of the same record request at the same time. (Search fee is included for the first copy of each record.)

If the precise information is not known in order to find the record, a five (5) year search will be made based in the information you provide. If the record is not found, the $10.00 search fee will be retained and a statement of search will be issued.

Method of Payment: Money order payable to: Kansas Vital Statistics
Credit Card: VISA, Mastercard, American Express, or Discover
For credit card orders call: (913) 296-1400
(Add a $5.00 service fee.)

Accompanying Documentation: Kansas vital records are not open to the public; therefore, you need to submit one of the following: an application signed by the person or the signature of an immediate family member, a signed release authorizing you to receive the certificate, a copy of power of attorney, a copy of conservatorship, or a copy of an insurance policy page or form showing you as the beneficiary, such as a copy of drivers license or social security card. Proof of relationship to the registrant must accompany the record request.

NOTES:

VITAL RECORDS

KENTUCKY

Agency:	Vital Statistics 275 E. Main St. Frankfort, KY 40621
Telephone:	(502) 564-4212
Fax:	(502) 227-0032
Available Records:	Births in Kentucky since January 1911 Deaths in Kentucky since January 1911 Marriages in Kentucky since June 1958 Divorces in Kentucky since June 1958 Marriage records prior to June 1958 are with the Clerk of County Court in the county where the license was issued. (See County Appendix S4.) Divorce records prior to June 1958 are kept with the Clerk of Circuit Court in the county in where their divorce was granted.
Fees:	Certified Birth: $7.00 each Certified Death/Marriage/Divorce: $6.00 each (Search fee is included for the first copy of each record.) If the precise information is not known in order to find the record, a five (5) year search will be made based on the information you provide. If a record is not found a search fee will be retained and a statement of search will be issue.
Method of Payment:	Money order payable to: Kentucky State Treasurer Credit Card: VISA, Mastercard, American Express, or Discover For credit card orders call: (502) 564-4212 (Add a $5.00 transfer fee.)
Accompanying Documentation:	If all of the specific information needed to obtain the record is known, a certified record will be issued. Proof of relationship to the registrant does not need to be included with record request.

NOTES:

VITAL RECORDS

LOUISIANA

Agency:	Vital Records Registry 325 Loyola Ave New Orleans, LA 70160
Telephone:	(504) 568-8353 (Direct) (504) 568-5152 (Recording)
Fax:	(504) 568-5391
Available Records:	Births in Louisiana since 1893 Deaths in Louisiana since 1943 Marriages in Louisiana since 1942 (New Orleans only) Marriage and divorce records are with the Clerk of Court in the parish where the event occurred.
Fees:	Certified Birth: $13.00 each Certified Death/ Marriage: $5.00 each cards: $7.00 each (Search fee is included for the first copy of each record.) If the precise information is not known in order to find the record, a three (3) year search will be made based on the information you provide. If the record is not found, a search fee will be retained and a statement of search will be issued.
Method of Payment:	Money order payable to: Vital Records Credit Card: VISA, Mastercard, American Express, or Discover For credit card orders call: (504) 568-8353 or (504) 568-5152 (Add $15.50 for Federal Express.)
Accompanying Documentation	Certified vital records are only issued to the registrant, the immediate family members of the registrant or legal representative of the registrant. Proof of relationship to the registrant must accompany the record request.

NOTES:

VITAL RECORDS

MAINE

Agency:	Dept. of Human Services Office of Vital Statistics State House Station 221 State St. Augusta, ME 04333-0011
Telephone:	(207) 287-3181 (Direct) (207) 289-3184 (Recording)
Fax:	(207) 287-1907
Available Records:	Births in Maine since 1923 Deaths in Maine since 1923 Marriages in Maine since 1923 Divorces in Maine since 1923
Fees:	Certified Birth/Death/Marriage/Divorce: $10.00 each $4.00 for a duplicate copy of the same record ordered at the same time. (Search fee is included for the first copy of each record.) If the precise information is not known in order to find the record, a five (5) year search will be made based on the information you provide. If the record is not found, the $10.00 search fee will be retained and a statement of search will be issued.
Method of Payment:	Money order payable to: Treasurer, State of Maine Credit Card: VISA, Mastercard, American Express, or Discover For credit card orders call: (207) 287-3181 (Add a $5.00 service fee for credit cards and $15.50 for Federal Express.)
Accompanying Documentation:	Most records in the state of Maine are open to the public. Proof of relationship is not required to obtain a certified record. Include all information possible in your request.

NOTES:

VITAL RECORDS

MARYLAND

Agency: Division of Vital Records
P.O. Box 68760
Baltimore, MD 21215-0020

Telephone: (410) 764-3038

Fax: (410) 764 5918

Toll Free: (800) 832-3277

Available Records: Births in Maryland since 1898
Deaths in Maryland since 1969
Marriages in Maryland since June 1951
Divorces in Maryland since January 1961 (verifications)
Marriage record prior to June 1951 are with the Clerk of Circuit Court in the county where the license was issued. (See County Appendix S4.) Certified divorce records are with the Clerk of Circuit Court in the county where the divorce was granted. (See County Appendix S4.)

Fees: Certified Birth/Death/Marriage: $4.00 each (non-refundable)
Divorce: verification only-no charge.
(Search fee is included for the first copy of each record.)

If the precise information is not known in order to find the record, a three (3) year search will be made based on the information you provide. If the record is not found, the $4.00 search fee will be retained and a statement of search will be issued.

Method of Payment: Money order payable to: Division of Vital Records
Credit Card: VISA, Mastercard, Discover, or American Express
For credit card orders call:
(410) 764-3038 (Add a $7.00 service fee.)

Accompanying Documentation: The issuance of an official transcript is restricted to the individual, a parent named on the certificate, the individual's legal guardian accompanied by a court order stating such, or the lawful representative of the individual who can provide evidence of his/her representation. Proof of relationship to the registrant must accompany the record request.

NOTES:

VITAL RECORDS

MASSACHUSETTS

Agency:	Massachusetts Dept. of Public Health Registry of Vital Records 470 Atlantic Ave., 2nd Floor Boston, MA 02210-2224
Telephone:	(617) 753-8600
Fax:	(617) 423-2038
Available Records:	Births in Massachusetts since 1901 Deaths in Massachusetts since 1901 Marriages in Massachusetts since 1901 Divorces in Massachusetts since 1952 (index only) Divorce records are with the Registrar of Probate Court in the county where the divorce was granted. Your name and year of divorce are needed. (See County Appendix S4.)
Fees:	Certified Birth/Death/Marriage: $6.00 each in person $11.00 each by mail (30 day turnaround; $14.00 rush) Divorce: verifications only-no charge If the precise information is not known in order to find the record, a ten (10) year search will be made based on the information you provide. If a record is not found, the search fee will be retained and a statement of search will be issued.
Method of Payment:	Money order payable to: Commonwealth of Massachusetts Credit Card: VISA, Mastercard, American Express, or Discover For credit card orders call: (617) 753-8600 (Add a $5.00 service fee; $19.00/record.)
Accompanying Documentation:	Most records in the state of Massachusetts are public information. Proof of relationship to the registrant does not have to accompany the record request.

NOTES:

VITAL RECORDS

MICHIGAN

Agency:	Michigan Dept. of Community Health Office of the State Registrar & Center for Health Statistics 3423 N. M.L. King Blvd. P.O. Box 30195 Lansing, MI 48909
Telephone:	(517) 335-8657(Direct) (517) 335-8655 (Recording)
Fax:	(517) 321-5884
Available Records:	Births in Michigan since 1867 Deaths in Michigan since 1867 Marriages in Michigan since 1867 Divorces in Michigan since 1897
Fees:	Certified Birth/Death/Marriage/Divorce: $13.00 each Senior Citizens records are $5.00 each $4.00 for a duplicate copy of the same record ordered at the same time. (Search fee is included for the first copy of each record.) If the precise information is not known in order to find the record, a three (3) year search will be made based on the information you provide. Add $4.00 for each additional year to be searched. If a record is not found, the search fee will be retained and a statement of search will be issued.
Method of Payment:	Money order payable to: State of Michigan Credit Card: VISA, Mastercard, Discover, or American Express For credit card orders call: (517) 335-8666 Total $32.00 - includes Federal Express, a certified record and a service fee for credit card use.
Accompanying Documentation:	Certified copies and certificates of registration can be issued only to the individual, the parent(s) named on the record, an heir, legal guardian, or legal representative of an eligible person upon written application and payment of fee. Proof of relationship to the registrant must accompany the record request.

NOTES:

VITAL RECORDS

MINNESOTA

Agency:	Minnesota Dept. of Health Section of Vital Statistics 717 Delaware St., S.E. P.O. Box 9441 Minneapolis, MN 55440
Telephone:	(612) 623-5120 (Direct) (612) 623-5121 (Recording)
Fax:	(612) 331-5776
Available Records:	Births in Minnesota since 1900 Deaths in Minnesota since 1908 Marriages in Minnesota since 1958 (index only) Divorces in Minnesota since 1970 (index only) Marriage inquiries will be forwarded to appropriate office for certification. Marriage and divorce records are with the Local Registrar in the county where the event occurred. (See County Appendix S4.)
Fees:	Certified Birth: $11.00 each $5.00 for a duplicate copy of the same birth record ordered at the same time. Certified Death: $8.00 for the first copy, $2.00 for a duplicate copy of the same death record ordered at the same time. Marriage/Divorce: verifications only-no charge (Search fee is included for the first copy of each record.) Search is made until the record is found or determined not to be on file in the office. If a record is not found, a search fee will be retained and a statement of search will be issued.
Method of Payment:	Money order payable to: Treasurer, State of Minnesota Credit Card: VISA, Mastercard, American Express, or Discover For credit card orders call: (612) 623-5120 $29.50 total for one certified birth record /$26.50 total for a death record and returned Federal Express. Used in emergency only.
Accompanying Documentation:	Most records in the state of Minnesota are public information. When requesting a birth certificate, proof of relationship to the registrant does not need to be included as long as the parents were married at the time of birth.

NOTES:

VITAL RECORDS

MISSISSIPPI

Agency:	Mississippi State Dept. of Health Vital Records 2423 N. State St. P.O. Box 1700 Jackson, MS 39215-1700
Telephone:	(601) 960-7981 (Direct) (601) 960-7450 (Recording)
Fax:	(601) 960-7948
Available Records:	Births in Mississippi since November 1912 Deaths in Mississippi since November 1912 Marriages in Mississippi from January 1926 to July 1938 and since 1942 (verifications only) Divorces in Mississippi since January 1926 (verifications only) Marriage records are with the Circuit Clerk in the county where the license was issued. (See County Appendix S4.) Divorce records are with the Chancery Clerk in the county where the divorce was granted. (See County Appendix S4.)
Fees:	Certified Birth: $12.00 each. $3.00 for a duplicate copy of the same birth record ordered at the same time. Certified Death: $10.00 each. $2.00 for a duplicate copy of the same death record ordered at the same time. Marriage: verifications only. $10.00 each (certified certificates). Divorce: $6.00 for each five (5) year increment. Book and page number for the county record will be verified. (Search fee is included for the first copy of each record.) If the precise information is not known in order to find the record, a five (5) year search will be made based on the information you provide. If record is not found, a $6.00 search fee will be retained and a statement of search will be issued.
Method of Payment:	Money order payable to: Mississippi State Dept. of Health Credit Card: VISA, Mastercard, Discover, or American Express For credit card orders call: (601) 960-7981 or Fax: (601) 352-0013 (There is a Federal Express fee and a $5.00 service fee.)
Accompanying Documentation:	Pursuant of Section 41-57-2 of the Mississippi Code of 1972, annotated and as defined by Mississippi State Board of Health Rules and Regulation, you must have a legitimate and tangible interest in the record request. Proof of relationship to the registrant must accompany the record requested.

NOTES:

VITAL RECORDS

MISSOURI

Agency:

Missouri Dept. of Health
Bureau of Vital Records
1730 E. Elm
P.O. Box 570
Jefferson City, MO 65102-0570

Telephone:

(573) 751-6387(Direct)
(573) 751-6374(Recording)

Fax:

(573) 751-6382

Available Records:

Births in Missouri since January 1910
Deaths in Missouri since January 1910
Marriages in Missouri since July 1948 (verifications only)
Divorces in Missouri since July 1948 (verifications only)
Marriage records are with the Recorder of Deeds in the county where the license was issued. (See County Appendix S4.)
Divorce records are with the Clerk of Circuit Court in the county where the divorce was granted. (See County Appendix S4.)

Fees:

Certified Birth/Death: $10.00 each
Marriage/Divorce: verifications only- no charge.
(Search fee is included for the first copy of each record.)

If the precise information is not known in order to find the record, a five (5) year search will be made based on the information you provide. If a record is not found, the $10.00 search fee will be retained and a statement of search will be issued.

Method of Payment:

Money order payable to: Missouri Dept. of Health
Credit Card: VISA, Mastercard, American Express, or Discover
For credit card orders call: (314) 751-6387 (please call before sending, emergency only)

Accompanying Documentation:

Statement of marriage and divorce are open to the general public. Birth and death records are confidential by law and can be released to the registrant, a member of his/her family, his/her legal guardian or one of their respective representatives. All family members, genealogists representing a family member and professionally recognized genealogists are eligible to receive copies of death certificates. Proof of relationship to the registrant must accompany the record request. If not a direct relative, there must be a notarized affidavit form.

NOTES:

VITAL RECORDS

MONTANA

Agency:	Vital Records & Statistics Bureau Health & Environmental Sciences 1400 Broadway P.O. Box 4210 Helena, MT 59604
Telephone:	(406) 444-4228 (Direct) (406) 444-2614 (Recording)
Fax:	(406) 444-1803
Available Records:	Births in Montana since 1907 Deaths in Montana since 1907 Marriages in Montana since July 1943 (verifications only) Divorces in Montana since July 1943 (verifications only) Marriage and divorce requests will be forwarded to appropriate offices. To obtain certified marriage or divorce records, contact the Clerk of District Court in the county where the event occurred. (See County Appendix S4.)
Fees:	Certified Birth/Death: $10.00 each Marriage/Divorce: verifications only-$10.00 each. (Search fee is included for the first copy of each record.) If the precise information is not known in order to find the record, a five (5) year search will be made based in the information you provide. If a record is not found, the $10.00 search fee will be retained and a statement of search will be issued.
Method of Payment:	Money order payable to: Montana Dept. of Health Credit Card: VISA, Mastercard, Discover, or American Express For credit card orders call:(406)444-4228 (Add a $5.00 service fee and a $10.50 Federal Express fee.)
Accompanying Documentation:	For birth and death records, you must have proof of relationship, legal representation and reason for wanting the certificate. Proof of relationship to the registrant must accompany the record request. Marriage and divorce records are public information. There is a picture I.D. required.

NOTES:

VITAL RECORDS

NEBRASKA

Agency:	Vital Health Records Management 14th & L, 3rd Floor P.O. Box 95065 Lincoln, NE 68509-5065
Telephone:	(402) 471-2872 (Direct) (402) 471-2871(Recording)
Fax:	(402) 471-0383
Available records:	Births in Nebraska since 1904 Deaths in Nebraska since 1904 Marriages in Nebraska since 1909 Divorces in Nebraska since 1909
Fees:	Certified Birth: $10.00 each Certified Death/ Marriage/ Divorce: $9.00 each (Search fee is included for the first copy of each record.) If the precise information is not known in order to find the record, a complete search will be made until the record is found or determined not to be on file in this office. If a record is not found, the search fee will be retained and statement of search will be issued.
Method of Payment:	Money order payable to: Bureau of Vital Statistics Credit Cards: VISA, Mastercard, Discover, or American Express For credit card orders call: (402) 471-2871 (press 7 at the prompt)
Accompanying Documentation:	Review of any record at the Bureau of Vital Statistics is open to the public. In order to get a certified copy of any record, you must show proof of relationship or legal representation. Proof of relationship to the registrant must accompany the record request. (Does not need to be notarized.)

NOTES:

VITAL RECORDS

NEVADA

Agency:	Nevada Office of Vital Statistics 505 E. King St., #102 Carson City, Nevada 89710
Telephone:	(702) 687-4481 (Direct) (702) 687-4480(Recording)
Fax:	(702) 887-6151
Toll Free:	(800) 992-0900 ext. 4481 (in Nevada only)
Available Records:	Births in Nevada since July 1911 Deaths in Nevada since July 1911 Marriages in Nevada since January 1968 (index only) Divorces in Nevada since January 1968 (index only) Marriage and divorce inquires will be forwarded to appropriate offices. Marriage records are with the County Recorder in the county where the license was issued. (See County Appendix S4.) Divorce records are with the County Clerk in the county where the divorce was granted. (See County Appendix S4.)
Fees:	Certified Birth: $11.00 each Certified Death: $8.00 each Marriage/Divorce: verifications only- $4.00 each (Search fee is included for the first copy of each record.) If the precise information is not known in order to find the record, a complete search will be made until the record is found or determined not on file in this office. If a record is not found, a $4.00 search fee will be retained and a statement of search will be issued.
Method of Payment:	Money order payable to: Office of Vital Statistics Credit Card: VISA, Mastercard, American Express, or Discover For credit card orders call: (702) 687-4481 (Add a $5.00 service fee.)
Accompanying Documentation:	Nevada law states that the applicant must establish relationship or a legal need for the use of the said certificate. Proof of relationship to the registrant and reason for wanting the documents, must accompany the record request.

NOTES

VITAL RECORDS

NEW HAMPSHIRE

Agency: Division of Public Health Services
Bureau of Vital Records
H&W Bldg.
6 Hazen Dr.
Concord, NH 03301-6527

Telephone: (603) 271-4650 (Direct)
(603) 271-4654 (Recording)

Fax: No Fax

Available Records: Births in New Hampshire since 1640
Deaths in New Hampshire since 1640
Marriages in New Hampshire since 1640
Divorces in New Hampshire since 1808

Fees: Certified Birth/Death: $10.00 each
$6.00 for a duplicate copy of the same birth or death record ordered at the same time.
Certified Marriage/Divorce: $10.00 each.
(Search fee is included for the first copy of each record.)
Search will continue until the record is found or determined not on file in this office. If a record is not found, the $10.00 search fee will be retained and a "NO RECORD STATEMENT" will be issued.

Method of Payment: Money order payable to: Treasurer, State of New Hampshire
Credit Card: VISA, Mastercard, American Express, or Discover
For credit card orders call: (603) 271-4650
(Add a $6.00 service fee.)

Accompanying Documentation: The registrant, a member of his/her immediate family, guardian, or their legal representative shall be considered to have a "direct and tangible interest" in the record and therefore may acquire a certified record. Proof of relationship to the registrant must accompany the record request.

NOTES

VITAL RECORDS

NEW JERSEY

Agency	Bureau of Vital Statistics CN 370 Trenton, NJ 08625-0370
Telephone:	(609) 292-4089
Fax:	(609) 392-4292 (limit of 3 requests per fax)
Available Records:	Births in New Jersey since June 1878 Deaths in New Jersey since June 1878 Marriages in New Jersey since June 1878 Divorce records, write to: Public Information Center CN 967 Trenton, NJ 08625
Telephone:	(609) 292-7834
Fax:	No Fax
	Divorce records, make money order for $10.00 payable to: Clerk of the Superior Court. If the county in which the event occurred is unknown call (609) 777-0093 for further assistance.
Fees:	Certified Birth/Death/Marriage: $4.00 each $2.00 for a duplicate copy of the same record ordered at the same time. (Search fee is included for the first copy of each record.) If the precise information is not known in order to find the record, they will only search the year on your request. Add $1.00 for each additional year that you need searched. If a record is not found, the $4.00 search fee will be retained and a statement of search will be issued.
Method of Payment:	Money order payable to: State Registrar Credit Card: VISA, Mastercard, American Express, or Discover For credit card orders call: (609) 633-2860 (Add a $5.00 service fee.) Use of a credit card limits the search to the year stated on the request.
Accompanying Documentation:	Most records in the state of New Jersey are public information. Proof of relationship is not required.

NOTES

VITAL RECORDS

NEW MEXICO

Agency:	Dept. of Health/P.H.D. Bureau of Vital Records & Health Statistics 1190 St. Francis Dr. P.O. Box 26110 Santa Fe, NM 87502-6110
Telephone:	(505) 827-0122 (Direct) (505) 827-2338 (Recording)
Fax:	(505) 984-1048
Available Records:	Births in New Mexico since 1920 Deaths in New Mexico since 1920 Marriage records are with the County Clerk in the county where the license was issued. (See County Appendix S4.) Divorce records are with the Clerk of Superior Court in the county where the divorce was granted. (See County Appendix S4.)
Fees:	Certified Birth: $10.00 each Certified Death: $5.00 each (Search fee is included for the first copy of each record.) If the precise information is not known in order to find the record, a ten (10) year search will be made based on the years you specify for the search and the other information you provide. If a record is not found, the search fee will be retained and a statement of search will be issued.
Method of Payment:	Money order payable to: Vital Statistics Credit Card: VISA, Mastercard, Discover, or American Express (birth certificates only) For credit card orders call: (505) 827-2897 (Add a $10.00 service fee.)
Accompanying Documentation:	The registrar, immediate family member of the registrar, or legal representative of the registrar, may obtain a certified vital record. Proof of relationship to the registrant and, if not a relative, a notarized affidavit must accompany the record request.

NOTES:

VITAL RECORDS

NEW YORK (except New York City)

Agency: New York State Dept. of Health
Vital Records Section
Empire State Plaza
Albany, NY 12237-0023

Telephone: (518) 474-3075

Fax: (518) 474-9168
(New York City records are with the City Clerk in the borough where the event occurred)

Available Records: Births in New York since 1881
Deaths in New York since 1881
Marriages in New York since 1881
Divorces in New York since 1963
Divorce records prior to January 1963 are with the County Clerk in the county where the divorce was granted. (See County Appendix S4.)

Fees: Certified Birth/Death/Divorce: $15.00 each
Certified Marriage: $5.00 each
(Search fee is included for the first copy of each record.)

If the precise information is not known in order to find the record, a three (3) year search will be made based on the information you provide. If a record is not found, the search fee will be retained and a statement of "No Record Certification" will be issued.

Method of Payment: Money order payable to: New York State Dept. of Health
Credit Card: VISA, Mastercard, American Express, or Discover (birth records only)
For credit card orders call: (518) 474-3075
$30.50 total by Federal Express

Accompanying Documentation: To obtain a certified record, you must show a specific request by the person(s), if 18 years of age or more, by an immediate family member, or other lawful representative of the person to whom the record relates. Proof of relationship to the registrant must accompany the record request.

NOTES

VITAL RECORDS

NORTH CAROLINA

Agency:	North Carolina Vital Records 225 N. McDowell St. P.O. Box 29537 Raleigh, NC 27626-0537
Telephone:	(919) 733-3526
Fax:	(919) 733-1511
Available Records:	Births in North Carolina since October 1913 Deaths in North Carolina since 1930 Marriages in North Carolina since July 1962 Divorces in North Carolina since 1958 Marriage records prior to July 1962 are with the Registrar of Deeds in the county where marriage was performed. (See County Appendix S4.) Divorce records prior to 1958 are with the Clerk of Superior Court in the county where the divorce was granted. (See County Appendix S4.)
Fees:	Certified Birth/Death/Marriage/Divorce: $10.00 each $5.00 for a duplicate copy of the same record ordered at the same time. (Search fee is included for the first copy of each record.) If the precise information is not known in order to find the record, a five (5) year search will be made based on the information you provide. Add $5.00 for each five (5) year search requested at the same time thereafter. If a record is not found, the $10.00 search fee will be retained and a statement of search will be issued.
Method of Payment:	Money order payable to: N.C. Vital Records Credit Card: VISA, Mastercard, American Express, or Discover For credit card orders call: (919) 733- 3526 A standard fee of $25.00 per expedited search applies, in addition to all commercial and shipping charges.
Accompanying Documentation:	Relationship to the person whose certificate is requested must be (1) self, (2) spouse, (3) brother/sister, (4) child, (5) parent/stepparent, (6) grandparent, or (7) authorized agent, attorney or legal representative of the person listed 1-6. Proof of relationship to the registrant must accompany the record request.

NOTES:

VITAL RECORDS

NORTH DAKOTA

Agency: North Dakota State Dept. of Health
Vital Records
State Capitol
600 E. Boulevard Ave.
Bismarck, ND 58505-0200

Telephone: (701) 328-2360

Fax: (701) 328-4727

Available Records: Births in North Dakota since 1870
Deaths in North Dakota since 1893
Marriages in North Dakota since July 1, 1925
Divorces in North Dakota since July 1, 1949 (index only)
Requests for marriage and divorce records prior to the dates above will be forwarded to the appropriate office.
Marriage records are with the County Judge in the county where the license was issued.(See County Appendix S4.)
Divorce records are with the Clerk of District Court in the county where the divorce was granted. (See County Appendix S4.)

Fees: Certified Birth: $7.00 each
$4.00 for a duplicate copy of the same birth record ordered at the same time.
Certified Marriage/Death: $5.00 each
$2.00 for a duplicate copy of the same death or marriage record ordered at the same time.
Divorce: verifications only-no charge. (Search fee is included for the first copy of each record.)
If the precise information is not known in order to find the record, a ten (10) year search will be made based in the information you provide. If the records are older the searches may take longer. If a record is not found, the search fee will be retained and a statement of search will be issued.

Method of Payment: Money order payable to: North Dakota State Dept. of Health
Credit Card: VISA, Mastercard, Discover, or American Express
For credit card order call: (701) 328-2360 (Add a $5.00 service fee.)

Accompanying Documentation: All vital records are by law confidential and information or copies can be furnished generally only to the individual himself, parent, legal guardian, or on court order. If the individual is living, you must obtain written authorization from that individual to be submitted with the request or secure the information you need directly from him/her. Proof of relationship to the registrant must accompany the record request.

NOTES:

VITAL RECORDS

OHIO

Agency: Bureau of Vital Statistics
Ohio Dept. of Health
P.O. Box 15098
Columbus, OH 43215-0098

Telephone: (614) 466-2531 (Recording)

Fax: No Fax

Available Records: Births in Ohio since December 20, 1908
Deaths in Ohio since January 1945
Marriages in Ohio since September 1949 (index only)
Divorces in Ohio since September 1949 (index only)
Certified marriage records are with the Probate Court Judge in the county where the license was issued. (See County Appendix S4.)
Certified divorce records are with the Clerk of Court of Common Pleas in the county where the divorce was granted. (See County Appendix S4.)

Fees: Certified Birth/Death: $7.00 each
Marriage/Divorce: verifications only-no charge. (Search fee is included for the first copy of each record.)

If the precise information is not known in order to find the record, a search will be made based on the years and information you provide. Add an additional $3.00 for each ten (10) year search. Fee will be refunded if the record is not located.

Method of Payment: Money order payable to: Treasury, State of Ohio
Credit Cards: not accepted

Accompanying Documentation: Most records in the state of Ohio are public information. Proof of relationship to the registrant is not needed in order to obtain a certified record.

NOTES:

VITAL RECORDS

OKLAHOMA

Agency:	Division of Vital Records Oklahoma State Dept. of Health 1000 N.E. 10th St. P.O. Box 53551 Oklahoma City, OK 73152-3551
Telephone:	(405) 271-4040 (Direct) (405) 271-5600 (General Info Line)
Fax:	No Fax
Available Records:	Births in Oklahoma since October 1908 Deaths in Oklahoma since 1908 Marriage and divorce records are with the Clerk of Court in the county where the event occurred. (See County Appendix S4.)
Fees:	Certified Birth/Death: $5.00/$10.00 each (Search fee is included for the first copy of each record.) If the precise information to find the record is not known, a search of five (5) to ten (10) years will be made based on the information you provide. If a record is not found, the search fee will be retained and a statement of search will be issued.
Method of Payment:	Money order payable to: State Dept. of Health or Vital Records Credit Cards: not accepted Orders by mail only or applications are available
Accompanying Documentation:	Certified records can only be issued to the registrant, next of kin or legal representative. Proof of relationship to the registrant must accompany the record request.
NOTES:	

VITAL RECORDS

OREGON

Agency:	Oregon Vital Records P.O. Box 14050 Portland, OR 97293
Telephone:	(503) 731-4108 (Direct) (503) 731-4095 (Recording)
Fax:	(503) 731-4084
Available Records:	Births in Oregon since 1903 Deaths in Oregon since 1903 Marriages in Oregon since 1906 Divorces in Oregon since 1925
Fees:	Certified Birth: $15.00 each Certified Death/Marriage/Divorce: $15.00 each. (Search fee is included for the first copy of each record; duplicate copy of the same record at the same time–$12.00.) If the precise information is not known in order to find the record, a five (5) year search will be made based on the information you provide. Add $1.00 for each additional year to be searched. If a record is not found, the search fee will be retained and a statement of search will be issued.
Method of Payment:	Money order Payable to: Oregon Health Division Credit Card: VISA, Mastercard, Discover, or American Express For credit card orders call: (503) 731-4108 (Add a $10.00 service fee.) Credit Card Fax: (503) 234-8417
Accompanying Documentation:	For birth records less than 100 years old, you must be an immediate family member or legal representative. For death records less than 50 years old, you must be an immediate family member, legal representative or have a direct and tangible interest in the record requested. Proof of relationship to the registrant must accompany the record request. Marriage and divorce records are public information.

NOTES:

VITAL RECORDS

PENNSYLVANIA

Agency:	Pennsylvania Dept. of Health Division of Vital Records 101 S. Mercer St. P.O. Box 1528 New Castle, PA 16013-1528
Telephone:	(412) 656-3100
Fax:	(412) 652-8951
Available Records:	Births in Pennsylvania since 1906 Deaths in Pennsylvania since 1906 Marriages records can be obtained by writing to the Marriage License Clerks, County Court House, in the county where the license was issued. (See County Appendix S4.) Divorce records can be obtained by writing to the Prothonotary, Court House, in the county seat of the county where divorce was granted. (See County Appendix S4.)
Fees:	Certified Birth: $4.00 each Certified Death: $3.00 each (Search fee is included for the first copy of each record.) If the precise information is not known in order to find the record, a three(3) year search for a birth record or a one (1) year search for a death record will be made based on the information you provide. If a record is not found, the search fee will be retained and a statement of search will be issued. A ten (10) year search can be made for a $20.00 fee plus the amount of the requested certificate.
Method of Payment:	Money order payable to: Vital Records Credit Card: VISA, Mastercard, Discover, or American Express For credit card orders call: (412) 656-3142 (Add a $5.00 service fee.)
Accompanying Documentation:	The regulations state that certified records may be issued only to the subject, parent, grandparent, spouse, brother, sister, child, guardian with court order, or their legal representative. Proof of relationship to the registrant must accompany the record request. (Need not be notarized.)

NOTES:

VITAL RECORDS

RHODE ISLAND

Agency: Rhode Island Dept. of Health
Division of Vital Records
3 Capitol Hill
Providence, RI 02908-5079

Telephone: (401) 277-2812 (Direct)
(401) 277-2811 (Recording)

Fax: No Fax

Available Records: Births in Rhode Island since 1894
Deaths in Rhode Island since 1944
Marriages in Rhode Island since 1894
Divorce records are obtained by writing to:
Clerk of Family Court
1 Dorrance Plaza
Providence, RI 02903
Fee: $1.00 each

Fees: Certified Birth\Death\Marriage: $15.00 each
$10 for a duplicate copy of the same record ordered at the same time.
(Search fee is included for the first copy of the each record.)
If the precise information is not known in order to find a record, a two (2) year search will be based on the information you provide. Add $.50 for each additional year searched. If a record is not found, the search fee will be retained and a statement of search will be issued.

Method of Payment: Money order payable to : General Treasure, State of Rhode Island
Credit Card: VISA, Mastercard, American Express, or Discover
For credit card orders call: (401) 277-2812
(Add $8.95 service fee.)

Accompanying Documentation: Rhode Island can only issue certified records to persons demonstrating a "direct and tangible" interest. You must furnish your relationship or the purpose for which the copy is to be used. Proof of relationship to the registrant must accompany the request. (Need not be notarized.)

NOTES:

VITAL RECORDS

SOUTH CAROLINA

Agency: South Carolina Dept. of Health and Environment Control (DHEC)
Office of Vital Records
2600 Bull St.
Columbia, SC 29201

Telephone: (803) 734-4830

Fax: (803) 799-0301

Available Records: Births in South Carolina since January 1915
Deaths in South Carolina since January 1915
Marriages in South Carolina since 1950
Divorces in South Carolina since 1962

Marriage records from July 1911 to July 1950 are with the Probate Judge in the county where the license was issued. (See County Appendix S4.) Divorce records from April 1949 to July 1962 are with the Clerk of the county where the petition was filed. (See County Appendix S4.)

Fees: Certified Birth\Death\Marriage\Divorce: $8.00 each
$3.00 for a duplicate copy of the same record ordered at the same time.
(Search fee is included for the first copy of each record.)

If the precise information is not known in order to find the record, a complete search of their records will be made based on the information you provide. If the record is determined not on file, the $8.00 search fee will be retained and a statement of search will be issued.

Method of Payment: Money order payable to: SC DHEC
Credit Card: VISA, Mastercard, Discover, or American Express
For credit card orders call: (803) 734-4830
Total $28.50-includes a certified copy, expedite fee and Federal Express delivery.
Expedite service: add $5.00. If record is located and correct, mailing is guaranteed within three working days of the receipt of proper request and correct fee.

Accompanying Documentation: Certified records may only be issued to the registrant, his\her immediate family, or legal representative or others who demonstrate a direct and tangible interest. Proof of relationship to the registrant must accompany the record request. (Need not be notarized.)

NOTES:

VITAL RECORDS

SOUTH DAKOTA

Agency:	South Dakota Dept. of Health Vital Records 445 E. Capitol Pierre, SD 57501-3185
Telephone:	(605) 773-4961 (Direct) (605) 773-3355 (Recording)
Fax:	(605) 773-5683
Available Records:	Births in South Dakota since July 1905 Deaths in South Dakota since July 1905 Marriages in South Dakota since July 1905 Divorces in South Dakota since July 1905 Certified Birth\Death\Marriage\Divorce: $7.00 each (Search fee is included for the first copy of each record.) To receive birth records, they need the exact date of birth. To receive a death, marriage or divorce record, they need an approximate date. Please be as specific as possible. If a record is not found, the $5.00 search fee will be retained and certified "no record" letter will be issued.
Method of Payment:	Money order payable to: South Dakota Dept. of Health Credit Card: VISA, Mastercard, Discover, or American Express For credit card orders call: (605) 773-4961 (Add a $5.00 service fee.)
Accompanying Documentation:	Most records in South Dakota are public information. Proof of relationship to the registrant is not required to obtain a certified record.

NOTES:

VITAL RECORDS

TENNESSEE

Agency:	Tennessee Dept. of Health Vital Records Tennessee Tower, 3rd Floor Nashville, TN 37247
Telephone:	(615) 741-1763
Fax:	(615) 741-9860
Available Records:	Births in Tennessee since 1914 Deaths in Tennessee since 1944 Marriages in Tennessee since 1945 Divorces in Tennessee since 1945 (If marriage and divorce documents are more then 50 years old they become public information and are sent to the public archive offices.) Marriage records prior to July 1945 are with the County Clerk in the county where the license was issued. (See County Appendix S4.) Divorce records prior to July 1945 are with the Clerk of Court in the county where the divorce was granted. (See County Appendix S4.)
Fees:	Certified Birth\Marriage\Divorce: $10.00 each $2.00 for a duplicate copy of the same record ordered at the same time. Certified Death: $5.00 each (Search fee is included for the first copy of each record.) If the precise information is not known in order to find a record, a three (3) year search will be made based on the information you provide. If a record is not found, the search fee will be retained and a statement of search will be issued.
Method of Payment:	Money order payable to:Tennessee Dept. of Health Credit Card: VISA, Mastercard, Discover, or American Express For credit card orders call: (615) 741-0778. (Add a $10.00 service fee.)
Accompanying Documentation:	Certified copies will be released to certain family members, legal representative, or person(s) named on the record. Proof of relationship to the registrant must accompany the record request.

NOTES:

VITAL RECORDS

TEXAS

Agency:	Bureau of Vital Statistics Texas Dept. of Health 1100 W. 49th St. P.O. Box 12040 Austin, TX 78711-2040
Telephone:	(512) 458-7468 (Direct) (512) 458-7111 (Recording)
Fax:	(512) 458-7711
Available Records:	Births in Texas since 1903 Deaths in Texas since 1903 Marriages in Texas since January 1966 (reports only) Divorces in Texas since January 1968 (reports only) Marriage and divorce reports with essential facts only. Certified marriage records can be obtained from the County Clerk in the county where the license was issued. (See County Appendix S4.) Certified divorce records can be obtained form the Clerk of District Court in the county where the divorce was granted. (See County Appendix S4.)
Fees:	Certified Birth: $11.00 each Certified Death: $9.00 each $3.00 for a duplicate copy of the same death record ordered at the same time. Marriage\Divorce: reports only-$9.00 each (Search fee is included for the first copy of each record.) If the precise information is not known in order to find a record, you must specify the block of years that you need searched to make it successful. If the record is not found, the search fee will be retained and a statement of search will be issued.
Method of Payment:	Money order payable to: Texas Dept. of Health Credit Card: VISA or Mastercard. For credit card orders call: (512) 458-7711 (fax only) (Add a $5.00 service fee plus $5.00 for Federal Express) Fax request: add a $5.00 service fee. Call (512) 458-7364 for additional information
Accompanying Documentation:	Birth records are confidential for 50 years and death records are confidential for 25 years: therefore, issuance is restricted. If the person requesting the information is not an immediate family member or properly qualified applicant, authorization from the registrant or an immediate family member must also be enclosed. Proof of relationship to the registrant must accompany the record request.

NOTES:

VITAL RECORDS

UTAH

Agency:	Bureau of Vital Records & Health Statistics 288 N. 1460 W. P.O. Box 142855 Salt Lake City, UT 84114-2855
Telephone:	(801) 538-6186 (Direct) (801) 538-6105 (Recording)
Fax:	(801) 538-7012
Available Records:	Births in Utah since 1905 Deaths in Utah since 1905 Marriages in Utah since 1978 Divorces in Utah since 1978 Marriage records prior to 1978 are with the County Clerk in the county where the license was issued. (See County Appendix S4.) Divorce records prior to 1978 are with the County Clerk in the county where the divorce was granted. (See County Appendix S4.) There are no phone verifications.
Fees:	Certified Birth: $12.00 each Certified Death\Marriage\Divorce: $9.00 each $5.00 for a duplicate copy of the same record ordered at the same time. (Search fee is included for the first copy of each record.) If the precise information is not known in order to find the record, a (5) year search will be based on the information you provide. If a record is not found, the search fee will be retained and a statement of search will be issued.
Method of Payment:	Money order payable to: Vital Records Credit Card: VISA, Mastercard, American Express, or Discover For credit card orders call: (801) 538-6386 (Add a $15.00 service fee.)
Accompanying Documentation:	The person whose record is requested, his/her parent, grandparent, sibling, or legal representative can obtain a certified record. Proof of relationship to the registrant must accompany the record request. If the applicant is not the person whose certificate is being requested, the reason for requesting the record must be provided.

NOTES:

VITAL RECORDS

VERMONT

Agency:	General Services Center Reference Research Section Drawer 33 Montpelier, VT 05633-7601
Telephone:	(802) 828-3286
Fax:	(802) 828-3710
Available Records:	Births in Vermont from 1760-1986 (or records older than 10 years) Deaths in Vermont from 1760-1983 Marriages in Vermont from 1770-1983 Divorces in Vermont from 1760-1983 Records within the past 10 years are kept at: Vital Records P.O. Box 70 Burlington, VT 05402
Telephone:	(802) 863-7275
Fax:	(802) 863-7425
Fees:	Certified Birth\Death\Marriage\Divorce: $5.00 each (Search fee is included for the first copy of each record.) If the precise information is not known on order to find the record, a search of the years you specify will be made. If you need additional years searched thereafter, add $2.00 per year. If the record is not found, a refund, if more than $5.00, will be returned.
Method of Payment:	Money order payable to: Vermont Dept. of Health Credit Card: VISA, Mastercard, American Express, or Discover For credit card orders call: (802) 828-3286 (Add a $5.00 service fee.)
Accompanying Documentation:	Most records in the state of Vermont are public information. Proof of relationship to the registrant is not required to obtain a certified record.

NOTES:

VITAL RECORDS

VIRGINIA

Agency:	Division of Vital Records P.O. Box 1000 Richmond, VA 23208-1000
Telephone:	(804) 644-2550
Fax:	No Fax
Available Records:	Births in Virginia since 1853-1996 Deaths in Virginia since 1853 Marriages in Virginia since 1853 Divorces in Virginia since 1853
Fees:	Certified Birth\Death\Marriage\Divorce: $8.00 each (Search fee is included for the first copy of each record.) If the precise information is not known in order to find the record, a ten (10) to fifteen (15) year search will be based in the information you provide. If a record is not found, the $8.00 search fee will be retained and a statement of search will be issued. Searches are only date back 20 years.
Method of payment:	Money order payable to: State Health Dept. Credit Cards: not accepted ($25.50 Federal Express fee and certificate.) No requests for genealogy
Accompanying Documentation:	Certifications may be issued to the individual registrant, members of the registrant's immediate family, the registrant's guardian, their respective legal representative, or by court order. Proof of relationship to the registrant must accompany the record request.
NOTES:	

VITAL RECORDS

WASHINGTON

Agency:	Dept. of Health Center for Health Statistics P.O. Box 9709 Olympia, WA 98507-9709
Telephone:	(306) 753-5936
Fax:	(360) 753-4135
Available Records:	Births in Washington since July 1907 Deaths in Washington since July 1907 Marriages in Washington since January 1968 Divorces in Washington since January 1968 Marriage records prior to January 1968 are with the County Auditor in the county where the license was issued. (See County Appendix S4.) Divorce records are with the County Clerk in the county where the divorce was granted. (See County Appendix S4.)
Fees:	Certified Birth\Death\Marriage\Divorce: $11.00 each (Search fee is included for the first copy of each record.) If the precise information is known in order to find the record, a ten (10) year search will be made based on the information you provide. If the record is not found, a $8.00 search fee will be retained and a statement of search will be issued.
Method of Payment:	Money order payable to : Dept. of Health Credit Card: VISA, Mastercard, American Express, or Discover For credit card orders call: (206) 753-5842 Total $21.00 (Add $11.00 if same person;$16.00 if different person.)
Accompanying Documentation:	Birth, death, (with the exception of cause of death) marriage and divorce records in Washington are public information. Proof of relationship to the registrant is not required in order to obtain a certified record. (Need not be notarized.)

NOTES:

VITAL RECORDS

WEST VIRGINIA

Agency	West Virgina Dept. of Health Vital Registration Office Capitol Complex Bldg. 3-Room 516 Charleston, WV 25305
Telephone:	(304) 558-2931
Fax:	(304) 558-1051
Available Records:	Births in West Virgina since 1800 Deaths in West Virginia since 1917 Marriages in West Virgina from 1921-1967 (verification index) Certified marriage records from 1967 to present Divorces in West Virginia since 1967 (verification index) Marriage records are with the County Clerk in the county where the license was issued. (See County Appendix S4.) Divorce records are with the Clerk of Circuit Court, Chancery Side, in the county where the divorce was granted. (See County Appendix S4.)
Fees:	Certified Birth/Death: $5.00 each Marriage/Divorce: verifications only-$5.00 each (Search fee is included in the first copy of each record.) If the precise information is not known, this office will only do a search of the year you have requested. If a record is not found, the $5.00 search fee will be retained and a statement of search will be issued. (Approx. three (3) year search, $5.00/year if no date.)
Method of Payment:	Money order payable to: Vital Registration Office Credit Card: VISA, Mastercard, Discover, or American Express For credit card orders call: (304) 558-2931 $15.00 each/$5.00 for a duplicate copy of the same record ordered at the same time.
Accompanying Documentation:	Must be immediate family or have a "vested interest" in the record. Proof of relationship to the registrant must accompany the record request.

NOTES:

VITAL RECORDS

WISCONSIN

Agency:	Division of Health Section of Vital Statistics 1 W. Wilson St. P.O. Box 309 Madison, WI 53701-0309
Telephone:	(608) 266-1372 (608) 266-1371(births)
Fax:	No Fax
Available Records:	Births in Wisconsin since October 1907 Deaths in Wisconsin since October 1907 Marriages in Wisconsin since October 1907 Divorces in Wisconsin since October 1907 (mail w/SASE)
Fees:	Certified Birth $12.00 each Certified/Death/Marriage/Divorce: $7.00 each $2.00 for duplicate copy of the same record ordered at the same time. (Search fee is included for the first copy of each record.) If the precise information is not known in order to find the record, a five (5) year search will be made based on the information you provide. If the record is not found, the search fee will be retained and a statement of search will be issued.
Method of Payment:	Money orders payable to: Vital Records Credit Cards: not accepted
Accompanying Documentation:	The registrant named on the record, a parent, legal guardian, an immediate family member, a legal representative, someone that can demonstrate that the information from the record is necessary for the determination or protection of a person or property, can obtain a certificate of the registrant. Proof of relationship to the registrant must accompany the record request.

NOTES:

VITAL RECORDS

WYOMING

Agency:	Vital Records Service Hathaway Bldg. Cheyenne, WY 82002
Telephone:	(307) 777-7591
Fax:	(307) 777-7739 Attn: Vital Records
Available records:	Births in Wyoming since 1909 Deaths in Wyoming since 1909 Marriages in Wyoming since May 1941 Divorces in Wyoming since 1941 Marriage records prior to May 1941 are with the County Clerk in the county where the license was issued. (See County Appendix S4.) Divorce records prior to May 1941 are with the Clerk of District Court in the county where the divorce took place. (See County Appendix S4.)
Fees:	Certified Birth/Marriage/Divorce: $11.00 each Certified Death: $9.00 each if the date is known $11.00 each if the date is not known. Search fee is included for the first copy of each record.) If the precise information is not known in order to find the record, a five (5) year search will be made based on the information you provide. If a record is not found, the search fee will be retained and a statement of search will be issued.
Method of Payment:	Money orders payable to : Vital Records Services Credit Cards: VISA, Mastercard, Discover, or American Express ($26.75 for Fed-ex)
Accompanying Documentation:	The records in Wyoming are confidential and certified copies are issued only to direct line descendants (surviving spouse, children, sibling, etc.). They will issue copies of birth certificates only upon written signature of the person named on the certificate or proof of that person's death. Proof of relationship to the registrant must accompany the record request. (Needs to be notarized.)

NOTES:

VITAL RECORDS

DISTRICT OF COLUMBIA

Agency:	Vital Records Branch 800 9th St. S.W., 1st Floor Washington, DC 20024
Telephone:	(202) 645-5962
Fax:	(202) 645-0531
Available Records:	Births in the District of Columbia since 1874 Deaths in the District of Columbia since 1974 Marriage records write to: Marriage Bureau 500 Indiana Ave N.W., Room 4485 Washington, DC 20001 Telephone: (202) 879-4840 Divorce records contact the Clerk of Superior Court for the record since September 16, 1956, or the Clerk of U.S. District Court for records prior to September 16, 1956.
Fees:	Certified Birth: $18.00 each Certified Death: $12.00 each (Search fee is included for the first copy of each record.) If the precise information is not known in order to find a record, a three (3) year search will be made based on the information you provide. If the record is not found, the search fee will be retained and a statement of search will be issued.
Method of Payment:	Money order payable to : DC Treasurer Credit Card: VISA, Mastercard, Discover, or American Express For credit card orders call: (800) 669-8309 (Add a $5.00 service fee.)
Accompanying Documentation:	The District of Columbia Law 4-34, the Vital Records Act of 1981 specified that the following persons are entitled to purchase a certified copy of a vital record: (1) the registrant, (2) a member of his/her immediate family, (3) a legal guardian, or (4) a legal representative. Proof of relationship to the registrant must accompany the record request. (Need not be notarized.)

NOTES:

APPENDIX S4

Counties

If you have very little information about your target relative, the place to begin is to locate the county where he/she died. If you are unable to establish this information from family records, call the Vital Statistics State Office (Appendix S3) in the state where he/she died. Once you know the county where the death took place, then look for that county's address in this Appendix.

Be sure to use the suggested form letter; it could result in substantial information on your target relative. It is very possible your target relative did business in other counties and therefore you could find probate action and money in more than one county.

SUGGESTED LETTER TO THE COUNTY

Date

Your Name
Address
City/State/Zip
Day Phone
Nights/Weekend Phone
Fax

County
Address (see County Appendix)

Re: Full Name
Last Known Address
City/State/Zip
Social Security Number
Time Lived in County

Dear Commissioner or Administrator,

The above named person is my relative (state relationship) and I am seeking information from the following county departments:

- County Assessor — (Did he/she own real estate in your county?)
- County Election — (How long did he/she vote in your county?)
- County Treasurer — (Did he/she pay taxes or have a vehicle registered in your county?)
- County Coroner — (Do you have a record associated with his/her death?)
- Other (specify)

Would you be so kind as to circulate a copy of my letter to each of the above county departments?

Please contact me at the address above if further information is needed.

Sincerely,

Signed

☛ This is public information.

County	Address	City, State	Zip Code	Phone	Fax
ALABAMA					
Autauga County	P.O. Box 89	Prattville AL	36067	334-361-3701	334-361-3724
Baldwin County	P.O. Box 1488	Bay Minette AL	36507	334-937-0264	334-587-2500
Barbour County	P.O. Box 398	Clayton AL	36016	205-775-3203	205-775-1102
Bibb County	Courthouse Square	Centreville AL	35042	205-926-3103	205-926-3110
Blount County	P.O. Box 668	Oneonta AL	35121	205-625-4160	205-625-5961
Bullock County	P.O Box 472	Union Springs AL	36089	205-738-3883	205-738-3839
Butler County	P.O. Box 756	Greenville AL	36037	334-382-3612	334-382-3506
Calhoun County	1702 Nobel St #103	Anniston AL	36201	205-236-3521	205-237-6956
Chambers County	18 Alabama Ave., E	LaFayette AL	36862	334-864-4310	334-864-4306
Cherokee County	Courthouse Annex	Centre AL	35960	205-927-3668	205-927-5226
Chilton County	P.O. Box 1948	Clanton AL	35046	205-775-1551	205-280-7204
Choctaw County	117 S. Mulberry, Suite 9	Butler AL	36904	205-459-2100	205-459-4248
Clark County	P.O. Box 548	Grove Hill AL	36451	334-275-3507	334-275-8517
Clay County	P.O. Box 187	Ashland AL	36251	205-354-7888	205-354-7835
Cleburne County	406 Vickery St	Heflin AL	36264	205-463-2951	205-463-7780
Coffee County	#2 County Complex	New Brockton AL	36351	334-894-5556	No Fax
Colbert County	201 N. Main St	Tuscumbia AL	35674	205-386-8500	205-386-8510
Conecuh County	P.O. Box 347	Evergreen AL	36407	334-578-2095	334-578-7002
Coosa County	P.O. Box 218	Rockford AL	35136	205-377-2420	205-377-2524
Covington County	P.O. Box 188	Andalusia AL	36420	334-222-3613	334-222-7603
Crenshaw County	P.O. Box 312	Luverne AL	36049	334-335-6568	334-335-3679
Cullman County	500 2nd Ave. S.W., Rm. 303	Cullman AL	35055	205-739-3530	No Fax
Dale County	1702 High, Suite C	Ozark AL	36360	334-774-6262	334-774-1841
Dallas County	P.O. Box 997	Selma AL	36702	334-874-2560	334-874-2587
De Kalb County	102 B Ave. S	Ft. Payne AL	35967	205-845-0404	205-845-8502
Elmore County	P.O. Box 280	Wetumpka AL	36092	334-567-1139	334-567-1144
Escambia County	P.O. Box 848	Brewton AL	36702	334-867-6162	334-867-0275
Etowah County	800 Forrest Ave.	Gadsden AL	35901	205-549-5300	205-549-5400
Fayette County	103 1st Ave. N.W., Suite 2	Fayette AL	35555	205-932-4510	205-932-6699
Franklin County	410 N. Jackson Ave	Russellville AL	35653	205-332-8850	205-332-8855
Geneva County	P.O. Box 430	Geneva AL	36340	334-684-2275	334-684-3583
Greene County	P.O. Box 656	Eutaw AL	35462	205-372-3349	205-372-0499
Hale County	P.O. Box 396	Greensboro AL	36744	334-624-4257	334-624-8725
Henry County	101 Court Sq., Suite A	Abbeville AL	36310	334-585-3257	334-585-5006
Houston County	P.O. Drawer 6406	Dothan AL	36302	334-677-4740	334-794-6633
Jackson County	P.O. Box 307	Scottsboro AL	35768	205-574-9280	205-574-9267
Jefferson County	716 21st St N.	Birmingham AL	35263	205-325-5300	205-325-5840
Lamar County	P.O. Box 338	Vernon AL	35592	205-695-7333	205-695-9253
Lauderdale County	P.O. Box 1059	Florence AL	35631	205-760-5750	205-760-5703
Lawrence County	750 Main St. #1	Moulton AL	35650	205-974-0663	205-974-2403

County	Address	City, State	Zip Code	Phone	Fax

ALABAMA *continued*

County	Address	City, State	Zip Code	Phone	Fax
Lee County	P.O. Box 666	Opelika AL	36803	334-745-9767	334-742-9478
Limestone County	310 W. Washington	Athens AL	36803	205-233-6400	205-233-6403
Lowndes County	P.O. Box 65	Hayneville AL	36040	334-548-2331	334-548-5101
Macon County	101 E. North Side	Tuskegee AL	36083	334-727-5120	334-727-3170
Madison County	100 North Side Sq.	Huntsville AL	35801	205-532-3492	205-532-6994
Marengo County	P.O. Box 480715	Linden AL	36748	334-295-2200	334-295-2254
Marion County	P.O. Box 460	Hamilton AL	35570	205-921-3172	205-921-5109
Marshall County	424 Blount Ave	Guntersville AL	35976	205-690-8605	205-690-7703
Mobile County	205 Goverment St.	Mobile AL	36644	334-690-8786	334-690-4770
Monroe County	P.O. Box 8	Monroeville AL	36461	334-743-4107	334-575-7934
Montgomery County	P.O. Box 1667	Montgomery AL	36102	334-832-4950	No Fax
Morgan County	P.O. Box 668	Decatur AL	35602	205-351-4737	205-351-4738
Perry County	P.O. Box 478	Marion AL	36756	334-683-2200	334-683-2201
Pickens County	P.O. Box 460	Carrollton AL	35447	205-367-2020	205-367-2025
Pike County	P.O. Box 1147	Troy AL	36081	334-566-6374	334-566-0142
Randolph County	P.O. Box 249	Wedowee AL	36278	205-357-4933	205-357-2790
Russell County	P.O. Box 518	Phenix City AL	36868	334-298-0516	No Fax
Shelby County	P.O. Box 467	Columbiana AL	35051	205-669-3740	205-669-3746
St. Clair County	P.O. Box 397	Ashville AL	35953	205-594-5116	205-594-2110
Sumter County	P.O. Box 936	Livingston AL	35470	205-652-2291	205-652-2213
Talladega County	P.O. Drawer 755	Talladega AL	35161	205-362-1357	205-761-2147
Tallapoosa County	125 N. Broadnax # 131	Dadeville AL	36853	205-825-4268	205-825-1009
Tuscaloosa County	714 Greensboro Ave	Tuscaloosa AL	35401	205-349-3870	205-758-6170
Walker County	P.O. Box 1447	Jasper AL	35502	205-384-7230	205-384-7003
Washington County	P.O. Box 146	Chatom AL	36518	334-847-2208	334-847-3677
Wilcox County	P.O. Box 488	Camden AL	36726	334-682-9112	334-682-4621
Winston County	P.O. Box 147	Double Springs AL	35553	205-489-5026	205-489-3090

ALASKA

County	Address	City, State	Zip Code	Phone	Fax
Bristol Bay Borough	P.O. Box 189	Naknek AK	99633	907-246-4224	907-246-6633
Haines Borough	P.O. Box 1209	Haines AK	99827	907-766-2711	907-766-2716
Juneau Borough	155 S. Seward St	Juneau AK	99801	907-586-5240	907-586-5385
Kenai Peninsula	144 N. Binkley St	Soldotna AK	99669	907-262-4441	907-262-8615
Ketchikan Borough	344 Front St	Ketchikan AK	99901	907-228-6605	907-247-8439
Kodiak Borough	710 Mill Bay Rd	Kodiak AK	99615	907-486-9311	907-486-9374
Matanuska-Susitna	350 E. Dahlia Ave.	Palmer AK	99645	907-745-4801	907-745-0886
Municipality of Anchorage	P.O. Box 196650	Anchorage AK	99519	907-343-4311	907-343-4780
North Slope Borough	P.O. Box 69	Barrow AK	99723	907-852-2611	907-852-0029
North Star Borough	809 Pioneer Rd	Fairbanks AK	99701	907-459-1000	907-451-6644
N.W. Arctic Borough	P.O. Box 1110	Kotzebue AK	99752	907-442-2500	907-442-2930

County	Address	City, State		Zip Code	Phone	Fax
ALASKA *continued*						
Sitka Borough	100 Lincoln St	Sitka	AK	99835	907-747-3294	907-747-7403
ARIZONA						
Apache County	P.O. Box 428	Saint Johns	AZ	85936	602-337-4364	602-337-2003
Cochise County	1415 W. Melody Ln.	Bisbee	AZ	85603	520-432-9200	520-432-5016
Coconino County	219 E. Cherry	Flagstaff	AZ	86001	602-779-6690	602-779-6687
Gila County	1400 E. Ash St	Globe	AZ	85501	520-425-3231	520-425-0319
Graham County	800 Main St.	Safford	AZ	85546	520-428-3250	520-428-0061
Greenlee County	P.O. Box 908	Clifton	AZ	85533	520-865-2310	520-865-4417
La Paz County	P.O. Box C	Parker	AZ	85344	520-669-6115	520-669-9709
Maricopa County	301 W. Jefferson,10th Fl	Phoenix	AZ	85003	602-506-3571	602-506-3328
Mohave County	P.O. Box 7000	Kingman	AZ	86401	520-753-0729	520-753-0732
Navajo County	P.O. Box 668	Holbrook	AZ	86025	602-524-4188	602-524-3094
Pima County	130 W. Congress St	Tucson	AZ	85701	602-740-8135	602-740-8171
Pinal County	P.O. Box 827	Florence	AZ	85232	602-868-6211	602-868-6512
Santa Cruz County	2100 N. Congress	Nogales	AZ	85621	520-761-7806	520-761-7934
Yavapai County	Gurley St & Cortez	Prescott	AZ	86301	520-771-3200	520-771-3111
Yuma County	198 S. Main St	Yuma	AZ	85364	520-329-2104	520-329-2001
ARKANSAS						
Arkansas County	P.O. Box 719	Stuttgart	AR	72160	501-946-4349	501-946-4349
Ashley County	205 E. Jefferson St	Hamburg	AR	71646	501-853-2020	501-853-2005
Baxter County	1 E. 7th St	Mountain Home	AR	72653	501-425-3475	501-424-5105
Benton County	215 E. Central St., Ste 217	Bentonville	AR	72712	501-271-1013	501-271-1019
Boone County	100 N. Main St	Harrison	AR	72601	501-741-8428	501-741-9724
Bradley County	101 E. Cedar	Warren	AR	71671	501-226-3464	501-226-8401
Calhoun County	P.O. Box 626	Hampton	AR	71744	501-798-2517	501-798-4944
Carroll County	210 W. Church St	Berryville	AR	72616	501-423-2022	501-423-3866
Chicot County	108 Main St.	Lake Village	AR	71653	501-265-8000	501-265-8018
Clark County	Courthouse Sq	Arkadelphia	AR	71923	501-246-4491	501-245-3092
Clay County	151 S. 2nd Ave	Piggott	AR	72454	501-598-2813	501-598-2819
Cleburne County	3rd & Main	Heber Springs	AR	72543	501-362-4620	501-362-4622
Cleveland County	P.O. Box 368	Rison	AR	71665	501-325-6521	501-325-6144
Columbia County	1 Court Sq	Magnolia	AR	71753	501-235-3774	501-235-3773
Conway County	117 S. Moose St	Morritton	AR	72110	501-354-9621	501-354-9610
Craighead County	511 S. Main St	Jonesboro	AR	72401	501-933-4520	501-933-4614
Crawford County	300 Main St.	Van Buren	AR	72956	501-474-1312	501-471-3236
Crittenden County	100 Court Sq	Marion	AR	72364	501-739-4434	501-739-3072
Cross County	705 E. Union Ave	Wynne	AR	72396	501-238-5735	501-238-5739
Dallas County	206 3rd St. W	Fordyce	AR	71742	501-352-2307	501-352-7179

County	Address	City, State	Zip Code	Phone	Fax
ARKANSAS *continued*					
Desha County	Robert Moore St	Arkansas City AR	71630	501-877-2323	501-877-2531
Drew County	210 S. Main St	Monticello AR	71655	501-460-6260	501-460-6246
Faulkner County	801 Locust St	Conway AR	72032	501-450-4909	501-450-4938
Franklin County	211 W. Commercial St	Ozark AR	72949	501-667-3607	501-667-4247
Fulton County	P.O. Box 485	Salem AR	72576	501-895-3310	501-895-3362
Garland County	501 Ouachita Ave	Hot Springs AR	71901	501-622-3610	501-623-0214
Grant County	101 W. Center	Sheridan AR	72150	501-942-2631	501-942-3564
Greene County	306 W. Court St	Paragould AR	72450	501-239-6345	501-239-3550
Hampstead County	400 S. Washington St	Hope AR	71801	501-777-2241	501-777-7814
Hot Spring County	3rd & Locust	Malvern AR	72104	501-332-2291	501-332-2221
Howard County	421 N. Main St	Nashville AR	71852	501-845-7502	501-845-7505
Independence County	192 E. Main St	Batesville AR	72501	501-793-8828	501-793-8803
Izard County	P.O. Box 95	Melbourne AR	72556	501-368-4316	501-368-5042
Jackson County	208 Main St.	Newport AR	72112	501-523-7420	501-523-7404
Jefferson County	101 E. Barraque St.	Pine Bluff AR	71601	501-541-5326	501-541-5324
Johnson County	215 W. Main St.	Clarksville AR	72830	501-754-3967	501-754-6098
Lafayette County	P.O. Box 945	Lewisville AR	71845	501-921-4633	501-921-4505
Lawrence County	P.O. Box 526	Walnut Ridge AR	72476	501-886-1111	501-886-1117
Lee County	15 E. Chestnut St.	Marianna AR	72360	501-295-7715	501-295-7766
Lincoln County	300 S. Drew St	Star City AR	71667	501-628-5114	501-628-4385
Little River County	351 N. 2nd St	Ashdown AR	71822	501-898-7208	501-898-7207
Logan County	25 County Courthouse	Paris AR	72855	501-963-2618	501-963-2590
Lonoke County	P.O. Box 188	Lonoke AR	72086	501-676-2368	501-676-3005
Madison County	P.O. Box 37	Huntsville AR	72740	501-738-2747	501-738-2735
Marion County	P.O. Box 385	Yellville AR	72687	501-449-6226	No Fax
Miller County	400 Laurel St	Texarkana AR	75502	501-774-1501	501-773-0923
Mississippi County	200 W. Walnut	Blytheville AR	72315	501-762-2411	501-763-0150
Monroe County	123 Madison St.	Clarendon AR	72029	501-747-3632	501-747-3710
Montgomery County	P.O. Box 377	Mount Ida AR	71957	501-867-3521	501-867-4354
Nevada County	P.O. Box 621	Prescott AR	71857	501-887-2710	501-887-5795
Newton County	Court St.	Jasper AR	72641	501-446-5125	501-446-2106
Ouachita County	P.O. Box 1041	Camden AR	71701	501-837-2220	501-837-2217
Perry County	P.O. Box 358	Perryville AR	72126	501-889-5126	501-889-5759
Phillips County	620 Cherry St	Helena AR	72342	501-338-5500	501-338-5504
Pike County	P.O. Box 219	Murfreesboro AR	71958	501-285-2231	501-285-3281
Poinsett County	401 Market St.	Harrisburg AR	72432	501-578-4410	501-578-2441
Polk County	507 Church St.	Mena AR	71953	501-394-8123	501-394-1975
Pope County	100 W. Main	Russellville AR	72801	501-968-6064	501-967-2291
Prairie County	P.O. Box 1011	Des Arc AR	72040	501-256-4434	501-256-4434
Pulaski County	P.O. Box 2659	Little Rock AR	72203	501-340-8330	501-340-8340

County	Address	City, State	Zip Code	Phone	Fax
ARKANSAS *continued*					
Randolph County	107 W. Broadway	Pocahontas AR	72455	501-892-5822	501-892-8794
Saint Francis County	313 S. Izard	Forrest City AR	72335	501-261-1725	501-630-1210
Saline County	215 N. Main St	Benton AR	72015	501-776-5630	501-776-5684
Scott County	P.O. Box 2165	Waldron AR	72958	501-637-2642	501-637-4199
Searcy County	P.O. Box 813	Marshall AR	72650	501-448-3807	No Fax
Sebastian County	35 S. 6th St	Fort Smith AR	72901	501-782-5065	501-784-1567
Sevier County	115 N. 3rd St.	De Queen AR	71832	501-642-2852	501-642-9638
Sharp County	P.O. Box 307	Ash Flat AR	72513	501-994-7361	501-994-7712
Stone County	P.O. Drawer 120	Mountain View AR	72560	501-269-3271	501-269-2303
Union County	101 N. Washington	El Dorado AR	71730	501-864-1910	501-864-1926
Van Buren County	P.O. Box 180	Clinton AR	72031	501-745-4140	501-745-6278
Washington County	280 N. College, Suite 300	Fayetteville AR	72701	501-444-1711	501-444-1894
White County	Courthouse Sq	Searcy AR	72143	501-279-6204	501-279-6233
Woodruff County	500 N. 3rd St.	Augusta AR	72006	501-347-2871	501-347-2915
Yell County	P.O. Box 219	Danville AR	72833	501-495-2414	501-495-3495
CALIFORNIA					
Alameda County	1224 Oak St	Oakland CA	94612	510-272-6347	No Fax
Alpine County	P.O. Box 158	Markleeville CA	96120	916-694-2281	916-694-2491
Amador County	108 Court St	Jackson CA	95642	209-223-6463	209-223-4286
Butte County	25 County Center Dr	Oroville CA	95965	916-538-7224	916-538-7120
Calaveras County	891 Mountain Ranch Rd	San Andreas CA	95249	209-754-6310	209-754-6561
Colusa County	546 Jay St	Colusa CA	95932	916-458-5146	916-458-0510
Contra Costa County	651 Pine St	Martinez CA	94553	510-646-4080	510-646-4098
Del Norte County	450 H St	Crescent City CA	95531	707-464-7205	707-465-4005
El Dorado County	360 Fair Ln., Building B	Placerville CA	95667	916-621-5490	916-621-2147
Fresno County	P.O. Box 1628	Fresno CA	93717	209-488-2708	209-488-1976
Glenn County	526 W. Sycamore St	Willows CA	95988	916-934-6407	916-934-6406
Humboldt County	825 5th St	Eureka CA	95501	707-445-7256	707-441-4500
Imperial County	939 Main St.	El Centro CA	92243	619-339-4217	619-352-3814
Inyo County	P.O. Drawer F.	Independence CA	93526	619-878-0218	619-878-2542
Kern County	1415 Truxtun Ave.	Bakersfield CA	93301	805-861-2621	805-324-6348
Kings County	1400 W. Lacey Blvd	Hanford CA	93230	209-582-3211	209-584-0319
Lake County	255 N. Forbes St.	Lakeport CA	95453	707-263-2372	707-263-2207
Lassen County	220 S. Lassen St	Susanville CA	96130	916-251-8228	916-257-9061
Los Angeles County	P.O. Box 30450	Los Angeles CA	90030	310-462-2716	310-868-5139
Madera County	209 W. Yosemite Ave	Madera CA	93637	209-675-7720	209-673-3302
Marin County	P.O. Box E.	San Rafael CA	94913	415-499-6416	415-499-7184
Mariposa County	P.O. Box 36	Mariposa CA	95338	209-966-5539	209-966-9496
Mendocino County	P.O. Box 148	Ukiah CA	94582	707-463-4370	707-463-4257
Merced County	2222 M St	Merced CA	95340	209-385-7501	209-385-7375

County	Address	City, State	Zip Code	Phone	Fax

CALIFORNIA *continued*

County	Address	City, State	Zip Code	Phone	Fax
Modoc County	P.O. Box 131	Alturas CA	96101	916-233-6200	916-233-2434
Mono County	P.O. Box 237	Bridgeport CA	93517	619-932-5240	No Fax
Monterey County	P.O. Box 1819	Salinas CA	93902	408-755-5030	408-759-6646
Napa County	900 Coombs St	Napa CA	94559	707-253-4481	No Fax
Nevada County	P.O. Box 6126	Nevada City CA	95959	916-265-1293	916-265-4178
Orange County	630 N. Broadway	Santa Ana CA	92701	714-834-2500	714-834-7534
Placer County	P.O. Box 5278	Auburn CA	95604	916-889-7983	916-887-0737
Plumas County	P.O. Box 10207	Quincy CA	95971	916-283-6305	916-283-6415
Riverside County	P.O. Box 751	Riverside CA	92501	909-275-1900	909-275-1954
Sacramento County	720 9th St	Sacramento CA	95814	916-440-5476	916-440-5620
San Benito County	Courthouse Rm. 206	Hollister CA	95023	408-637-3786	408-636-2939
San Bernardino County	385 N. Arrowhead	San Bernardino CA	92415	909-387-3922	No Fax
San Diego County	220 W. Broadway, Rm. 3005	San Diego CA	92101	619-685-6677	No Fax
San Francisco County	633 Folsom St., Rm. 26	San Francisco CA	94107	415-554-7878	415-554-6955
San Joaquin County	24 S. Hunter, Rm. 304	Stockton CA	95201	209-468-2362	No Fax
San Luis Obispo County	1144 Monterey St	San Luis Obispo CA	93408	805-781-5241	No Fax
San Mateo County	401 Marshall St., 6th Fl.	Redwood City CA	94063	415-363-4713	415-363-4843
Santa Barbara County	P.O. Box 159	Santa Barbara CA	93102	805-568-2250	No Fax
Santa Clara County	191 N. First St	San Jose CA	95113	408-299-2074	408-298-0582
Santa Cruz County	701 Ocean St., Rm. 110	Santa Cruz CA	95060	408-454-2020	No Fax
Shasta County	P.O. Box 880	Redding CA	96099	916-245-6714	No Fax
Sierra County	P.O. Box D.	Downieville CA	95936	916-289-3295	916-289-3300
Siskiyou County	P.O. Box 338	Yreka CA	96097	916-842-8084	916-842-8093
Solano County	600 Texas St	Fairfield CA	94533	707-421-7485	707-421-6311
Sonoma County	2300 County Dr	Santa Rosa CA	95403	707-527-3800	No Fax
Stanislaus County	P.O. Box 1670	Modesto CA	95353	209-558-6419	209-525-5207
Sutter County	433 2nd St	Yuba City CA	95991	916-822-7120	916-822-7214
Tehama County	P.O. Box 250	Red Bluff CA	96080	916-527-3350	916-529-0980
Trinity County	P.O. Box 1258	Weaverville CA	96093	916-623-1222	916-623-3762
Tulare County	221 S. Mooney Blvd., Rm. 203	Visalia CA	93291	209-733-6421	209-730-2621
Tuolumne County	2 S. Green St.	Sonora CA	95370	209-533-5551	209-553-5627
Ventura County	800 S. Victoria Ave	Ventura CA	93009	805-654-2267	No Fax
Yolo County	P.O. Box 1130	Woodland CA	95776	916-666-8264	916-666-8121
Yuba County	935 14th St	Marysville CA	95901	916-741-6341	916-741-6285

COLORADO

County	Address	City, State	Zip Code	Phone	Fax
Adams County	450 S. 4th Ave.	Brighton CO	80601	970-659-2120	970-654-6011
Alamosa County	P.O. Box 178	Alamosa CO	81101	719-589-5887	719-589-6118
Arapahoe County	1790 W. Littleton Blvd.	Littleton CO	80166	970-785-4571	No Fax
Archuleta County	P.O. Box 1507	Pagosa Springs CO	81147	970-264-2536	970-264-4896
Baca County	741 Main St.	Springfield CO	81073	719-523-4372	719-523-4735

County	Address	City, State		Zip Code	Phone	Fax

COLORADO *continued*

County	Address	City	State	Zip Code	Phone	Fax
Bent County	P.O. Box 350	Las Animas	CO	81054	719-456-2009	719-456-2223
Boulder County	P.O. Box 8020	Boulder	CO	80306	303-441-3515	303-441-4864
Chaffee County	104 Crestone Ave	Salida	CO	81201	719-539-4004	719-539-7442
Cheyenne County	P.O. Box 567	Cheyenne Wells	CO	80810	719-767-5685	719-767-5540
Clear Creek County	P.O. Box 2000	Georgetown	CO	80444	303-569-3251	No Fax
Conejos County	P.O. Box 127	Conejos	CO	81129	719-376-5422	719-376-5661
Costilla County	P.O. Box 308	San Luis	CO	81152	719-672-3301	719-672-3692
Crowley County	110 E. 6th St	Ordway	CO	81063	719-267-4643	719-267-4608
Custer County	205 S. 6th St	Westcliffe	CO	81252	719-783-2441	719-783-2885
Delta County	501 Palmer, Suite 211	Delta	CO	81416	970-874-2150	970-874-2161
Denver County	1437 Bannock St.	Denver	CO	80202	303-640-2641	303-640-3628
Dolores County	P.O. Box 58	Dove Creek	CO	81324	907-677-2381	970-677-2815
Douglas County	301 Wilcox	Castle Rock	CO	80104	303-660-7469	303-688-3060
Eagle County	P.O. Box 537	Eagle	CO	81631	970-328-8710	970-328-8716
El Paso County	200 S. Cascade	Colorado Springs	CO	80903	719-520-6200	719-520-6212
Elbert County	P.O. Box 597	Kiowa	CO	80117	303-621-3115	303-621-2343
Fremont County	615 Macon, Rm. 100	Canon City	CO	81212	719-275-1522	719-275-7626
Garfield County	109 8th St.,St 200	Glenwood Springs	CO	81601	970-945-2377	970-945-7785
Gilpin County	P.O. Box 429	Central City	CO	80427	303-582-5321	303-582-5440
Grand County	308 Byers Ave	Hot Sulphur Springs	CO	80451	970-725-3347	970-725-3303
Gunnison County	200 E. Virginia Ave	Gunnison	CO	81230	970-641-3500	970-641-6826
Hinsdale County	P.O. Box 9	Lake City	CO	81235	970-944-2228	970-944-2202
Huerfano County	401 Main St.	Walsenburg	CO	81089	719-738-2380	719-738-2370
Jackson County	P.O. Box 337	Walden	CO	80480	970-723-4334	No Fax
Jefferson County	100 Jefferson Cnty Pkwy	Golden	CO	80419	303-271-8168	303-271-8197
Kiowa County	P.O. Box 37	Eads	CO	81036	719-438-5421	719-438-5327
Kit Carson County	P.O. Box 249	Burlington	CO	80807	719-346-8638	719-346-7242
La Plata County	1060 E. 2nd Ave	Durango	CO	81301	970-382-6280	970-382-6299
Lake County	505 Harrison Ave	Leadville	CO	80461	719-486-1410	719-486-3972
Larimer County	P.O. Box 1280	Fort Collins	CO	80522	970-498-7860	970-498-7830
Las Animas County	1st & Maple St	Trinidad	CO	81082	719-846-2221	719-846-9367
Lincoln County	P.O. Box 67	Hugo	CO	80821	719-743-2444	719-743-2838
Logan County	4th Main St.	Sterling	CO	80751	970-522-1544	970-522-2875
Mesa County	P.O. Box 20000	Grand Junction	CO	81502	970-243-1136	No Fax
Mineral County	P.O. Box 70	Creede	CO	81130	970-658-2440	970-658-2764
Moffat County	221 W. Victory Way	Craig	CO	81625	970-824-5517	970-824-3995
Montezuma County	109 W. Main	Cortez	CO	81321	970-565-3728	970-564-0215
Montrose County	P.O. Box 1289	Montrose	CO	81402	970-249-7755	970-249-7761
Morgan County	P.O. Box 1399	Fort Morgan	CO	80701	970-867-5616	970-867-6485
Otero County	P.O. Box 511	La Junta	CO	81050	719-384-8701	719-384-4221

County	Address	City, State	Zip Code	Phone	Fax
COLORADO *continued*					
Ouray County	Bin C	Ouray CO	81427	970-325-4961	970-325-0452
Park County	P.O. Box 220	Fairplay CO	80440	719-836-2771	719-836-4204
Phillips County	221 S. Interocean	Holyoke CO	80734	970-854-3131	970-854-3811
Pitkin County	530 E. Main, Suite 101	Aspen CO	81611	303-920-5180	303-920-5196
Prowers County	P.O. Box 889	Lamar CO	81052	719-336-4337	719-336-2255
Pueblo County	215 W. 10th St	Pueblo CO	81003	719-583-6000	719-583-6549
Rio Blanco County	P.O. Box 1067	Meeker CO	81641	970-878-5068	970-878-5796
Rio Grande County	P.O. Box 160	Del Norte CO	81132	719-657-3334	719-657-2514
Routt County	P.O. Box 773598	Steamboat Springs CO	80477	970-879-0108	970-879-3992
Saguache County	P.O. Box 655	Saguache CO	81149	719-655-2231	719-655-2635
San Jaun County	P.O. Box 466	Silverton CO	81433	970-387-5671	970-387-5671
San Miguel County	P.O. Box 548	Telluride CO	81435	970-725-3954	970-728-4397
Sedgwick County	P.O. Box 50	Julesburg CO	80737	970-474-3346	970-474-0954
Summit County	P.O. Box 1538	Breckenridge CO	80424	970-453-2561	970-453-5461
Teller County	P.O. Box 1010	Cripple Creek CO	80813	719-689-2574	719-689-3268
Washington County	150 Ash Ave	Akron CO	80720	970-345-2701	970-245-6607
Weld County	1402 N. 17 Ave	Greeley CO	80631	970-353-3840	970-353-1964
Yuma County	P.O. Box 426	Wray CO	80758	970-332-5809	970-332-3411
CONNECTICUT					
Town of Andover	P.O. Box 328	Andover CT	06232	203-742-7305	203-742-7535
Town of Ansonia	253 Main Street	Ansonia CT	06401	203-736-5980	203-734-3853
Town of Ashford	25 Pompey Hollow Rd	Ashford CT	06278	203-429-7044	No Fax
Town of Avon	60 W. Main St	Avon CT	06001	203-677-2634	203-678-1635
Town of Barkhamsted	P.O. Box 185	Pleasant Valley CT	06063	203-379-8665	203-379-9284
Town of Beacon Falls	10 Maple Ave	Beacon Falls CT	06403	203-729-4340	203-720-1078
Town of Berlin	P.O. Box 1	Kensington CT	06037	203-828-7035	203-828-8628
Town of Bethany	40 Peck Rd	Bethany CT	06524	203-393-0820	203-393-0821
Town of Bethel	P.O. Box 3	Bethel CT	06801	203-794-8500	203-794-8552
Town of Bethlehem	P.O. Box 160	Bethlehem CT	06751	203-266-7510	203-266-7677
Town of Bloomfield	P.O. Box 337	Bloomfield CT	06002	860-769-3507	No Fax
Town of Bolton	222 Bolton Center Rd	Bolton CT	06043	203-643-4756	203-643-0021
Town of Bozrah	Town Hall 1 River Rd	Bozrah CT	06334	203-889-2689	203-887-5449
Town of Branford	P.O. Box 150	Branford CT	06405	203-488-6305	203-481-5561
Town of Bridgeport	45 Lyon Terrace	Bridgeport CT	06752	203-576-7207	No Fax
Town of Bridgewater	P.O. Box 216	Bridgewater CT	06752	203-354-5102	No Fax
Town of Bristol	111 N. Main St	Bristol CT	06010	203-584-7656	203-584-3827
Town of Brookfield	P.O. Box 5106	Brookfield Ctr. CT	06804	203-775-7313	No Fax
Town of Brooklyn	P.O. Box 356	Brooklyn CT	06234	203-774-9543	203-779-3744
Town of Burlington	200 Spielman Hwy	Burlington CT	06013	203-673-2108	203-675-9312

CONNECTICUT *continued*

County	Address	City, State	Zip Code	Phone	Fax
Town of Canaan	P.O. Box 155	Falls Village CT	06031	203-824-0707	203-824-4506
Town of Canterbury	P.O. Box 27	Canterbury CT	06331	860-546-9377	860-546-7805
Town of Canton	P.O. Box 168	Collinsville CT	06022	860-693-7870	860-693-7840
Town of Chaplin	P.O. Box 268	Chaplin CT	06235	860-455-9455	860-455-0027
Town of Cheshire	84 S. Main St.	Cheshire CT	06410	203-271-6601	No Fax
Town of Chester	P.O. Box 328	Chester CT	06412	860-526-0006	860-526-0014
Town of Clinton	54 E. Main St	Clinton CT	06413	860-669-9101	No Fax
Town of Colchester	127 Norwich Ave	Colchester CT	06415	203-537-7215	No Fax
Town of Colebrook	P.O. Box 5	Colebrook CT	06021	860-379-3359	860-379-7215
Town of Columbia	P.O. Box 165	Columbia CT	06237	860-228-3284	860-228-1952
Town of Cornwall	Pine St. Box 97	Cornwall CT	06753	860-672-2709	No Fax
Town of Coventry	P.O. Box 189	Coventry CT	06238	860-742-7966	860-742-8911
Town of Cromwell	41 W. St.	Cromwell CT	06416	203-632-3440	No Fax
City of Danbury	155 Deer Hill Ave	Danbury CT	06810	203-797-4530	No Fax
Town of Darien	2 Renshaw Rd	Darien CT	06820	203-656-7307	No Fax
Town of Deep River	174 Main St.	Deep River CT	06417	860-526-6024	860-526-6023
Town of Derby	35 5th St	Derby CT	06418	203-736-1462	203-736-1458
Town of Durham	P.O. Box 428	Durham CT	06422	860-349-3452	860-349-8391
Town of East Granby	P.O. Box TC	East Granby CT	06026	860-653-6528	860-653-4017
Town of East Haddam	P.O. Box K.	East Haddam CT	06423	860-873-5027	860-203-5025
Town of East Hampton	20 E. High St	East Hampton CT	06424	860-267-2519	860-267-1027
Town of East Hartford	740 Main St.	East Hartford CT	06108	860-291-7231	860-289-0831
Town of East Haven	250 Main St.	East Haven CT	06512	203-468-3201	No Fax
Town of East Lyme	108 Pennsylvania Ave	Niantic CT	06357	860-739-6931	860-739-6930
Town of East Windsor	P.O. Box 213	Broad Brook CT	06016	860-623-9467	No Fax
Town of Eastford	P.O. Box 273	Eastford CT	06242	860-974-1885	860-974-0624
Town of Easton	225 Center Rd	Easton CT	06612	203-268-6291	203-261-6080
Town of Ellington	P.O. Box 187	Ellington CT	06029	860-875-3190	860-875-0788
Town of Enfield	820 Enfield St	Enfield CT	06082	860-253-6300	860-253-6310
Town of Essex	P.O. Box 98	Essex CT	06426	860-767-8201	860-767-8509
Town of Fairfield	611 Old Post Rd	Fairfield CT	06430	203-256-3090	No Fax
Town of Farmington	1 Monteith Dr	Farmington CT	06032	860-673-8247	860-675-7410
Town of Franklin	7 Meeting House Hill Rd	N Franklin CT	06254	860-642-7352	860-642-6606
Town of Glastonbury	2155 Main St.	Glastonbury CT	06033	860-652-7710	No Fax
Town of Goshen	P.O. Box 54	Goshen CT	06756	860-491-3647	860-491-9162
Town of Granby	15 N. Granby Rd.	Granby CT	06035	203-653-4817	No Fax
Town of Greenwich	P.O. Box 2540	Greenwich CT	06836	203-622-7897	203-622-3767
Town of Griswold	P.O. Box 369	Jewett City CT	06351	860-376-7063	860-376-7070
Town of Groton	45 Fort Hill Rd	Groton CT	06340	860-445-8551	860-441-6678
Town of Guilford	31 Park St	Guilford CT	06437	203-453-8001	203-453-8467

County	Address	City, State	Zip Code	Phone	Fax
CONNECTICUT *continued*					
Town of Haddam	P.O. Box 87	Haddam CT	06438	860-345-8531	860-345-3730
Town of Hamden	2372 Whitney Ave	Hamden CT	06518	203-287-2517	203-387-2517
Town of Hampton	P.O. Box 143	Hampton CT	06247	860-455-9132	860-455-0517
Town of Hartford	550 Main St.	Hartford CT	06103	860-522-4888	860-722-8041
Town of Hartland	22 South Rd	East Hartland CT	06027	860-653-3542	860-653-7919
Town of Harwinton	100 Bentley Dr	Harwinton CT	06791	860-485-9613	No Fax
Town of Hebron	10 Gilead St	Hebron CT	06248	860-228-9406	860-228-4859
Town of Kent	P.O. Box 678	Kent CT	06757	860-927-3433	No Fax
Town of Killingly	172 Main St.	Danielson CT	06239	860-774-8601	860-779-5394
Town of Killingworth	323 Route 81	Killingworth CT	06419	860-663-1616	860-663-3305
Town of Lebanon	579 Exeter Rd	Lebanon CT	06249	860-642-7319	860-642-7716
Town of Ledyard	P.O. Box 38	Ledyard CT	06339	860-464-8740	860-464-1126
Town of Lisbon	One Newent Rd	Lisbon CT	06351	860-376-2708	860-373-6545
Town of Litchfield	P.O. Box 488	Litchfield CT	06759	860-567-7561	No Fax
Town of Lyme	480 Hamburg Rd	Old Lyme CT	06371	860-434-7733	860-434-2989
Town of Madison	8 Campus Dr.	Madison CT	06443	203-245-5672	203-245-5609
Town of Manchester	P.O. Box 191	Manchester CT	06045	860-647-3037	860-647-3099
Town of Mansfield	4 S. Eagleville Rd	Mansfield CT	06268	860-429-3302	No Fax
Town of Marlborough	P.O. Box 29	Marlborough CT	06447	860-295-9547	860-295-0317
Town of Meriden	142 E Main St.	Meriden CT	06450	203-630-4030	203-630-4095
Town of Middlebury	1212 Whittemore Rd	Middlebury CT	06762	203-758-2557	No Fax
Town of Middlefield	P.O. Box 179	Middlefield CT	06455	860-349-7116	860-349-7115
Town of Middletown	245 Dekoven Dr & Ct St	Middletown CT	06457	860-344-3459	860-344-0136
Town of Milford	70 W. River St.	Milford CT	06460	203-783-3210	No Fax
Town of Monroe	7 Fan Hill Rd	Monroe CT	06468	203-452-5417	203-261-6197
Town of Montville	310 Norwich-New London	Uncasville CT	06382	860-848-1349	860-848-4534
Town of Morris	P.O. Box 66	Morris CT	06763	860-567-5387	860-567-3678
Town of Naugatuck	229 Church St.	Naugatuck CT	06770	203-729-4571	203-723-1297
Town of New Britain	27 W. Main St.	New Britian CT	06051	860-826-3344	No Fax
Town of New Canaan	P.O. Box 447	New Canaan CT	06840	203-972-2323	203-966-0309
Town of New Fairfield	4 Brush Hill Rd.	New Fairfield CT	06812	203-746-8110	No Fax
Town of New Hartford	P.O. Box 316	New Hartford CT	06057	860-379-5037	860-379-0940
Town of New Haven	200 Orange St., #202	New Haven CT	06510	203-787-8339	203-946-6974
Town of New London	181 State St	New London CT	06320	860-447-5205	860-447-1644
Town of New Milford	P.O. Box 360	New Milford CT	06776	860-355-6020	860-355-6002
Town of Newington	131 Cedar St	Newington CT	06111	860-666-4661	No Fax
Town of Newtown	45 Main St.	Newtown CT	06470	203-270-4200	203-270-4205
Town of Norfolk	P.O. Box 552	Norfolk CT	06058	860-542-5679	No Fax
Town of North Branford	P.O. Box 287	North Branford CT	06471	203-481-5369	203-483-1245
Town of North Canaan	P.O. Box 338	Canaan CT	06018	860-824-3138	No Fax

County	Address	City, State	Zip Code	Phone	Fax
CONNECTICUT *continued*					
Town of North Haven	18 Church St.	North Haven CT	06473	203-239-5321	203-234-2130
Town of No. Stonington	40 Main St.	North Stonington CT	06359	860-535-2877	860-535-4554
Town of Norwalk	P.O. Box 5125	Norwalk CT	06856	203-854-7746	No Fax
Town of Norwich	100 Broadway	Norwich CT	06360	860-823-3700	860-823-3790
Town of Old Lyme	P.O. Box 338	Old Lyme CT	06371	860-434-1655	860-434-9283
Town of Old Saybrook	302 Main St.	Old Saybrook CT	06475	860-395-3135	No Fax
Town of Orange	617 Orange Center Rd	Orange CT	06477	203-891-2122	203-891-2185
Town of Oxford	486 Oxford Rd.	Oxford CT	06478	203-888-2543	203-888-2136
Town of Plainfield	8 Community Ave	Plainfield CT	06374	860-564-4075	No Fax
Town of Plainville	1 Central Sq	Plainville CT	06062	860-793-0221	860-793-2285
Town of Plymouth	80 Main St.	Terryville CT	06786	860-585-4039	860-585-4015
Town of Pomfret	5 Haven Rd	Pomfret Center CT	06259	860-974-0343	860-974-3950
Town of Portland	P.O. Box 71	Portland CT	06480	860-342-6743	860-342-0001
Town of Preston	389 Rt 2	Preston CT	06365	860-887-9821	860-885-1905
Town of Prospect	36 Center St	Prospect CT	06712	203-758-4461	203-758-4466
Town of Putnam	126 Church St.	Putnam CT	06260	860-963-6807	860-963-6814
Town of Redding	P.O. Box 1028	Redding Center CT	06875	203-938-2377	203-938-8816
Town of Ridgefield	400 Main St.	Ridgefield CT	06877	203-431-2783	203-431-2722
Town of Rocky Hill	P.O. Box 657	Rocky Hill CT	06067	860-258-2705	860-258-7638
Town of Roxbury	P.O. Box 203	Roxbury CT	06783	860-354-3328	860-354-0560
Town of Salem	270 Hardford Rd.	Salem CT	06420	860-859-3875	860-859-1184
Town of Salisbury	P.O. Box 548	Salisbury CT	06068	860-435-5182	No Fax
Town of Scotland	P.O. Box 122	Scotland CT	06264	203-423-9634	203-423-3666
Town of Seymour	1 First St	Seymour CT	06483	203-888-0519	203-881-2765
Town of Sharon	P.O. Box 224	.Shanon CT	06069	203-364-5224	No Fax
Town of Shelton	54 Hill St.	Shelton CT	06484	203-924-1562	203-924-0185
Town of Sherman	P.O. Box 39	Sherman CT	06784	860-354-5281	860-355-6943
Town of Simsbury	P.O. Box 495	Simsbury CT	06070	860-658-3200	860-658-9467
Town of Somers	P.O. Box 308	Somers CT	06071	860-763-8206	860-763-0973
Town of South Windsor	1540 Sullivan Ave.	South Windsor CT	06074	860-644-2511	860-644-3781
Town of Southbury	501 Main St. S	Southbury CT	06488	203-262-0600	203-264-9762
Town of Southington	75 Main St.	Southington CT	06489	860-276-6211	860-628-8669
Town of Sprague	P.O. Box 162	Baltic CT	06330	860-822-3001	No Fax
Town of Stafford	P.O. Box 11	Stafford Springs CT	06076	860-684-2532	860-864-9845
Town of Stamford	P.O. Box 891	Stamford CT	06904	203-977-4055	No Fax
Town of Sterling	P.O. Box 157	Oneco CT	06373	860-564-2657	860-564-1660
Town of Stonington	P.O. Box 352	Stonington CT	06378	860-535-4721	860-535-0602
Town of Stratford	2725 Main St., #101	Stratford CT	06497	203-385-4020	203-385-4108
Town of Suffield	83 Mountain Rd	Suffield CT	06078	860-668-3880	860-668-3878
Town of Thomaston	158 Main St.	Thomaston CT	06787	860-283-4141	860-283-1013

County	Address	City, State	Zip Code	Phone	Fax

CONNECTICUT *continued*

County	Address	City, State	Zip Code	Phone	Fax
Town of Thompson	815 Riverside Dr.	N. Grosvenor Dale CT	06255	860-923-9900	860-923-3836
Town of Tolland	21 Tolland Green	Tolland CT	06084	860-871-3630	No Fax
Town of Torrington	140 Main St.	Torrington CT	06790	860-489-2241	No Fax
Town of Trumbull	5866 Main St.	Trumbull CT	06611	203-452-5037	203-452-5038
Town of Union	1024 Buckley Highway	Union CT	06076	860-684-3770	No Fax
Town of Vernon	P.O. Box 245	Rockville CT	06066	860-872-8591	860-871-9459
Town of Voluntown	P.O. Box 96	Voluntown CT	06384	860-376-4089	860-376-3295
Town of Wallingford	P.O. Box 427	Wallingford CT	06492	203-294-2145	203-294-2073
Town of Warren	P.O. Box 1025	Warren CT	06754	860-868-0090	No Fax
Town of Washington	Bryan Mem Twn Hall	Washington Depot CT	06794	203-868-2786	No Fax
Town of Waterbury	235 Grand St.	Waterbury CT	06702	203-574-6806	203-574-6887
Town of Waterford	15 Rope Ferry Rd	Waterford CT	06385	860-442-0553	860-437-0352
Town of West Hartford	50 S. Main St	West Hartford CT	06107	860-523-3143	860-523-3522
Town of West Haven	355 Main St.	West Haven CT	06516	203-937-3535	No Fax
Town of Westbrook	P.O. Box G.	Westbrook CT	06498	860-399-3044	860-399-9568
Town of Weston	P.O. Box 1007	Weston CT	06883	203-222-2616	No Fax
Town of Westport	P.O. Box 549	Westport CT	06881	203-226-8311	203-226-6085
Town of Wethersfield	505 Silas Deane Hwy	Wethersfield CT	06109	860-721-2880	860-721-2994
Town of Willington	40 Old Farms Rd	Willington CT	06279	860-429-9965	860-429-9778
Town of Wilton	238 Danbury Rd	Wilton CT	06897	203-834-9205	203-834-9211
Town of Winchester	338 Main St.	Winsted CT	06098	860-379-2713	860-738-7053
Town of Windham	979 Main St.	Willimantic CT	06226	860-465-3013	860-465-3012
Town of Windsor Locks	50 Church St.	Windsor Locks CT	06096	860-627-1441	No Fax
Town of Windsor	P.O. Box 472	Windsor CT	06095	860-285-1900	860-285-1909
Town of Wolcott	10 Kenea Ave	Wolcott CT	06716	203-879-8100	No Fax
Town of Woodbridge	11 Meetinghouse Ln.	Woodbridge CT	06525	203-389-3422	No Fax
Town of Woodbury	P.O. Box 369	Woodbury CT	06798	203-263-2144	203-263-5477
Town of Woodstock	P.O. Box 123	Woodstock CT	06281	860-928-6595	860-963-7557

DELAWARE

County	Address	City, State	Zip Code	Phone	Fax
Kent County	414 Federal St	Dover DE	19901	302-736-2040	No Fax
New Castle County	800 N. French St	Wilmington DE	19801	302-471-4180	No Fax
Sussex County	P.O. Box 756	Georgetown DE	19947	302-856-5740	302-856-5739

FLORIDA

County	Address	City, State	Zip Code	Phone	Fax
Alachua County	P.O. Box 2877	Gainesville FL	32602	352-374-5210	352-338-7363
Baker County	55 N. 3rd St.	Macclenny FL	32063	904-259-3613	904-259-7610
Bay County	P.O. Box 1818	Panama City FL	32402	904-784-4015	904-784-4026
Bradford County	P.O. Drawer B.	Starke FL	32091	904-964-6280	904-964-4454
Brevard County	2725 Jameson Way	Viera FL	32940	407-633-2001	407-633-2115

FLORIDA *continued*

County	Address	City, State		Zip Code	Phone	Fax
Broward County	115 S. Andrews	Fort Lauderdale	FL	33301	305-357-7362	305-357-7360
Calhoun County	425 E. Central	Blountstown	FL	32424	904-674-4545	904-674-5553
Charlotte County	18500 Murdock Cir.	Port Charlotte	FL	33948	941-743-1320	941-743-1554
Citrus County	111 W. Main St	Inverness	FL	34450	352-637-9810	352-637-9803
Clay County	P.O. Box 1366	Green Cove Springs	FL	32043	904-284-6313	904-278-4731
Collier County	3301 Tamiami Trail E	Naples	FL	34112	941-774-8383	941-774-4010
Columbia County	P.O. Drawer 1529	Lake City	FL	32056	904-755-4100	904-758-2182
Dade County	111 N.W. 1st #2910	Miami	FL	33128	305-375-5311	305-375-4658
DeSoto County	P.O. Drawer 2076	Arcadia	FL	34265	941-993-4800	941-993-4809
Dixie County	P.O. Box 1206	Cross City	FL	32628	352-498-1206	352-498-1207
Duval County	220 E. Bay St	Jacksonville	FL	32202	904-630-1776	904-630-2391
Escambia County	P.O. Box 1591	Pensacola	FL	32597	904-436-5781	904-436-5802
Flagler County	P.O. Box 787	Bunnell	FL	32110	904-437-7414	904-437-7399
Franklin County	33 Marek St., Suite 203	Apalachicola	FL	32320	904-653-8862	904-653-2261
Gadsden County	P.O. Box 1799	Quincy	FL	32353	904-875-8650	904-875-8655
Gilchrist County	P.O. Box 37	Trenton	FL	32693	352-463-3170	352-463-3166
Glades County	P.O. Box 1018	Moore Haven	FL	33471	941-946-2140	941-946-1091
Gulf County	1000 5th St	Port Saint Joe	FL	32456	904-229-6112	904-229-8461
Hamilton County	207 N.E. 1st St., Rm. 106	Jasper	FL	32052	904-792-1288	904-792-3524
Hardee County	P.O. Drawer 1749	Wauchula	FL	33873	941-773-4174	941-773-0958
Hendry County	P.O. Box 1760	La Belle	FL	33935	941-675-5201	941-675-5238
Hernando County	20 N. Main St	Brooksville	FL	34601	352-754-4000	352-754-4477
Highlands County	P.O. Box 1926	Sebring	FL	33871	941-386-6500	941-386-6507
Hillsborough County	P.O. Box 1110	Tampa	FL	33601	813-276-8100	813-272-6518
Holmes County	201 N. Oklahoma St	Bonifay	FL	32425	904-547-1100	904-547-6630
Indian River County	1840 25th St	Vero Beach	FL	32960	407-567-8000	407-770-5095
Jackson County	P.O. Drawer 510	Marianna	FL	32447	904-482-9552	904-482-7849
Jefferson County	County Courthouse, Rm 10	Monticello	FL	32344	904-342-0218	904-342-0222
Lafayette County	P.O. Box 88	Mayo	FL	32066	904-294-1600	904-294-4231
Lake County	P.O. Box 7800	Tavares	FL	32778	352-343-9888	352-343-9495
Lee County	P.O. Box 398	Fort Myers	FL	33902	941-335-2221	941-335-2262
Leon County	301 S. Monroe St	Tallahassee	FL	32301	904-488-9962	904-488-1670
Levy County	P.O. Box 610	Bronson	FL	32621	352-486-5100	352-486-5766
Liberty County	P.O. Box 399	Bristol	FL	32321	904-643-2215	904-643-2866
Madison County	P.O. Box 539	Madison	FL	32341	904-973-3179	904-973-6880
Manatee County	P.O. Box 1000	Bradenton	FL	34206	941-745-3717	941-745-3790
Marion County	601 S.E. 25th Ave	Ocala	FL	34471	352-620-3340	352-620-3344
Martin County	2401 S.E. Monterey Rd	Stuart	FL	34996	407-288-5422	407-288-5432
Monroe County	5100 College Rd	Key West	FL	33040	904-292-4441	904-292-4544
Nassau County	P.O. Box 456	Fernandina Beach	FL	32035	904-321-5708	904-321-5723

County	Address	City, State	Zip Code	Phone	Fax
FLORIDA *continued*					
Okaloosa County	1804 Lewisturner Blvd	Ft. Walton FL	32547	904-651-7105	904-651-7142
Okeechobee County	304 N.W. 2nd St	Okeechobee FL	34972	941-763-6441	941-763-9529
Orange County	P.O. Box 1393	Orlando FL	32802	407-836-7370	407-836-7399
Osceola County	17 S Vernon Ave, Rm 231C	Kissimmee FL	34741	407-847-1300	407-847-1509
Palm Beach County	P.O. Box 1989	West Palm Beach FL	33402	407-355-2030	407-355-3982
Pasco County	7530 Little Rd	New Port Richey FL	34654	813-847-8115	813-847-8021
Pinellas County	315 Court St	Clearwater FL	34616	813-464-3485	813-464-4384
Polk County	P.O. Box 9000, Drawer CC-1	Bartow FL	33831	941-534-4000	941-534-4089
Putnam County	P.O. Box 758	Palatka FL	32178	904-329-0212	904-329-1216
Saint Johns County	P.O. Drawer 349	Saint Augustine FL	32085	904-823-2400	904-823-2362
Saint Lucie County	2300 Virginia Ave	Fort Pierce FL	34982	561-462-4450	561-462-2131
Santa Rosa County	801 Caroline St. S.E	Milton FL	32570	904-623-0135	904-623-1684
Sarasota County	P.O. Box 3079	Sarasota FL	34230	941-364-4326	941-364-4453
Seminole County	P.O. Drawer C	Sanford FL	32772	352-323-4330	352-330-0218
Sumter County	209 N. Florida St	Bushnell FL	33513	352-793-0215	352-793-0218
Suwannee County	200 S. Ohio Ave	Live Oak FL	32060	904-364-3498	904-362-2421
Taylor County	P.O. Box 620	Perry FL	32347	904-838-3506	904-838-3507
Union County	County Crthouse,Rm 103	Lake Butler FL	32054	904-496-3711	904-496-1535
Volusia County	123 W. Indiana Ave	De Land FL	32720	904-736-5907	904-882-5707
Wakulla County	P.O. Box 1263	Crawfordville FL	32326	904-926-8876	904-926-2071
Walton County	P.O. Box 1260	De Funiak Springs FL	32435	904-892-8155	904-892-8130
Washington County	201 W. Cypress #B	Chipley FL	32428	904-638-6289	904-638-6297
GEORGIA					
Appling County	100 Oak St	Baxley GA	31513	912-367-8100	912-367-8161
Atkinson County	P.O. Box 518	Pearson GA	31642	912-422-3391	912-422-3429
Bacon County	502 W. 12th St	Alma GA	31510	912-632-5214	912-632-2757
Baker County	P.O. Box 607	Newton GA	31770	912-734-3000	912-734-8822
Baldwin County	201 W. Hancock #6	Milledgeville GA	31061	912-453-4791	912-453-6320
Banks County	P.O. Box 130	Homer GA	30547	706-677-2320	706-677-4330
Barrow County	30 N. Broad Rd., Suite 321	Winder GA	30680	770-307-3111	770-867-4800
Bartow County	135 W. Cherokee, Ste 233	Cartersville GA	30120	770-387-5025	No Fax
Ben Hill County	401 E. Central Ave	Fitzgerald GA	31750	912-423-2455	912-423-5715
Berrien County	P.O. Box 446	Nashville GA	31639	912-686-5421	912-686-2785
Bibb County	P.O. Box 4708	Macon GA	31298	912-749-6345	912-749-6329
Bleckley County	306 2nd St. S.E	Cochran GA	31014	912-934-3200	912-934-3205
Brantley County	P.O. Box 398	Nahunta GA	31553	912-462-5256	912-462-5538
Brooks County	P.O. Box 272	Quitman GA	31643	912-263-5561	912-263-9345
Bryan County	P.O. Box H	Pembroke GA	31321	912-653-4681	912-653-4691
Bulloch County	P.O. Box 334	Statesboro GA	30459	912-764-6245	912-764-8634

County	Address	City, State		Zip Code	Phone	Fax

GEORGIA *continued*

County	Address	City, State		Zip Code	Phone	Fax
Burke County	P.O. Box 803	Waynesboro	GA	30830	706-554-2279	706-554-0350
Butts County	P.O. Box 320	Jackson	GA	30233	770-775-8215	770-775-8211
Calhoun County	P.O. Box 226	Morgan	GA	31766	912-849-4835	912-849-2100
Camden County	P.O. Box 578	Woodbine	GA	31569	912-576-5601	912-576-5647
Candler County	705 N. Lewis St	Metter	GA	30439	912-685-2835	912-685-4823
Carroll County	P.O. Box 338	Carrollton	GA	30117	770-830-5800	770-830-5808
Catoosa County	206 E. Nashville St.	Ringgold	GA	30736	706-935-4231	No Fax
Charlton County	100 S. 3rd St	Folkston	GA	31537	912-496-2549	912-496-1156
Chatham County	124 Bull St., Suite 210	Savannah	GA	31412	912-652-7175	No Fax
Chattahoochee County	P.O. Box 299	Cusseta	GA	31805	706-989-3602	706-989-2005
Chattooga County	P.O. Box 159	Summerville	GA	30747	706-857-0706	No Fax
Cherokee County	90 North St., Suite 310	Canton	GA	30114	770-479-0449	770-720-6361
Clarke County	P.O. Box 1868	Athens	GA	30613	706-613-3031	706-613-3033
Clay County	P.O. Box 550	Fort Gaines	GA	31751	912-768-2631	912-768-3443
Clayton County	121 S. McDonough	Jonesboro	GA	30236	404-477-3028	404-473-5969
Clinch County	100 Court Sq	Homerville	GA	31634	912-487-2667	912-487-3658
Cobb County	12 E. Park Sq	Marietta	GA	30090	770-528-1211	No Fax
Coffee County	109 S. Peterson	Douglas	GA	31533	912-384-4799	912-384-0291
Colquitt County	155 S. 1st St	Moultrie	GA	31776	912-758-4104	912-890-2988
Columbia County	P.O. Box 498	Evans	GA	30809	706-868-3379	706-868-3348
Cook County	212 N. Parrish	Adel	GA	31620	912-896-2266	912-896-7629
Coweta County	22 E. Broad St.	Newnan	GA	30263	770-254-2601	770-254-2606
Crawford County	P.O. Box 59	Roberta	GA	31078	912-836-3782	912-836-3232
Crisp County	210 S. 7th St	Cordele	GA	31015	912-276-2672	912-276-2675
Dade County	P.O. Box 613	Trenton	GA	30752	706-657-4625	706-657-5116
Dawson County	P.O. Box 192	Dawsonville	GA	30534	706-265-3164	706-265-2358
Decatur County	P.O. Box 735	Bainbridge	GA	31717	912-248-3030	912-246-2062
DeKalb County	556 N. McDough St	Decatur	GA	30030	770-371-2261	No Fax
Dodge County	P.O. Box 818	Eastman	GA	31023	912-374-4361	912-374-8121
Dooly County	P.O. Box 322	Vienna	GA	31092	912-268-4228	912-268-4230
Dougherty County	P.O. Box 1827	Albany	GA	31702	912-431-2121	912-438-3967
Douglas County	6754 Broad St	Douglasville	GA	30134	404-920-7266	404-920-7357
Early County	P.O. Box 693	Blakely	GA	31723	912-723-4304	912-723-8684
Echois County	P.O. Box 190	Statenville	GA	31648	912-559-6538	912-559-5792
Effingham County	P.O. Box 307	Springfield	GA	31329	912-754-6071	912-754-6023
Elbert County	10 W. Church St	Elberton	GA	30635	706-283-2000	706-283-1818
Emanuel County	P.O. Box 787	Swainsboro	GA	30401	912-237-3881	912-237-2593
Evans County	P.O. Box 711	Claxton	GA	30417	912-739-1141	912-739-0111
Fannin County	P.O. Box 487	Blue Ridge	GA	30513	706-632-2203	706-632-2507
Fayette County	140 Stonewall	Fayetteville	GA	30214	770-461-4703	No Fax

County	Address	City, State Zip Code	Phone	Fax

GEORGIA *continued*

County	Address	City, State Zip Code	Phone	Fax
Floyd County	P.O. Box 946	Rome GA 30162	706-291-5110	706-291-5248
Forsyth County	100 Courthouse Sq	Cumming GA 30130	770-781-2120	No Fax
Franklin County	P.O. Box 159	Carnesville GA 30521	706-384-2483	706-384-7089
Fulton County	141 Pryor St. S.W.	Atlanta GA 30303	404-730-8200	404-730-8258
Gilmer County	1 Westside Sq	Ellijay GA 30540	706-635-4361	706-635-4359
Glascock County	P.O. Box 66	Gibson GA 30810	706-598-2671	No Fax
Glynn County	P.O. Box 879	Brunswick GA 31521	912-267-5600	912-267-5691
Gordon County	P.O. Box 580	Calhoun GA 30703	706-629-3795	706-629-9516
Grady County	250 N. Broad St	Cairo GA 31728	912-377-1512	912-377-4127
Greene County	201 N. Main St	Greensboro GA 30642	706-453-7716	706-453-9555
Gwinnett County	75 Langley Dr	Lawrenceville GA 30245	770-822-8564	770-822-8566
Habersham County	555 Monroe, Unit 20	Clarkesville GA 30523	706-754-6264	706-754-1014
Hall County	P.O. Box 1435	Gainesville GA 30503	770-531-7000	770-531-6711
Hancock County	Courthouse Sq	Sparta GA 31087	706-444-5746	706-444-6221
Haralson County	P.O. Box 186	Buchanan GA 30113	770-646-2018	770-646-2017
Harris County	P.O. Box 365	Hamilton GA 31811	706-628-4958	706-628-9223
Hart County	P.O. Box 279	Hartwell GA 30643	706-376-2024	706-376-9477
Heard County	P.O. Box 40	Franklin GA 30217	706-675-3821	706-675-0819
Henry County	345 Phillips Dr	McDonough GA 30253	770-954-2400	770-954-2418
Houston County	200 Carl Vinson	Warner Robins GA 31088	912-542-2115	912-923-5697
Irwin County	P.O. Box 287	Ocilla GA 31774	912-468-9441	912-468-9672
Jackson County	67 Acton St	Jefferson GA 30549	706-367-1199	706-367-9083
Jasper County	County Courthouse	Monticello GA 31064	706-468-4900	706-468-4942
Jeff Davis County	P.O. Box 602	Hazlehurst GA 31539	912-375-6611	912-375-0378
Jefferson County	P.O. Box 658	Louisville GA 30434	912-625-3332	912-625-4007
Jenkins County	P.O. Box 797	Millen GA 30442	912-982-2563	912-982-4750
Johnson County	P.O. Box 269	Wrightsville GA 31096	912-864-3388	912-864-9441
Jones County	P.O. Box 1359	Gray GA 31032	912-986-6405	912-986-1985
Lamar County	326 Thomaston St	Barnesville GA 30204	770-358-5218	770-358-5149
Lanier County	100 Main St.	Lakeland GA 31635	912-482-2088	912-482-8333
Laurens County	P.O. Box 2011	Dublin GA 31040	912-272-4755	912-272-3895
Lee County	P.O. Box 56	Leesburg GA 31763	912-759-6000	912-759-6050
Liberty County	P.O. Box 829	Hinesville GA 31313	912-876-2164	912-369-0204
Lincoln County	P.O. Box 340	Lincolnton GA 30817	706-359-4444	706-359-4729
Long County	P.O. Box 476	Ludowici GA 31316	912-545-2143	912-545-2150
Lowndes County	P.O. Box 1349	Valdosta GA 31603	912-333-5116	912-245-5222
Lumpkin County	280 Courthouse Hill	Dahlonega GA 30533	706-864-3742	706-864-4760
Macon County	P.O. Box 297	Oglethorpe GA 31068	912-472-7021	912-472-5643
Madison County	P.O. Box 247	Danielsville GA 30633	706-795-3351	706-795-5668
Marion County	P.O. Box 481	Buena Vista GA 31803	912-649-2603	912-649-3702

County	Address	City, State	Zip Code	Phone	Fax

GEORGIA *continued*

County	Address	City, State	Zip Code	Phone	Fax
McDuffle County	P.O. Box 28	Thomson GA	30824	706-595-2100	706-595-4710
McIntosh County	P.O. Box 584	Darien GA	31305	912-437-6671	912-437-6416
Meriwether County	P.O. Box 428	Greenville GA	30222	706-672-1314	706-672-1886
Miller County	155 S. 1st St	Colquitt GA	31737	912-758-4104	912-758-2229
Mitchell County	P.O. Box 187	Camilla GA	31730	912-336-2000	912-336-2003
Monroe County	P.O. Box 189	Forsyth GA	31029	912-994-7000	912-994-7055
Montgomery County	P.O. Box 295	Mount Vernon GA	30445	912-583-2363	912-583-2026
Morgan County	P.O. Box 168	Madison GA	30650	706-342-0725	706-342-7806
Murray County	P.O. Box 1129	Chatsworth GA	30705	706-695-2413	706-695-8721
Muscogee County	P.O. Box 1340	Columbus GA	31902	706-571-4860	706-571-5850
Newton County	1124 Clark St	Covington GA	30209	770-784-2035	No Fax
Oconee County	P.O. Box 145	Watkinsville GA	30677	706-769-5120	706-769-0705
Oglethorpe County	P.O. Box 261	Lexington GA	30648	706-743-5270	706-743-5270
Paulding County	11 Courthouse Sq	Dallas GA	30132	770-443-7527	No Fax
Peach County	P.O. Box 468	Fort Valley GA	31030	912-825-2535	912-825-2678
Pickens County	52 N. Main St, Suite 201	Jasper GA	30143	706-692-2121	706-692-2850
Pierce County	P.O. Box 679	Blackshear GA	31516	912-449-2022	912-449-2024
Pike County	P.O. Box 377	Zebulon GA	30295	770-567-3406	770-567-2006
Polk County	100 Prior St.	Cedartown GA	30125	770-749-2130	770-748-5520
Pulaski County	P.O. Box 29	Hawkinsville GA	31036	912-783-4154	912-892-3308
Putnam County	108 S. Madison	Eatonton GA	31024	706-485-5826	706-485-5578
Quitman County	P.O. Box 114	Georgetown GA	31754	912-334-0903	912-334-2151
Rabun County	25 Courthouse Sq., Box 8	Clayton GA	30525	706-782-5271	706-782-7588
Randolph County	P.O. Box 221	Cuthbert GA	31740	912-732-6440	912-732-5364
Richmond County	801 City-County Bldg.	Augusta GA	30911	706-821-2400	706-821-2819
Rockdale County	922 Court St	Conyers GA	30207	770-929-4019	No Fax
Schley County	P.O. Box 352	Ellaville GA	31806	912-937-2609	912-937-2609
Screven County	P.O. Box 159	Sylvania GA	30467	912-564-7535	912-564-2562
Seminole County	County Courthouse	Donalsonville GA	31745	912-524-2878	912-524-8984
Spalding County	P.O. Box 1046	Griffin GA	30224	770-228-9900	No Fax
Stephens County	P.O. Box 386	Toccoa GA	30577	706-886-9491	706-886-2185
Stewart County	P.O. Box 157	Lumpkin GA	31815	706-838-6769	706-838-6769
Sumter County	P.O. Box 295	Americus GA	31709	912-924-6725	912-924-2541
Talbot County	P.O. Box 155	Talbotton GA	31827	706-665-3220	706-665-8199
Tallaferro County	P.O. Box 114	Crawfordville GA	30631	706-456-2494	706-456-2904
Tattnall County	P.O. Box 25	Reidsville GA	30453	912-557-4335	912-557-6088
Taylor County	P.O. Box 278	Butler GA	31006	912-862-3336	912-862-2871
Telfair County	Courthouse Sq	McRae GA	31055	912-868-5688	No Fax
Terrell County	P.O. Box 525	Dawson GA	31742	912-995-4476	912-995-4320
Thomas County	P.O. Box 920	Thomasville GA	31799	912-225-4100	912-226-3430

County	Address	City, State		Zip Code	Phone	Fax
GEORGIA *continued*						
Tift County	P.O. Box 826	Tifton	GA	31793	912-386-7850	912-386-7955
Toombs County	P.O. Box 112	Lyons	GA	30436	912-526-3311	912-526-1004
Towns County	48 River St	Hiawassee	GA	30546	706-896-2276	706-896-1772
Treutlen County	P.O. Box 88	Soperton	GA	30457	912-529-3664	912-529-6062
Troup County	P.O. Box 866	LaGrange	GA	30241	706-883-1740	No Fax
Turner County	P.O. Box 191	Ashburn	GA	31714	912-567-4313	912-567-4794
Twiggs County	P.O. Box 202	Jeffersonville	GA	31044	912-945-3629	912-945-3988
Union County	114 Courthouse St., Box 1	Blairsville	GA	30512	706-745-9655	706-745-1311
Upson County	P.O. Box 889	Thomaston	GA	30286	706-647-7145	716-647-7030
Walker County	P.O. Box 445	La Fayette	GA	30728	706-638-1437	706-638-1453
Walton County	P.O. Box 774	Monroe	GA	30655	770-207-4192	770-267-1402
Ware County	P.O. Box 1069	Waycross	GA	31502	912-287-4300	912-287-4301
Warren County	P.O. Box 46	Warrenton	GA	30828	706-465-2171	706-465-1300
Washington County	P.O. Box 271	Sandersville	GA	31082	912-552-2325	912-552-7424
Wayne County	P.O. Box 217	Jesup	GA	31598	912-427-5900	912-427-5906
Webster County	P.O. Box 29	Preston	GA	31824	912-828-5775	912-828-2105
Wheeler County	P.O. Box 38	Alamo	GA	30411	912-568-7137	No Fax
White County	59 S. Main St	Cleveland	GA	30528	706-865-2235	706-865-1324
Whitfield County	P.O. Box 248	Dalton	GA	30722	706-275-7500	706-275-7501
Wilcox County	103 N. Broad St	Abbeville	GA	31001	912-467-2737	912-467-2000
Wilkes County	23 E. Court St	Washington	GA	30673	706-678-2511	706-678-1300
Wilkinson County	P.O. Box 161	Irwinton	GA	31042	912-946-2236	912-946-3767
Worth County	201 W. Main, Rm. 110	Sylvester	GA	31791	912-776-8200	912-776-8232
HAWAII						
Hawaii County	25 Aupuni St	Hilo	HI	96720	808-961-8255	808-969-3291
Honolulu County	530 S. King St	Honolulu	HI	96813	808-523-4352	808-527-6888
Kauai County	4396 Rice St., Suite 206	Lihue	HI	96766	808-241-6371	808-241-6349
Maui County	200 S. High St	Wailuku	HI	96793	808-243-7825	808-243-7686
IDAHO						
Ada County	650 Main St	Boise	ID	83702	208-364-2323	208-364-2331
Adams County	P.O. Box 48	Council	ID	83612	208-253-4561	208-253-4880
Bannock County	624 E. Center St	Pocatello	ID	83201	208-236-7333	208-236-7345
Bear Lake County	P.O. Box 190	Paris	ID	83261	208-945-2212	208-945-2780
Benewah County	701 College Ave	Saint Maries	ID	83861	208-245-3212	208-245-3046
Bingham County	501 N. Maple St	Blackfoot	ID	83221	208-785-5005	208-785-5199
Blaine County	P.O. Box 1006	Hailey	ID	83333	208-788-5521	208-788-8527
Boise County	P.O. Box B. C.	Idaho City	ID	83631	208-392-4431	208-392-4473
Bonner County	215 S. 1st Ave	Sandpoint	ID	83864	208-265-1432	208-263-0896
Bonneville County	605 N Capital Ave	Idaho Falls	ID	83402	208-529-1363	208-528-5509

County	Address	City, State	Zip Code	Phone	Fax
IDAHO *continued*					
Boundary County	P.O. Box 419	Bonners Ferry ID	83805	208-267-2242	208-267-7814
Butte County	P.O. Box 737	Arco ID	83213	208-527-3021	208-527-3916
Camas County	P.O. Box 430	Fairfield ID	83327	208-764-2242	208-764-2349
Canyon County	1115 Albany St	Caldwell ID	83605	208-454-7300	208-454-7272
Caribou County	P.O. Box 775	Soda Springs ID	83276	208-547-4324	208-547-4759
Cassia County	County Courthouse	Burley ID	83318	208-678-4367	208-677-1003
Clark County	P.O. Box 205	Dubois ID	83423	208-374-5304	208-374-5609
Clearwater County	P.O. Box 586	Orofino ID	83544	208-476-5615	208-476-7835
Custer County	P.O. Box 385	Challis ID	83226	208-879-2360	208-879-5246
Elmore County	150 S. 4th East	Mountain Home ID	83647	208-587-2130	208-587-2159
Franklin County	39 W. Oneida St	Preston ID	83263	208-852-1090	208-852-1094
Fremont County	151 W. 1st North	Saint Anthony ID	83445	208-624-7332	208-624-7335
Gem County	415 E. Main	Emmett ID	83617	208-365-4561	208-365-6172
Gooding County	P.O. Box 417	Gooding ID	83330	208-934-4841	208-934-4408
Idaho County	320 W. Main	Grangeville ID	83530	208-983-2751	208-983-1418
Jefferson County	134 N. Clark	Rigby ID	83442	208-745-7756	208-745-9212
Jerome County	300 N. Lincoln	Jerome ID	83338	208-324-8811	208-324-2719
Kootenai County	501 N. Government W	Coeur dAlene ID	83814	208-769-4400	208-667-8534
Latah County	P.O. Box 8068	Moscow ID	83843	208-882-8580	208-883-4338
Lemhi County	206 Courthouse Dr	Salmon ID	92467	208-756-2815	208-756-8424
Lewis County	P.O. Box 39	Nezperce ID	83543	208-937-2661	208-937-2661
Lincoln County	111 W. B St	Shoshone ID	83352	208-886-7641	208-886-2851
Madison County	P.O. Box 389	Rexburg ID	83440	208-356-3662	208-356-8396
Minidoka County	715 G St.	Rupert ID	83350	208-436-9511	208-436-9561
Nez Perce County	P.O. Box 896	Lewiston ID	83501	208-799-3020	208-799-3037
Oneida County	10 Court St	Malad City ID	83252	208-766-4116	208-766-4285
Owyhee County	P.O. Box 128	Murphy ID	83650	208-495-2421	208-495-1173
Payette County	P.O. Box D.	Payette ID	83661	208-642-6000	208-642-6011
Power County	543 Bannock Ave	American Falls ID	83211	208-226-7611	208-226-7612
Shoshone County	700 Bank St	Wallace ID	83873	208-752-1264	208-753-2711
Teton County	P.O. Box 756	Driggs ID	83422	208-354-2905	208-354-8410
Twin Falls County	P.O. Box 126	Twin Falls ID	83303	208-736-4004	208-736-4182
Valley County	P.O. Box 737	Cascade ID	83611	208-382-4297	208-382-4955
Washington County	P.O. Box 670	Weiser ID	83672	208-549-2092	208-549-3925
ILLINOIS					
Adams County	521 Vermont St.	Quincy IL	62301	217-223-6300	217-223-2186
Alexander County	2000 Washington Ave	Cairo IL	62914	618-734-7000	618-734-7003
Bond County	200 W. College	Greenville IL	62246	618-664-0449	618-664-4676
Boone County	601 N. Main St	Belvedere IL	61008	815-544-3103	815-547-8701
Brown County	County Courthouse	Mount Sterling IL	62353	217-773-3421	217-773-2233

County	Address	City, State	Zip Code	Phone	Fax

ILLINOIS *continued*

County	Address	City, State	Zip Code	Phone	Fax
Bureau County	700 S. Main St	Princeton IL	61356	815-875-2014	815-879-4803
Calhoun County	P.O. Box 187	Hardin IL	62047	618-576-2351	No Fax
Carroll County	301 N. Main	Mount Carroll IL	61053	815-244-9171	815-244-3709
Cass County	County Courthouse	Virginia IL	62691	217-452-7217	217-452-7219
Champaign County	204 E. Elm St	Urbana IL	61801	217-384-3720	217-384-1241
Christian County	P.O. Box 647	Taylorville IL	62568	217-824-4969	217-824-5105
Clark County	Courthouse	Marshall IL	62441	217-826-8311	217-826-5674
Clay County	P.O. Box 160	Louisville IL	62858	618-665-3626	618-665-3155
Clinton County	P.O. Box 308	Carlyle IL	62231	618-594-2464	618-594-8715
Coles County	P.O. Box 227	Charleston IL	61920	217-348-0501	217-348-7337
Cook County	50 W. Washington	Chicago IL	60602	312-443-4743	312-443-4707
Crawford County	P.O. Box 602	Robinson IL	62454	618-546-1212	618-546-0140
Cumberland County	P.O. Box 146	Toledo IL	62468	217-849-2631	217-849-2968
De Witt County	201 W. Washington	Clinton IL	61727	217-935-2119	217-935-4596
DeKalb County	110 E. Sycamore St	Sycamore IL	60178	815-895-7149	815-895-7129
Douglas County	401 S. Center St	Tuscola IL	61953	217-253-2411	No Fax
Du Page County	421 N. County Farm Rd.	Wheaton IL	60187	708-682-7035	708-682-7409
Edgar County	115 W. Court, Rm. J.	Paris IL	61944	217-465-4151	217-463-3137
Edwards County	50 E. Main St	Albion IL	62806	618-445-2115	618-445-3505
Effingham County	P.O. Box 628	Effingham IL	62401	217-342-6535	217-342-3577
Fayette County	221 S. 7th St	Vandalia IL	62471	618-283-5000	618-283-5004
Ford County	200 W. State St.	Paxton IL	60957	217-379-2721	217-379-3258
Franklin County	P.O. Box 607	Benton IL	62812	618-438-3221	618-439-4119
Fulton County	100 N. Main St	Lewistown IL	61542	309-547-3041	309-547-3636
Gallatin County	P.O. Box 550	Shawneetown IL	62984	618-269-3025	618-269-4324
Greene County	519 N. Main St	Carrollton IL	62016	217-942-5443	217-942-6211
Grundy County	111 E. Washington St	Morris IL	60450	815-941-3222	815-942-2222
Hamilton County	County Courthouse	McLeansboro IL	62859	618-643-2721	No Fax
Hancock County	P.O. Box 39	Carthage IL	62321	217-357-3911	No Fax
Hardin County	P.O. Box 187	Elizabethtown IL	62931	618-287-2251	618-287-7833
Henderson County	P.O. Box 308	Oquawka IL	61469	309-867-2911	309-867-2033
Henry County	100 S. Main St	Cambridge IL	61238	309-937-2426	309-937-2796
Iroquois County	1001 E. Grant St.	Watseka IL	60970	815-432-6960	815-432-6984
Jackson County	County Courthouse	Murphysboro IL	62966	618-687-7360	No Fax
Jasper County	100 W. Jourdan St	Newton IL	62448	618-783-3124	618-783-4137
Jefferson County	100 S. 10th St	Mount Vernon IL	62864	618-244-8020	618-244-8029
Jersey County	201 W. Pearl St.	Jerseyville IL	62052	618-498-5571	618-498-6128
Jo Daviess County	330 N. Bench St	Galena IL	61036	815-777-0161	815-777-3688
Johnson County	P.O. Box 96	Vienna IL	62995	618-658-3611	618-658-2908
Kane County	P.O. Box 70	Geneva IL	60134	708-232-5950	708-232-5870

ILLINOIS *continued*

County	Address	City, State	Zip Code	Phone	Fax
Kankakee County	189 E. Court St	Kankakee IL	60901	815-937-2990	815-973-3918
Kendall County	111 W. Fox St	Yorkville IL	60560	708-553-4104	708-553-4119
Knox County	200 S. Cherry St	Galesburg IL	61401	309-345-3829	309-343-7002
Lake County	18 N. County St	Waukegan IL	60085	847-360-3610	847-360-6735
LaSalle County	707 E. Etna Rd	Ottawa IL	61350	815-434-8202	815-434-8319
Lawrence County	County Courthouse	Lawrenceville IL	62439	618-943-2346	618-943-5205
Lee County	P.O. Box 385	Dixon IL	61021	815-288-3309	815-288-6492
Livingston County	112 W. Madison St	Pontiac IL	61764	815-844-2006	815-842-1844
Logan County	P.O. Box 278	Lincoln IL	62656	217-732-4148	217-732-6064
Macon County	141 S. Main St., Rm. 104	Decatur IL	62523	217-424-1305	217-423-0922
Macoupin County	County Courthouse	Carlinville IL	62626	217-854-3214	612-854-8461
Madison County	157 N. Main St	Edwardsville IL	62025	618-692-6290	618-692-8903
Marion County	P.O. Box 637	Salem IL	62881	618-548-3400	618-548-2226
Marshall County	122 N. Prairie St.	Lacon IL	61540	309-246-6325	309-246-3667
Mason County	County Courthouse	Havana IL	62644	309-543-3634	309-543-2085
Massac County	P.O. Box 429	Metropolis IL	62960	618-524-5213	618-524-4230
McDonough County	County Courthouse	Macomb IL	61455	309-833-2474	309-836-3013
McHenry County	2200 N. Seminary Ave	Woodstock IL	60098	815-334-4242	815-334-4242
McLean County	104 W. Front St	Bloomington IL	61701	309-888-5183	309-888-5209
Menard County	P.O. Box 465	Petersburg IL	62675	217-632-2415	217-632-4124
Mercer County	P.O. Box 66	Aledo IL	61231	309-582-7021	309-582-7022
Monroe County	100 S. Main St	Waterloo IL	62298	618-939-8681	618-939-5132
Montgomery County	P.O. Box C	Hillsboro IL	62049	217-532-9541	217-532-9903
Morgan County	300 W. State St	Jacksonville IL	62650	217-243-8581	217-243-8368
Moultrie County	County Courthouse	Sullivan IL	61951	217-728-4389	217-728-8178
Ogle County	P.O. Box 357	Oregon IL	61061	815-732-3201	815-732-6273
Peoria County	324 Main St.	Peoria IL	61602	309-672-6059	309-672-6063
Perry County	P.O. Box 438	Pinckneyville IL	62274	618-357-5116	618-357-3194
Piatt County	101 W. Washington	Monticello IL	61856	217-762-9487	217-762-7563
Pike County	County Courthouse	Pittsfield IL	62363	217-285-6812	217-285-4726
Pope County	P.O. Box 216	Golconda IL	62938	618-683-4466	618-683-2211
Pulaski County	P.O. Box 109	Mound City IL	62963	618-748-9360	618-748-9338
Putnam County	County Courthouse	Hennepin IL	61327	815-925-7129	815-925-7549
Randolph County	1 Taylor St	Chester IL	62233	618-826-5000	618-826-3750
Richland County	9423 W. Main	Olney IL	62450	618-392-3111	618-274-3636
Rock Island County	1504 3rd Ave	Rock Island IL	61201	309-786-4451	309-786-7381
Saint Clair County	10 Public Sq	Belleville IL	62220	618-277-6600	618-277-8783
Saline County	10 E. Poplar	Harrisburg IL	62946	618-253-8197	618-252-3073
Sangamon County	200 S. 9th	Springfield IL	62701	217-753-6706	217-753-6672
Schuyler County	P.O. Box 200	Rushville IL	62681	217-322-4734	217-322-6164

County	Address	City, State	Zip Code	Phone	Fax
ILLINOIS *continued*					
Scott County	101 E. Market	Winchester IL	62694	217-742-3178	217-742-5853
Shelby County	P.O. Box 230	Shelbyville IL	62565	217-774-4421	217-774-2690
Stark County	130 W. Main St	Toulon IL	61483	309-286-5911	309-286-6091
Stephenson County	15 N. Galena Ave	Freeport IL	61032	815-235-8289	No Fax
Tazewell County	11 S. 4th St	Pekin IL	61554	309-477-2264	309-346-4415
Union County	P.O. Box H	Jonesboro IL	62952	618-833-5711	No Fax
Vermillion County	6 N. Vermillion	Danville IL	61832	217-431-2607	217-431-2806
Wabash County	P.O. Box 277	Mount Carmel IL	62863	618-262-4561	618-263-4441
Warren County	100 W. Broadway	Monmouth IL	61462	309-734-8592	309-734-7406
Washington County	101 E. St Louis St	Nashville IL	62263	618-327-8314	618-327-3378
Wayne County	300 E. Main St	Fairfield IL	62837	618-842-5182	618-842-2556
White County	P.O. Box 339	Carmi IL	62821	618-382-7211	618-382-2322
Whiteside County	200 E. Knox St	Morrison IL	61270	815-772-5189	815-772-7673
Will County	302 N. Chicago St	Joliet IL	60431	815-740-4615	815-740-4699
Williamson County	200 W. Jefferson St	Marion IL	62959	618-997-1301	618-993-2071
Winnebago County	404 Elm St	Rockford IL	61101	815-987-3050	815-969-0259
Woodford County	115 N. Main St #202	Eureka IL	61530	309-467-2822	309-467-5211
INDIANA					
Adams County	112 S. 2nd St	Decatur IN	46733	219-724-2600	219-724-9189
Allen County	715 S. Calhoun	Fort Wayne IN	46802	219-449-7245	No Fax
Bartholomew County	P.O. Box 924	Columbus IN	47202	812-379-1600	812-379-1675
Benton County	706 E. 5th St	Fowler IN	47944	317-884-0930	317-884-2013
Blackford County	110 W. Washington	Hartford City IN	47348	317-348-3213	No Fax
Boone County	212 Courthouse Sq	Lebanon IN	46052	317-482-3510	No Fax
Brown County	P.O. Box 85	Nashville IN	47448	812-988-5510	812-988-5562
Carroll County	101 W. Main St	Delphi IN	46923	317-564-4485	317-564-6907
Cass County	200 Court Pk	Logansport IN	46947	219-753-7700	219-753-3512
Clark County	501 E. Court Ave	Jeffersonville IN	47130	812-285-6200	812-285-6363
Clay County	P. O. Box 33	Brazil IN	47834	812-448-9024	No Fax
Clinton County	265 Courthouse Sq	Frankfort IN	46041	317-659-6335	No Fax
Crawford County	P.O. Box 375	English IN	47118	812-338-2565	812-338-2507
Daviess County	P.O. Box 739	Washington IN	47501	812-254-8664	No Fax
Dearborn County	215-B W. High St	Lawrenceburg IN	47025	812-537-1040	812-537-5534
Decatur County	150 Courthouse Sq, Suite 5	Greensburg IN	47240	812-663-2546	812-663-2242
DeKalb County	100 S. Main St	Auburn IN	46706	219-925-2362	219-925-0060
Delaware County	P.O. Box 1089	Muncie IN	47308	317-747-7726	317-747-7768
Dubois County	1 Courthouse Sq	Jasper IN	47546	812-481-7035	812-481-7044
Elkhart County	101 N. Main, Rm 204	Goshen IN	46526	219-535-6433	219-535-6471
Elkhart County	315 S. 2nd	Elkhart IN	46516	219-523-2233	219-523-2323

INDIANA *continued*

County	Address	City, State	Zip Code	Phone	Fax
Fayette County	P.O. Box 607	Connersville IN	47331	317-825-1813	No Fax
Floyd County	311 W. 1st St.	New Albany IN	47150	812-948-5411	812-948-4711
Fountain County	P.O. Box 183	Covington IN	47932	317-793-2192	317-793-5002
Franklin County	459 Main St.	Brookville IN	47012	317-647-5111	317-647-3224
Fulton County	P.O. Box 524	Rochester IN	46975	219-223-2911	219-223-8304
Gibson County	101 N. Main	Princeton IN	47670	812-385-4927	812-386-1173
Grant County	County Courthouse	Marion IN	46952	317-668-8121	317-668-6541
Greene County	P.O. Box 229	Bloomfield IN	47424	812-384-8532	812-384-8458
Hamilton County	1 Hamilton County Sq	Noblesville IN	46060	317-776-9629	317-776-9727
Hancock County	9 E. Main St,Rm 208	Greenfield IN	46140	317-462-1106	317-462-1712
Harrison County	300 N. Capitol Ave	Corydon IN	47112	812-738-8241	812-738-3788
Hendricks County	P.O. Box 599	Danville IN	46122	317-745-9231	317-745-9306
Henry County	P.O. Box B	New Castle IN	47362	317-529-6401	317-529-3000
Howard County	117 N. Main	Kokomo IN	46901	317-456-2204	317-456-2267
Huntington County	201 N. Jefferson St	Huntington IN	46750	219-358-4822	219-358-4823
Jackson County	P.O. Box 122	Brownstown IN	47220	812-358-6116	No Fax
Jasper County	Courthouse Box 5	Rensselaer IN	47978	219-866-4930	219-866-4940
Jay County	120 N. Court St.	Portland IN	47371	219-726-4951	No Fax
Jefferson County	300 E. Main St	Madison IN	47250	812-265-8921	812-265-8950
Jennings County	County Courthouse	Vernon IN	47282	812-346-5977	812-346-4605
Johnson County	5 E. Jefferson St	Franklin IN	46131	317-736-5000	317-736-3749
Knox County	P.O. Box 906	Vincennes IN	47591	812-885-2521	812-886-2401
Kosciusko County	100 W. Center St	Warsaw IN	46580	219-267-4444	No Fax
La Porte County	813 Lincolnway	La Porte IN	46350	219-326-6808	219-326-5615
LaGrange County	114 W. Michigan St	LaGrange IN	46761	219-463-2183	219-463-7853
Lake County	2293 N. Main St	Crown Point IN	46307	219-755-3440	219-755-3520
Lawrence County	County Courthouse	Bedford IN	47421	812-275-7543	812-277-2024
Madison County	16 E. 9th St.	Anderson IN	46016	317-641-9419	317-641-9486
Marion County	200 E. Washington St	Indianapolis IN	46204	317-236-3200	317-327-3873
Marshall County	112 W. Jefferson St	Plymouth IN	46563	219-935-8510	219-936-4863
Martin County	P.O. Box 120	Shoals IN	47581	812-247-3651	812-247-3901
Miami County	County Courthouse	Peru IN	46970	317-472-3901	317-472-1412
Monroe County	301 N. College	Bloomington IN	47401	812-349-2612	812-333-3610
Montgomery County	100 E. Main St	Crawfordsville IN	47933	317-364-6434	317-364-6430
Morgan County	10 W. Washington	Martinsville IN	46151	317-342-1025	317-342-1111
Newton County	201 N. 3rd St.	Kentland IN	47951	219-474-6081	219-474-6086
Noble County	101 N. Orange St	Albion IN	46701	219-636-2736	No Fax
Ohio County	413 Main St.	Rising Sun IN	47040	812-438-2062	812-438-4590
Orange County	Court St.	Paoli IN	47454	812-723-2649	812-723-4603
Owen County	County Courthouse	Spencer IN	47460	812-829-5015	812-829-5034

County	Address	City, State	Zip Code	Phone	Fax
INDIANA *continued*					
Parks County	116 W. High St. #204	Rockville IN	47872	317-569-5132	317-569-4037
Perry County	2219 Payne St.	Tell City IN	47586	812-547-3741	812-547-9782
Pike County	801 Main St.	Petersburg IN	47567	812-354-6025	812-354-3552
Porter County	16 E. Lincolnway	Valparaiso IN	46383	219-465-3400	219-465-3592
Posey County	300 Main St.	Mount Vernon IN	47620	812-838-1300	812-838-1344
Pulaski County	112 E. Main St	Winamac IN	46996	219-946-3313	219-946-4953
Putnam County	1 W. Washington	Greencastle IN	46135	317-653-4603	317-653-5992
Randolph County	County Courthouse	Winchester IN	47394	317-584-7070	317-584-2958
Ripley County	P.O. Box 177	Versailles IN	47042	812-689-6115	812-689-6000
Rush County	P.O. Box 429	Rushville IN	46173	317-932-2086	317-938-1163
Saint Joseph County	101 S. Main	South Bend IN	46601	219-235-9635	219-235-9838
Scott County	1 E. McClain Ave	Scottsburg IN	47170	812-752-4769	812-752-5459
Shelby County	407 S. Harrison St	Shelbyville IN	46176	317-392-6330	317-392-6393
Spencer County	P.O. Box 12	Rockport IN	47635	812-649-6027	812-649-6030
Starke County	53 Washington St	Knox IN	46534	219-772-9128	219-772-9160
Steuben County	55 S. Public Sq	Angola IN	46703	219-665-2361	No Fax
Sullivan County	100 Courthouse Sq., Rm 304	Sullivan IN	47882	812-268-4657	No Fax
Switzerland County	212 W. Main St.	Vevay IN	47043	812-427-3175	812-427-2017
Tippecanoe County	20 N. 3rd St.	Lafayette IN	47901	317-423-9215	317-423-9196
Tipton County	County Courthouse	Tipton IN	46072	317-675-2795	317-675-7797
Union County	26 W. Union St	Liberty IN	47353	317-458-6121	317-458-5263
Vanderburg County	P.O. Box 3356	Evansville IN	47732	812-435-5160	812-435-5849
Vermillion County	P.O. Box 8	Newport IN	47966	317-492-3500	No Fax
Vigo County	P.O. Box 8449	Terre Haute IN	47807	812-462-3211	812-235-7558
Wabash County	1 W. Hill St	Wabash IN	46992	219-563-0661	219-563-3451
Warren County	125 N. Monroe #11	Williamsport IN	47993	317-762-3510	317-762-7222
Warrick County	109 W. Main St.	Boonville IN	47601	812-897-6120	812-897-6189
Washington County	99 Public Sq	Salem IN	47167	812-883-5748	812-883-1933
Wayne County	401 E. Main St	Richmond IN	47374	317-973-9200	317-973-9250
Wells County	102 W. Market St	Bluffton IN	46714	219-824-6470	219-824-6511
White County	P.O. Box 350	Monticello IN	47960	219-583-7032	No Fax
Whitley County	101 W. Van Buren St	Columbia City IN	46725	219-248-3100	219-248-3137
IOWA					
Adair County	400 Public Sq	Greenfield IA	50849	515-743-6111	515-743-2565
Adams County	P.O. Box 484	Corning IA	50841	515-322-4711	515-322-4523
Allamakee County	P.O. Box 248	Waukon IA	52172	319-568-6351	319-568-6353
Appanoose County	P.O. Box 400	Centerville IA	52544	515-856-6101	515-856-2282
Audubon County	318 Leroy #6	Audubon IA	50025	712-563-4275	712-563-4276
Benton County	P.O. Box 719	Vinton IA	52349	319-472-2766	No Fax

IOWA *continued*

County	Address	City, State	Zip Code	Phone	Fax
Black Hawk County	316 E. 5th St	Waterloo IA	50703	319-291-4826	319-291-2516
Boone County	201 State St	Boone IA	50036	515-433-0561	515-433-0563
Bremer County	415 E. Bremer Ave	Waverly IA	50677	319-352-5661	319-352-1054
Buchanan County	P.O. Box 259	Independence IA	50644	319-334-2196	319-334-7455
Buena Vista County	P.O Box 220	Storm Lake IA	50588	712-749-2545	712-732-2603
Butler County	P.O. Box 307	Allison IA	50602	319-267-2487	No Fax
Calhoun County	416 4th St	Rockwell City IA	50579	712-297-8122	712-297-5607
Carroll County	114 E. 6th	Carroll IA	51401	712-792-4327	712-792-4328
Cass Coumty	5 W. 7th St	Atlantic IA	50022	712-243-2105	712-243-4661
Cedar County	P.O. Box 111	Tipton IA	52772	319-886-2101	319-886-3594
Cerro Gordo County	220 N. Washington	Mason City IA	50401	515-424-6431	515-424-3726
Cherokee County	6th & W. Main, Courthouse	Cherokee IA	51012	712-225-6744	712-225-6749
Chickasaw County	P.O. Box 467	New Hampton IA	50659	515-394-2106	515-394-5106
Clarke County	100 S. Main St	Osceola IA	50213	515-342-6096	515-342-2463
Clay County	215 W. 4th St	Spencer IA	51301	712-262-4335	No Fax
Clayton County	111 High St. N.E	Elkader IA	52043	319-245-2204	319-245-1794
Clinton County	P.O. Box 2957	Clinton IA	52733	319-243-6210	No Fax
Crawford County	1202 Broadway	Denison IA	51442	712-263-2242	712-263-5753
Dallas County	801 Court St	Adel IA	50003	515-993-5816	515-993-4752
Davis County	111 W. Franklin	Bloomfield IA	52537	515-664-2260	No Fax
Decatur County	207 N. Main St	Leon IA	50144	515-446-4331	515-446-3759
Delaware County	301 E. Main St	Manchester IA	52057	319-927-4942	319-927-3074
Des Moines County	513 N. Main	Burlington IA	52601	319-753-8203	319-753-8721
Dickinson County	1802 Hill Ave	Spirit Lake IA	51360	712-336-2677	712-336-2677
Debuque County	720 Central Ave	Dubuque IA	52001	319-589-4441	319-589-4478
Emmet County	609 1st Ave. N.	Estherville IA	51334	712-362-3325	712-362-5329
Fayette County	P.O. Box 458	West Union IA	52175	319-422-5694	319-422-3137
Floyd County	101 S. Main St	Charles City IA	50616	515-257-6129	515-257-6150
Franklin County	P.O. Box 28	Hampton IA	50441	515-456-5626	515-456-5628
Fremont County	506 Filmore	Sidney IA	51652	712-374-2415	712-374-2826
Greene County	114 N. Chestnut	Jefferson IA	50129	515-386-2552	515-386-2216
Grundy County	706 G Ave	Grundy Center IA	50638	319-824-5813	319-824-6098
Guthrie County	200 N. 5th St.	Guthrie Center IA	50115	515-747-3512	515-747-3346
Hamilton County	2300 Superior St.	Webster City IA	50595	515-832-9530	515-832-9530
Hancock County	855 State St	Garner IA	50438	515-923-3421	515-923-3912
Hardin County	P.O. Box 495	Eldora IA	50627	515-858-2328	515-858-2320
Harrison County	111 N. 2nd Ave	Logan IA	51546	712-644-3123	712-644-2643
Henry County	100 E. Washington	Mount Pleasant IA	52641	319-385-0761	319-385-0778
Howard County	137 N. Elm St	Cresco IA	52136	319-547-3404	319-547-2629
Humboldt County	203 Main	Dakota City IA	50529	515-332-1571	515-332-1738

County	Address	City, State		Zip Code	Phone	Fax
IOWA *continued*						
Ida County	401 Moorehead St	Ida Grove	IA	51445	712-364-2632	712-364-2746
Iowa County	P.O. Box 126	Marengo	IA	52301	319-642-3041	319-642-7637
Jackson County	201 W. Platt St	Maquoketa	IA	52060	319-652-3181	319-652-6975
Jasper County	101 1st St. N	Newton	IA	50208	515-792-7016	515-792-1053
Jefferson County	51 W. Briggs Ave	Fairfield	IA	52556	515-472-2851	515-472-6695
Johnson County	417 S. Clinton St	Iowa City	IA	52240	319-356-6060	319-356-6086
Jones County	P.O. Box 109	Anamosa	IA	52205	319-462-2378	No Fax
Keokuk County	101 S. Main	Sigourney	IA	52591	515-622-2902	515-622-2286
Kossuth County	114 W. State St	Algona	IA	50511	515-295-2718	515-295-9304
Lee County	P.O. Box 190	Fort Madison	IA	52627	319-372-6557	319-372-7033
Linn County	930 1st St. S.W	Cedar Rapids	IA	52404	319-398-3421	319-398-3905
Louisa County	117 S. Main St	Wapello	IA	52653	319-523-3372	319-523-3713
Lucas County	916 Braden Ave	Chariton	IA	50049	515-774-2018	515-774-2993
Lyon County	206 S. 2nd Ave	Rock Rapids	IA	51246	712-472-2623	712-472-2422
Madison County	P.O. Box 152	Winterset	IA	50273	515-462-3225	515-462-2506
Mahaska County	106 South 1st	Oskaloosa	IA	52577	515-673-3469	515-673-8979
Marion County	214 E. Main	Knoxville	IA	50138	515-828-2231	515-828-8453
Marshall County	1 E. Main St	Marshalltown	IA	50158	515-754-6330	515-754-6231
Mills County	418 Sharp St	Glenwood	IA	51534	712-527-4729	712-527-5124
Mitchell County	508 State St	Osage	IA	50461	515-732-5861	515-732-5218
Monona County	610 Iowa Ave	Onawa	IA	51040	712-423-1585	712-423-3034
Monroe County	Benton Ave. E	Albia	IA	52531	515-932-7706	515-932-2863
Montgomery County	105 Coolbaugh	Red Oak	IA	51566	712-623-5127	712-623-2346
Muscatine County	401 E. 3rd St	Muscatine	IA	52761	319-263-5821	319-263-7248
OBrien County	P.O. Box M	Primghar	IA	51245	712-757-3225	712-757-3045
Osceola County	300 7th St	Sibley	IA	51249	712-754-2241	712-754-3743
Page County	112 E. Main	Clarinda	IA	51632	712-542-5018	712-542-5019
Palo Alto County	1010 Broadway	Emmetsburg	IA	50536	712-852-3603	712-852-2274
Plymouth County	215 4th Ave. S.E	Le Mars	IA	51031	712-546-9571	712-546-5784
Pocahontas County	99 Court Sq	Pocahontas	IA	50574	712-335-3361	712-335-4502
Polk County	111 Court Ave	Des Moines	IA	50309	515-286-3119	515-323-5225
Pottawattamie County	227 S. 6th St	Council Bluffs	IA	51501	712-328-5644	712-328-4740
Poweshiek County	P.O. Box 57	Montezuma	IA	50171	515-623-5723	515-623-2363
Ringgold County	109 W. Madison	Mount Ayr	IA	50854	515-464-3244	515-464-2568
Sac County	100 N. West State St	Sac City	IA	50583	712-662-7401	712-662-7129
Scott County	416 W. 4th St	Davenport	IA	52801	319-326-8702	319-328-3285
Shelby County	612 Court St	Harlan	IA	51537	712-755-3733	712-755-2519
Sioux County	P.O. Box 18	Orange City	IA	51041	712-737-2131	712-737-2537
Story County	900 6th St	Nevada	IA	50201	515-382-6581	515-382-3962
Tama County	100 W. High St	Toledo	IA	52342	515-484-3980	515-484-5127

County	Address	City, State		Zip Code	Phone	Fax

IOWA *continued*

County	Address	City, State		Zip Code	Phone	Fax
Taylor County	405 Jefferson	Bedford	IA	50833	712-523-2060	712-523-3262
Union County	300 N. Pine St	Creston	IA	50801	515-782-7315	712-782-8241
Van Buren County	P.O. Box 475	Keosauqua	IA	52565	319-293-3129	319-293-3828
Wapello County	101 W. 4th St	Ottumwa	IA	52501	515-683-0060	515-683-0064
Warren County	115 N. Howard	Indianola	IA	50125	515-961-1028	515-961-1013
Washington County	P.O. Box 889	Washington	IA	52353	319-653-7711	319-653-7788
Wayne County	P.O. Box 435	Corydon	IA	50060	515-872-2221	515-872-2843
Webster County	703 Central Ave	Fort Dodge	IA	50501	515-573-7175	515-574-3714
Winnebago County	126 S. Clark St	Forest City	IA	50436	515-582-3412	515-582-2891
Winneshiek County	201 W. Main St	Decorah	IA	52101	319-382-2469	319-382-0603
Woodbury County	620 Douglas	Sioux City	IA	51101	712-279-6525	712-279-6577
Worth County	1000 Central Ave	Northwood	IA	50459	515-324-1337	515-324-2316
Wright County	115 N. Main	Clarion	IA	50525	515-532-3262	515-532-2669

KANSAS

County	Address	City, State		Zip Code	Phone	Fax
Allen County	1 N. Washington St	Iola	KS	66749	316-365-1407	316-365-1414
Anderson County	100 E. 4th Ave	Garnett	KS	66032	913-448-6841	913-448-5621
Atchison County	423 N. 5th	Atchison	KS	66002	913-367-1653	913-367-0227
Barber County	120 E. Washington	Medicine Lodge	KS	67104	316-886-3961	316-886-5425
Barton County	1400 Main	Great Bend	KS	67530	316-793-1835	316-793-1807
Bourbon County	210 S. National Ave	Fort Scott	KS	66701	316-223-3800	316-223-5241
Brown County	601 Oregon	Hiawatha	KS	66434	913-742-2581	913-742-3255
Butler County	205 W. Central Ave	El Dorado	KS	67042	316-321-1960	316-321-1011
Chase County	P.O. Box 547	Cottonwood Falls	KS	66845	316-273-6423	316-273-6617
Chautauqua County	215 N. Chautauqua	Sedan	KS	67361	316-725-5800	316-725-3256
Cherokee County	P.O. Box 14	Columbus	KS	66725	316-429-2042	316-429-1042
Cheyenne County	P.O. Box 985	Saint Francis	KS	67756	913-332-8800	913-332-8825
Clark County	P.O. Box 886	Ashland	KS	67831	316-635-2813	316-635-2393
Clay County	P.O. Box 98	Clay Center	KS	67432	913-632-2552	913-632-5856
Cloud County	811 Washington	Concordia	KS	66901	913-243-8110	913-243-8123
Coffey County	110 S. 6th St	Burlington	KS	66839	316-364-2191	316-364-8975
Comanche County	P.O. Box 776	Coldwater	KS	67029	316-582-2361	316-582-2426
Cowley County	311 E. 9th Ave	Winfield	KS	67156	316-221-4066	316-221-5498
Crawford County	P.O. Box 249	Girard	KS	66743	316-724-6115	316-724-6007
Decatur County	P.O. Box 28	Oberlin	KS	67749	913-475-8102	913-475-8150
Dickinson County	109 E. 1st	Abilene	KS	67410	913-263-3774	913-263-1512
Doniphan County	P.O. Box 278	Troy	KS	66087	913-985-3513	913-985-3723
Douglas County	1100 Massachusetts St	Lawrence	KS	66044	913-832-5281	913-832-5912
Edwards County	312 Massachusetts Ave	Kinsley	KS	67547	316-659-3000	316-659-2583
Elk County	P.O. Box 606	Howard	KS	67349	316-374-2490	316-374-2771

County	Address	City, State	Zip Code	Phone	Fax
KANSAS *continued*					
Ellis County	P.O. Box 720	Hays KS	67601	913-628-9410	913-628-9413
Ellsworth County	210 N. Kansas	Ellsworth KS	67439	913-472-4161	913-472-3818
Finney County	P.O. Box M	Garden City KS	67846	316-272-3524	316-272-3599
Ford County	100 Gunsmoke	Dodge City KS	67801	316-227-4550	316-227-4699
Franklin County	315 S. Main	Ottawa KS	66067	913-229-3410	913-229-3419
Geary County	139 E. 8th St	Junction City KS	66441	913-238-3912	913-238-5419
Gove County	520 Washington	Gove KS	67736	913-938-2300	913-938-4486
Graham County	410 N. Pomeroy St	Hill City KS	67642	913-674-3453	913-674-5463
Grant County	108 S. Glenn St	Ulysses KS	67880	316-356-1335	316-356-3081
Gray County	P.O. Box 487	Cimarron KS	67835	316-855-3618	316-855-3107
Greely County	P.O. Box 277	Tribune KS	67879	316-376-4256	316-376-2294
Greenwood County	311 N. 9th	Eureka KS	67045	316-583-8121	316-583-8124
Hamilton County	P.O. Box 1167	Syracuse KS	67878	316-384-5629	316-384-5853
Harper County	201 N. Jennings	Anthony KS	67003	316-842-5555	316-842-3455
Harvey County	P.O. Box 687	Newton KS	67114	316-284-6840	316-284-6856
Haskell County	P.O. Box 518	Sublette KS	67877	316-675-2263	316-675-8142
Hodgeman County	P.O. Box 247	Jetmore KS	67854	316-357-6421	316-357-6161
Jackson County	400 New York	Holton KS	66436	913-364-2891	913-364-4204
Jefferson County	P.O. Box 321	Oskaloosa KS	66066	913-863-2272	913-863-3135
Jewell County	307 N. Commercial	Mankata KS	66956	913-378-4020	913-378-4075
Johnson County	111 S. Cherry St	Olathe KS	66061	913-764-4020	913-791-5111
Kearny County	P.O. Box 86	Lakin KS	67860	316-355-6422	316-355-7382
Kingman County	130 N. Spruce	Kingman KS	67068	316-532-2521	316-532-2037
Kiowa County	211 E. Florida Ave	Greensburg KS	67054	316-723-3366	316-723-3302
Labette County	501 Merchant	Oswego KS	67356	316-795-2138	316-795-2928
Lane County	144 S. Lane	Dighton KS	67839	316-397-5356	316-397-5937
Leavenworth County	300 Walnut	Leavenworth KS	66048	913-684-0422	913-684-0406
Lincoln County	216 E. Lincoln Ave	Lincoln KS	67455	913-524-4757	913-524-4108
Linn County	P.O Box 350	Mound City KS	66056	913-795-2668	913-795-2889
Logan County	710 W. 2nd St	Oakley KS	67748	913-672-4244	913-672-3517
Lyon County	402 Commercial St	Emporia KS	66801	316-342-4950	316-342-2652
Marion County	P.O. Box 219	Marion KS	66861	316-382-2185	316-382-3420
Marshall County	1201 Broadway	Marysville KS	66508	913-562-5361	913-562-5685
McPherson County	P.O. Box 425	McPherson KS	67460	316-241-3656	316-241-1372
Meade County	P.O. Box 278	Meade KS	67864	316-873-8700	316-873-8713
Miami County	120 S. Pearl St	Paola KS	66071	913-294-3976	913-294-9515
Mitchell County	P.O. Box 190	Beloit KS	67420	913-738-3652	913-738-5844
Montgomery County	P.O. Box 138	Independence KS	67301	316-330-1200	316-330-1202
Morris County	501 W. Main St	Council Grove KS	66846	316-767-5518	316-767-5703
Morton County	P.O. Box 1116	Elkhart KS	67950	316-697-2157	316-697-2159

County	Address	City, State		Zip Code	Phone	Fax
KANSAS *continued*						
Nemaha County	607 Nemaha St	Seneca	KS	66538	913-336-2170	913-336-3373
Neosho County	P.O. Box 138	Erie	KS	66733	316-244-3811	316-244-3860
Ness County	202 W. Sycamore St	Ness City	KS	67560	913-798-2401	913-798-3829
Norton County	105 S. Kansas	Norton	KS	67654	913-877-5710	913-877-5703
Osage County	717 Topeka Ave	Lyndon	KS	66451	913-828-4812	913-828-4749
Osborn County	423 W. Main St	Osborne	KS	67473	913-346-2431	913-346-5992
Ottawa County	307 N. Concord St	Minneapolis	KS	67467	913-392-2279	913-392-3605
Pawnee County	715 Broadway	Larned	KS	67550	316-285-3721	316-285-3802
Phillips County	301 State	Phillipsburg	KS	67661	913-543-6825	913-543-6897
Pottawatomie County	P.O. Box 187	Westmoreland	KS	66549	913-457-3314	913-457-3507
Pratt County	P.O. Box 885	Pratt	KS	67124	316-672-4110	316-672-9541
Rawlins County	607 Main St.	Atwood	KS	67730	913-626-3351	913-626-9019
Reno County	206 W. 1st Ave	Hutchinson	KS	67501	316-694-2934	316-694-2944
Republic County	P.O. Box 429	Belleville	KS	66935	913-527-5691	913-527-2717
Rice County	101 W. Commercial St	Lyons	KS	67554	316-257-2232	316-257-3039
Riley County	110 Courthouse Plaza	Manhattan	KS	66502	913-537-6301	913-537-6394
Rooks County	115 N. Walnut St	Stockton	KS	67669	913-425-6391	913-425-7124
Rush County	P.O. Box 220	La Crosse	KS	67548	913-222-2731	913-222-3559
Russell County	P.O. Box 113	Russell	KS	67665	913-483-4641	913-483-5725
Saline County	300 W. Ash St	Salina	KS	67401	913-826-6550	913-826-6629
Scott County	303 Court St	Scott City	KS	67871	316-872-2420	316-872-7145
Sedgwick County	525 N. Main St	Wichita	KS	67203	316-383-7666	316-383-7961
Seward County	415 N. Washington Ave	Liberal	KS	67901	316-626-3201	316-626-3211
Shawnee County	200 E. 7th St	Topeka	KS	66603	913-233-8200	913-291-4912
Sheridan County	P.O. Box 899	Hoxie	KS	67740	913-675-3361	913-675-3050
Sherman County	813 Broadway	Goodland	KS	67735	913-899-4800	913-899-4844
Smith County	218 S. Grant St	Smith Center	KS	66967	913-282-5110	913-282-5175
Stafford County	209 N. Broadway St	Saint John	KS	67576	316-549-3509	316-549-3481
Stanton County	P.O. Box 190	Johnson	KS	67855	316-492-2140	316-492-2688
Stevens County	200 E. 6th St	Hugoton	KS	67951	316-544-2541	316-544-4081
Sumner County	501 N. Washington	Wellington	KS	67152	316-326-3395	316-326-8172
Thomas County	300 N. Court Ave	Colby	KS	67701	913-462-4500	913-462-4512
Trego County	216 Main St.	WaKeeney	KS	67672	913-743-5773	913-743-2461
Wabaunsee County	215 Kansas	Alma	KS	66401	913-765-3414	913-765-3704
Wallace County	P.O. Box 70	Sharon Springs	KS	67758	913-852-4282	913-852-4783
Washington County	214 C St.	Washington	KS	66968	913-325-2974	913-325-2830
Witchita County	P.O. Drawer 968	Leoti	KS	67861	316-375-2731	316-375-4350
Wilson County	615 Madison St.	Fredonia	KS	66736	316-378-2186	316-378-3841
Woodson County	105 W. Rutledge St.	Yates Center	KS	66783	316-625-2179	316-625-8670
Wyandotte County	710 N. 7th St.	Kansas City	KS	66101	913-573-2874	913-321-0237

County	Address	City, State	Zip Code	Phone	Fax

KENTUCKY

County	Address	City, State	Zip Code	Phone	Fax
Adair County	424 Public Sq, Ste 5	Columbia KY	42728	502-384-2801	502-384-4805
Allen County	P.O. Box 336	Scottsville KY	42164	502-237-3706	502-237-9155
Anderson County	151 S. Main St	Lawrenceburg KY	40342	502-839-3041	502-839-3043
Ballard County	P.O. Box 145	Wickliffe KY	42087	502-335-5168	502-335-3010
Barren County	103 Courthouse Sq.	Glasgow KY	42141	502-651-5200	502-651-1083
Bath County	P.O. Box 609	Owingsville KY	40360	606-674-2613	No Fax
Bell County	P.O. Box 156	Pineville KY	40977	606-337-6143	606-337-5415
Boone County	P.O. Box 874	Burlington KY	41005	606-334-2112	606-334-2193
Bourbon County	P.O. Box 312	Paris KY	40361	606-987-2142	606-987-5660
Boyd County	P.O. Box 523	Catlettsburg KY	41129	606-739-5116	606-739-6357
Boyle County	321 W. Main St Rm. 123	Danville KY	40422	606-238-1110	606-238-1114
Bracken County	P.O. Box 147	Brooksville KY	41004	606-735-2952	606-735-2925
Breathitt County	1137 Main St.	Jackson KY	41339	606-666-3810	606-666-3807
Breckinridge County	P.O. Box 538	Hardinsburg KY	40143	502-756-2246	502-756-1569
Bullitt County	P.O. Box 6	Shephersville KY	40165	502-543-2513	502-543-9121
Butler County	P.O. Box 448	Morgantown KY	42261	502-526-5676	502-526-2658
Caldwell County	100 E. Market St. #3	Princeton KY	42445	502-365-6754	502-365-7447
Calloway County	101 S. 5th St	Murray KY	42071	502-753-3923	502-759-9611
Campbell County	340 York St	Newport KY	41071	606-292-3845	606-292-0615
Carlisle County	P.O. Box 176	Bardwell KY	42023	502-628-3233	502-628-0191
Carroll County	Courthouse, 440 Main St	Carrollton KY	41008	502-732-7005	502-732-7007
Carter County	Courthouse Room 232	Grayson KY	41143	606-474-5188	606-474-5180
Casey County	P.O. Box 310	Liberty KY	42539	606-787-6471	606-787-6471
Christian County	511 S. Main St	Hopkinsville KY	42240	502-887-4105	No Fax
Clark County	P.O. Box 744	Winchester KY	40391	606-745-0280	606-745-4251
Clay County	316 Main St. Suite 143	Manchester KY	40962	606-598-2544	606-598-7119
Clinton County	County Courthouse	Albany KY	42602	606-387-5943	606-387-5258
Crittenden County	107 S. Main St	Marion KY	42064	502-965-3403	502-965-3447
Cumberland County	P.O. Box 275	Burkesville KY	42717	502-864-3726	502-864-5884
Daviess County	P.O. Box 609	Owensboro KY	42302	502-685-8434	502-686-7111
Edmonson County	P.O. Box 414	Brownsville KY	42210	502-597-2624	No Fax
Elliott County	P.O. Box 225	Sandy Hook KY	41171	606-738-5421	606-738-4462
Estill County	P.O. Box 59	Irvine KY	40336	606-723-5156	606-723-5108
Fayette County	162 E. Main St	Lexington KY	40507	606-253-3344	606-231-9619
Fleming County	100 Court Sq	Flemingsburg KY	41041	606-845-8461	606-845-0212
Floyd County	P.O. Box 1089	Prestonsburg KY	41653	606-886-3816	606-886-8089
Franklin County	P.O. Box 338	Frankfort KY	40602	502-875-8708	502-875-8718
Fulton County	P.O. Box 126	Hickman KY	42050	502-236-2727	502-236-3933
Gallatin County	P.O. Box 616	Warsaw KY	41095	606-567-5411	606-567-4764
Garrard County	Public Sq	Lancaster KY	40444	606-792-3071	606-792-2010

KENTUCKY *continued*

County	Address	City, State	Zip Code	Phone	Fax
Grant County	P.O. Box 469	Williamstown KY	41097	606-824-3321	No Fax
Graves County	County Courthouse	Mayfield KY	42066	502-247-1676	502-247-1274
Grayson County	10 Public Sq	Leitchfield KY	42754	502-259-3201	502-259-9264
Green County	203 W. Court St	Greensburg KY	42743	502-932-5386	502-932-3635
Greenup County	P.O. Box 686	Greenup KY	41144	606-473-7394	606-473-5354
Hancock County	P.O. Box 146	Hawesville KY	42348	502-927-6117	502-927-8639
Hardin County	P.O. Box 10	Elizabethtown KY	42702	502-765-2171	502-769-2682
Harlan County	P.O. Box 670	Harlan KY	40831	606-573-3636	606-573-0064
Harrison County	190 WPike St	Cynthiana KY	41031	606-234-7130	606-234-8049
Hart County	P.O. Box 277	Munfordville KY	42765	502-524-2751	502-524-0458
Henderson County	P.O. Box 374	Henderson KY	42420	502-826-3906	502-826-9677
Henry County	P.O. Box 615	New Castle KY	40050	502-845-5705	502-845-5708
Hickman County	Courthouse Sq	Clinton KY	42031	502-653-2131	502-653-4248
Hopkins County	P.O. Drawer 737	Madisonville KY	42431	502-821-7361	502-825-5009
Jackson County	P.O. Box 700	McKee KY	40447	606-287-7800	606-287-3277
Jefferson County	527 W. Jefferson St	Louisville KY	40202	502-574-5700	502-574-5566
Jessamine County	101 N. Main	Nicholasville KY	40356	606-885-9464	No Fax
Johnson County	Courthouse	Paintsville KY	41240	606-789-2557	606-789-2559
Kenton County	P.O. Box 1109	Covington KY	41012	606-491-0702	606-491-6316
Knott County	P.O. Box 446	Hindman KY	41822	606-785-5651	606-785-0996
Knox County	401 Court Sq. Suite 102	Barbourville KY	40906	606-546-3568	606-546-3589
Larue County	W. High St.	Hodgenville KY	42748	502-358-3544	502-358-4528
Laurel County	101 S. Main Courthouse #203	London KY	40741	606-864-5158	606-864-7369
Lawrence County	122 S. Main Cross.	Louisa KY	41230	606-638-4108	606-638-0638
Lee County	Courthouse Rm. 11.	Beattyville KY	41311	606-464-4115	606-464-4102
Leslie County	P.O. Box 916	Hyden KY	41749	606-672-2193	606-672-4264
Letcher County	P.O. Box 58	Whitesburg KY	41858	606-633-2432	606-633-7105
Lewis County	P.O. Box 129	Vanceburg KY	41179	606-796-3062	606-796-6511
Lincoln County	102 E. Main St	Stanford KY	40484	606-365-4570	606-365-4572
Livingston County	P.O. Box 400	Smithland KY	42081	502-928-2162	502-928-4612
Logan County	P.O. Box 358	Russellville KY	42276	502-726-6061	502-726-4355
Lyon County	P.O. Box 350	Eddyville KY	42038	502-388-2331	502-388-0715
Madison County	101 W. Main St.	Richmond KY	40475	606-624-4703	606-623-3071
Magoffin County	P.O. Box 530	Salyersville KY	41465	606-349-2216	606-349-2328
Marion County	120 W. Main St.	Lebanon KY	40033	502-692-2651	502-692-9811
Marshall County	1101 Main St.	Benton KY	42025	502-527-4740	502-527-4738
Martin County	P.O. Box 485	Inez KY	41224	606-298-2810	606-298-0143
Mason County	P.O. Box 234	Maysville KY	41056	606-564-3341	606-564-8979
McCracken County	P.O. Box 609	Paducah KY	42002	502-444-4700	502-444-4704
McCreary County	P.O. Box 699	Whitley City KY	42653	606-376-2411	606-376-3898

County	Address	City, State		Zip Code	Phone	Fax
KENTUCKY *continued*						
McLean County	P.O. Box 57	Calhoun	KY	42327	502-273-3082	502-273-5084
Meade County	P.O. Box 614	Brandenburg	KY	40108	502-422-2152	502-422-2158
Menifee County	P.O. Box 123	Frenchburg	KY	40322	606-768-3512	606-734-6309
Mercer County	P.O. Box 426	Harrodsburg	KY	40330	606-734-6310	606-734-6309
Metcalfe County	P.O. Box 850	Edmonton	KY	42129	502-432-4821	502-432-5176
Monroe County	P.O. Box 188	Tompkinsville	KY	42167	502-487-5471	502-487-5976
Montgomery County	P.O. Box 414	Mount Sterling	KY	40353	606-498-8700	606-498-8729
Morgan County	P.O. Box 26	West Liberty	KY	41472	606-743-3949	606-743-2111
Muhlenberg County	P.O. Box 525	Greenville	KY	42345	502-338-1441	502-338-1774
Nelson County	P.O. Box 312	Bardstown	KY	40004	502-348-1820	502-348-1822
Nicholas County	P.O. Box 227	Carlisle	KY	40311	606-289-3730	606-289-3705
Ohio County	P.O. Box 85	Hartford	KY	42347	502-298-4422	502-298-4425
Oldham County	100 W. Jefferson	La Grange	KY	40031	502-222-9311	502-222-3208
Owen County	P.O. Box 338	Owenton	KY	40359	502-484-2213	502-484-1002
Owsley County	P.O. Box 500	Booneville	KY	41314	606-593-5735	606-593-5737
Pendleton County	P.O. Box 112	Falmouth	KY	41040	606-654-3380	No Fax
Perry County	P.O. Box 150	Hazard	KY	41702	606-436-4614	606-439-0557
Pike County	320 Main	Pikeville	KY	41501	606-432-6211	606-432-6222
Powell County	P.O. Box 548	Stanton	KY	40380	606-663-6444	606-663-6406
Pulaski County	P.O. Box 724	Somerset	KY	42501	606-679-2042	606-678-0073
Robertson County	P.O. Box 75	Mount Olivet	KY	41064	606-724-5212	No Fax
Rockcastle County	P.O. Box 365	Mount Vernon	KY	40456	606-256-2831	606-256-4302
Rowan County	627 E. Main St	Morehead	KY	40351	606-784-5212	606-784-2923
Russell County	P.O. Box 579	Jamestown	KY	42629	502-343-2125	502-343-4700
Scott County	101 E. Main St	Georgetown	KY	40324	502-863-7875	502-863-7898
Shelby County	P.O. Box 819	Shelbyville	KY	40066	502-633-4410	502-633-7887
Simpson County	P.O. Box 268	Franklin	KY	42134	502-586-8161	502-586-6464
Spencer County	P.O. Box 544	Taylorsville	KY	40071	502-477-3215	502-477-3216
Taylor County	203 N. Court #5	Campbellsville	KY	42718	502-465-6677	502-789-1144
Todd County	P.O. Box 307	Elkton	KY	42220	502-265-2363	502-265-2588
Trigg County	P.O. Box 1310	Cadiz	KY	42211	502-522-6661	502-522-6662
Trimble County	P.O. Box 262	Bedford	KY	40006	502-255-7174	502-255-7045
Union County	P.O. Box 119	Morganfield	KY	42437	502-389-1334	502-389-0406
Warren County	429 E. 10th St	Bowling Green	KY	42101	502-842-9416	502-843-5319
Washington County	P.O. Box 446	Springfield	KY	40069	606-336-5425	606-336-5408
Wayne County	P.O. Box 565	Monticello	KY	42633	606-348-5721	606-348-8303
Webster County	P.O. Box 19	Dixon	KY	42409	502-639-7006	502-639-7006
Whitley County	P.O. Box 8	Williamsburg	KY	40769	606-549-6002	606-549-2790
Wolfe County	P.O. Box 400	Campton	KY	41301	606-668-3515	606-668-3367
Woodford County	103 Main St.	Versailles	KY	40383	606-873-3421	No Fax

County	Address	City, State		Zip Code	Phone	Fax
LOUISIANA						
Acadia Parish	P.O. Box A	Crowley	LA	70527	318-788-8800	318-788-2421
Allen Parish	P.O. Drawer G	Oberlin	LA	70655	318-639-4328	318-639-4326
Ascension Parish	P.O. Box 351	Donaldsonville	LA	70346	504-473-4815	504-473-9931
Assumption Parish	P.O. Box 518	Napoleonville	LA	70390	504-369-7435	318-369-2972
Avoyelles Parish	301 N. Main St	Marksville	LA	71351	318-253-9208	318-253-4614
Beauregard Parish	P.O. Box 310	DeRidder	LA	70634	318-463-7019	318-462-2567
Bienville Parish	P.O. Box 479	Arcadia	LA	71001	318-263-2019	318-263-7404
Bossier Parish	P.O. Box 68	Benton	LA	71006	318-965-2329	318-965-3703
Caddo Parish	501 Texas St	Shreveport	LA	71101	318-226-6596	318-226-6909
Calcasieu Parish	P.O. Drawer 3287	Lake Charles	LA	70602	318-437-3500	318-437-3345
Caldwell Parish	P.O. Box 1737	Columbia	LA	71418	318-649-2681	318-649-5930
Cameron Parish	P.O. Box 366	Cameron	LA	70631	318-775-5718	318-775-5567
Catahoula Parish	P.O. Box 258	Harrisonburg	LA	71340	318-744-5435	318-744-5568
Claiborne Parish	P.O. Box 270	Homer	LA	71040	318-927-2222	318-927-2727
Concordia Parish	4001 Carter St. #1	Vidalia	LA	71373	318-336-7151	318-336-9915
Desoto Parish	P.O. Box 898	Mansfield	LA	71052	318-872-0738	318-872-5343
East Baton Rouge Parish	P.O. Box 1471	Baton Rouge	LA	70821	504-389-3123	504-389-3127
East Carroll Parish	400 1st St	Lake Providence	LA	71254	318-559-2256	318-559-1502
East Feliciana Parish	P.O. Box 427	Clinton	LA	70722	504-683-8577	504-683-3100
Evangeline Parish	Courthouse Bldg	Ville Platte	LA	70586	318-363-5651	318-363-5652
Franklin Parish	6558 Main St.	Winnsboro	LA	71295	318-435-9429	318-435-9420
Grant Parish	200 Main St.	Colfax	LA	71417	318-627-3157	318-487-5755
Iberia Parish	121 Decuir	New Iberia	LA	70560	318-365-8246	318-369-7424
Iberville Parish	P.O. Box 389	Plaquemine	LA	70764	504-687-5190	504-687-5250
Jackson Parish	500 E. Court St	Jonesboro	LA	71251	318-259-2361	No Fax
Jefferson Parish	1221 Elmwood Park, 10th Fl.	Harahan	LA	70123	504-736-6400	504-736-6638
Jefferson Davis Parish	P.O. Box 1409	Jennings	LA	70546	318-824-4792	318-824-8908
Lafayette Parish	P.O. Drawer 4508	Lafayette	LA	70502	318-233-6220	318-267-7007
Lafourche Parish	P.O. Drawer 5548	Thibodaux	LA	70302	504-446-8427	504-446-8459
LaSalle Parish	P.O. Box 57	Jena	LA	71342	318-992-2101	318-992-2103
Lincoln Parish	P.O. Box 979	Ruston	LA	71273	318-251-5150	318-251-5149
Livingston Parish	P.O. Box 427	Livingston	LA	70754	504-686-2266	504-686-7079
Madison Parish	P.O. Box 1710	Tallulah	LA	71282	318-574-0655	318-574-3961
Morehouse Parish	P.O. Drawer 543	Bastrop	LA	71221	318-281-3343	318-283-3775
Natchitoches Parish	P.O. Box 476	Natchitoches	LA	71457	318-352-8152	318-352-9321
Orleans Parish	1300 Perdido St	New Orleans	LA	70112	504-565-6300	504-565-6299
Ouachita Parish	P.O. Box 1862	Monroe	LA	71210	318-323-5188	318-327-1462
Plaquemines Parish	P.O. Box 129	Port Sulphur	LA	70083	504-682-0081	504-392-6690
Pointe Coupee Parish	P.O. Box 290	New Roads	LA	70760	504-638-9556	504-627-6750
Rapides Parish	P.O. Box 1150	Alexandria	LA	71309	318-473-6660	318-473-6670

County	Address	City, State	Zip Code	Phone	Fax
LOUISIANA *continued*					
Red River Parish	P.O. Drawer 709	Coushatta LA	71019	318-932-5719	318-932-5080
Richland Parish	P.O. Box 668	Rayville LA	71269	318-728-2061	318-728-7004
Sabine Parish	400 Courthouse St	Many LA	71449	318-256-5637	318-256-9652
Saint Bernard Parish	8201 Judge Perez Dr	Chaimette LA	70043	504-278-4200	504-278-4329
Saint Charles Parish	P.O. Box 302	Hahnville LA	70057	504-783-5000	504-783-2067
Saint Helena Parish	P.O. Box 339	Greensburg LA	70441	504-222-4549	504-222-6405
Saint James Parish	P.O. Box 106	Convent LA	70723	504-562-2260	504-562-2279
Saint John Parish	1801 W. Airline Hwy	LaPlace LA	70068	504-652-9569	504-652-4131
Saint Landry Parish	P.O. Box 750	Opelousas LA	70571	318-942-5606	318-948-7265
Saint Martin Parish	P.O. Box 9	Saint Martinville LA	70582	318-394-2200	318-394-2203
Saint Mary Parish	P.O. Drawer 1231	Franklin LA	70538	318-828-4100	318-828-2509
Saint Tammany Parish	P.O. Box 628	Covington LA	70434	504-898-2362	504-898-5237
Tanglpahoa Parish	P.O. Box 215	Amite LA	70422	504-748-3211	504-748-7576
Tensas Parish	P.O. Box 6168	St Joseph LA	71366	318-766-3542	318-766-4580
Terrebonne Parish	P.O. Box 1569	Houma LA	70361	504-873-6401	No Fax
Union Parish	P.O. Box 723	Farmerville LA	71241	318-368-3296	318-368-8342
Vermilion Parish	P.O. Box 430	Abbeville LA	70511	318-898-4300	318-898-4309
Vernon Parish	P.O. Box 1548	Leesville LA	71446	318-238-0324	318-238-0240
Washington Parish	Washington & Main	Franklinton LA	70438	504-839-3420	No Fax
Webster Parish	P.O. Box 389	Minden LA	71058	318-377-7564	318-371-2366
West Baton Rouge	Parish P.O. Box 757	Port Allen LA	70767	504-383-4755	504-387-0218
West Carroll Parish	P.O. Box 1014	Oak Grove LA	71263	318-428-3390	318-428-4556
West Feliciana Parish	P.O. Box 1921	Saint Francisville LA	70775	504-635-3864	504-635-6161
Winn Parish	P.O. Box 951	Winnfield LA	71483	318-628-5824	318-628-7336
MAINE					
Androscoggin County	2 Turner St	Auburn ME	04210	207-784-8390	207-782-5367
Aroostook County	240 Sweden St., Suite 1	Caribou ME	04736	207-493-3318	207-493-3491
Cumberland County	142 Federal St., Suite 102	Portland ME	04101	207-871-8380	207-871-8292
Franklin County	38 Main St.	Farmington ME	04938	207-778-6614	207-778-5899
Hancock County	60 State St	Ellsworth ME	04605	207-667-9542	207-667-1414
Kennebec County	125 State St	Augusta ME	04330	207-622-0971	207-623-4083
Knox County	P.O. Box 546	Rockland ME	04841	207-594-0304	207-594-9481
Lincoln County	P.O. Box 249	Wiscasset ME	04578	207-882-6311	207-882-4320
Oxford County	26 Western Ave.	South Paris ME	04281	207-743-6359	207-743-2656
Penobscot County	97 Hammond St	Bangor ME	04401	207-942-8535	207-945-6027
Piscataquis County	51 E. Main St	Dover-Foxcroft ME	04426	207-564-2161	207-564-7708
Sagadshoc County	P.O. Box 246	Bath ME	04530	207-443-8200	207-443-8212
Somerset County	Court St.	Skowhegan ME	04976	207-474-9861	No Fax
Waldo County	137 Church St.	Belfast ME	04915	207-338-3282	207-338-6360
Washington County	P.O. Box 297	Machias ME	04654	207-255-3127	207-255-8636

County	Address	City, State	Zip Code	Phone	Fax
MAINE *continued*					
York County	Court St.	Alfred ME	04002	207-324-1571	207-324-9494
MARYLAND					
Allegany County	701 Kelly Rd	Cumberland MD	21502	301-777-5911	301-777-5819
Anne Arundel County	P.O. Box 2700	Annapolis MD	21401	410-222-7000	No Fax
Baltimore City	111 N. Calvert.	Baltimore MD	21202	410-396-3100	410-752-5274
Baltimore County	400 Washington Ave	Towson MD	21204	410-887-3196	410-887-5791
Calvert County	175 Main St.	Prince Frederick MD	20678	410-535-1600	410-535-1787
Caroline County	109 Market St., Rm. 109	Denton MD	21629	410-479-0660	410-479-4060
Carroll County	55 N. Court St.	Westminster MD	21157	410-848-1124	410-876-5354
Cecil County	129 E. Main St	Elkton MD	21921	410-996-5200	410-996-5210
Charles County	P.O. Box B.	La Plata MD	20646	301-645-0550	301-645-0560
Dorchester County	P.O. Box 26	Cambridge MD	21613	410-228-1700	410-228-9641
Frederick County	12 E. Church St	Frederick MD	21701	301-694-1100	301-694-1849
Garrett County	203 S. 4th St	Oakland MD	21550	301-334-8970	301-334-5000
Harford County	20 W. Court Ln	Bel Air MD	21014	410-638-3426	410-879-6449
Howard County	3451 Court House Dr	Ellicott City MD	21043	410-461-0203	No Fax
Kent County	103 N. Cross St.	Chestertown MD	21620	410-778-4600	410-778-7482
Montgomery County	27 Courthouse Sq	Rockville MD	20850	301-340-0160	No Fax
Prince Georges County	7911 Anchor St	Landover MD	20785	301-350-9700	No Fax
Queen Annes County	107 N. Liberty St	Centreville MD	21617	410-758-4098	410-758-1170
Saint Marys County	Rt. 245 Washington St. N	Leonardtown MD	20650	301-475-5621	301-475-4489
Somerset County	P.O. Box 37	Princess Anne MD	21853	410-651-0320	410-651-0366
Talbot County	11 N. Washington St	Easton MD	21601	410-822-2401	410-822-8697
Washington County	P.O. Box 229	Hagerstown MD	21741	301-791-3085	301-791-1151
Wicomico County	P.O. Box 198	Salisbury MD	21803	410-543-6551	410-548-5150
Worcester County	1 W. Market St	Snow Hill MD	21863	410-632-1194	410-632-3131
MASSACHUSETTS					
Barnstable County	P.O. Box 427	Barnstable MA	02630	508-362-2511	No Fax
Berkshire County	76 E. St	Pittsfield MA	01201	413-448-8424	413-499-0213
Bristol County	9 Court St	Taunton MA	02780	508-823-6588	No Fax
Dukes County	P.O. Box 190	Edgartown MA	02539	508-627-5535	508-627-9554
Essex County	36 Federal St	Salem MA	01970	508-741-0200	508-741-5763
Franklin County	425 Main St.	Greenfield MA	01301	413-774-4015	413-774-3169
Hampden County	50 State St	Springfield MA	01103	413-748-7855	413-747-4822
Hampshire County	15 Gothic St	Northampton MA	01060	413-584-7400	413-586-1980
Middlesex County	40 Thorndike St	East Cambridge MA	02141	617-494-4010	No Fax
Nantucket County	Town & County Bldg	Nantucket MA	02554	508-228-0460	508-325-5759
Norfolk County	650 High St.	Dedham MA	02026	617-326-1600	617-326-3871

County	Address	City, State	Zip Code	Phone	Fax
MASSACHUSETTS *continued*					
Plymouth County	Court St.	Plymouth MA	02360	508-747-6911	508-830-0676
Suffolk County	55 Pemberton Sq	Boston MA	02108	617-725-8000	617-725-8137
Worcester County	2 Main St.	Worcester MA	01608	508-756-2441	508-798-7741
MICHIGAN					
Alcona County	P.O. Box 308	Harrisville MI	48740	517-724-6807	517-724-5684
Alger County	101 Court St	Munising MI	49862	906-387-2076	906-387-2156
Allegan County	113 Chestnut St	Allegan MI	49010	616-673-0450	616-673-0298
Alpena County	720 Chisholm St	Alpena MI	49707	517-356-0115	517-356-6559
Antrim County	P.O. Box 520	Bellaire MI	49615	616-533-8607	616-533-8392
Arenac County	P.O. Box 747	Standish MI	48658	517-846-4626	No Fax
Baraga County	16 N. 3rd St.	LAnse MI	49946	906-524-6183	906-524-6186
Barry County	200 W. State St.	Hastings MI	49058	616-948-4810	616-948-4884
Bay County	515 Center Ave	Bay City MI	48708	517-895-4280	517-895-4284
Benzie County	P.O. Box 398	Beulah MI	49617	616-882-9671	616-882-5941
Berrien County	811 Port St	St Joseph MI	49085	616-983-7111	616-982-8642
Branch County	31 Division St	Coldwater MI	49036	517-279-8411	517-278-4130
Calhoun County	315 W. Green St	Marshall MI	49068	616-781-0730	616-781-3007
Cass County	120 N. Broadway	Cassopolis MI	49031	616-445-8621	616-445-8978
Charlevoix County	203 Antrim St	Charlevoix MI	49720	616-547-7200	616-547-7217
Cheboygan County	P.O. Box 70	Cheboygan MI	49721	616-627-8808	616-627-8881
Chippewa County	319 Court St	Sault Sainte Marie MI	49783	906-635-6300	906-635-6851
Clare County	P.O. Box 438	Harrison MI	48625	517-539-7131	517-539-6166
Clinton County	P.O. Box 69	Saint Johns MI	48879	517-224-5140	517-224-5254
Crawford County	200 W. Michigan	Grayling MI	49738	517-348-2841	517-348-7582
Delta County	310 Ludington St	Escanaba MI	49829	906-789-5103	906-789-5196
Dickinson County	P.O. Box 609	Iron Mountain MI	49801	906-774-0988	906-774-4660
Eaton County	1045 Independence Blvd	Charlotte MI	48813	517-485-6444	517-543-7377
Emmet County	200 Division St	Petoskey MI	49770	616-348-1744	616-348-0633
Genesee County	900 S. Saginaw	Flint MI	48502	810-257-3252	810-239-9280
Gladwin County	4011 W. Cedar Ave	Gladwin MI	48624	517-426-7351	517-426-4281
Gogebic County	200 N. Moore	Bessemer MI	49911	906-663-4518	906-663-4660
Grand Traverse County	400 Boardman Ave	Traverse City MI	49684	616-922-4760	616-922-4658
Gratiot County	P.O. Drawer 437	Ithaca MI	48847	517-875-5215	517-875-5285
Hillsdale County	29 N. Howell St.	Hillsdale MI	49242	517-437-3391	No Fax
Houghton County	401 E. Houghton Ave	Houghton MI	49931	906-482-1150	906-482-7238
Huron County	250 E. Huron Ave	Bad Axe MI	48413	517-269-9942	517-269-6160
Ingham County	P.O. Box 179	Mason MI	48854	517-676-7255	517-676-7254
Ionia county	100 Main St.	Ionia MI	48846	616-527-5322	616-527-5380
Iosco County	P.O. Box 838	Tawas City MI	48764	517-362-3497	No Fax

County	Address	City, State		Zip Code	Phone	Fax

MICHIGAN *continued*

County	Address	City	State	Zip Code	Phone	Fax
Iron County	2 S. 6th St	Crystal Falls	MI	49920	906-875-3221	906-875-6775
Isabella County	200 N. Main St	Mount Pleasant	MI	48858	517-772-0911	517-773-7431
Jackson County	312 S. Jackson, 4th Fl	Jackson	MI	49201	517-788-4267	517-788-4601
Kalamazoo County	201 W. Kalamazoo Ave	Kalamazoo	MI	49007	616-383-8840	616-383-8862
Kalkaska County	P.O. Box 10	Kalkaska	MI	49646	616-258-3300	No Fax
Kent County	300 Monroe N.W.	Grand Rapids	MI	49503	616-336-3550	616-336-2885
Keweenaw County	HC 1, Box 607	Eagle River	MI	49924	906-337-2229	No Fax
Lake County	P.O. Drawer B.	Baldwin	MI	49304	616-745-4641	616-745-2241
Lapeer County	255 Clay St	Lapeer	MI	48446	810-667-0296	810-667-0297
Leelanau County	P.O. Box 467	Leland	MI	49654	616-256-9824	616-256-7850
Lenawee County	425 N. Main St	Adrian	MI	49221	517-263-8831	517-265-5721
Livingston County	200 E. Grand River	Howell	MI	48843	517-546-0500	517-546-0500
Luce County	E. Court St	Newberry	MI	49868	906-293-5521	906-293-3581
Mackinac County	100 N. Marley St	St Ignace	MI	49781	906-643-7300	906-643-7302
Macomb County	40 N. Main St	Mt Clemens	MI	48043	810-469-5155	No Fax
Manistee County	415 3rd St	Manistee	MI	49660	616-723-3331	616-723-1492
Marquette County	232 W. Baraga Ave	Marquette	MI	49855	906-228-1525	906-228-1500
Mason County	304 E. Ludington Ave.	Ludington	MI	49431	616-843-8202	616-843-1972
Mecosta County	400 Elm St	Big Rapids	MI	49307	616-592-0787	616-592-0193
Menominee County	839 10th Ave	Menominee	MI	49858	906-863-9968	906-863-8839
Midland County	220 W. Ellsworth St	Midland	MI	48640	517-832-6739	517-832-6680
Missaukee County	P.O. Box 800	Lake City	MI	49651	616-839-4967	616-839-3684
Monroe County	106 E. 1st St	Monroe	MI	48161	313-243-7081	313-243-7107
Montcalm County	P.O. Box 368	Stanton	MI	48888	517-831-5226	517-831-7474
Montmorency County	P.O. Box 415	Atlanta	MI	49709	517-785-4794	517-785-2266
Muskegon County	990 Terrace	Muskegon	MI	49442	616-724-6221	616-724-6262
Newaygo County	P.O. Box 885	White Cloud	MI	49349	616-689-7235	616-689-7205
Oakland County	1200 N. Telegraph Rd	Pontiac	MI	48341	810-858-0564	810-858-1533
Oceana County	P.O. Drawer 153	Hart	MI	49420	616-873-4328	616-873-5914
Ogemaw County	806 W. Houghton Ave	West Branch	MI	48661	517-345-0215	517-345-4939
Ontonagon County	725 Greenland Rd.	Ontonagon	MI	49953	906-884-4255	906-884-5914
Osceola County	301 W. Upton	Reed City	MI	49677	616-832-3261	616-832-6149
Oscoda County	P.O. Box 399	Mio	MI	48647	517-826-1100	517-826-3657
Otsego County	225 W. Main St	Gaylord	MI	49735	517-732-6484	517-732-6066
Ottawa County	414 Washington	Grand Haven	MI	49417	616-846-8310	616-846-8138
Presque Isle County	P.O. Box 110	Rogers City	MI	49779	517-734-3288	517-734-7635
Roscommon County	P.O. Box 98	Roscommon	MI	48653	517-275-5923	517-275-8640
Saginaw County	111 S. Michigan Ave.	Saginaw	MI	48602	517-790-5251	517-790-5254
St Clair County	201 McMorran Blvd	Port Huron	MI	48060	810-985-2200	810-985-2030
St Joseph County	P.O. Box 189	Centreville	MI	49032	616-467-5532	616-467-5628

County	Address	City, State	Zip Code	Phone	Fax
MICHIGAN *continued*					
Sanilac County	60 W. Sanilac	Sandusky MI	48471	810-648-3212	810-648-5466
Schoolcraft County	300 Walnut Room 164	Manistique MI	49854	906-341-3618	906-341-5680
Shiawassee County	208 N. Shiawassee St.	Corunna MI	48817	517-743-2279	517-743-2241
Tuscola County	440 N. State St	Caro MI	48723	517-673-5999	517-673-8164
Van Buren County	212 E. Paw Paw St.	Paw Paw MI	49079	616-657-8218	616-657-7573
Washtenaw County	P.O. Box 8645	Ann Arbor MI	48107	313-994-2507	313-994-1690
Wayne County	211 City County Bldg.	Detroit MI	48226	313-224-6262	313-224-5364
Wexford County	437 E. Division St.	Cadillac MI	49601	616-779-9450	616-779-0292
MINNESOTA					
Aitkin County	209 2nd St. N.W	Aitkin MN	56431	218-927-7354	218-927-7324
Anoka County	2100 3rd Ave	Anoka MN	55303	612-323-5680	612-323-5682
Becker County	P.O. Box 787	Detroit Lakes MN	56502	218-846-7301	218-846-7257
Beltrami County	619 Beltrami Ave. N.W	Bemidji MN	56601	218-759-4109	No Fax
Benton County	531 Dewey St	Foley MN	56329	320-968-6254	320-968-7626
Big Stone County	20 2nd St. S.E	Ortonville MN	56278	320-839-2525	320-839-6253
Blue Earth County	204 S. 5th St. #8608	Mankato MN	56002	507-389-8235	507-389-8344
Brown County	P.O. Box 248	New Ulm MN	56073	507-359-7900	507-359-1430
Carlton County	P.O. Box 130	Carlton MN	55718	218-384-9127	218-384-9181
Carver County	600 E. 4th St	Chaska MN	55318	612-361-1510	612-361-1581
Cass County	P.O. Box 3000	Walker MN	56484	218-547-3300	218-547-2440
Chippewa County	629 N. 11th St.	Montevideo MN	56265	320-269-7447	320-269-7412
Chisago County	313 N. Main St	Center City MN	55012	612-257-1300	612-257-0454
Clay County	807 11th St. N.	Moorhead MN	56560	218-299-5002	218-299-5195
Clearwater County	213 N. Main Ave.	Bagley MN	56621	218-694-6520	218-694-6244
Cook County	P.O. Box 1048	Grand Marais MN	55604	218-387-2282	No Fax
Cottonwood County	900 3rd Ave.	Windom MN	56101	507-831-5669	507-831-3675
Crow Wing County	326 Laurel St	Brainerd MN	56401	218-828-3970	218-828-2917
Dakota County	1590 Hwy. 55 W	Hastings MN	55033	612-438-4418	612-438-4347
Dodge County	P.O. Box 38	Mantorville MN	55955	507-635-6230	507-635-6265
Douglas County	305 8th Ave. W	Alexandria MN	56308	612-762-2381	612-762-2389
Faribault County	P.O. Box 130	Blue Earth MN	56013	507-526-6226	507-526-6227
Fillmore County	P.O. Box 466	Preston MN	55965	507-765-4566	No Fax
Freeborn County	411 S. Broadway Ave	Albert Lea MN	56007	507-377-5299	No Fax
Goodhue County	509 W. 5th St	Red Wing MN	55066	612-385-3001	No Fax
Grant County	10 2nd St. N.E	Elbow Lake MN	56531	218-685-4520	218-685-4521
Hennepin County	A2303 Govt. Center	Minneapolis MN	55487	612-348-3000	No Fax
Houston County	304 S. Marshall St	Caledonia MN	55921	507-724-5803	507-724-2647
Hubbard County	301 Court St	Park Rapids MN	56470	218-732-3196	218-732-3645
Isanti County	18th Ave. S.W.	Cambridge MN	55008	612-689-3859	612-689-8226

County	Address	City, State	Zip Code	Phone	Fax

MINNESOTA *continued*

County	Address	City, State	Zip Code	Phone	Fax
Itasca County	123 N.E. 4th St	Grand Rapids MN	55744	218-327-2847	218-327-2848
Jackson County	405 4th St	Jackson MN	56143	507-847-2763	507-847-4718
Kanabec County	18 N. Vine St.	Mora MN	55051	320-679-1030	320-679-9994
Kandiyohi County	1900 Hwy. 294 NE, Ste 2020	Willmar MN	56201	320-231-6215	320-231-7899
Kittson County	P.O. Box 848	Hallock MN	56728	218-843-2655	218-843-2020
Koochiching County	4th St. & 6th Ave.	International Falls MN	56649	218-283-6252	218-283-6262
Lac Qui Parle County	600 6th St	Madison MN	56256	612-598-3536	612-598-7444
Lake County	601 3rd Ave	Two Harbors MN	55616	218-834-8320	No Fax
Lake of the Woods County	P.O. Box 808	Baudette MN	56623	218-634-2836	218-634-2509
Le Sueur County	88 S. Park	Le Center MN	56057	507-357-2251	507-357-6375
Lincoln County	319 N. Rebecca #29	Ivanhoe MN	56142	507-694-1529	507-694-1198
Lyon County	607 Main St. W	Marshall MN	56258	507-537-6728	507-537-6091
Mahnomen County	P.O. Box 379	Mahnomen MN	56557	218-935-5669	218-935-5946
Marshall County	208 E. Colvin Ave	Warren MN	56762	218-745-4851	218-745-4343
Martin County	201 Lake Ave. #955	Fairmont MN	56031	507-238-3211	507-238-2359
McLeod County	830 11th St. E	Glencoe MN	55336	320-864-5551	320-864-3410
Meeker County	325 N. Sibley Ave	Litchfield MN	55355	320-693-5200	320-693-5444
Mille Lacs County	635 2nd St. S.E	Milaca MN	56353	320-983-8310	320-983-8336
Morrison County	213 S.E. 1st Ave	Little Falls MN	56345	320-632-0132	320-632-0139
Mower County	201 1st St. N.E	Austin MN	55912	507-437-9545	507-437-9471
Murray County	P.O. Box 57	Slayton MN	56172	507-836-6148	507-836-6019
Nicollet County	P.O. Box 496	Saint Peter MN	56082	507-931-6800	507-931-4278
Nobles County	315 10th St. #757	Worthington MN	56187	507-372-8231	507-372-8223
Norman County	16 3rd Ave. E	Ada MN	56510	218-784-3851	No Fax
Olmsted County	Govt Center 1st Floor	Rochester MN	55902	507-285-8115	507-285-8106
Otter Tail County	121 W. Junius Ave	Fergus Falls MN	56537	218-739-2271	218-739-3721
Pennington County	P.O. Box 616	Thief River Falls MN	56701	218-681-4011	218-681-1235
Pine County	315 6th St	Pine City MN	55063	320-629-6781	320-629-7319
Pipestone County	416 S. Hiawatha Ave	Pipestone MN	56164	507-825-4494	507-825-4699
Polk County	612 N. Broadway, Suite 215	Crookston MN	56716	218-281-5408	218-281-3808
Pope County	P.O. Box 195	Glenwood MN	56334	320-634-5301	320-634-5527
Ramsey County	15 W. Kellogg, Suite 250	Saint Paul MN	55102	612-266-8009	612-266-8039
Red Lake County	100 Langavin St	Red Lake Falls MN	56750	218-253-2598	218-253-2656
Redwood County	P.O. Box 130	Redwood Falls MN	56283	507-637-3207	507-637-5112
Renville County	500 DePue Ave. E	Olivia MN	56277	320-523-2071	320-523-3679
Rice County	218 3rd St. N.W	Faribault MN	55021	507-332-6100	507-332-6199
Rock County	P.O. Box 509	Luverne MN	56156	507-283-9165	507-283-9504
Roseau County	216 Center St. W	Roseau MN	56751	218-463-1282	No Fax
Saint Louis County	100 N. 5th Ave. W	Duluth MN	55802	218-726-2448	218-726-2469
Scott County	428 Holmes St., Rm. 110	Shakopee MN	55379	612-496-8100	612-496-8257

County	Address	City, State	Zip Code	Phone	Fax

MINNESOTA *continued*

County	Address	City, State	Zip Code	Phone	Fax
Sherburne County	13880 Hwy. 10	Elk River MN	55330	612-241-2701	612-241-2995
Sibley County	400 Court St	Gaylord MN	55334	507-237-2369	507-237-2957
Stearns County	705 Courthouse Sq #121	Saint Cloud MN	56303	320-656-3601	320-656-3977
Steele County	111 E. Main St	Owatonna MN	55060	507-451-8040	507-451-6803
Stevens County	P.O. Box 530	Morris MN	56267	320-589-7417	320-589-2036
Swift County	301 14th St. N.	Benson MN	56215	320-843-4069	320-843-2299
Todd County	215 1st Ave. S	Long Prairie MN	56347	320-732-4469	320-732-4001
Traverse County	P.O. Box 428	Wheaton MN	56296	320-563-4242	320-563-4424
Wabasha County	625 Jefferson Ave	Wabasha MN	55981	612-565-2648	612-565-2774
Wadena County	415 S. Jefferson St.	Wadena MN	56482	218-631-2425	218-631-2428
Waseca County	307 N. State St	Waseca MN	56093	507-835-0630	507-835-0633
Washington County	14900 61st St. N	Stillwater MN	55082	612-430-6000	612-430-6017
Watonwan County	710 2nd Ave. S	Saint James MN	56081	507-375-1210	507-315-3547
Wilkin County	5th St. S.	Breckenridge MN	56520	218-643-4981	218-643-2230
Winona County	171 W. 3rd St	Winona MN	55987	507-457-6350	507-457-6469
Wright County	10 2nd St. NW.	Buffalo MN	55313	612-682-7377	612-682-6178
Yellow Medicine County	415 9th Ave	Granite Falls MN	56241	320-564-3132	320-564-4165

MISSISSIPPI

County	Address	City, State	Zip Code	Phone	Fax
Adams County	P.O. Box 1006	Natchez MS	39121	601-446-6684	601-445-7913
Alcorn County	P.O. Box 69	Corinth MS	38835	601-286-7700	601-286-7706
Amite County	P.O. Box 680	Liberty MS	39645	601-657-8022	601-657-8288
Attala County	230 W. Washington	Kosciusko MS	39090	601-289-2921	601-289-7662
Benton County	P.O. Box 218	Ashland MS	38603	601-224-6300	601-224-6303
Boliver County	P.O. Box 789	Cleveland MS	38732	601-843-2071	601-846-5880
Calhoun County	P.O. Box 8	Pittsboro MS	38951	601-983-3117	601-983-3128
Carroll County	P.O. Box 60	Carrollton MS	38917	601-237-9274	No Fax
Chickasaw County	101 N. Jefferson	Houston MS	38851	601-456-2513	601-456-5295
Choctaw County	P.O. Box 250	Ackerman MS	39735	601-285-6329	601-285-3444
Claiborne County	P.O. Box 449	Port Gibson MS	39150	601-437-4992	601-437-4330
Clarke County	P.O. Box 689	Quitman MS	39355	601-776-2126	601-776-1013
Clay County	P.O. Box 815	West Point MS	39773	601-494-3124	No Fax
Coahoma County	P.O. Box 98	Clarksdale MS	38614	601-624-3000	601-624-3029
Copiah County	P.O. Box 507	Hazlehurst MS	39083	601-894-3021	601-894-3026
Covington County	P.O. Box 1679	Collins MS	39428	601-765-4242	601-765-1052
De Soto County	2535 Hwy. 51 S.	Hernando MS	38632	601-429-1318	601-429-1311
Forrest County	P.O. Box 1310	Hattiesburg MS	39403	601-545-6000	601-545-6095
Franklin County	P.O. Box 297	Meadville MS	39653	601-384-2330	601-384-5864
George County	200 Courthouse Sq, Suite A.	Lucedale MS	39452	601-947-4801	601-947-4812
Greene County	P.O. Box 610	Leakesville MS	39451	601-394-2377	601-394-2334

MISSISSIPPI *continued*

County	Address	City, State	Zip Code	Phone	Fax
Grenada County	P.O. Box 1208	Grenada MS	38901	601-226-1821	601-226-0427
Hancock County	P.O. Box 429	Bay Saint Louis MS	39520	601-467-5404	601-466-5994
Harrison County	P.O. Drawer CC	Gulfport MS	39502	601-865-4036	601-868-1480
Hinds County	P.O. Box 686	Jackson MS	39205	601-968-6501	601-968-6794
Holmes County	P.O. Box 239	Lexington MS	39095	601-834-2508	601-834-3020
Humphreys County	102 Castleman	Belzoni MS	39038	601-247-1740	601-247-0101
Issaquena County	P.O. Box 27	Mayersville MS	39113	601-873-2761	601-873-2061
Itawamba County	213 Wiygul St	Fulton MS	38843	601-862-3421	601-862-4006
Jackson County	P.O. Box 998	Pascagoula MS	39567	601-769-3000	601-769-3357
Jasper County	P.O. Box 1047	Bay Springs MS	39422	601-764-3368	601-764-3468
Jefferson County	P.O. Box 145	Fayette MS	39069	601-786-3021	601-786-6009
Jefferson Davis County	P.O. Box 1137	Prentiss MS	39474	601-792-4204	601-792-2894
Jones County	P.O. Box 1468	Laurel MS	39441	601-428-0527	No Fax
Kemper County	P.O. Box 188	De Kalb MS	39328	601-743-2460	601-743-2789
Lafayette County	P.O. Box 1240	Oxford MS	38655	601-234-7563	601-234-5402
Lamar County	P.O. Box 247	Purvis MS	39475	601-794-8504	601-794-1049
Lauderdale County	P.O. Box 1587	Meridian MS	39305	601-482-9701	601-484-3976
Lawrence County	P.O. Box 40	Monticello MS	39654	601-587-7162	601-587-3003
Leake County	P.O. Drawer 72	Carthage MS	39051	601-267-7371	601-267-6312
Lee County	P.O. Box 7127	Tupelo MS	38802	601-841-9100	601-680-6091
Leflore County	P.O. Box 250	Greenwood MS	38935	601-453-6203	601-455-7965
Lincoln County	P.O. Box 555	Brookhaven MS	39601	601-835-3411	601-835-3423
Lowndes County	P.O. Box 684	Columbus MS	39703	601-329-5800	No Fax
Madison County	P.O. Box 404	Canton MS	39046	601-859-1177	601-859-5875
Marion County	250 Broad St., Suite 2	Columbia MS	39429	601-736-2691	601-736-1232
Marshall County	P.O. Box 219	Holly Springs MS	38635	601-252-4431	601-252-0004
Monroe County	P.O. Box 578	Aberdeen MS	39730	601-369-8143	601-369-7928
Montgomery County	P.O. Box 71	Winona MS	38967	601-283-2333	601-283-2233
Neshoba County	401 E. Beacon St.	Philadelphia MS	39350	601-656-3581	601-650-3280
Newton County	P.O. Box 68	Decatur MS	39327	601-635-2367	601-635-3210
Noxubee County	505 S. Jefferson	Macon MS	39341	601-726-4243	601-726-2938
Oktibbeha County	Courthouse	Starkville MS	39759	601-323-5834	601-338-1065
Panola County	151 Public Sq	Batesville MS	38606	601-563-6205	601-563-8233
Pearl River County	P.O. Box 431	Poplarville MS	39470	601-795-3001	601-795-3024
Perry County	P.O. Box 198	New Augusta MS	39462	601-964-8398	601-964-8265
Pike County	P.O. Box 309	Magnolia MS	39652	601-783-3362	601-783-4010
Pontotoc County	P.O. Box 209	Pontotoc MS	38863	601-489-3900	No Fax
Prentiss County	P.O. Box 477	Booneville MS	38829	601-728-8151	601-728-2007
Quitman County	230 Chestnut St	Marks MS	38646	601-326-2661	601-326-8004
Rankin County	P.O. Box 700	Brandon MS	39043	601-825-1469	No Fax

County	Address	City, State Zip Code	Phone	Fax
MISSISSIPPI *continued*				
Scott County	P.O. Box 630	Forest MS 39074	601-469-1922	601-469-3514
Sharkey County	P.O. Box 218	Rolling Fork MS 39159	601-873-2755	601-873-6045
Simpson County	P.O. Box 367	Mendenhall MS 39114	601-847-2626	601-847-7004
Smith County	P.O. Box 39	Raleigh MS 39153	601-782-9811	601-782-4002
Stone County	P.O. Drawer 7	Wiggins MS 39577	601-928-5266	601-928-5248
Sunflower County	P.O. Box 988	Indianola MS 38751	601-887-4703	601-887-7054
Tallahatchie County	P.O. Box 350	Charleston MS 38921	601-647-5551	601-647-8490
Tate County	201 S. Ward St	Senatobia MS 38668	601-562-5661	601-562-7486
Tippah County	Courthouse	Ripley MS 38663	601-837-7374	601-837-1030
Tishomingo County	1008 Battleground Dr	Iuka MS 38852	601-423-7010	601-423-7005
Tunica County	P.O. Box 217	Tunica MS 38676	601-363-2451	601-363-2593
Union County	P.O. Box 847	New Albany MS 38652	601-534-1900	601-534-1907
Walthall County	P.O. Box 351	Tylertown MS 39667	601-876-3553	601-876-6688
Warren County	P.O. Box 351	Vicksburg MS 39181	601-636-4415	601-634-4815
Washington County	P.O. Box 309	Greenville MS 38702	601-332-1595	601-334-2725
Wayne County	1 Azalea Dr	Waynesboro MS 39367	601-735-2873	601-735-6248
Webster County	P.O. Box 398	Walthall MS 39771	601-258-4131	601-258-6657
Wilkinson County	P.O. Box 516	Woodville MS 39669	601-888-4381	601-888-6776
Winston County	P.O. Drawer 69	Louisville MS 39339	601-773-3631	601-773-8825
Yalobusha County	P.O. Box 664	Water Valley MS 38965	601-473-2091	601-473-5020
Yazoo County	P.O. Box 68	Yazoo City MS 39194	601-746-2661	No Fax
MISSOURI				
Adair County	County Courthouse	Kirksville MO 63501	816-665-3350	816-785-3213
Andrew County	P.O. Box 206	Savannah MO 64485	816-324-3624	816-324-5667
Atchison County	P.O. Box 280	Rock Port MO 64482	816-744-6214	816-744-5705
Audrain County	101 N. Jefferson	Mexico MO 65265	314-473-5820	314-581-2380
Barry County	P.O. Box G	Cassville MO 65625	417-847-2400	417-847-5311
Barton County	223 N.E. 80th Rd	Sheldon MO 64784	417-884-2804	No Fax
Bates County	Rt 1, P.O. Box 78	Butler MO 64730	816-679-5257	816-679-4446
Benton County	P.O. Box 1238	Warsaw MO 65355	816-438-7326	816-438-2062
Bollinger County	P.O. Box 110	Marble Hill MO 63764	573-238-2126	573-238-4511
Boone County	P.O. Box 7716	Columbia MO 65201	573-886-4190	573-886-4193
Buchanan County	411 Jules St	Saint Joseph MO 64501	816-271-1442	816-271-1563
Butler County	County Courthouse	Poplar Bluff MO 63901	314-686-8078	314-785-0701
Caldwell County	P.O. Box 67	Kingston MO 64650	816-586-2571	816-586-2103
Callaway County	10 E. 5th St	Fulton MO 65251	573-642-0730	573-642-7181
Camden County	P.O. Box 1258	Camdenton MO 65020	314-346-4440	314-346-5181
Cape Girardeau County	1 Barton Sq	Jackson MO 63755	573-243-1052	573-243-6893
Carroll County	County Courthouse	Carrollton MO 64633	816-542-3276	816-542-1539

County	Address	City, State Zip Code	Phone	Fax
MISSOURI *continued*				
Carter County	P.O. Box 517	Van Buren MO 63965	314-323-4527	314-323-8577
Cass County	102 E. Wall	Harrisonville MO 64701	816-380-1500	816-380-5136
Cedar County	P.O. Box 129	Stockton MO 65785	417-276-3514	417-276-5135
Chariton County	306 Cherry	Keytesville MO 65261	816-288-3273	816-288-3612
Christian County	County Clerk Office	Ozark MO 65721	417-581-6360	417-581-8331
Clark County	Rt 1, P.O. Box 63-B	Canton MO 63435	816-727-3283	816-727-1088
Clay County	Administration Bldg.	Liberty MO 64068	816-792-7637	816-792-7777
Clinton County	P.O. Box 24.	Plattsburg MO 64477	816-539-3713	816-539-2346
Cole County	301 E. High St	Jefferson City MO 65101	314-634-9106	314-634-8031
Cooper County	200 Main St.	Booneville MO 65233	816-882-2114	816-882-2043
Crawford County	P.O. Box AS.	Steelville MO 65565	573-775-2376	573-775-2126
Dade County	225 S. Water	Greenfield MO 65661	417-637-2724	417-637-2224
Dallas County	P.O. Box 436	Buffalo MO 65622	417-345-2632	417-345-5321
Daviess County	Rt 1	Galamont MO 64620	816-663-2641	816-663-3322
De Kalb County	P.O. Box 248	Maysville MO 64469	816-449-5402	816-449-2440
Dent County	400 N. Main	Salem MO 65560	573-729-4144	573-729-6106
Douglas County	P.O. Box 395	Ava MO 65608	417-683-4714	417-683-3100
Dunklin County	P.O. Box 62	Kennett MO 63857	573-888-2379	573-888-1504
Franklin County	P.O. Box 311	Union MO 63084	573-583-6355	573-583-3500
Gasconade County	119 E. 1st St. Rm 2	Herman MO 65066	573-486-5427	573-486-8893
Gentry County	County Courthousel	Albany MO 64402	816-726-3525	816-726-4102
Greene County	940 Boonville Ave	Springfield MO 65802	417-868-4000	417-868-4050
Grundy County	700 Main St.	Trenton MO 64683	816-359-6305	816-359-3761
Harrison County	P.O. Box 525	Bethany MO 64424	816-425-6424	816-425-3772
Henry County	100 W. Franklin St.	Clinton MO 64735	816-885-6963	816-885-8456
Hickory County	P.O. Box 3	Hematay MO 65779	417-745-6450	417-745-6670
Holt County	Rt 1, P.O. Box 13-A.	Oregon MO 64473	816-446-3033	816-446-3409
Howard County	200 Cooper	Fayette MO 65248	816-248-5161	816-248-3905
Howell County	Rm. 001, Courthouse	West Plains MO 65775	417-256-2591	417-256-2512
Iron County	P.O Box 42	Ironton MO 63650	573-546-2912	573-546-6499
Jackson County	415 E. 12th St	Kansas City MO 64106	816-881-3242	816-881-3340
Jasper County	601 S. Pearl	Joplin MO 64801	417-625-4360	No Fax
Jefferson County	P.O. Box 100	Hillsboro MO 63050	314-789-5478	314-789-5360
Johnson County	County Courthouse	Warrensburg MO 64093	816-747-6161	816-747-9332
Knox County	107 N. 4th	Edina MO 63537	816-397-2184	816-397-3331
Laclede County	200 N. Adams Ave.	Lebenon MO 65536	417-532-5471	417-588-9288
Lafayette County	1001 Main	Lexington MO 64067	816-259-4315	816-259-6109
Lawrence County	P.O. Box 431	Mount Vernon MO 65712	417-466-2273	417-466-3697
Lewis County	P.O. Box 67	Monticello MO 63457	573-767-5476	No Fax
Lincoln County	201 Main St.	Troy MO 63379	314-528-4415	314-528-5528

County	Address	City, State Zip Code	Phone	Fax
MISSOURI *continued*				
Linn County	108 N. High St.	Linneus MO 64653	816-895-5417	No Fax
Livingston County	700 Webster, Ste 10	Chillicothe MO 64601	816-646-2293	816-646-6139
Macon County	101 E Washington	Macon MO 63552	816-385-2913	816-385-7203
Madison County	#1 Courthouse Sq.	Fredericktown MO 63645	573-783-2176	573-783-5351
Maries County	P.O. Box 165	Vienna MO 65582	573-422-3388	573-422-3100
Marion County	100 S. Main	Palmyra MO 63461	573-769-2549	573-769-4312
McDonald County	P.O. Box 665	Pineville MO 64856	417-223-4717	417-223-4072
Mercer County	County Courthouse	Princeton MO 64673	816-748-3625	816-748-3180
Miller County	P.O Box 11	Tuscumbia MO 65082	573-369-2303	573-369-2910
Mississippi County	P.O. Box 369	Charleston MO 63834	573-683-2146	573-683-3904
Moniteau County	200 E. Main St	California MO 65018	314-796-4704	314-796-3082
Monroe County	300 N. Main	Paris MO 65275	816-327-5106	816-327-5781
Montgomery County	211 E. 3rd	Montgomery City MO 63361	573-564-3357	573-564-8088
Morgan County	100 E. Newton	Versailles MO 65084	573-378-5436	573-378-5790
New Madrid County	P.O.Box 68	New Madrid MO 63869	573-748-2524	573-748-7214
Newton County	101 S. Wood	Neosho MO 64850	417-451-8220	417-451-7434
Nodaway County	P.O. Box 218	Marville MO 64468	816-582-2251	816-582-5282
Oregon County	P.O. Box 363	Alton MO 65606	417-778-7475	417-778-6641
Osage County	P.O Box 862	Linn MO 65051	573-897-2139	573-897-2285
Ozark County	P.O. Box 416	Gainsville MO 65635	417-273-4012	417-679-3209
Pemiscot County	610 Ward Ave	Caruthersville MO 63830	573-333-4203	573-333-0440
Perry County	321 N. Main St. #8	Perryville MO 63775	573-547-4242	573-547-7367
Pettis County	415 S. Ohio Ave	Sedalia MO 65301	816-826-5395	816-826-8637
Phelps County	210 N. Main St.	Rolla MO 65401	573-364-1891	573-364-0436
Pike County	15 W. Main St.	Bowling Green MO 63334	573-324-2412	573-324-5152
Platte County	328 Main St.Box SCH	Platte MO 64079	816-858-3481	816-858-3392
Polk County	102 E. Broadway	Bolivar MO 65613	417-326-4031	417-326-4194
Pulaski County	P.O. Box 554	Crocker MO 65452	573-774-6609	573-774-5601
Putnam County	Rm. 204 Courthouse	Unionville MO 63565	816-947-2674	816-947-3700
Ralls County	P.O. Box 400	New London MO 63459	573-985-7111	No Fax
Randolph County	110 S. Main	Huntsville MO 65259	816-277-4717	816-277-3246
Ray County	100 W. Main St.	Richmond MO 64085	816-776-4502	816-776-6016
Reynolds County	P.O. Box 10	Centerville MO 63633	573-648-2494	573-648-2296
Ripley County	County Courthouse	Doniphan MO 63935	573-996-3215	573-996-5014
Saint Charles County	201 N. 2nd	Saint Charles MO 63301	314-949-7550	314-949-7552
Saint Clair County	P.O. Box 405	Osceola MO 64776	417-646-2315	417-646-8080
Saint Francois County	Courthouse 2nd Fl	Hunnington MO 63640	573-756-5411	573-756-2817
Saint Louis County	41 S. Central	Clayton MO 63105	573-889-2000	573-889-3727
Sainte Genevieve County	55 S. 3rd	Sainte Genevieve MO 63670	573-883-5589	573-883-9636
Saline County	156 W. North	Marshall MO 65340	816-886-8699	816-886-4227

County	Address	City, State	Zip Code	Phone	Fax
MISSOURI *continued*					
Schuyler County	P.O. Box 187	Lancaster MO	63548	816-457-3843	816-457-3016
Scotland County	County Courthouse	Memphis MO	63555	816-465-7027	816-465-8640
Scott County	P.O. Box 188	Benton MO	63736	573-545-3549	573-545-3540
Shannon County	P.O. Box 187	Eminence MO	65466	573-226-3414	573-226-5321
Shelby County	P.O. Box 186	Shelbyville MO	63469	573-633-2181	573-633-2142
Stoddard County	P.O. Drawer H	Bloomfield MO	63825	573-568-3339	573-568-2194
Stone County	P.O. Box 45	Galena MO	65633	417-357-6127	417-357-6861
Sullivan County	109 N. Main	Milan MO	63556	816-265-3786	816-265-4711
Taney County	P.O. Box 364	Forsyth MO	65653	417-546-3340	417-546-3170
Texas County	210 N. Grand	Houston MO	65483	417-967-2112	417-967-3837
Vernon County	County Courthouse	Nevada MO	64772	417-448-2570	417-448-2512
Warren County	105 S. Market	Warrenton MO	63383	573-456-3331	573-456-1801
Washington County	102 N. Missouri	Potosi MO	63664	573-438-4901	573-438-4038
Wayne County	P.O. Box 168	Greenville MO	63944	573-224-3221	573-224-5609
Webster County	Rm. 11 County Courthouse	Marshfield MO	65706	417-468-2223	417-468-5307
Worth County	P.O. Box 38	Grant City MO	64456	816-786-2229	816-564-2432
Wright County	P.O. Box 169	Mansfield MO	65704	417-924-3233	417-924-3679
City of St. Louis	10 N. Tucker Blvd	St Louis MO	63101	573-622-4395	No Fax
MONTANA					
Beaverhead County	2 S. Pacific	Dillon MT	59725	406-683-5245	406-683-5776
Big Horn County	P.O. Drawer H	Hardin MT	59034	406-665-3520	406-665-1608
Blaine County	P.O. Box 278	Chinook MT	59523	406-357-3250	406-327-2199
Broadwater County	515 Broadway	Townsend MT	59644	406-266-3405	406-266-3674
Carbon County	P.O. Box 887	Red Lodge MT	59068	406-446-1595	406-446-2640
Carter County	P.O. Box 315	Ekalaka MT	59324	406-775-8749	406-775-8750
Cascade County	Courthouse Annex-111	Great Falls MT	59401	406-454-6810	406-454-6945
Chouteau County	P.O. Box 459	Fort Benton MT	59442	406-622-3631	406-622-3631
Custer County	1010 Main St.	Miles City MT	59301	406-233-3457	406-233-3452
Daniels County	P.O. Box 247	Scobey MT	59263	406-487-5561	406-487-5502
Dawson County	207 W. Bell St	Glendive MT	59330	406-365-3562	406-365-2022
Deer Lodge County	800 S. Main St	Anaconda MT	59711	406-563-4000	406-563-4001
Fallon County	P.O. Box 846	Baker MT	59313	406-778-2883	406-778-3431
Fergus County	712 W. Main St	Lewistown MT	59457	406-538-5119	406-538-9220
Flathead County	800 S. Main St	Kalispell MT	59901	406-758-5503	406-758-5861
Gallatin County	311 W. Main St #204	Bozeman MT	59715	406-582-3050	406-582-3037
Garfield County	P.O. Box 7	Jordan MT	59337	406-557-2760	406-557-2625
Glacier County	512 E. Main St	Cut Bank MT	59427	406-873-5063	406-873-2125
Golden Valley County	P.O. Box 10	Ryegate MT	59074	406-568-2231	406-568-2598
Granite County	P.O. Box B	Phillipsburg MT	59858	406-859-3771	406-859-3817

County	Address	City, State	Zip Code	Phone	Fax
MONTANA *continued*					
Hill County	315 4th St	Havre MT	59501	406-265-5481	406-265-5487
Jefferson County	P.O. Box H	Boulder MT	59632	406-225-4251	406-225-3275
Judith Basin County	Courthouse	Stanford MT	59479	406-566-2277	406-566-2211
Lake County	106 4th Ave E	Polson MT	59860	406-883-7204	406-883-7283
Lewis & Clark County	316 N. Park Ave	Helena MT	59601	406-447-8304	406-447-8370
Liberty County	P.O. Box 459	Chester MT	59522	406-759-5365	406-759-5395
Lincoln County	512 California Ave	Libby MT	59923	406-293-7781	406-293-8577
Madison County	P.O. Box 278	Virginia City MT	59755	406-843-5392	406-843-5517
McCone County	P.O. Box 199	Circle MT	59215	406-485-3500	406-485-2689
Meagher County	P.O. Box 309	White Sulphur Springs MT	59645	406-547-3612	406-547-3388
Mineral County	P.O. Box 669	Superior MT	59872	406-822-3540	406-822-3579
Missoula County	200 W. Broadway St.	Missoula MT	59802	406-721-5700	406-721-4043
Musselshell County	506 Main St.	Roundup MT	59072	406-323-1104	406-323-1710
Park County	414 E. Callendar.	Livingston MT	59047	406-222-6120	406-222-4199
Petroleum County	P.O. Box 226	Winnett MT	59087	406-429-5311	406-429-6328
Phillips County	P.O. Box 360	Malta MT	59538	406-654-2429	406-654-2429
Pondera County	20 4th Ave. SW	Conrad MT	59425	406-278-4026	406-278-4070
Powder River County	P.O. Box 270	Broadus MT	59317	406-436-2657	406-436-2151
Powell County	409 Missouri Ave	Deer Lodge MT	59722	406-846-3680	406-846-2742
Prairie County	P.O. Box 125	Terry MT	59349	406-637-5575	406-637-5546
Ravalli County	P.O. Box 5001	Hamilton MT	59840	406-363-4790	406-363-1880
Richland County	201 W. Main St.	Sidney MT	59270	406-482-1706	406-482-3731
Roosevelt County	400 2nd Ave. S	Wolf Point MT	59201	406-653-1590	406-653-3100
Rosebud County	P.O. Box 47	Forsyth MT	59327	406-356-2251	406-356-7551
Sanders County	P.O. Box 519	Thompson Falls MT	59873	406-827-4391	406-827-4388
Sheridan County	100 W. Laurel Ave	Plentywood MT	59254	406-765-1660	406-765-2129
Silver Bow County	155 W. Granite St.	Butte MT	59701	406-723-8262	406-782-6637
Stillwater County	P.O. Box 149	Columbus MT	59019	406-322-4546	406-322-4698
Sweet Grass County	P.O. Box 460	Big Timber MT	59011	406-932-5152	406-932-4777
Teton County	P.O. Box 610	Choteau MT	59422	406-466-2151	406-466-2138
Toole County	226 1st St. S	Shelby MT	59474	406-434-5121	406-434-2467
Treasure County	P.O. Box 392	Hysham MT	59038	406-342-5547	406-342-5212
Valley County	501 Courtsquare #1	Glasgow MT	59230	406-228-8221	406-228-9027
Wheatland County	P.O. Box 1903	Harlowton MT	59036	406-632-4891	406-632-4719
Wibaux County	P.O. Box 199	Wibaux MT	59353	406-795-2481	406-795-2625
Yellowstone County	P.O. Box 35000	Billings MT	59107	406-256-2701	406-256-6947
NEBRASKA					
Adams County	Courthouse	Hastings NE	68901	402-461-7107	402-461-7118
Antelope County	501 Main St.	Neligh NE	68756	402-887-4410	402-887-4719

County	Address	City, State	Zip Code	Phone	Fax
NEBRASKA *continued*					
Arthur County	P.O. Box 126	Arthur NE	69121	308-764-2203	308-764-2216
Banner County	P.O. Box 67	Harrisburg NE	69345	308-436-5268	308-436-4180
Blaine County	P.O. Box 136	Brewster NE	68821	308-547-2222	308-547-2228
Boone County	222 S. 4th St	Albion NE	68620	402-395-2055	402-395-6592
Box Butte County	P.O. Box 678	Alliance NE	69301	308-762-6565	308-762-2867
Boyd County	401 Thayer St	Butte NE	68722	402-775-2391	402-775-2146
Brown County	148 W. 4th St	Ainsworth NE	69210	402-387-2705	402-387-0918
Buffalo County	P.O. Box 1270	Kearney NE	68848	308-236-1226	308-236-1291
Burt County	111 N. 13th St.	Tekamah NE	68061	402-374-1955	402-374-1955
Butler County	P.O. Box 289	David City NE	68632	402-367-7430	402-367-3329
Cass County	346 Main St.	Plattsmouth NE	68048	402-296-9300	402-296-9327
Cedar County	P.O. Box 47	Hartington NE	68739	402-254-7411	402-254-7410
Chase County	P.O. Box 1299	Imperial NE	69033	308-882-5266	308-882-5679
Cherry County	P.O. Box 120	Valentine NE	69201	402-376-2771	402-376-1680
Cheyenne County	P.O. Box 217	Sidney NE	69162	308-254-2141	308-254-4293
Clay County	111 W. Fairfield St	Clay Center NE	68933	402-762-3463	402-762-3250
Colfax County	411 E. 11th St	Schuyler NE	68661	402-352-3434	402-352-3287
Cuming County	P.O. Box 290	West Point NE	68788	402-372-6003	402-372-2311
Custer County	431 S. 10th St	Broken Bow NE	68822	308-872-5701	No Fax
Dakota County	P.O. Box 39	Dakota City NE	68731	402-987-2126	402-987-2173
Dawes County	451 Main St.	Chadron NE	69337	308-432-0100	308-432-0115
Dawson County	P.O. Box 370	Lexington NE	68850	308-324-2127	308-324-5614
Deuel County	P.O. Box 327	Chappell NE	69129	308-874-3308	308-874-3472
Dixon County	P.O. Box 546	Ponca NE	68770	402-755-2208	402-755-4276
Dodge County	435 N. Park Ave	Fremont NE	68025	402-727-2767	402-727-2753
Douglas County	1819 Farnam St	Omaha NE	68183	402-444-7150	402-444-6456
Dundy County	P.O. Box 506	Benkelman NE	69021	308-423-2058	308-423-2325
Fillmore County	P.O. Box 307	Geneva NE	68361	402-759-4931	402-759-4429
Franklin County	P.O. Box 146	Franklin NE	68939	308-425-6202	308-425-6289
Frontier County	1 Wellington St	Stockville NE	69042	308-367-8641	308-367-8730
Furnas County	P.O. Box 387	Beaver City NE	68926	308-268-4145	No Fax
Gage County	P.O. Box 429	Beatrice NE	68310	402-223-1300	402-223-1371
Garden County	P.O. Box 486	Oshkosh NE	69154	308-772-3924	308-772-4143
Garfield County	P.O. Box 218	Burwell NE	68823	308-346-4161	No Fax
Gosper County	P.O. Box 136	Elwood NE	68937	308-785-2611	308-785-2036
Grant County	P.O. Box 139	Hyannis NE	69350	308-458-2488	308-458-2485
Greeley County	P.O. Box 287	Greeley NE	68842	308-428-3625	308-428-4905
Hall County	121 S. Pine St	Grand Island NE	68801	308-381-5080	308-381-5094
Hamilton County	1111 13th St., Suite 1	Aurora NE	68818	402-694-3443	402-694-2250
Harlan County	P.O. Box 698	Alma NE	68920	308-928-2173	308-928-2592

County	Address	City, State	Zip Code	Phone	Fax
NEBRASKA *continued*					
Hayes County	P.O. Box 370	Hayes Center NE	69032	308-286-3413	No Fax
Hitchcock County	P.O. Box 248	Trenton NE	69044	308-334-5646	308-334-5351
Holt County	P.O. Box 329	ONeill NE	68763	402-336-1762	No Fax
Hooker County	P.O. Box 184	Mullen NE	69152	308-546-2244	308-546-2490
Howard County	P.O. Box 25	Saint Paul NE	68873	308-754-4343	308-754-4727
Jefferson County	411 4th St	Fairbury NE	68352	402-729-2323	402-729-2016
Johnson County	P.O. Box 416	Tecumseh NE	68450	402-335-3246	402-335-3975
Kearney County	P.O. Box 339	Minden NE	68959	308-832-2719	308-832-1748
Keith County	P.O. Box 149	Ogallala NE	69153	308-284-4726	308-284-6277
Keya Paha County	P.O. Box 349	Springview NE	68778	402-497-3791	402-497-3799
Kimball County	114 E. 3rd St	Kimball NE	69145	308-235-2241	308-235-3131
Knox County	P.O. Box 166	Center NE	68724	402-288-4282	402-288-4263
Lancaster County	P.O. Drawer 70	Lincoln NE	68508	402-441-7482	402-441-8728
Lincoln County	301 N. Jeffers	North Platte NE	69101	308-534-4350	No Fax
Logan County	P.O. Box 8	Stapleton NE	69163	308-636-2311	No Fax
Loup County	P.O. Box 187	Taylor NE	68879	308-942-3135	308-942-6015
Madison County	P.O. Box 290	Madison NE	68748	402-454-3311	402-454-3816
McPherson County	P.O. Box 122	Tryon NE	69167	308-587-2363	No Fax
Merrick County	P.O. Box 27	Central City NE	68826	308-946-2881	308-946-2332
Morrill County	P.O. Box 610	Bridgeport NE	69336	308-262-0860	308-262-0352
Nance County	P.O. Box 309	Fullerton NE	68638	308-536-2331	308-536-2453
Nemaha County	1824 N. St	Auburn NE	68305	402-274-4213	402-274-4605
Nuckolls County	P.O. Box 366	Nelson NE	68961	402-225-4361	402-225-3014
Otoe County	P.O. Box 249	Nebraska City NE	68410	402-873-3586	402-873-3340
Pawnee County	P.O. Box 431	Pawnee City NE	68420	402-852-2962	402-852-2963
Perkins County	P.O. Box 156	Grant NE	69140	308-352-4643	308-352-2455
Phelps County	P.O. Box 404	Holdrege NE	68949	308-995-4469	308-995-6412
Pierce County	111 W. Court St., Rm 1	Pierce NE	68767	402-329-4225	402-329-6412
Platt County	2610 14th St	Columbus NE	68601	402-563-4904	402-563-4900
Polk County	P.O. Box 276	Osceola NE	68651	402-747-5431	402-747-5981
Red-Willow County	500 Norris Ave	McCook NE	69001	308-345-1552	308-345-1503
Richardson County	1700 Stone St	Falls City NE	68355	402-245-2911	402-245-3327
Rock County	P.O. Box 367	Bassett NE	68714	402-684-3933	402-684-2741
Saline County	P.O. Box 865	Wilber NE	68465	402-821-2374	402-821-3381
Sarpy County	1210 Golden Gate Dr	Papillion NE	68046	402-593-2106	402-593-4360
Saunders County	P.O. Box 61	Wahoo NE	68066	402-443-8101	402-443-5010
Scotts Bluff County	1825 10th St	Gering NE	69341	308-436-6600	308-436-3178
Seward County	P.O. Box 190	Seward NE	68434	402-643-2883	402-643-4614
Sheridan County	P.O. Box 39	Rushville NE	69360	308-327-2633	308-327-2712
Sherman County	P.O. Box 456	Loup City NE	68853	308-745-1513	308-745-1820

County	Address	City, State	Zip Code	Phone	Fax
NEBRASKA *continued*					
Sioux County	P.O. Box 158	Harrison NE	69346	308-668-2443	308-668-2443
Stanton County	P.O. Box 347	Stanton NE	68779	402-439-2222	402-439-2229
Thayer County	P.O. Box 208	Hebron NE	68370	402-768-6126	402-768-7232
Thomas County	P.O. Box 226	Thedford NE	69166	308-645-2261	308-645-2623
Thurston County	P.O. Box G.	Pender NE	68047	402-385-2343	402-385-2762
Valley County	125 S. 15th St	Ord NE	68862	308-728-3700	308-728-5320
Washington County	P.O. Box 466	Blair NE	68008	402-426-6822	402-426-6825
Wayne County	P.O. Box 248	Wayne NE	68787	402-375-2288	402-375-3702
Webster County	621 N. Cedar St	Red Cloud NE	68970	402-746-2716	402-746-2710
Wheeler County	P.O. Box 127	Bartlett NE	68622	308-654-3235	308-654-3442
York County	510 Lincoln Ave	York NE	68467	402-362-7759	402-362-2651
NEVADA					
Carson City	198 N. Carson St	Carson City NV	89701	702-887-2082	No Fax
Churchill County	10 W. Williams Ave, Ste A.	Fallon NV	89406	702-423-6028	702-423-7069
Clark County	200 S. 3rd St	Las Vegas NV	89155	702-455-3156	No Fax
Douglas County	P.O. Box 218	Minden NV	89423	702-782-9020	702-782-9016
Elko County	571 Idaho St., 3rd Fl	Elko NV	89801	702-738-3044	702-753-3044
Esmeralda County	P.O. Box 547	Goldfield NV	89013	702-485-6367	702-485-6376
Eureka County	P.O. Box 677	Eureka NV	89316	702-237-5262	702-237-5707
Humboldt County	Courthouse, Room 207	Winnemucca NV	89445	702-623-6343	702-623-6302
Lander County	315 S. Humboldt	Battle Mountain NV	89820	702-635-5738	702-635-5761
Lincoln County	P.O. Box 90	Pioche NV	89043	702-962-5390	702-962-5180
Lyon County	P.O. Box 816	Yerington NV	89447	702-463-6501	No Fax
Mineral County	P.O. Box 1450	Hawthorne NV	89415	702-945-2446	702-945-0706
Nye County	P.O. Box 1031	Tonopah NV	89049	702-482-8134	702-482-8133
Pershing County	P.O. Box 820	Lovelock NV	89419	702-273-2208	702-273-7058
Storey County	P.O. Box D.	Virginia City NV	89440	702-847-0969	702-847-0949
Washoe County	P.O. Box 11130	Reno NV	89520	702-328-3260	702-328-3582
White Pine County	P.O. Box 659	Ely NV	89301	702-289-2341	702-289-2544
NEW HAMPSHIRE					
Belknap County	64 Court St	Laconia NH	03246	603-524-3579	603-524-1748
Carroll County	P.O. Box 152	Ossipee NH	03864	603-539-2428	603-539-4287
Cheshire County	12 Court St..	Keene NH	03431	603-352-6902	No Fax
Coos County	P.O. Box 309	Lancaster NH	03584	603-788-4900	603-788-2223
Grafton County	R.R. #1 Box 67	North Heveihill NH	03774	603-787-6941	No Fax
Hillsborough County	300 Chestnut St	Manchester NH	03101	603-669-7410	No Fax
Merrimack County	163 N. Main St	Concord NH	03301	603-228-0331	603-244-2665
Rockingham County	119 North Rd	Brentwood NH	03833	603-679-2256	603-679-2514

County	Address	City, State Zip Code	Phone	Fax
NEW HAMPSHIRE *continued*				
Strafford County	P.O. Box 799	Dover NH 03821	603-742-1458	603-743-4407
Sullivan County	14 Main St.	Newport NH 03773	603-863-2560	603-863-9314
NEW JERSEY				
Atlantic County	1201 Backarach Blvd	Atlantic City NJ 08401	609-345-6700	609-343-2326
Bergen County	10 Main St, Rm 118	Hackensack NJ 07601	201-646-2101	201-646-0267
Burlington County	County Office Bldg	Mount Holly NJ 08060	609-265-5020	609-265-5022
Camden County	101 5th & Mickel Blvd.	Camden NJ 08103	609-225-7300	609-225-7100
Cape May County	7 N. Main	Cape May Court House NJ 08210	609-465-1010	609-465-6189
Cumberland County	790 E. Commerce St.	Bridgeton NJ 08302	609-453-2138	609-451-8243
Essex County	465 Dr. M.L. King Jr. Blvd	Newark NJ 07102	201-621-4925	201-621-5915
Gloucester County	P.O. Box 337	Woodbury NJ 08096	609-853-3275	609-853-3308
Hudson County	595 Newark Ave	Jersey City NJ 07306	201-795-6000	No Fax
Hunterdon County	71 Main St.	Flemington NJ 08822	908-788-1221	908-782-4068
Mercer County	P.O. Box 8068	Trenton NJ 08650	609-989-6502	609-695-5124
Middlesex County	Admin Bldg	New Brunswick NJ 08903	908-745-3040	908-745-4199
Monmouth County	Main St	Freehold NJ 07728	908-431-7324	908-409-7566
Morris County	P.O. Box 900	Morristown NJ 07960	201-285-6040	201-285-5266
Ocean County	P.O. Box 2191	Toms River NJ 08754	908-929-2128	908-349-4336
Passaic County	401 Grand St.	Paterson NJ 07505	201-881-4405	201-881-2853
Salem County	92 Market St.	Salem NJ 08079	609-935-7510	609-935-9102
Somerset County	P.O. Box 3000	Somerville NJ 08876	908-231-7040	908-231-1740
Sussex County	4 Park Place	Newton NJ 07860	201-579-0250	201-383-7493
Union County	Admin Bldg.	Elizabeth NJ 07207	908-527-4200	908-289-0180
Warren County	413 2nd St.	Belvidere NJ 07823	908-475-6211	No Fax
NEW MEXICO				
Bernalillo County	P.O. Box 542	Albuquerque NM 87103	505-768-4090	505-768-4631
Catron County	P.O. Box 197	Reserve NM 87830	505-533-6400	505-533-6400
Chaves County	P.O. Box 580	Roswell NM 88201	505-624-6614	505-624-6523
Cibola County	P.O. Box 758	Grants NM 87020	505-287-8831	505-285-5755
Colfax County	P.O. Box 159	Raton NM 87740	505-445-5551	505-445-4031
Curry County	P.O. Box 1168	Clovis NM 88102	505-763-5591	505-763-4232
De Baca County	P.O. Box 347	Fort Sumner NM 88119	505-355-2601	505-355-2441
Dona Ana County	251 W. Amador Ave	Las Cruces NM 88005	505-525-6659	505-647-7464
Eddy County	P.O. Box 850	Carlsbad NM 88221	505-885-3383	505-887-1039
Grant County	P.O. Box 898	Silver City NM 88062	505-538-2979	505-538-8926
Guadalupe County	420 Parker Ave	Santa Rosa NM 88435	505-472-3791	505-472-3735
Harding County	P.O. Box 1002	Mosquero NM 87733	505-673-2301	505-673-2922
Hidalgo County	300 S. Shakespeare St	Lordsburg NM 88045	505-542-9213	505-542-3414

County	Address	City, State	Zip Code	Phone	Fax

NEW MEXICO *continued*

County	Address	City, State	Zip Code	Phone	Fax
Lea County	P.O. Box 1507	Lovington NM	88260	505-396-8521	505-396-5684
Lincoln County	P.O. Box 338	Carrizozo NM	88301	505-648-2394	505-648-2576
Los Alamos County	P.O. Box 30	Los Alamos NM	87544	505-662-8010	505-662-8008
Luna County	P.O. Box 1838	Deming NM	88031	505-546-0491	505-546-4708
McKinley County	P.O. Box 1268	Gallup NM	87305	505-863-6866	505-863-1419
Mora County	P.O. Box 360	Mora NM	87732	505-387-2448	505-387-9022
Otero County	1000 New York Ave	Alamogordo NM	88310	505-437-4942	505-434-2509
Quay County	P.O. Box 1225	Tucumcari NM	88401	505-461-0510	505-461-0513
Rio Arriba County	P.O. Box 158	Tierra Amarilla NM	87575	505-588-7724	505-588-7418
Roosevelt County	County Courthouse	Portales NM	88130	505-356-8562	505-356-3560
San Juan County	P.O. Box 550	Aztec NM	87410	505-334-9471	505-334-3635
San Miguel County	County Courthouse	Las Vegas NM	87701	505-425-9331	505-425-7019
Sandoval County	P.O. Box 40	Bernalillo NM	87004	505-867-7572	505-867-7600
Santa Fe County	P.O. Box 1985	Santa Fe NM	87504	505-986-6286	505-986-6206
Sierra County	311 Date St	Truth or Consequences NM	87901	505-894-2840	505-894-2516
Socorro County	P.O. Box I	Socorro NM	87801	505-835-3263	505-835-1043
Taos County	105 Albright St., Suite D	Taos NM	87571	505-758-8836	505-751-3391
Torrance County	P.O. Box 48	Estancia NM	87016	505-384-2221	505-384-5294
Union County	P.O. Box 430	Clayton NM	88415	505-374-9491	505-374-2763
Valencia County	P.O. Box 969	Los Lunas NM	87031	505-866-2073	505-866-2002

NEW YORK

County	Address	City, State	Zip Code	Phone	Fax
Albany County	Courthouse	Albany NY	12207	518-487-5100	518-487-5099
Allegany County	7 Court St	Belmont NY	14813	716-268-7270	716-268-9659
Bronx County	851 Grand Concourse	Bronx NY	10451	718-590-3646	718-590-8122
Broome County	44 Hawley St.	Binghamton NY	13902	607-778-2451	607-778-2243
Cattaraugus County	303 Court St	Little Valley NY	14755	716-938-9111	716-938-6009
Cayuga County	160 Genesee St	Auburn NY	13021	315-253-1271	315-253-1006
Chautauqua County	P.O. 170	Mayville NY	14757	716-753-4331	716-753-4310
Chemung County	210 Lake St.	Elmirea NY	14901	607-737-2920	607-737-2897
Chenango County	5 Court St	Norwich NY	13815	607-337-1430	607-336-6551
Clinton County	137 Margaret St	Plattsburgh NY	12901	518-565-4700	518-565-4680
Columbia County	401 Union St.	Hudson NY	12534	518-828-3339	518-822-1110
Cortland County	P.O. Box 5590	Cortland NY	13045	607-753-5052	607-753-5392
Delaware County	P.O. Box 426	Delhi NY	13753	607-746-2123	No Fax
Dutchess County	22 Market St.	Poughkeepsie NY	12601	914-486-2120	914-486-1876
Erie County	25 Delaware Ave.	Buffalo NY	14202	716-858-8865	716-858-6550
Essex County	P.O. Box 247	Elizabethtown NY	12932	518-873-3600	518-873-3548
Franklin County	63 W. Main St.	Malone NY	12953	518-483-6767	518-483-9143
Fulton County	P.O. Box 485	Johnstone NY	12095	518-762-0555	518-762-3839

County	Address	City, State	Zip Code	Phone	Fax

NEW YORK *continued*

County	Address	City, State	Zip Code	Phone	Fax
Genessee County	P.O. Box 379	Batavia NY	14021	716-344-2550	716-334-8521
Greene County	P.O. Box 446	Catskill NY	12414	518-943-2050	518-943-2146
Hamilton County	P.O. Box 104	Lake Pleasant NY	12108	518-548-7111	No Fax
Herkimer County	P.O. Box 111	Herkimer NY	13350	315-867-1209	315-866-1802
Jefferson County	175 Arsenal St	Watertown NY	13601	315-785-3081	No Fax
Kings County	360 Adams St	Brooklyn NY	11201	718-643-7037	718-643-8187
Lewis County	P.O. Box 232	Lowville NY	13367	315-376-5333	315-376-3768
Livingston County	#6 Court St	Geneseo NY	14454	716-243-7010	No Fax
Madison County	P.O. Box 668	Wampsville NY	13163	315-366-2269	315-366-2302
Monroe County	39 W. Main St.	Rochester NY	14614	716-428-5151	No Fax
Montgomery County	P.O. Box 1500	Fonda NY	12068	518-853-3431	518-853-8220
Nassau County	240 Old County Rd	Mineola NY	11501	516-571-2661	516-742-4099
New York County	60 Centre St	New York NY	10007	212-374-8359	No Fax
Niagara County	175 Hawley St.	Lockport NY	14094	716-439-7022	716-439-7066
Oneida County	800 Park Ave	Utica NY	13501	315-798-5790	315-798-6440
Onondaga County	401 Montgomery St., Rm. 200	Syracuse NY	13202	315-435-2226	315-435-3455
Ontario County	25 Pleasant St.	Canandaigua NY	14424	716-396-4200	716-396-4245
Orange County	255-275 Main St	Goshen NY	10924	914-294-5151	914-294-3171
Orleans County	3 S. Main St	Albion NY	14411	716-589-5334	No Fax
Oswego County	46 E. Bridge St	Oswego NY	13126	315-349-8385	315-349-8383
Otaego County	197 Main St.	Cooperstown NY	13326	607-547-4275	No Fax
Putnam County	40 Gleneida Ave	Carmel NY	10512	914-225-3641	914-228-0231
Queens County	88-11 Sutphin Blvd	Jamaica NY	11435	718-520-3136	718-520-4731
Rensselaer County	Courthouse	Troy NY	12180	518-270-4080	518-271-7998
Richmond County	18 Richmond Terrace	Staten Island NY	10301	718-390-5393	718-390-5269
Rockland County	27 New Hempstead Rd.	New City NY	10956	914-638-5072	914-638-5647
Saint Lawrence County	48 Court St	Canton NY	13617	315-379-2237	315-379-2302
Saratoga County	40 McMasters St.	Ballston Spa NY	12020	518-885-2213	518-884-4726
Schenectady County	620 State St	Schenectady NY	12305	518-388-4222	518-388-4224
Schoharie County	P.O. Box 549	Schoharie NY	12157	518-295-8316	518-295-8338
Schuyler County	105 9th St	Watkins Glen NY	14891	607-535-8133	607-535-8109
Seneca County	1 DiPronio Dr	Waterloo NY	13165	315-539-5655	315-539-9479
Steuben County	3 Pulteney Sq	Bath NY	14810	607-776-9631	607-776-9631
Suffolk County	310 Center Dr.	Riverhead NY	11901	516-852-1400	516-852-2004
Sullivan County	County Office Bldg	Monticello NY	12701	914-794-3000	914-794-3459
Tioga County	P.O. Box 307	Owego NY	13827	607-687-8660	607-687-4612
Tompkins County	320 N. Tioga St.	Ithaca NY	14850	607-274-5431	607-274-5429
Ulster County	P.O. Box 1800	Kingston NY	12402	914-340-3288	914-340-3299
Warren County	Municiple Bldg., Rt. 9	Lake George NY	12845	518-761-6429	518-761-6551
Washington County	383 Upper Broadway	Fort Edward NY	12828	518-746-2170	518-746-2166

County	Address	City, State	Zip Code	Phone	Fax
NEW YORK *continued*					
Wayne County	P.O. Box 608	Lyons NY	14489	315-946-5870	518-946-5978
Westchester County	110 Grove St	White Plains NY	10601	914-285-3080	No Fax
Wyoming County	P.O. Box 70	Warsaw NY	14569	716-786-8810	716-786-3703
Yates County	110 Court St	Penn Yan NY	14527	315-536-5120	315-536-5545
NORTH CAROLINA					
Alamance County	124 W. Elm St.	Graham NC	27253	910-228-1312	910-227-0439
Alexander County	255 Liledon Rd	Taylorsville NC	28681	704-632-9332	704-632-0059
Alleghany County	P.O. Box 366	Sparta NC	28675	910-372-4179	910-372-5969
Anson County	Courthouse Rm 30	Wadesboro NC	28170	704-694-2796	704-694-7015
Ashe County	P.O. Box 633	Jefferson NC	28640	910-246-8841	910-246-8427
Avery County	P.O. Box 115	Newland NC	28657	704-733-2910	704-733-8410
Beaufort County	P.O. Box 1027	Washington NC	27889	919-946-0079	919-946-7722
Bertie County	P.O. Box 530	Windsor NC	27983	919-794-5300	919-794-5327
Bladen County	166 Courthouse Sq	Elizabethtown NC	28337	910-862-6700	910-862-6767
Brunswick County	P.O. Box 249	Bolivia NC	28422	910-253-2000	910-253-2022
Buncombe County	1 Oak Plaza	Asheville NC	28801	704-255-5650	704-255-5461
Burke County	201 Southgrade St	Morganton NC	28655	704-432-2811	No Fax
Cabarrus County	65 Church St. S.E.	Concord NC	28025	704-788-8100	704-788-8146
Caldwell County	P.O. Box 2200	Lenoir NC	28645	704-757-1300	704-757-1295
Camden County	P.O. Box 190	Camden NC	27921	919-338-1919	704-333-1603
Carteret County	Courthouse Sq	Beaufort NC	28516	919-728-8450	910-728-2092
Caswell County	P.O. Box 98, Courthouse	Yanceyville NC	27379	910-694-4193	910-694-1405
Catawba County	P.O. Box 389	Newton NC	28658	704-465-8201	704-465-8392
Chatham County	P.O. Box 368	Pittsboro NC	27312	919-542-3240	919-542-1402
Cherokee County	201 Peachtree St.	Murphy NC	28906	704-837-5527	No Fax
Chowan County	P.O. Box 1030	Edenton NC	27932	919-482-8431	919-482-4925
Clay County	P.O. Box 118	Hayesville NC	28904	704-389-6301	704-389-9749
Cleveland County	P.O. Box 1210	Shelby NC	28151	704-484-4800	704-484-4935
Columbus County	Administration Bldg.	Whiteville NC	28472	910-642-5700	910-642-2386
Craven County	406 Craven St	New Bern NC	28560	919-636-6600	919-636-6638
Cumberland County	P.O. Box 1829	Fayetteville NC	28302	910-678-7723	910-678-7717
Currituck County	P.O. Box 39	Currituck NC	27929	919-232-2075	919-232-3551
Dare County	P.O. Box 1849	Manteo NC	27954	919-473-2950	919-473-1620
Davidson County	P.O. Box 1067	Lexington NC	27293	704-242-2200	704-246-8440
Davie County	123 S. Main St	Mocksville NC	27028	704-634-5513	704-634-7408
Duplin County	P.O. Box 910	Kenansville NC	28349	910-296-2100	910-296-2107
Durham County	200 E. Main St	Durham NC	27701	919-560-0000	919-560-0020
Edgecombe County	P.O. Box 10	Tarboro NC	27886	919-641-7833	919-641-0456
Forsyth County	700 Hall of Justice	Winston Salem NC	27101	910-727-2797	910-727-8446

County	Address	City, State Zip Code	Phone	Fax

NORTH CAROLINA *continued*

County	Address	City, State Zip Code	Phone	Fax
Franklin County	P.O. Box 529	Louisburg NC 27549	919-496-5994	919-496-2683
Gaston County	P.O. Box 1578	Gastonia NC 28053	704-866-3100	704-866-3147
Gates County	P.O. Box 141	Gatesvile NC 27938	919-357-1240	919-357-0073
Graham County	P.O. Box 1179	Robbinsville NC 28771	704-479-7961	704-479-6417
Granville County	P.O. Box 906	Oxford NC 27565	919-693-5286	919-690-1766
Greene County	229 Kingold Blvd	Snow Hill NC 28580	919-747-3446	919-747-3884
Guilford County	301 W. Market St	Greensboro NC 27401	910-373-3383	910-333-6833
Halifax County	P.O. Box 38	Halifax NC 27839	919-583-1131	919-583-9921
Harnett County	P.O. Box 759	Lillington NC 27546	910-893-7555	910-893-4992
Haywood County	215 N. Main St	Waynesville NC 28786	704-452-6625	704-452-6725
Henderson County	100 N. King St	Hendersonville NC 28792	704-697-4809	704-692-9855
Hertford County	P.O. Box 116	Winton NC 27986	919-358-7805	919-358-7806
Hoke County	P.O. Drawer 266	Raeford NC 28376	910-875-8751	910-875-9222
Hyde County	P.O. Box 188	Swanquarter NC 27885	919-926-5711	919-926-1286
Iredell County	P.O. Box 788	Statesville NC 28687	704-878-3050	704-878-3032
Jackson County	401 Grindstaff Cove Rd	Sylva NC 28779	704-586-4055	704-586-9009
Johnston County	P.O. Box 1049	Smithfield NC 27577	919-989-5100	919-989-5100
Jones County	266 Courthouse	Trenton NC 28585	919-448-7571	919-448-1072
Lee County	106 Hillcrest Dr	Sanford NC 27331	919-774-8403	919-774-8407
Lenoir County	3289 Courthouse	Kinston NC 28501	919-523-7659	919-527-3656
Lincoln County	115 W. Main	Lincolnton NC 28092	704-736-8471	704-735-0273
Macon County	5 W. Main St	Franklin NC 28734	704-349-2000	704-524-9522
Madison County	Courthouse, P.O. Box 217	Marshall NC 28753	704-649-2531	704-649-2829
Martin County	P.O. Box 668	Williamston NC 27892	919-792-1901	919-792-7477
McDowell County	1 S. Main St	Marion NC 28752	704-652-7121	No Fax
Macklenburg County	600 E. 4th St	Charlotte NC 28231	704-336-2472	704-336-5887
Mitchell County	Administration Bldg.	Bakersville NC 28705	704-688-2139	704-688-3666
Montgomery County	P.O. Box 425	Troy NC 27371	910-576-4221	910-576-2209
Moore County	Old Courthouse	Carthage NC 28327	910-947-6363	910-947-1874
Nash County	Rm. 104, Nash Courthouse	Nashville NC 27856	919-459-9801	919-459-9817
New Hanover County	320 Chestnut	Wilmington NC 28401	910-341-7184	910-341-4027
Northampton County	P.O. Box 808	Jackson NC 27845	919-534-2501	919-534-1166
Onslow County	521 Mill Ave	Jacksonville NC 28540	910-347-4717	910-455-7878
Orange County	200 S. Cameron St	Hillsborough NC 27278	919-732-8181	919-644-3004
Pamlico County	P.O. Box 776	Bayboro NC 28515	919-745-3133	919-745-5514
Pasquotank County	P.O. Box 39	Elizabeth City NC 27907	919-335-0865	919-335-0866
Pender County	P.O. Box 5	Burgaw NC 28425	910-259-1200	910-259-1402
Perquimans County	P.O. Box 45	Hertford NC 27944	919-426-8484	919-426-4034
Person County	304 Morgan St., Rm. 212	Roxboro NC 27573	910-597-5120	910-599-1609
Pitt County	1717 W 5th St	Greenville NC 27834	919-830-6302	919-830-6311

County	Address	City, State	Zip Code	Phone	Fax
NORTH CAROLINA *continued*					
Polk County	P.O. Box 308	Columbus NC	28722	704-894-3301	704-894-2263
Randolph County	P.O. Box 4728	Asheboro NC	27204	910-318-6300	910-318-6853
Richmond County	P.O. Box 504	Rockingham NC	28380	910-997-8211	910-997-8208
Robeson County	Administration Bldg.	Lumberton NC	28358	910-671-3022	910-671-3010
Rockingham County	P.O. Box 206	Reidsville NC	27320	910-342-8101	910-342-8105
Rowan County	130 W. Innes St	Salisbury NC	28144	704-636-0361	704-638-3092
Rutherford County	601 N. Main St	Rutherfordton NC	28139	704-287-6060	704-287-6262
Sampson County	435 Rowen Rd	Clinton NC	28328	910-592-6308	910-592-1945
Scotland County	P.O. Box 489	Laurinburg NC	28353	910-277-2406	910-277-2411
Stanley County	201 S. 2nd St.	Albemarle NC	28001	704-983-7200	704-983-3133
Stokes County	Government Ctr	Danbury NC	27016	910-593-2811	910-593-2346
Surry County	P.O. Box 345	Dobson NC	27017	910-386-8131	910-386-9879
Swain County	P.O. Drawer A.	Bryson City NC	28713	704-488-9273	704-488-2754
Transylvania County	28 E .Main St	Brevard NC	28712	704-884-3100	704-877-3119
Tyrrell County	P.O. Box 406	Columbia NC	27925	919-796-6281	919-796-0008
Union County	P.O. Box 218	Monroe NC	28111	704-283-3810	704-282-0121
Vance County	122 Young St., Suite B	Henderson NC	27536	919-492-2141	919-492-5873
Wake County	P.O. Box 550	Raleigh NC	27602	919-856-6160	919-856-6168
Warren County	P.O. Box 619	Warrenton NC	27589	919-257-3115	919-257-5971
Washington County	P.O. Box 1007	Plymouth NC	27962	919-793-5823	919-793-9788
Watauga County	842 King St., Suite 1	Boone NC	28607	704-265-8000	704-265-8018
Wayne County	P.O. Box 227	Goldsboro NC	27533	919-731-1435	919-731-1446
Wilkes County	110 North St.	Wilkesboro NC	28697	910-651-7345	910-651-7546
Wilson County	P.O. Box 61008	Wilson NC	27893	919-291-7502	919-291-8635
Yadkin County	P.O. Box 146, Willow St.	Yadkinville NC	27055	910-679-4200	910-679-6005
Yancey County	County Courthouse	Burnsville NC	28714	704-682-3971	704-682-4301
NORTH DAKOTA					
Adams County	P.O. Box 589	Hettinger ND	58639	701-567-4363	701-567-2910
Barnes County	230 4th St. N.W., Rm 202	Valley City ND	58072	701-845-8500	701-845-8538
Benson County	P.O. Box 206	Minnewaukan ND	58351	701-473-5340	701-473-5571
Billings County	P.O. Box 168	Medora ND	58645	701-623-4377	701-623-4896
Bottineau County	314 W. 5th St	Bottineau ND	58318	701-228-2225	701-228-2336
Bowman County	P.O. Box 439	Bowman ND	58623	701-523-3130	701-523-5443
Burke County	P.O. Box 310	Bowbells ND	58721	701-377-2861	701-377-2020
Burleigh County	P.O. Box 5518	Bismarck ND	58506	701-222-6714	701-222-6717
Cass County	P.O. Box 2806	Fargo ND	58108	701-241-5600	701-241-5728
Cavalier County	P.O. Box 469	Langdon ND	58249	701-256-2229	701-256-2566
Dickey County	P.O. Box 215	Ellendale ND	58436	701-349-3249	701-349-4639
Divide County	P.O. Box 49	Crosby ND	58730	701-965-6351	701-965-6943

County	Address	City, State Zip Code	Phone	Fax

NORTH DAKOTA *continued*

County	Address	City, State Zip Code	Phone	Fax
Dunn County	P.O. Box 105	Manning ND 58642	701-573-4448	701-573-4311
Eddy County	524 Central Ave	New Rockford ND 58356	701-947-2434	701-947-2279
Emmons County	P.O. Box 128	Linton ND 58552	701-254-4807	701-254-4012
Foster County	P.O. Box 104	Carrington ND 58421	701-652-2441	701-652-2173
Golden Valley County	P.O. Box 67	Beach ND 58621	701-872-4331	701-872-4383
Grand Forks County	P.O. Box 5726	Grand Forks ND 58206	701-780-8200	701-780-8212
Grant County	P.O. Box 227	Carson ND 58529	701-622-3275	701-622-3717
Griggs County	P.O. Box 511	Cooperstown ND 58425	701-797-3117	701-797-3170
Hettinger County	P.O. Box 668	Mott ND 58646	701-824-2515	701-824-2717
Kidder County	P.O. Box 167	Steele ND 58482	701-475-2632	701-475-2202
La Moure County	P.O. Box 5	La Moure ND 58458	701-883-5301	701-883-5304
Logan County	301 Broadway	Napoleon ND 58561	701-754-2425	701-754-2270
McHenry County	P.O. Box 147	Towner ND 58788	701-537-5724	701-537-5969
McIntosh County	P.O. Box D.	Ashley ND 58413	701-288-3347	701-288-3671
McKenzie County	P.O. Box 543	Watford City ND 58854	701-842-3616	701-842-4113
McLean County	P.O. Box D.	Washburn ND 58577	701-462-8541	701-462-3441
Mercer County	P.O. Box 39	Stanton ND 58571	701-745-3292	701-745-3364
Morton County	210 2nd Ave. NW	Mandan ND 58554	701-667-3300	701-667-3296
Mountrall County	P.O. Box 69	Stanley ND 58784	701-628-2145	701-628-3975
Nelson County	P.O. Box 585	Lakota ND 58344	701-247-2463	701-247-2412
Oliver County	P.O. Box 188	Center ND 58530	701-794-8721	701-794-3476
Pembina County	301 Dakota St. W. #1	Cavalier ND 58220	701-265-4231	701-265-4876
Pierce County	240 2nd St. S.E	Rugby ND 58368	701-776-5225	701-776-5707
Ramsey County	524 4th Ave	Devils Lake ND 58301	701-662-7007	701-662-7049
Ransom County	P.O. Box 668	Lisbon ND 58054	701-683-5823	701-683-5827
Renville County	P.O. Box 68	Mohall ND 58761	701-756-6301	701-756-7158
Richland County	418 2nd Ave. N	Wahpeton ND 58075	701-642-7700	701-642-7701
Rolette County	P.O. Box 939	Rolla ND 58367	701-477-5665	701-477-3484
Sargent County	P.O. Box 177	Forman ND 58032	701-724-6241	701-724-6244
Sheridan County	P.O. Box 636	McClusky ND 58463	701-363-2205	701-363-2953
Sioux County	P.O. Box L	Fort Yates ND 58538	701-854-3481	701-854-3854
Slope County	P.O. Box NN	Amidon ND 58620	701-879-6276	701-879-6278
Stark County	P.O. Box 130	Dickinson ND 58602	701-264-7630	701-264-7628
Steele County	P.O. Box 275	Finley ND 58230	701-524-2110	701-524-1715
Stutsman County	511 2nd Ave. SE	Jamestown ND 58401	701-252-9035	701-251-1603
Towner County	P.O. Box 603	Cando ND 58324	701-968-4340	701-968-4342
Traill County	P.O. Box 429	Hillsboro ND 58045	701-436-4458	701-436-4308
Walsh County	600 Cooper Ave	Grafton ND 58237	701-352-2851	701-352-1104
Ward County	315 3rd St. S.E	Minot ND 58701	701-857-6420	701-857-6520
Wells County	P.O. Box 37	Fessenden ND 58438	701-547-3521	701-547-3719

County	Address	City, State	Zip Code	Phone	Fax
NORTH DAKOTA *continued*					
Williams County	P.O. Box 2047	Williston ND	58801	701-572-1700	701-572-1763
OHIO					
Adams County	110 W. Main St	West Union OH	45693	513-544-2344	513-544-8911
Allen County	301 N. Main St	Lima OH	45801	419-228-3700	419-222-8427
Ashland County	110 Cottage St	Ashland OH	44805	419-289-0000	No Fax
Ashtabula County	25 W. Jefferson St	Jefferson OH	44047	216-576-9090	216-576-2344
Athens County	P.O. Box 290	Athens OH	45701	614-592-3242	614-592-3282
Auglaize County	201 Willipie St., Ste. G-11	Wapakoneta OH	45895	419-738-3612	419-738-4713
Belmont County	100 W. Main St	Saint Clairsville OH	43950	614-695-2121	
Brown County	800 Mt Otab Pike	Georgetown OH	45121	513-378-3956	513-378-6324
Butler County	130 High St	Hamilton OH	45011	513-887-3000	513-887-3568
Carroll County	119 Public Sq	Carrollton OH	44615	216-627-2250	216-627-7555
Champaign County	200 N. Main	Urbana OH	43078	513-653-2701	513-653-7696
Clark County	101 N. Limestone St	Springfield OH	45502	513-328-2458	513-328-2436
Clermont County	101 E. Main St	Batavia OH	45103	513-732-7300	513-732-7826
Clinton County	46 S. South St	Wilmington OH	45177	513-382-2103	513-383-2884
Columbiana County	105 S. Market St	Lisbon OH	44432	303-424-9511	330-424-3960
Coshocton County	349 1/2 Main St	Coshocton OH	43812	614-622-1753	614-622-4917
Crawford County	112 E. Mansfield St	Bucyrus OH	44820	419-562-5876	419-562-3171
Cuyahoga County	1200 Ontario St	Cleveland OH	44113	216-443-7950	No Fax
Darke County	504 S. Broadway	Greenville OH	45331	513-547-7370	513-547-7323
Defiance County	500 Court St	Defiance OH	43512	419-782-4761	419-782-8449
Delaware County	91 N. Sandusky St	Delaware OH	43015	614-368-1850	614-368-1849
Erie County	323 Columbus Ave	Sandusky OH	44870	419-627-7705	419-624-6873
Fairfield County	224 E. Main St	Lancaster OH	43130	614-687-7030	614-687-0158
Fayette County	110 E. Court	Washington CrtHse OH	43160	614-335-0720	614-333-3530
Franklin County	373 S. High St	Columbus OH	43215	614-462-3322	614-462-5999
Fulton County	125 Courthouse Plaza	Wauseon OH	43567	419-337-9255	419-337-9285
Gallia County	18 Locust St	Gallipolis OH	45631	614-446-4374	614-446-4804
Geauga County	100 Short Court	Chardon OH	44024	216-285-2222	No Fax
Greene County	45 N. Detroit St	Xenia OH	45385	513-376-5290	513-376-5309
Guernsey County	128 E. 8th St #101	Cambridge OH	43725	614-432-9200	614-432-9359
Hamilton County	138 E. Court St	Cincinnati OH	45202	513-632-8222	513-632-5797
Hancock County	300 S. Main St	Findlay OH	45840	419-424-7037	No Fax
Hardin County	1 Courthouse Sq #100	Kenton OH	43326	419-674-2205	419-674-2272
Harrison County	100 W. Market St	Cadiz OH	43907	614-942-8861	614-942-4693
Henry County	P.O. Box 546	Napoleon OH	43545	419-592-4876	419-592-4016
Highland County	114 Governor Foraker	Hillsboro OH	45133	513-393-1911	513-393-5850
Hocking County	1 E. Main St	Logan OH	43138	614-385-5195	614-385-1105

County	Address	City, State Zip Code	Phone	Fax

OHIO *continued*

County	Address	City, State Zip Code	Phone	Fax
Holmes County	34D S. Clay	Millersburg OH 44654	216-674-0286	330-674-0566
Huron County	2 E. Main St	Norwalk OH 44857	419-668-5113	419-663-4048
Jackson County	226 Main St.	Jackson OH 45640	614-286-3301	614-286-4061
Jefferson County	301 Market St.	Steubenville OH 43952	614-283-8500	614-283-8599
Knox County	110 E. High St	Mount Vernon OH 43050	614-393-6703	614-393-6806
Lake County	P.O. Box 490	Painesville OH 44077	216-350-2500	No Fax
Lawrence County	P.O. Box 208	Ironton OH 45638	614-533-4353	No Fax
Licking County	20 S. 2nd St.	Newark OH 43055	614-349-6000	614-349-6179
Logan County	101 S Main, 2nd Fl, #12	Bellefontaine OH 43311	513-599-7258	No Fax
Lorain County	P.O. Box 749	Elyria OH 44036	216-329-5536	216-329-5404
Lucas County	700 Adams St	Toledo OH 43604	419-245-4484	419-245-4487
Madison County	County Courthouse	London OH 43140	614-852-2972	614-852-7144
Mahoning County	120 Market St.	Youngstown OH 44503	216-740-2104	No Fax
Marion County	100 N. Main St	Marion OH 43302	614-387-5871	614-383-1190
Medina County	93 Public Sq	Medina OH 44256	216-725-9722	No Fax
Meigs County	100 E. 2nd St	Pomeroy OH 45769	614-992-2895	614-992-2270
Mercer County	101 N .Main St #107	Celina OH 45822	419-586-3178	419-586-1714
Miami County	201 W. Main St.	Troy OH 45373	513-332-6800	513-339-9882
Monroe County	101 N. Main St	Woodsfield OH 43793	614-472-5181	No Fax
Montgomery County	41 N. Perry St #104	Dayton OH 45422	513-225-4512	513-796-7220
Morgan County	19 E. Main St	McConnelsville OH 43756	614-962-4752	614-962-4589
Morrow County	48 E. High St	Mount Gilead OH 43338	419-947-4085	419-947-1860
Muskingum County	P.O. Box 268	Zanesville OH 43702	614-455-7104	No Fax
Noble County	County Courthouse, Rm. 210	Caldwell OH 43724	614-732-2969	614-732-5702
Ottawa County	315 Madison St #103	Port Clinton OH 43452	419-734-6710	419-734-6898
Paulding County	115 N. Williams St	Paulding OH 45879	419-399-8210	419-399-8299
Perry County	121 W. Brown St.	New Lexington OH 43764	614-342-2045	614-342-5505
Pickaway County	207 S. Court St	Circleville OH 43113	614-474-6093	614-474-8988
Pike County	100 E. 2nd St	Waverly OH 45690	614-947-2715	614-947-5665
Portage County	449 S. Meridian St	Ravenna OH 44266	330-297-3600	330-297-3610
Preble County	100 Main St.	Eaton OH 45320	513-456-8160	513-456-9548
Putnam County	245 E. Main St	Ottawa OH 45875	419-523-3656	419-523-9213
Richland County	50 Park Ave E.	Mansfield OH 44902	419-774-5510	No Fax
Ross County	N. Paint St	Chillicothe OH 45601	614-773-5115	614-774-1602
Sandusky County	100 N. Park Ave	Fremont OH 43420	419-334-6100	419-334-6104
Scioto County	602 7th St	Portsmouth OH 45662	614-355-8210	614-354-2057
Seneca County	81 Jefferson St	Tiffin OH 44883	419-447-4550	419-447-0556
Shelby County	129 E. Court St., Suite 100	Sidney OH 45365	513-498-7226	513-498-1293
Stark County	115 Central Plaza N.	Canton OH 44702	330-438-0799	330-438-0852
Summit County	53 University Ave.	Akron OH 44308	216-643-2217	No Fax

County	Address	City, State		Zip Code	Phone	Fax
OHIO *continued*						
Trumbull County	160 High St. NW	Warren	OH	44481	330-615-2557	330-343-4682
Tuscarawas County	125 E. High	New Philadelphia	OH	44663	216-364-8811	No Fax
Union County	233 W. 6th St	Marysville	OH	43040	513-645-3012	513-645-3002
Van Wert County	121 E. Main St	Van Wert	OH	45891	419-238-6159	419-238-1022
Vinton County	100 E. Main St.	McArthur	OH	45651	614-596-4571	614-596-4702
Warren County	550 Justice Dr.	Lebanon	OH	45036	513-932-4040	513-933-2990
Washington County	205 Putnam St	Marietta	OH	45750	614-373-6623	614-373-2085
Wayne County	P.O. Box 507	Wooster	OH	44691	216-287-5590	No Fax
Williams County	County Courthouse Sq	Bryan	OH	43506	419-636-1551	419-636-7877
Wood County	P.O. Box 829	Bowling Green	OH	43402	419-354-9280	419-354-9241
Wyandot County	County Courthouse	Upper Sandusky	OH	43351	419-294-1432	No Fax
OKLAHOMA						
Adair County	P.O. Box 169	Stilwell	OK	74960	918-696-7198	918-696-2603
Alfalfa County	300 S. Grand Ave	Cherokee	OK	73728	405-596-2392	405-596-2254
Atoka County	200 E. Court St	Atoka	OK	74525	405-889-2643	405-889-3527
Beaver County	P.O. Box 56	Beaver	OK	73932	405-625-3151	405-625-3430
Beckham County	P.O. Box 67	Sayre	OK	73662	405-928-2457	405-928-2467
Blaine County	P.O. Box 138	Watonga	OK	73772	405-623-5890	No Fax
Bryan County	402 W. Evergreen	Durant	OK	74701	405-924-2201	405-924-3094
Caddo County	County Courthouse	Anadarko	OK	73005	405-247-3105	405-247-3611
Canadian County	201 N. Choctaw Ave	El Reno	OK	73036	405-262-1070	405-422-2429
Carter County	Arst & B S.W	Ardmore	OK	73401	405-223-8162	No Fax
Cherokee County	213 W. Delaware St	Tahlequah	OK	74464	918-456-3171	918-458-6586
Choctaw County	300 E. Duke	Hugo	OK	74743	405-326-5337	405-326-6787
Cimarrron County	P.O. Box 145	Boise City	OK	73933	405-544-2251	405-544-3420
Cleveland County	200 S. Peters	Norman	OK	73069	405-321-6402	No Fax
Coal County	4 N. Main St	Coalgate	OK	74538	405-927-3122	No Fax
Comanche County	315 S. W. 5th St	Lawton	OK	73501	405-355-5214	No Fax
Cotton County	301 N. Broadway St	Walters	OK	73572	405-875-3026	405-875-3756
Craig County	P.O. Box 397	Vinita	OK	74301	918-256-2507	918-256-3617
Creek County	222 E. Dewey Ave	Sapulpa	OK	74066	918-227-2525	918-227-5030
Custer County	P.O. Box 300	Arapaho	OK	73620	405-323-4420	405-323-4421
Delaware County	P.O. Box 309	Jay	OK	74346	918-253-4520	No Fax
Dewey County	P.O. Box 368	Taloga	OK	73667	405-328-5390	405-328-5559
Ellis County	P.O. Box 197	Arnett	OK	73832	405-885-7301	405-885-7258
Garfield County	County Courthouse	Enid	OK	73701	405-237-0227	405-249-5951
Garvin County	201 W. Grant	Pauls Valley	OK	73075	405-238-2772	405-238-6283
Grady County	P.O. Box 1009	Chickasha	OK	73018	405-224-7388	405-222-4506
Grant County	112 E. Guthrie	Medford	OK	73759	405-395-2214	405-395-2603

County	Address	City, State	Zip Code	Phone	Fax

OKLAHOMA *continued*

County	Address	City, State	Zip Code	Phone	Fax
Greer County	P.O. Box 207	Mangum OK	73554	405-782-2329	405-782-3803
Harmon County	County Courthouse	Hollis OK	73550	405-688-3658	405-688-9784
Harper County	P.O. Box 3619	Buffalo OK	73834	405-735-2012	No Fax
Haskell County	202 E. Main St	Stigler OK	74462	918-967-2884	918-967-3290
Hughes County	200 N. Broadway, Suite 7	Holdenville OK	74848	405-379-2746	405-379-6739
Jackson County	P.O. Box 515	Altus OK	73522	405-482-4070	No Fax
Jefferson County	220 N. Main St	Waurika OK	73573	405-228-2241	405-228-3418
Johnston County	414 W. Main	Tishomingo OK	73460	405-371-3058	405-371-2174
Kay County	County Courthouse	Newkirk OK	74647	405-362-2537	405-362-3300
Kingfisher County	101 S. Main, Rm. 9	Kingfisher OK	73750	405-375-3808	405-375-6033
Kiowa County	P.O. Box 73	Hobart OK	73651	405-726-5286	405-726-6033
Latimer County	109 N. Central St	Wilburton OK	74578	918-465-2021	918-465-4001
Le Flore County	P.O. Box 607	Poteau OK	74953	918-647-2527	918-647-8930
Lincoln County	County Courthouse	Chandler OK	74834	405-258-1264	No Fax
Logan County	301 E. Harrison Ave	Guthrie OK	73044	405-282-2124	405-282-6090
Love County	County Courthouse	Marietta OK	73448	405-276-3059	405-276-3726
Major County	P.O. Box 379	Fairview OK	73737	405-227-4732	405-227-2736
Marshall County	County Courthouse	Madill OK	73446	405-795-3165	405-795-3165
Mayes County	P.O. Box 97	Pryor OK	74362	918-825-2426	918-825-2913
McClain County	County Courthouse	Purcell OK	73080	405-527-3360	No Fax
McCurtain County	P.O. Box 1078	Idabel OK	74745	405-286-2370	No Fax
McIntosh County	P.O. Box 110	Eufaula OK	74432	918-689-2362	918-689-2620
Murray County	P.O. Box 240	Sulphur OK	73086	405-622-3777	405-622-6209
Muskogee County	P.O. Box 1008	Muskogee OK	74401	918-682-7781	No Fax
Noble County	300 Courthouse Dr	Perry OK	73077	405-336-2771	405-336-3024
Nowata County	229 N. Maple St	Nowata OK	74048	918-273-0175	918-273-1936
Okfuskee County	P.O. Box 26	Okemah OK	74859	918-623-0939	918-623-0739
Oklahoma County	320 Robert S. Kerr	Oklahoma City OK	73102	405-236-2727	405-278-1850
Okmulgee County	300 W. 7th Ave	Okmulgee OK	74447	918-756-0788	918-758-1202
Osage County	County Courthouse	Pawhuska OK	74056	918-287-3136	No Fax
Ottawa County	County Courthouse	Miami OK	74354	918-542-9408	918-542-9408
Pawnee County	500 Harrison St	Pawnee OK	74058	918-762-3741	918-762-3714
Payne County	606 S. Husband, Rm. 101	Stillwater OK	74074	405-624-9300	405-624-9325
Pittsburg County	County Courthouse	McAlester OK	74501	918-423-6865	918-423-7321
Pontotoc County	P.O. Box 1425	Ada OK	74820	405-332-1425	405-436-5613
Pottawatomie County	Commision, 325 N. Broadway	Shawnee OK	74801	405-273-4305	405-273-6207
Pushmataha County	304 S.W. B St	Antlers OK	74523	405-298-2512	405-298-3626
Roger Mills County	P.O. Box 708	Cheyenne OK	73628	405-497-3365	405-497-3488
Rogers County	219 S. Missouri	Claremore OK	74017	918-341-2518	918-342-3646
Seminole County	P.O. Box 1180	Wewoka OK	74884	405-257-2501	405-257-6422

County	Address	City, State		Zip Code	Phone	Fax
OKLAHOMA *continued*						
Sequoyah County	120 E. Chickasaw Ave	Sallisaw	OK	74955	918-775-5539	918-775-5530
Stephens County	101 S. 11th St	Duncan	OK	73533	405-255-4193	405-255-1771
Texas County	319 N. Main St	Guymon	OK	73942	405-338-3233	405-338-4311
Tillman County	P.O. Box 992	Frederick	OK	73542	405-335-3421	405-335-3795
Tulsa County	500 S. Denver Ave	Tulsa	OK	74103	918-596-5000	918-587-4767
Wagoner County	307 E. Cherokee St.	Wagoner	OK	74467	918-485-2141	918-485-8677
Washington County	420 S. Johnston Ave	Bartlesville	OK	74003	918-337-2840	918-337-2894
Washita County	111 E. Main.	Cordell	OK	73632	405-832-2284	405-832-3526
Woods County	P.O. Box 386	Alva	OK	73717	405-327-2126	No Fax
Woodward County	1600 Main St.	Woodward	OK	73802	405-256-8097	405-254-6803
OREGON						
Baker County	1995 3rd St	Baker City	OR	97814	503-523-8207	503-523-8201
Benton County	120 N.W. 4th St	Corvallis	OR	97330	503-757-6756	503-757-6757
Clackamas County	906 Main St.	Oregon City	OR	97045	503-655-8698	503-655-8461
Clatsop County	749 Commercial	Astoria	OR	97103	503-325-8511	503-325-8606
Columbia County	County Courthouse	Saint Helens	OR	97051	503-397-3796	503-397-7266
Coos County	250 N. Baxter St.	Coquille	OR	97423	503-396-3121	503-396-4861
Crook County	300 E. 3rd St.	Prineville	OR	97754	503-447-6553	503-447-1051
Curry County	P.O. Box 746	Gold Beach	OR	97444	503-247-7011	503-247-2718
Deschutes County	1130 N.W. Harriman	Bend	OR	97701	503-388-6546	503-389-6830
Douglas County	1036 S.E. Douglas Ave	Roseburg	OR	97470	503-440-4323	No Fax
Gilliam County	221 S. Oregon	Condon	OR	97823	503-384-2311	503-384-2166
Grant County	200 S. Canyon Blvd	Canyon City	OR	97820	503-575-1675	503-575-2248
Harney County	450 N. Buena Vista	Burns	OR	97720	503-573-6641	503-573-8389
Hood River County	309 State St	Hood River	OR	97031	503-386-1442	503-386-9392
Jackson County	10 S. Oakdale Ave	Medford	OR	97501	503-776-7181	503-776-7028
Jefferson County	75 S.E. "C" St	Madras	OR	97741	503-475-4451	503-475-4454
Josephine County	N.W. 6th C	Grants Pass	OR	97526	503-474-5240	503-474-5246
Klamath County	500 Klamath Ave	Klamath Falls	OR	97601	503-883-5311	503-883-5399
Lake County	513 Center St	Lakeview	OR	97630	503-947-6006	503-947-6015
Lane County	125 E. 8th St.	Eugene	OR	97401	503-687-4234	503-465-2303
Lincoln County	225 W. Olive St., Rm 201	Newport	OR	97365	503-265-4131	503-265-4950
Linn County	300 4th Ave. S.W	Albany	OR	97321	503-967-3831	503-926-5109
Malheur County	251 "B" St. W	Vale	OR	97918	503-473-5151	503-473-5136
Marion County	100 High St. N.E	Salem	OR	97301	503-588-5225	503-373-4408
Morrow County	100 Court St	Heppner	OR	97836	503-676-9061	503-676-9876
Multnomah County	1021 S.W. 4th Ave	Portland	OR	97204	503-248-3511	503-248-3425
Polk County	850 Main St.	Dallas	OR	97338	503-623-9217	503-623-0717
Sherman County	500 Court St	Moro	OR	97039	503-565-3606	503-565-3312

County	Address	City, State	Zip Code	Phone	Fax
OREGON *continued*					
Tillamook County	201 Laurel Ave	Tillamook OR	97141	503-842-3402	503-842-2721
Umatilla County	216 S.E. 4th St	Pendleton OR	97801	503-276-7111	503-278-5463
Union County	1001 4th St., Suite D	La Grande OR	97850	503-963-1006	503-963-1039
Wallows County	101 S. River St	Enterprise OR	97828	503-426-4543	503-426-5901
Wasco County	511 Washington St	The Dalles OR	97058	503-296-6159	503-298-1002
Washington County	155 N. 1st Ave.	Hillsboro OR	97123	503-648-8670	503-693-4854
Wheeler County	701 Adams St	Fossil OR	97830	503-763-2400	503-763-2026
Yamhill County	535 E. 5th St	McMinnville OR	97128	503-434-7518	503-434-7520
PENNSYLVANIA					
Adams County	111 Baltimore St.	Gettysburg PA	17325	717-334-6781	717-334-2091
Allegheny County	Courthouse, Rm. 115	Pittsburg PA	15219	412-350-5323	412-350-7359
Armstrong County	500 E. Market St	Kittanning PA	16201	412-543-2500	No Fax
Beaver County	810 3rd St	Beaver PA	15009	412-728-5700	412-728-8853
Bedford County	230 S. Juliana St	Bedford PA	15522	814-623-4807	814-623-0991
Berks County	633 Court St	Reading PA	19601	610-478-6100	610-478-6139
Blair County	423 Allegheny St	Hollidaysburg PA	16648	814-695-5541	814-696-9214
Bradford County	301 Main St.	Towanda PA	18848	717-265-1727	717-265-1729
Bucks County	Main & Court Sts	Doylestown PA	18901	215-348-6000	215-348-6740
Butler County	P.O. Box 1208	Butler PA	16003	412-285-4731	412-284-5474
Cambria County	200 S. Center St	Ebensburg PA	15931	814-472-5440	814-472-6940
Cameron County	20 E. 5th St	Emporium PA	15834	814-486-2315	814-486-0464
Carbon County	P.O. Box 129	Jim Thorpe PA	18229	717-325-3611	717-325-3622
Centre County	420 Holmes St.	Bellefonte PA	16823	814-355-6700	814-355-6980
Chester County	2 N. High St	West Chester PA	19380	610-344-6135	610-344-6605
Clarion County	420 Main St.	Clarion PA	16214	814-226-4000	814-226-8069
Clearfield County	1 N. 2nd & Market	Clearfield PA	16830	814-765-2641	814-765-6089
Clinton County	County Courthouse	Lock Haven PA	17745	717-893-4000	717-893-4041
Columbia County	P.O. Box 380	Bloomsburg PA	17815	717-389-5600	717-784-0257
Crawford County	903 Diamond Pk	Meadville PA	16335	814-336-1151	814-337-0457
Cumberland County	1 Courthouse Sq	Carlisle PA	17013	717-240-6150	717-240-6448
Dauphin County	Front & Market Sts	Harrisburg PA	17101	717-255-2741	717-257-1604
Delaware County	201 W. Front St	Media PA	19063	610-891-4259	No Fax
Elk County	Main St	Ridgway PA	15853	814-776-1161	814-776-5379
Erie County	140 W. 6th St	Erie PA	16501	814-451-6000	814-451-6323
Fayette County	61 E. Main St	Uniontown PA	15401	412-430-1201	412-430-1265
Forest County	526 Elm St	Tionesta PA	16353	814-755-3537	814-755-8837
Franklin County	157 Lincoln Way E	Chambersburg PA	17201	717-264-4125	717-267-3438
Fulton County	201 N. 2nd St	McConnellsburg PA	17233	717-485-4212	717-485-9411
Greene County	93 E. High St	Waynesburg PA	15370	412-852-5223	412-627-5428

County	Address	City, State		Zip Code	Phone	Fax
PENNSYLVANIA *continued*						
Huntingdon County	223 Penn St.	Huntingdon	PA	16652	814-643-3091	814-643-8152
Indiana County	825 Philadelphia St	Indiana	PA	15701	412-465-3800	412-465-3953
Jefferson County	200 Main St.	Brookville	PA	15825	814-849-8031	814-849-4084
Juniata County	P.O. Box 68	Mifflintown	PA	17059	717-436-8991	717-436-5543
Lackawanna County	200 N. Washington Ave	Scranton	PA	18503	717-963-6723	717-963-6812
Lancaster County	50 N. Duke St	Lancaster	PA	17602	717-299-8300	717-293-7208
Lawrence County	430 Court St	New Castle	PA	16101	412-658-2541	412-652-9646
Lebannon County	400 S. 8th St	Lebanon	PA	17042	717-274-2801	717-274-8094
Lehigh County	P.O. Box 1548	Allentown	PA	18105	610-820-3001	610-820-3615
Luzerne County	200 N. River St	Wilkes-Barre	PA	18711	717-825-1500	717-825-1843
Lycoming County	48 W. 3rd St	Williamsport	PA	17701	717-327-2200	717-327-2511
McKean County	500 W. Main St.	Smethport	PA	16749	814-887-5571	814-887-2242
Mercer County	112 Mercer County Court House.	Mercer	PA	16137	610-250-1825	610-662-1530
Mifflin County	20 N. Wayne St.	Lewistown	PA	17044	717-248-6733	717-248-3695
Monroe County	1 Quaker Plaza, Rm. 201	Stroudsburg	PA	18360	717-420-3400	717-420-3458
Montgomery County	Swede & Airy Sts	Norristown	PA	19404	215-278-3000	No Fax
Montour County	29 Mill St.	Danville	PA	17821	717-271-3012	717-271-3088
Northampton County	7th & Washington Sts	Easton	PA	18042	610-250-1825	No Fax
Northumberland County	230-A Market St.	Sunbury	PA	17801	717-988-4111	717-988-4286
Perry County	P.O. Box 37	New Bloomfield	PA	17068	717-582-8984	717-582-7069
Philadelphia County	Broad & Market Sts	Philadelphia	PA	19107	215-683-7707	No Fax
Pike County	506 Broad St	Milford	PA	18337	717-296-7613	717-296-6055
Potter County	1 E. 2nd St	Coudersport	PA	16915	814-274-8290	814-274-8284
Schuylkill County	401 N. 2nd St	Pottsville	PA	17901	717-622-5570	717-628-1108
Snyder County	9 W. Market St	Middleburg	PA	17842	717-837-4207	717-837-4282
Somerset County	P.O. Box 494	Somerset	PA	15501	814-445-5154	814-445-7991
Sullivan County	Main & Muncy Sts	Laporte	PA	18626	717-946-5201	717-946-4421
Tioga County	118 Main St.	Wellsboro	PA	16901	717-723-8191	717-724-6819
Union County	103 S. 2nd St.	Lewisburg	PA	17837	717-524-8600	717-524-8635
Venango County	Liberty & 12th Sts	Franklin	PA	16323	814-432-9577	814-432-9569
Warren County	204 4th Ave	Warren	PA	16365	814-723-7550	814-723-8115
Washington County	100 W. Beau St	Washington	PA	15301	412-228-6700	412-228-6965
Wayne County	925 Court St	Honesdale	PA	18431	717-253-5970	717-253-2943
Westmoreland County	2 N. Main St	Greensburg	PA	15601	412-830-3000	412-830-3042
Wyoming County	1 Courthouse Sq	Tunkhannock	PA	18657	717-836-3200	717-836-7244
York County	1 W. Market Way, 4th Fl	York	PA	17401	717-771-9675	717-771-9804
RHODE ISLAND						
Bristol County	514 Main St.	Warren	RI	02885	401-245-7421	401-245-7421
Kent County	222 Quaker Ln	Warwick	RI	02886	401-822-1311	401-823-9655

County	Address	City, State		Zip Code	Phone	Fax

RHODE ISLAND *continued*

County	Address	City	State	Zip Code	Phone	Fax
Newport County	45 Washington Sq.	Newport	RI	02840	401-841-8330	No Fax
Providence County	250 Benefit St	Providence	RI	02903	401-277-3220	401-277-2701
Washington County	4800 Tower Hill Rd	Wakefield	RI	02879	401-782-4121	No Fax

SOUTH CAROLINA

County	Address	City	State	Zip Code	Phone	Fax
Abbeville County	P.O. Box 579	Abbeville	SC	29620	864-459-5312	864-459-4982
Aiken County	828 Richland Ave. W	Aiken	SC	29801	803-642-2013	803-642-2124
Allendale County	P.O. Box 677	Allendale	SC	29810	803-584-3438	803-584-7042
Anderson County	P.O. Box 8002	Anderson	SC	29622	864-260-4031	864-260-4106
Bamberg County	P.O. Box 149	Bamberg	SC	29003	803-245-5191	803-245-3027
Barnwell County	1609 Main St.	Barnwell	SC	29812	803-541-1000	803-541-1005
Beaufort County	P.O. Box 1228	Beaufort	SC	29901	803-525-7151	803-525-7181
Berkeley County	223 N. Live Oak Dr	Moncks Corner	SC	29461	803-761-6900	803-899-7929
Calhoun County	302 S. FrHuff Dr. Ste 108	St Matthews	SC	29135	803-874-2435	803-874-1242
Charleston County	2 Courthouse Sq	Charleston	SC	29401	803-723-6761	803-720-2224
Cherokee County	210 N. Limestone St.	Gaffney	SC	29340	864-487-2560	864-487-2594
Chester County	P.O. Box 580	Chester	SC	29706	803-385-5133	803-385-2022
Chesterfield County	200 W. Main St.	Chesterfield	SC	29709	803-623-2535	803-623-3945
Clarendon County	P.O. Box 486	Manning	SC	29102	803-435-8424	803-435-8258
Colleton County	P.O. Box 157	Walterboro	SC	29488	803-549-5221	803-549-7215
Darlington County	1 Public Square	Darlington	SC	29532	803-398-4100	803-398-4172
Dillon County	P.O. Box 449	Dillon	SC	29536	803-774-1400	803-774-1443
Dorchester County	P.O. Box 416	Saint George	SC	29477	803-563-0100	803-563-0137
Edgefield County	215 Jeter St.	Edgefield	SC	29824	803-637-4000	803-637-4056
Fairfield County	P.O. Drawer 60	Winnsboro	SC	29180	803-635-1415	803-635-5969
Florence County	180 N. Irby St	Florence	SC	29501	803-665-3035	803-665-3042
Georgetown County	P.O. Box 1270	Georgetown	SC	29442	803-546-4189	803-546-4730
Greenville County	County Sq, Ste 100	Greenville	SC	29601	864-467-7105	864-467-7201
Greenwood County	Box P-103 600 Monument St.	Greenwood	SC	29646	864-942-8502	864-942-8566
Hampton County	201 Jackson St. W	Hampton	SC	29924	803-943-7500	803-943-7502
Horry County	P.O. Box 1236	Conway	SC	29526	803-248-1203	803-248-1378
Jasper County	P.O. Drawer F	Ridgeland	SC	29936	803-726-7700	803-726-7800
Kershaw County	Courthouse, Room 202	Camden	SC	29020	803-425-1500	803-425-7673
Lancaster County	P.O. Box 1809	Lancaster	SC	29721	803-285-1565	803-285-3361
Laurens County	P.O. Box 445	Laurens	SC	29360	864-984-5484	864-984-3726
Lee County	P.O. Box 387	Bishopville	SC	29010	803-484-5341	803-484-6512
Lexington County	212 S. Lake Dr	Lexington	SC	29072	803-359-8100	803-359-8101
Marion County	P.O. Box 183	Marion	SC	29571	803-423-3904	803-423-8306
Marlboro County	P.O. Box 419	Bennettsville	SC	29512	803-479-5600	803-479-5639
McCormick County	1330 S. Mine St., Rm. 102	McCormick	SC	29835	864-465-2195	864-465-0071

County	Address	City, State		Zip Code	Phone	Fax

SOUTH CAROLINA *continued*

County	Address	City	State	Zip Code	Phone	Fax
Newberry County	P.O. Box 156	Newberry	SC	29108	803-321-2100	803-321-2102
Oconee County	208 Booker Dr.	Walhalla	SC	29691	864-638-4242	864-638-4241
Orangeburg County	P.O. Drawer 9000	Orangeburg	SC	29116	803-533-6101	803-533-6104
Pickens County	1022 McDaniel Ave	Pickens	SC	29671	864-898-5900	864-898-5924
Richland County	P.O. Box 192	Columbia	SC	29202	803-748-4616	803-748-4644
Saluda County	108 S Rudolph St	Saluda	SC	29138	864-445-2635	864-445-8829
Spartanburg County	P.O. Box 5666	Spartanburg	SC	29304	864-596-2526	864-596-2232
Sumter County	141 N. Main St	Sumter	SC	29150	803-436-2102	803-436-2223
Union County	P.O. Box 200	Union	SC	29379	864-429-1600	864-429-1603
Williamsburg County	P.O. Box 330	Kingstree	SC	29556	803-354-5188	803-354-2106
York County	P.O. Box 66	York	SC	29745	803-684-8511	803-684-8550

SOUTH DAKOTA

County	Address	City	State	Zip Code	Phone	Fax
Aurora County	P.O. Box 397	Plankinton	SD	57368	605-942-7752	605-942-7751
Beadle County	P.O. Box 845	Huron	SD	57350	605-352-8436	605-352-1328
Bennett County	P.O. Box 460	Martin	SD	57551	605-685-6931	605-685-6311
Bon Homme County	P.O. Drawer E.	Tyndall	SD	57066	605-589-4212	605-589-4209
Brookings County	314 6th Ave	Brookings	SD	57006	605-692-6284	605-692-7397
Brown County	25 Market St.	Aberdeen	SD	57401	605-626-7110	605-626-4010
Brule County	300 S. Courtland St	Chamberlain	SD	57325	605-734-6521	605-734-6110
Buffalo County	P.O. Box 146	Gannvalley	SD	57341	605-293-3217	605-293-3240
Butte County	839 5th Ave	Belle Fourche	SD	57717	605-892-4485	605-892-4525
Campbell County	P.O. Box 37	Mound City	SD	57646	605-955-3366	605-955-3308
Charles Mix County	P.O. Box 490.	Lake Andes	SD	57356	605-487-7131	605-626-4010
Clark County	P.O. Box 294	Clark	SD	57225	605-532-5921	605-532-5931
Clay County	P.O. Box 403	Vermillion	SD	57069	605-677-7120	605-677-7105
Codington County	16 1st Ave. S.E	Watertown	SD	57201	605-882-6297	605-882-6288
Corson County	P.O. Box 255	McIntosh	SD	57641	605-273-4229	605-273-4355
Custer County	420 Mt. Rushmore Rd	Custer	SD	57730	605-673-4815	No Fax
Davison County	200 E. 4th	Mitchell	SD	57301	605-996-2474	605-996-4651
Day County	710 W. 1st St.	Webster	SD	57274	605-345-3102	605-345-4162
Deuel County	P.O. Box 616	Clear Lake	SD	57226	605-874-2312	605-874-2916
Dewey County	P.O. Box 277	Timber Lake	SD	57656	605-865-3672	605-865-3787
Douglas County	P.O. Box 159	Armour	SD	57313	605-724-2423	605-724-2204
Edmunds County	P.O. Box 97	Ipswich	SD	57451	605-426-6762	605-426-6164
Fall River County	906 N. River St	Hot Springs	SD	57747	605-745-5130	605-745-3855
Faulk County	P.O. Box 309	Faulkton	SD	57438	605-598-6224	No Fax
Grant County	210 E. 5th Ave	Milbank	SD	57252	605-432-6711	605-432-9004
Gregory County	P.O. Box 413	Burke	SD	57523	605-775-2664	605-775-2596
Hakon County	P.O. Box 698	Philip	SD	57567	605-859-2800	605-859-2830

County	Address	City, State	Zip Code	Phone	Fax

SOUTH DAKOTA *continued*

County	Address	City, State	Zip Code	Phone	Fax
Hamlin County	P.O. Box 237	Hayti SD	57241	605-783-3201	605-783-3201
Hand County	415 W. 1st Ave	Miller SD	57362	605-853-2182	605-853-2769
Hanson County	P.O. Box 500	Alexandria SD	57311	605-239-4714	605-239-4296
Harding County	P.O. Box 26	Buffalo SD	57720	605-375-3313	605-375-3318
Hughes County	104 E. Capitol Ave	Pierre SD	57501	605-773-7451	605-773-7479
Hutchinson County	140 Euclid Rm. 128	Olivet SD	57052	605-387-4212	605-387-4209
Hyde County	P.O. Box 379	Highmore SD	57345	605-852-2519	605-852-2171
Jackson County	P.O. Box 280	Kadoka SD	57543	605-837-2422	605-837-2147
Jerauld County	P.O. Box 422	Wessington Springs SD	57382	605-539-9301	605-539-9125
Jones County	P.O. Box 307	Murdo SD	57559	605-669-2242	No Fax
Kingsbury County	P.O. Box 196	De Smet SD	57231	605-854-3832	605-854-3833
Lake County	200 E. Center St	Madison SD	57042	605-256-7600	605-256-7622
Lawrence County	P.O. Box F	Deadwood SD	57732	605-578-1941	605-578-1065
Lincoln County	100 E. 5th St	Canton SD	57013	605-987-2581	605-987-5932
Lyman County	P.O. Box 38	Kennebec SD	57544	605-869-2247	605-869-2203
Marshall County	P.O. Box 130	Britton SD	57430	605-448-2401	605-448-2116
McCook County	P.O. 190	Salem SD	57058	605-425-2791	605-425-2791
McPherson County	P.O. Box L	Leola SD	57456	605-439-3314	605-439-3394
Meade County	1425 Sherman St	Sturgis SD	57785	605-347-2360	605-347-5925
Mellette County	P.O. Box C	White River SD	57579	605-259-3291	605-259-3194
Miner County	P.O. Box 86	Howard SD	57349	605-772-4671	605-772-4148
Minnehaha County	415 N. Dakota Ave	Sioux Falls SD	57104	605-367-4220	605-367-8314
Moody County	P.O. Box 152	Flandreau SD	57028	605-997-3161	No Fax
Pennington County	315 St. Joseph St	Rapid City SD	57701	605-394-2153	605-394-6840
Perkins County	P.O. Box 126	Bison SD	57620	605-244-5624	605-244-7110
Potter County	201 S. Exene St.	Gettysburg SD	57442	605-765-9408	605-765-2412
Roberts County	411 2nd Ave. E	Sisseton SD	57262	605-698-7336	605-698-4277
Sanborn County	P.O. Box 7	Woonsocket SD	57385	605-796-4513	605-796-4509
Shannon County	906 N. River St	Hot Springs SD	57747	605-745-5130	605-745-3855
Spink County	210 E. 7th Ave	Redfield SD	57469	605-472-1825	605-472-2301
Stanley County	P.O. Box 595	Fort Pierre SD	57532	605-223-2673	605-223-9948
Sully County	P.O. Box 265	Onida SD	57564	605-258-2541	605-258-2884
Todd County	200 E. 3rd	Winner SD	57580	605-842-3727	605-842-2224
Tripp County	200 E. 3rd St	Winner SD	57580	605-842-3727	605-842-2224
Turner County	P.O. Box 370	Parker SD	57053	605-297-3153	605-297-5556
Union County	P.O. Box 519	Elk Point SD	57025	605-356-2101	605-356-3356
Walworth County	P.O. Box 199	Selby SD	57472	605-649-7878	605-649-7867
Yankton County	P.O. Box 137	Yankton SD	57078	605-665-2143	No Fax
Ziebach County	P.O. Box 68	Dupree SD	57623	605-365-5157	605-365-5204

County	Address	City, State	Zip Code	Phone	Fax
TENNESSEE					
Anderson County	100 Main St.	Clinton TN	37716	423-457-5400	423-463-0737
Bedford County	1 Public Sq	Shelbyville TN	37160	615-684-7944	615-684-4628
Benton County	P.O. Box 298	Camden TN	38320	901-584-6011	901-584-4640
Bledsoe County	P.O. Box 149	Pikeville TN	37367	423-447-6855	423-447-6856
Blount County	341 Court St	Maryville TN	37804	423-982-1302	423-977-1276
Bradley County	P.O. Box 1167	Cleveland TN	37364	423-476-0600	423-476-0696
Campbell County	P.O. Box 435	Jacksboro TN	37757	423-562-2526	423-562-2075
Cannon County	County Courthouse	Woodbury TN	37190	615-563-2320	615-563-4502
Carroll County	P.O. Box 110	Huntingdon TN	38344	901-986-1960	901-986-1935
Carter County	801 Elk Ave.	Elizabethton TN	37643	423-542-1801	423-542-9279
Cheatham County	100 Public Sq	Ashland City TN	37015	615-792-4316	615-792-2001
Chester County	P.O. Box 262	Henderson TN	38340	901-989-7171	901-989-7176
Claiborne County	P.O. Drawer K	Tazewell TN	37879	423-626-5236	423-626-1661
Clay County	P.O. Box 218	Celina TN	38551	615-243-2249	No Fax
Cocke County	360 E. Main.	Newport TN	37821	423-623-8791	423-623-8792
Coffee County	300 Hillsboro Blvd, Box 8	Manchester TN	37355	615-723-5100	615-723-5152
Crockett County	County Courthouse	Alamo TN	38001	901-696-5460	901-696-4101
Cumberland County	101 S. Main St, Box 1	Crossville TN	38555	615-484-6165	615-484-5374
Davidson County	107 Metro Courthouse	Nashville TN	37201	615-862-6000	615-862-6040
Decatur County	P.O. Box 488	Decaturville TN	38329	901-852-2131	901-852-2130
DeKalb County	County Courthouse, Rm 204	Smithville TN	37166	615-597-5175	615-597-7420
Dickson County	P.O. Box 220	Charlotte TN	37036	615-789-4171	615-789-6075
Dyer County	P.O. Box 1360	Dyersburg TN	38024	901-286-7800	901-286-6462
Fayette County	P.O. Box 218	Somerville TN	38068	901-465-5202	901-465-5229
Fentress County	P.O. Box 1128	Jamestown TN	38556	615-879-7713	615-879-1579
Franklin County	1 S. Jefferson St	Winchester TN	37398	615-967-2905	615-962-1473
Gibson County	1 Court Sq	Trenton TN	38382	901-855-7613	901-855-7650
Giles County	P.O. Box 678	Pulaski TN	38478	615-363-5300	615-424-6101
Grainger County	P.O. Box 126	Rutledge TN	37861	423-828-3513	423-828-4284
Greene County	101 S. Main St	Greeneville TN	37743	423-638-8118	423-638-8119
Grundy County	P.O. Box 177	Altamont TN	37301	615-692-3718	615-692-2400
Hamblen County	511 W. 2nd North St	Morristown TN	37814	423-586-1931	423-587-9798
Hamilton County	Courthouse, Rm. 201	Chattanooga TN	37402	423-209-6500	423-209-6501
Hancock County	P.O. Box 347	Sneedville TN	37869	423-733-4341	423-733-4348
Hardeman County	P.O. Box 250	Bolivar TN	38008	901-658-3266	901-658-5721
Hardin County	601 Main St.	Savannah TN	38372	901-925-9078	901-925-0338
Hawkins County	150 Washington St.	Rogersville TN	37857	423-272-7359	423-272-1867
Haywood County	1 N. Washington St	Brownsville TN	38012	901-772-1432	901-772-3864
Henderson County	P.O. Box 528	Lexington TN	38351	901-968-0122	901-965-9085
Henry County	P.O. Box 7	Paris TN	38242	901-642-5212	901-642-6531

County	Address	City, State	Zip Code	Phone	Fax
TENNESSEE *continued*					
Hickman County	5 Public Sq	Centerville TN	37033	615-729-2492	615-729-6150
Houston County	P.O. Box 366	Erin TN	37061	615-289-3633	615-289-3633
Humphreys County	Rm.1 Courthouse Annex	Waverly TN	37185	615-296-7795	615-296-5011
Jackson County	P.O. Box 716	Gainesboro TN	38562	615-268-9888	615-268-9060
Jefferson County	P.O. Box 710	Dandridge TN	37725	423-397-3800	423-397-3839
Johnson County	222 W. Main St	Mountain City TN	37683	423-727-9696	423-727-7047
Knox County	Rm 615C — C Building	Knoxville TN	37902	423-215-2005	423-215-2002
Lake County	229 Church St	Tiptonville TN	38079	901-253-7382	901-253-9815
Lauderdale County	100 Court Sq	Ripley TN	38063	901-635-3500	901-635-9682
Lawrence County	240 W Gaines St	Lawrenceburg TN	38464	615-762-7700	615-766-2219
Lewis County	Park Ave N	Hohenwald TN	38462	615-796-3378	615-796-6010
Lincoln County	P.O. Box 32	Fayetteville TN	37334	615-433-3045	615-433-9979
Loudon County	100 River Rd	Loudon TN	37774	423-458-4664	423-458-6508
Macon County	Public Sq. Courthouse, Rm. 104	Lafayette TN	37083	615-666-2333	615-666-5323
Madison County	100 E. Main	Jackson TN	38301	901-423-6020	901-988-3820
Marion County	P.O. Box 789	Jasper TN	37347	423-942-2552	423-942-1327
Marshall County	Commerce St	Lewisburg TN	37091	615-359-1279	901-359-0543
Maury County	41 Public Sq	Columbia TN	38401	615-381-3690	615-380-2168
McMinn County	6 W. Madison Ave	Athens TN	37303	423-745-7634	423-745-0095
McNairy County	County Courthouse	Selmer TN	38375	901-645-3472	901-380-2168
Meigs County	P.O. Box 156	Decatur TN	37322	423-334-5850	423-334-4819
Monroe County	105 College St	Madisonville TN	37354	423-442-3981	423-442-7279
Montgomery County	P.O. Box 368	Clarksville TN	37040	615-648-5787	615-553-5177
Moore County	P.O. Box 206	Lynchburg TN	37352	615-759-7076	615-759-7028
Morgan County	P.O. Box 387	Wartburg TN	37887	423-346-6288	423-346-3609
Obion County	P.O. Box 236	Union City TN	38261	901-885-9611	901-885-7515
Overton County	317 E. University St	Livingston TN	38570	615-823-5630	615-823-7036
Perry County	P.O. Box 16	Linden TN	37096	615-589-2216	615-589-2350
Pickett County	P.O. Box 280	Byrdstown TN	38549	615-864-3798	615-864-6615
Polk County	P.O. Box 128	Benton TN	37307	423-338-4527	423-338-4558
Putnam County	300 E. Spring St	Cookeville TN	38501	615-526-2161	615-528-1300
Rhea County	1475 Market St	Dayton TN	37321	423-775-7801	423-775-5553
Roane County	P.O. Box 643	Kingston TN	37763	423-376-5578	423-376-4318
Robertson County	501 Main	Springfield TN	37172	615-384-2476	615-384-0617
Rutherford County	Courthouse Rm. 101	Murfreesboro TN	37130	615-898-7745	615-898-7747
Scott County	P.O. Box 69	Huntsville TN	37756	423-663-2000	423-663-3803
Sequatchie County	P.O. Box 595	Dunlap TN	37327	423-949-3479	423-949-2579
Sevier County	125 Court Ave	Sevierville TN	37862	423-453-6136	423-453-6830
Shelby County	160 N. Main, Suite 850	Memphis TN	38103	901-576-4500	901-576-4759
Smith County	207 A Main St	Carthage TN	37030	615-735-2294	615-735-8240

County	Address	City, State		Zip Code	Phone	Fax

TENNESSEE *continued*

County	Address	City	State	Zip Code	Phone	Fax
Stewart County	P.O. Box 487	Dover	TN	37058	615-232-5371	615-232-3111
Sullivan County	P.O. Box 509	Blountville	TN	37617	423-323-6417	423-279-2867
Sumner County	355 N. Belvedere Dr.	Gallatin	TN	37066	615-452-3604	615-452-0393
Tipton County	P.O. Box 686	Covington	TN	38019	901-476-0200	901-476-0227
Trousdale County	P.O. Box 69	Hartsville	TN	37074	615-374-2461	615-374-1100
Unicoi County	P.O. Box 169	Erwin	TN	37650	423-743-9391	423-743-8007
Union County	P.O. Box 278	Maynardville	TN	37807	423-992-3061	423-992-1937
Van Buren County	P.O. Box 217	Spencer	TN	38585	615-946-2314	615-946-2388
Warren County	P.O. Box 639	McMinnville	TN	37110	615-473-2505	615-473-3726
Washington County	P.O. Box 219	Jonesborough	TN	37659	423-753-1666	423-753-1718
Wayne County	P.O. Box 848	Waynesboro	TN	38485	615-722-3653	615-722-5994
Weakley County	County Courthouse, Rm. 106	Dresden	TN	38225	901-364-5413	901-364-5389
White County	County Courthouse, Rm 205	Sparta	TN	38583	615-836-3203	615-836-3204
Williamson County	1320 W. Main St.	Franklin	TN	37064	615-790-5700	615-790-5818
Wilson County	228 E. Main St, Rm. 104	Lebannon	TN	37087	615-444-1383	615-443-1714

TEXAS

County	Address	City	State	Zip Code	Phone	Fax
Anderson County	County Courthouse	Palestine	TX	75801	903-723-7432	903-723-2493
Andrews County	P.O. Box 727	Andrews	TX	79714	915-524-1426	915-524-1470
Angelina County	P.O. Box 908	Lufkin	TX	75901	409-634-8339	409-634-5915
Aransas County	301 N. Live Oak	Rockport	TX	78382	512-790-0122	512-790-0125
Archer County	P.O. Box 815	Archer City	TX	76351	817-574-4615	817-574-4625
Armstrong County	P.O. Box 309	Claude	TX	79019	806-226-2081	806-226-3221
Atascosa County	Rm. 6-1, Circle Dr.	Jourdanton	TX	78026	210-769-2511	210-769-2349
Austin County	1 E. Main.	Bellville	TX	77418	409-865-5911	409-865-8786
Bailey County	300 S 1st St.	Muleshoe	TX	79347	806-272-3044	806-272-3879
Bandera County	P.O. Box 823	Bandera	TX	78003	210-796-3332	210-796-8323
Bastrop County	P.O. Box 577	Bastrop	TX	78602	512-321-4443	No Fax
Baylor County	P.O. Box 689	Seymour	TX	76380	817-888-3322	No Fax
Bee County	105 W. Corpus Christi, Rm. 103	Beeville	TX	78102	512-358-3664	512-362-3247
Bell County	P.O. Box 480	Belton	TX	76513	817-933-5165	817-939-5176
Bexar County	100 Dolorosa, Suite 108	San Antonio	TX	78205	210-220-2216	No Fax
Blanco County	P.O. Box 65	Johnson City	TX	78636	210-868-7357	No Fax
Borden County	P.O. Box 124	Gail	TX	79738	806-756-4312	806-756-4405
Bosque County	P.O. Box 617	Meridian	TX	76665	817-435-2201	817-435-2152
Bowie County	P.O. Box 248	New Boston	TX	75570	903-628-2571	903-628-2426
Brazoria County	111 E. Locust St	Angleton	TX	77515	409-849-5711	409-849-1358
Brazos County	County Courthouse	Bryan	TX	77803	409-775-7400	409-823-6993
Brewster County	P.O. Drawer 119	Alpine	TX	79831	915-837-3366	915-837-5036
Briscoe County	County Courthouse	Silverton	TX	79257	806-823-2134	806-823-2359
Brooks County	P.O. Box 427	Falfurrias	TX	78355	512-325-5604	No Fax

County	Address	City, State	Zip Code	Phone	Fax
TEXAS *continued*					
Brown County	200 S. Broadway St	Brownwood TX	76801	915-643-2594	No Fax
Burleson County	County Courthouse	Caldwell TX	77836	409-567-4326	No Fax
Burnet County	220 S. Pierce St.	Burnet TX	78611	512-756-5406	512-756-5410
Caldwell County	P.O. Box 749	Lockhart TX	78644	512-398-1805	No Fax
Calhoun County	211 S. Ann St	Port Lavaca TX	77979	512-553-4411	No Fax
Callahan County	100 W. 4th St., Suite 104	Baird TX	79504	915-854-1217	No Fax
Cameron County	964 E. Harrison	Brownsville TX	78520	210-544-0815	210-550-7287
Camp County	126 Church St.	Pittsburg TX	75686	903-856-2731	903-856-0811
Carson County	P.O. Box 487	Panhandle TX	79068	806-537-3873	806-537-3724
Cass County	P.O. Box 468	Linden TX	75563	903-756-5071	No Fax
Castro County	County Courthouse	Dimmitt TX	79027	806-647-3338	806-647-2189
Chambers County	County Courthouse	Anahuac TX	77514	409-267-8309	No Fax
Cherokee County	County Courthouse	Rusk TX	75785	903-683-2350	No Fax
Childress County	Courthouse Box 4	Childress TX	79201	817-937-6143	817-937-3479
Clay County	100 N. Bridge St	Henrietta TX	76365	817-538-4631	No Fax
Cochran County	County Courthouse	Morton TX	79346	806-266-5450	806-266-5629
Coke County	P.O. Box 150	Robert Lee TX	76945	915-453-2631	915-453-2157
Coleman County	P.O. Box 591	Coleman TX	76834	915-625-2889	No Fax
Collin County	200 S. McDolad St., Suite 120	McKinney TX	75069	214-548-4134	No Fax
Collingsworth County	County Courthouse	Wellington TX	79095	806-447-2408	806-447-5418
Colorado County	P.O. Drawer 68	Columbus TX	78934	409-732-2155	409-732-8852
Comal County	100 Main Plaza	New Braunfels TX	78130	210-620-5513	210-620-3410
Comanche County	County Courthouse	Comanche TX	76442	915-356-2655	No Fax
Concho County	P.O. Box 98	Paint Rock TX	76866	915-732-4322	915-732-4307
Cooke County	100 Dixon	Gainesville TX	76240	817-668-5420	No Fax
Coryell County	P.O. Box 237	Gatesville TX	76528	817-865-5016	817-865-8631
Cottle County	P.O. Box 717	Paducah TX	79248	806-492-3823	No Fax
Crane County	P.O. Box 578	Crane TX	79731	915-558-3581	No Fax
Crockett County	P.O. Drawer C.	Ozona TX	76943	915-392-2022	915-392-2022
Crosby County	P.O. Box 218	Crosbyton TX	79322	806-675-2334	806-675-2804
Culberson County	P.O. Box 158	Van Horn TX	79855	915-283-2058	915-283-9234
Dallam County	P.O. Box 1352	Dalhart TX	79022	806-249-4751	806-249-2252
Dallas County	509 Main St.	Dallas TX	75202	214-653-7131	214-653-7176
Dawson County	P.O. Drawer 1268	Lamesa TX	79331	806-872-3778	806-872-3395
Deaf Smith County	205 E. 3rd, Rm. 203	Hereford TX	79045	806-363-7077	806-364-8830
Delta County	County Courthouse	Cooper TX	75432	903-395-4110	903-395-2178
Denton County	401 W. Hickory St	Denton TX	76201	817-565-8646	No Fax
DeWitt County	307 N. Gonzales St	Cuero TX	77954	512-275-3724	512-275-8994
Dickens County	P.O. Box 120	Dickens TX	79229	806-623-5531	806-623-5319
Dimmit County	County Courthouse	Carrizo Springs TX	78834	210-876-3569	210-876-5036

County	Address	City, State		Zip Code	Phone	Fax

TEXAS *continued*

County	Address	City, State		Zip Code	Phone	Fax
Donley County	300 S. Sully	Clarendon	TX	79226	806-874-3436	806-874-5146
Duval County	P.O. Box 248	San Diego	TX	78384	512-279-3322	No Fax
Eastland County	P.O. Box 110	Eastland	TX	76448	817-629-1583	817-629-8125
Ector County	County Courthouse	Odessa	TX	79761	915-335-3045	No Fax
Edwards County	P.O. Box 184	Rocksprings	TX	78880	210-683-2235	210-683-5376
Ellis County	P.O. Box 250	Waxahachie	TX	75165	214-923-5070	No Fax
El Paso County	City-County Building, Rm. 105	El Paso	TX	79901	915-546-2071	915-546-2012
Erath County	County Courthouse	Stephenville	TX	76401	817-965-1482	817-965-5732
Falls County	P.O. Box 458	Marlin	TX	76661	817-883-2061	No Fax
Fannin County	101 E. San Rayburn	Bonham	TX	75418	903-583-7486	903-583-7811
Fayette County	P.O. Box 59	La Grange	TX	78945	409-968-3251	No Fax
Fisher County	P.O. Box 368	Roby	TX	79543	915-776-2401	915-776-2815
Floyd County	P.O. Box 476	Floydada	TX	79235	806-983-4900	806-983-2400
Foard County	P.O. Box 539	Crowell	TX	79227	817-684-1365	817-684-1947
Fort Bend County	301 Jackson	Richmond	TX	77469	713-341-8685	713-341-8669
Franklin County	P.O. Box 68	Mount Vernon	TX	75457	903-537-4252	No Fax
Freestone County	P.O. Box 1017	Fairfield	TX	75840	903-389-2635	No Fax
Frio County	500 E. San Antonio St., Box 6	Pearsall	TX	78061	210-334-2214	210-334-4881
Gaines County	101 S. Main, Rm. 107	Seminole	TX	79360	915-758-4003	No Fax
Galveston County	722 Moody	Galveston	TX	77550	409-766-2200	No Fax
Garza County	P.O. Box 366	Post	TX	79356	806-495-4430	806-495-4431
Gillespie County	101 W. Main St.	Fredericksburg	TX	78624	210-997-6515	210-997-9958
Glasscock County	P.O. Box 190	Garden City	TX	79739	915-354-2371	No Fax
Goliad County	P.O. Box 5	Goliad	TX	77963	512-645-3294	512-645-3858
Gonzales County	P.O. Box 77	Gonzales	TX	78629	210-972-2801	210-672-2636
Gray County	P.O. Box 1902	Pampa	TX	79066	806-669-8004	806-669-8054
Grayson County	100 W. Houston St., Suite 15	Sherman	TX	75090	903-813-4228	903-870-0829
Gregg County	County Courthouse	Longview	TX	75601	903-236-8430	903-237-2574
Grimes County	P.O. Box 209	Anderson	TX	77830	409-873-2111	409-873-2499
Guadalupe County	101 E. Court	Seguin	TX	78155	210-303-4188	210-410-0300
Hale County	500 Broadway, Rm. 140	Plainview	TX	79072	806-291-5261	806-291-9810
Hall County	County Courthouse	Memphis	TX	79245	806-259-2627	806-259-5078
Hamilton County	County Courthouse	Hamilton	TX	76531	817-386-3518	817-386-8727
Hansford County	P.O. Box 397	Spearman	TX	79081	806-659-2666	806-659-2025
Hardeman County	P.O. Box 30	Quanah	TX	79252	817-663-2901	No Fax
Hardin County	P.O. Box 38	Kountze	TX	77625	409-246-5185	No Fax
Harris County	1001 Preston	Houston	TX	77002	713-755-6411	713-755-4977
Harrison County	200 W. Houston	Marshall	TX	75670	903-935-4858	No Fax
Hartley County	County Courthouse	Channing	TX	79018	806-235-3582	806-235-2316
Haskell County	P.O. Box 725	Haskell	TX	79521	817-864-2451	No Fax

TEXAS *continued*

County	Address	City, State	Zip Code	Phone	Fax
Hays County	137 N. Guadalupe	San Marcos TX	78666	512-396-2601	No Fax
Hemphill County	P.O. Box 867	Canadian TX	79014	806-323-6212	No Fax
Henderson County	P.O. Box 632	Athens TX	75751	903-675-6140	903-675-6190
Hidalgo County	100 N. Closner Blvd	Edinburg TX	78539	210-318-2000	210-318-2105
Hill County	P.O. Box 398	Hillsboro TX	76645	817-582-2161	No Fax
Hockley County	802 Houston, Suite 213	Levelland TX	79336	806-894-3185	806-894-6917
Hood County	P.O. Box 339	Granbury TX	76048	817-579-3222	817-579-3227
Hopkins County	County Courthouse	Sulphur Springs TX	75482	903-885-3929	903-885-2794
Houston County	P.O. Box 370	Crockett TX	75835	409-544-3255	409-544-8053
Howard County	P.O. Box 1468	Big Spring TX	79720	915-264-2213	915-264-2215
Hudspeth County	P.O. Box A	Sierra Blanca TX	79851	915-369-2301	915-369-2361
Hunt County	P.O. Box 1316	Greenville TX	75403	903-408-4130	No Fax
Hutchinson County	P.O. Box 1186	Stinnett TX	79083	806-878-4002	No Fax
Irion County	P.O. Box 736	Mertzon TX	76941	915-835-2421	915-835-2008
Jack County	100 Main St.	Jacksboro TX	76458	817-567-2111	No Fax
Jackson County	115 W. Main St, Rm. 101	Edna TX	77957	512-782-3563	No Fax
Jasper County	P.O. Box 2070	Jasper TX	75951	409-384-2632	No Fax
Jeff Davis County	P.O. Box 836	Fort Davis TX	79734	915-426-3251	915-426-3760
Jefferson County	1149 Pearl	Beaumont TX	77701	409-835-8475	409-839-2394
Jim Hogg County	P.O. Box 878	Hebbronville TX	78361	512-527-4031	512-527-5843
Jim Wells County	P.O. Box 1459	Alice TX	78333	512-668-5702	No Fax
Johnson County	P.O. Box 662	Cleburne TX	76033	817-556-6323	817-556-6326
Jones County	P.O. Box 552	Anson TX	79501	915-823-3762	915-823-4223
Karnes County	101 N. Panamaria, Suite 9	Karnes City TX	78118	210-780-3938	210-780-4538
Kaufman County	100 W. Mulbury	Kaufman TX	75142	214-932-4331	214-932-7628
Kendall County	204 E. San Antionio St.	Boerne TX	78006	210-249-9343	210-249-9478
Kenedy County	County Courthouse	Sarita TX	78385	512-294-5220	512-294-5218
Kent County	County Courthouse	Jayton TX	79528	806-237-3881	806-237-3306
Kerr County	County Courthouse	Kerrville TX	78028	210-792-2255	210-792-2274
Kimble County	501 Main	Junction TX	76849	915-446-3353	915-446-4361
King County	P.O. Box 135	Guthrie TX	79236	806-596-4412	806-596-4664
Kinney County	P.O. Drawer 9	Brackettville TX	78832	210-563-2521	210-563-2644
Kleberg County	P.O. Box 1327	Kingsville TX	78364	512-595-8548	No Fax
Knox County	P.O. Box 196	Benjamin TX	79505	817-454-2441	817-454-2022
Lamar County	119 N. Main	Paris TX	75460	903-737-2420	903-737-2451
Lamb County	County Courthouse, Rm. 103	Littlefield TX	79339	806-385-4222	806-385-6485
Lampasas County	P.O. Box 327	Lampasas TX	76550	512-556-8271	512-556-8270
LaSalle County	P.O. Box 340	Cotulla TX	78014	210-879-2117	210-879-2933
Lavaca County	P.O. Box 326	Hallettsville TX	77964	512-798-3612	No Fax
Lee County	P.O. Box 419	Giddings TX	78942	409-542-3684	409-542-2623

County	Address	City, State	Zip Code	Phone	Fax
TEXAS *continued*					
Leon County	County Courthouse	Centerville TX	75833	903-536-2352	No Fax
Liberty County	P.O. Box 369	Liberty TX	77575	409-336-4671	409-336-4640
Limestone County	P.O. Box 350	Groesbeck TX	76642	817-729-5504	817-729-2915
Lipscomb County	County Courthouse	Lipscomb TX	79056	806-862-3091	806-862-2603
Live Oak County	P.O. Box 208	George West TX	78022	512-449-2103	No Fax
Llano County	107 W. Sandstone	Llano TX	78643	915-247-4455	No Fax
Loving County	County Courthouse	Mentone TX	79754	915-377-2441	915-377-2701
Lubbock County	County Courthouse, Rm. 207	Lubbock TX	79408	806-767-1042	806-767-1381
Lynn County	County Courthouse	Tahoka TX	79373	806-998-4750	806-998-4151
Madison County	101 W. Main St	Madisonville TX	77864	409-348-2638	409-348-5858
Marion County	P.O. Box F	Jefferson TX	75657	903-665-3971	No Fax
Martin County	P.O. Box 906	Stanton TX	79782	915-756-3412	915-756-2992
Mason County	P.O. Box 702	Mason TX	76856	915-347-5253	915-347-6868
Matagorda County	1700 7th St	Bay City TX	77414	409-244-7680	409-244-7688
Maverick County	County Courthouse	Eagle Pass TX	78852	210-773-2829	No Fax
McCulloch County	County Courthouse	Brady TX	76825	915-597-0733	915-597-1731
McLennan County	P.O. Box 1727	Waco TX	76703	817-757-5078	817-757-5196
McMullen County	P.O. Box 235	Tilden TX	78072	512-274-3215	512-274-3618
Medina County	1600 Ave. M	Hondo TX	78861	210-426-3378	210-426-5189
Menard County	P.O. Box 1028	Menard TX	76859	915-396-4682	915-396-2047
Midland County	P.O. Box 211	Midland TX	79701	915-688-1070	915-688-8973
Milam County	100 S. Fannin	Cameron TX	76520	817-697-6596	817-697-4433
Mills County	P.O. Box 646	Goldthwaite TX	76844	915-648-2711	915-648-2806
Mitchell County	349 Oak St., Rm. 103	Colorado City TX	79512	915-728-3481	915-728-8697
Montague County	P.O. Box 77	Montague TX	76251	817-894-2461	817-894-3110
Montgomery County	P.O. Box 959	Conroe TX	77305	409-539-7885	409-760-6990
Moore County	County Courthouse	Dumas TX	79029	806-935-6164	806-935-9004
Morris County	County Courthouse	Daingerfield TX	75638	903-645-3911	903-645-5729
Motley County	County Courthouse	Matador TX	79244	806-347-2621	806-347-2220
Nacogdoches County	101 W. Main	Nacogdoches TX	75961	409-560-7733	No Fax
Navarro County	P.O. Box 423	Corsicana TX	75151	903-654-3035	No Fax
Newton County	P.O. Box 484	Newton TX	75966	409-379-5341	409-379-2107
Nolan County	P.O. Drawer 98	Sweetwater TX	79556	915-235-2462	No Fax
Nueces County	901 Leopard St	Corpus Christi TX	78401	512-888-0580	512-888-0329
Ochiltree County	511 S. Main St	Perryton TX	79070	806-435-8105	806-435-2081
Oldham County	P.O. Box 360	Vega TX	79092	806-267-2667	806-267-2362
Orange County	County Courthouse	Orange TX	77631	409-883-7740	409-883-0379
Palo Pinto County	P.O. Box 219	Palo Pinto TX	76484	817-659-1277	No Fax
Panola County	County Courthouse, Rm. 201	Carthage TX	75633	903-693-0302	903-693-2726
Parker County	P.O. Box 819	Weatherford TX	76086	817-594-7461	No Fax

County	Address	City, State	Zip Code	Phone	Fax
TEXAS *continued*					
Parmer County	P.O. Box 356	Farwell TX	79325	806-481-3691	806-481-3305
Pecos County	103 W. Callaghan St	Fort Stockton TX	79735	915-336-7555	915-336-7557
Polk County	P.O. Box 2119	Livingston TX	77351	409-327-6804	No Fax
Potter County	P.O. Box 9638	Amarillo TX	79105	806-379-2275	806-379-2296
Presidio County	P.O. Box 789	Marfa TX	79843	915-729-4812	915-729-4313
Rains County	100 Quitman St	Emory TX	75440	903-473-2461	No Fax
Randall County	P.O. Box 660	Canyon TX	79015	806-655-6330	No Fax
Reagan County	P.O. Box 100	Big Lake TX	76932	915-884-2442	915-884-2252
Real County	P.O. Box 656	Leakey TX	78873	210-232-5202	210-232-6040
Red River County	200 N. Walnut	Clarksville TX	75426	903-427-2401	No Fax
Reeves County	P.O. Box 749	Pecos TX	79772	915-445-5467	915-445-9403
Refugio County	P.O. Box 704	Refugio TX	78377	512-526-2233	512-526-5100
Roberts County	P.O. Box 477	Miami TX	79059	806-868-2341	806-868-3381
Robertson County	P.O. Box 1029	Franklin TX	77856	409-828-4130	No Fax
Rockwoll County	1101 Ridge Rd., Suite 101	Rockwall TX	75087	214-771-5141	214-722-0242
Runnels County	P.O. Box 189	Ballinger TX	76821	915-365-2720	915-365-3408
Rusk County	115 N. Main St	Henderson TX	75652	903-657-0330	No Fax
Sabine County	P.O. Box 580	Hemphill TX	75948	409-787-3786	409-787-2044
San Augustine County	106 Courthouse	San Augustine TX	75972	409-275-2452	No Fax
San Jacinto County	P.O. Box 669	Coldspring TX	77331	409-653-2324	No Fax
San Patricio County	P.O. Box 578	Sinton TX	78387	512-364-6290	No Fax
San Saba County	County Courthouse	San Saba TX	76877	915-372-3614	915-372-5746
Schleicher County	P.O. Box 580	Eldorado TX	76936	915-853-2833	915-853-2603
Scurry County	1806 25th St., Suite 300	Snyder TX	79549	915-573-5332	915-573-1266
Shackelford County	P.O. Box 247	Albany TX	76430	915-762-2232	915-762-3432
Shelby County	P.O. Box 1987	Center TX	75935	409-598-6361	409-598-3701
Sherman County	P.O. Box 270	Stratford TX	79048	806-396-2371	806-396-5670
Smith County	P.O. Box 1018	Tyler TX	75710	903-535-0630	903-535-0684
Somervell County	P.O. Box 1098	Glen Rose TX	76043	817-897-4427	No Fax
Starr County	Courthouse Rm. 201	Rio Grande City TX	78582	210-487-2954	210-487-6227
Stephens County	201 W. Walker	Breckenridge TX	76424	817-559-3700	No Fax
Sterling County	P.O. Box 55	Sterling City TX	76951	915-378-5191	No Fax
Stonewall County	P.O. Box P	Aspermont TX	79502	817-989-2272	817-989-3566
Sutton County	301 E. Oak, Suite 3	Sonora TX	76950	915-387-3815	No Fax
Swisher County	County Courthouse	Tulia TX	79088	806-995-3294	806-995-2214
Tarrant County	County Courthouse	Fort Worth TX	76196	817-884-1111	No Fax
Taylor County	P.O. Box 5497	Abilene TX	79608	915-674-1202	915-674-1267
Terrell County	P.O. Box 410	Sanderson TX	79848	915-345-2391	915-345-2653
Terry County	500 W. Main, Rm. 105	Brownfield TC	79316	806-637-8551	806-637-4874
Throckmorton County	P.O. Box 309	Throckmorton TX	76483	817-849-2501	817-849-3220

County	Address	City, State		Zip Code	Phone	Fax
TEXAS *continued*						
Titus County	100 W. 1st, Suite 204	Mount Pleasant	TX	75455	903-577-6796	903-577-6793
Tom Green County	122 W. Beauregard	San Angelo	TX	76903	915-659-6556	No Fax
Travis County	P.O. Box 1748	Austin	TX	78767	512-473-9188	512-473-9075
Trinity County	P.O. Box 456	Groveton	TX	75845	409-642-1208	409-642-2609
Tyler County	100 Courthouse	Woodville	TX	75979	409-283-2281	409-283-7296
Upshur County	P.O. Box 730	Gilmer	TX	75644	903-843-3083	903-843-5492
Upton County	P.O. Box 465	Rankin	TX	79778	915-693-2861	915-693-2129
Uvalde County	P.O. Box 284	Uvalde	TX	78802	210-278-6614	No Fax
Val Verde County	100 E. Broadway	Del Rio	TX	78840	210-774-7564	210-775-9198
Van Zandt County	121 E. Dallas	Canton	TX	75103	903-567-6503	903-567-6722
Victoria County	115 N. Bridge	Victoria	TX	77901	512-575-1478	512-575-6276
Walker County	P.O. Box 1207	Huntsville	TX	77340	409-291-9500	409-291-2815
Waller County	County Courthouse	Hempstead	TX	77445	409-826-3357	409-826-8317
Ward County	County Courthouse	Monahans	TX	79756	915-943-3294	915-943-6054
Washington County	100 E. Main St	Brenham	TX	77834	409-277-6200	409-277-6278
Webb County	P.O. Box 29	Laredo	TX	78042	210-721-2640	210-721-2515
Wharton County	P.O. Box 69	Wharton	TX	77488	409-532-2381	No Fax
Wheeler County	County Courthouse	Wheeler	TX	79096	806-826-5544	806-826-3282
Wichita County	P.O. Box 1679	Wichita Falls	TX	76307	817-766-8144	No Fax
Wilbarger County	County Courthouse, R.m. 15	Vernon	TX	76384	817-552-5486	817-553-4702
Willacy County	540 Misty Hidalgo	Raymondville	TX	78580	210-689-2710	No Fax
Williamson County	P.O. Box 18	Georgetown	TX	78627	512-930-4300	512-930-4461
Wilson County	P.O. Box 27	Floresville	TX	78114	210-393-7308	210-393-7319
Winkler County	P.O. Box 1007	Kermit	TX	79745	915-586-3401	No Fax
Wise County	P.O. Box 359	Decatur	TX	76234	817-627-3351	817-627-2138
Wood County	P.O. Box 338	Quitman	TX	75783	903-763-2711	903-763-2902
Yoakum County	P.O. Box 309	Plains	TX	79355	806-456-2721	806-456-6175
Young County	516 4th St., Rm. 104	Graham	TX	76450	817-549-8432	817-549-2031
Zapata County	P.O. Box 789	Zapata	TX	78076	210-765-9915	210-765-9933
Zavala County	County Courthouse	Crystal City	TX	78839	210-374-2331	210-374-3007
UTAH						
Beaver County	P.O. Box 392	Beaver	UT	84713	801-438-6463	801-438-6481
Box Elder County	1 S. Main St	Brigham City	UT	84302	801-734-2031	801-734-2038
Cache County	170 N. Main St	Logan	UT	84321	801-752-3542	801-752-3597
Carbon County	120 E. Main St	Price	UT	84501	801-637-4700	801-636-3210
Daggett County	P.O. Box 219	Manila	UT	84046	801-784-3154	801-784-3335
Davis County	P.O. Box 618	Farmington	UT	84025	801-451-3214	801-451-3202
Duchesne County	P.O. Box 270	Duchesne	UT	84021	801-738-2435	801-738-5522
Emery County	P.O. Box 907	Castle Dale	UT	84513	801-381-2139	801-381-5183

County	Address	City, State		Zip Code	Phone	Fax
UTAH *continued*						
Garfield County	P.O. Box 77	Panguitch	UT	84759	801-676-8826	801-676-8239
Grand County	125 E. Center St	Moab	UT	84532	801-259-1321	801-259-2959
Iron County	P.O. Box 429	Parowan	UT	84761	801-477-3375	801-477-8847
Juab County	160 N. Main St	Nephi	UT	84648	801-623-0271	801-623-5936
Kane County	76 N. Main	Kanab	UT	84741	801-644-2458	801-644-2052
Millard County	765 S. HWY 99, S.R. Box 55.	Fillmore	UT	84631	801-743-6223	801-743-6923
Morgan County	P.O. Box 886	Morgan	UT	84050	801-829-6811	801-829-6176
Piute County	P.O. Box 99	Junction	UT	84740	801-577-2840	801-577-2433
Rich County	P.O. Box 218	Randolph	UT	84064	801-793-2415	801-793-2410
Salt Lake County	2001 State St	Salt Lake City	UT	84190	801-468-3530	801-468-3440
San Juan County	P.O. Box 338	Monticello	UT	84535	801-587-3223	801-587-2425
Sanpete County	160 N. Main St	Manti	UT	84642	801-835-2131	801-835-2135
Sevier County	P.O. Box 517	Richfield	UT	84701	801-896-9262	801-896-8888
Summit County	P.O. Box 128	Coalville	UT	84017	801-336-4451	801-336-4450
Tooele County	47 S. Main St	Tooele	UT	84074	801-882-9140	801-882-7317
Uintah County	147 E. Main	Vernal	UT	84078	801-781-5360	801-781-5319
Utah County	100 East Center #3600	Provo	UT	84601	801-370-8237	801-370-8146
Wasatch County	25 N. Main St	Heber City	UT	84032	801-654-3211	801-654-5116
Washington County	197 E. Tabernacle St	Saint George	UT	84770	801-634-5712	801-634-5753
Wayne County	18 S. Main	Loa	UT	84747	801-836-2731	801-836-2479
Weber County	2549 Washington Blvd	Ogden	UT	84401	801-399-8110	801-399-8300
VERMONT						
Addison	RD 1, Box 1330	Vergennes	VT	05491	802-759-2020	802-759-2233
Albany	P.O. Box 284	Albany	VT	05820	802-755-6100	No Fax
Alburg	P.O. Box 346	Alburg	VT	05440	802-796-3468	802-796-3939
Andover	RD 1, Box 179	Chester	VT	05143	802-875-2765	802-875-2765
Arlington	P.O. Box 304	Arlington	VT	05250	802-375-2332	802-375-6474
Athens	RR 3, Box 195-C	Athens	VT	05143	802-869-3370	No Fax
Bakersfield	P.O. Box 203	Bakersfield	VT	05441	802-827-4495	No Fax
Baltimore	RD 4, Box 365	Chester	VT	05143	802-885-5599	No Fax
Barnard	P.O. Box 274	Barnard	VT	05031	802-234-9211	No Fax
Barnet	P.O. Box 15	Barnet	VT	05821	802-633-2256	802-633-2256
Barre City	P.O. Box 418	Barre	VT	05641	802-476-0242	802-476-0264
Barre Town	P.O. Box 124	Websterville	VT	05678	802-479-9392	802-479-9332
Barton	P.O. Box 657	Barton	VT	05822	802-525-6222	No Fax
Belvidere	RR 1 Box 1062	Belvidere Center	VT	05442	802-644-2498	No Fax
Bennington	205 South St	Bennington	VT	05201	802-442-1043	802-442-1068
Benson	P.O. Box 163	Benson	VT	05731	802-537-2611	802-537-2611
Berkshire	RFD #1, Box 2560	Enosburg Falls	VT	05450	802-933-2335	No Fax

VERMONT *continued*

County	Address	City, State	Zip Code	Phone	Fax
Berlin	RD #4, Box 2375	Montpelier VT	05602	802-229-9298	No Fax
Bethel	RR 2, Box 85	Bethel VT	05032	802-234-9722	802-234-6840
Bloomfield	P.O. Box 336	N. Stratford VT	03590	802-962-5191	No Fax
Bolton	RD 1, Box 445	Waterbury VT	05676	802-434-5075	802-434-6404
Bradford	P.O. Box 339	Bradford VT	05033	802-222-4727	802-222-4728
Braintree	RD 1, Box 361A	Randolph VT	05060	802-728-9787	No Fax
Brandon	49 Center St	Brandon VT	05733	802-247-5721	802-247-5481
Brattleboro	230 Main St.	Brattleboro VT	05301	802-254-4541	802-257-2322
Bridgewater	P.O. Box 14	Bridgewater VT	05034	802-672-3334	802-672-5395
Bridport	P.O. Box 27	Bridport VT	05734	802-758-2483	No Fax
Brighton	P.O. Box 377	Island Pond VT	05846	802-723-4405	802-723-4405
Bristol	P.O. Box 249	Bristol VT	05443	802-453-2486	802-453-8188
Brookfield	P.O. Box 463	Brookfield VT	05036	802-276-3352	No Fax
Brookline	Grassy Brook Road	Brookline VT	05345	802-365-4648	No Fax
Brownington	RFD #2, Box 158	Orleans VT	05860	802-754-8401	No Fax
Brunswick	RFD #1, Box 470	Guildhall VT	05905	802-962-5283	No Fax
Burke	P.O. Box 248	W Burke VT	05871	802-467-3717	802-467-8623
Burlington	City Hall Room 20	Burlington VT	05401	802-865-7140	No Fax
Cabot	Box 36	Cabot VT	05647	802-563-2279	No Fax
Calais	RR #1, Box 35	Calais VT	05648	802-223-5952	No Fax
Cambridge	P.O. Box 127	Jeffersonville VT	05464	802-644-2251	No Fax
Canaan	P.O. Box 159	Canaan VT	05903	802-266-3370	802-266-7085
Castleton	P.O. Box 115	Castleton VT	05735	802-468-2212	802-468-5482
Cavendish	P.O. Box 126	Cavendish VT	05142	802-226-7292	802-226-7291
Charleston	HCR 61, Box 26	W. Charleston VT	05872	802-895-2814	No Fax
Charlotte	P.O. Box 119	Charlotte VT	05445	802-425-3071	802-425-4241
Chelsea	P.O. Box 266	Chelsea VT	05038	802-685-4460	No Fax
Chester	P.O. Box 370	Chester VT	05143	802-875-2173	802-875-2237
Chittenden	Holden Road	Chittenden VT	05737	802-483-6647	No Fax
Clarendon	P.O. Box 30	N. Clarendon VT	05759	802-775-4274	802-775-4274
Cokchester	P.O. Box 55	Colchester VT	05446	802-655-0811	802-655-0811
Concord	P.O. Box 317	Concord VT	05824	802-695-2220	No Fax
Corinth	P.O. Box 461	Corinth VT	05039	802-439-5850	No Fax
Cornwall	RD 4, Box 680	Middlebury VT	05753	802-462-2775	No Fax
Coventry	P.O. Box 104	Coventry VT	05825	802-754-2288	No Fax
Craftsbury	P.O. Box 55	Craftsbury VT	05826	802-586-2823	802-586-2823
Danby	P.O. Box 231	Danby VT	05739	802-293-5136	802-293-5311
Danville	P.O. Box 183	Danville VT	05828	802-684-3352	802-684-9606
Derby	P.O. Box 25	Derby VT	05829	802-766-4906	No Fax
Dorset	Mad Tom Road	E. Dorset VT	05253	802-362-1178	No Fax

County	Address	City, State Zip Code	Phone	Fax
VERMONT *continued*				
Dover	P.O. Box 527, Rte 100	W. Dover VT 05356	802-464-5100	802-464-8721
Putney	RR 2, Box 995	Putney VT 05346	802-257-1496	802-257-4671
Waterbury	RR 2, Box 1260	Waterbury VT 05676	802-244-6660	No Fax
East Haven	P.O. Box 10	East Haven VT 05837	802-467-3772	No Fax
E. Montpelier	P.O. Box 157	E. Montpelier VT 05651	802-223-3313	No Fax
Eden Mills	P.O. Box 11	Eden Mills VT 05653	802-635-2528	802-635-7201
Lake Elmore	P.O. Box 123	Lake Elmore VT 05657	802-888-2637	802-888-2637
Enosburg Falls	P.O. Box 465	Enosburg Falls VT 05450	802-933-4421	No Fax
Essex Jct	81 Main St.	Essex Jct. VT 05452	802-879-0413	802-878-1353
Fairfax	P.O. Box 27	Fairfax VT 05454	802-849-6111	No Fax
Fairfield	P.O. Box 5	Fairfield VT 05455	802-827-3261	No Fax
Fair Haven	3 North Park Pl	Fair Haven VT 05743	802-265-3610	No Fax
Fairlee	P.O. Box 95	Fairlee VT 05045	802-333-4363	802-333-4363
Moretown	RR 1, Box 1594	Moretown VT 05660	802-496-2454	No Fax
Ferrisburgh	P.O. Box 6	Ferrisburgh VT 05456	802-877-3429	No Fax
Cambridge	RR 1, Box 1550	Cambridge VT 05444	802-849-6616	No Fax
Franklin	P.O. Box 82	Franklin VT 05457	802-285-2101	No Fax
Georgia	RD 2, Box 319	St Albans VT 05478	802-524-3524	802-524-9794
Glover	P.O. Box 226	Glover VT 05839	802-525-6227	No Fax
Goshen	RR #3, Box 3384	Goshen VT 05733	802-247-6455	No Fax
Grafton	P.O. Box 180	Grafton VT 05146	802-843-2419	802-843-6100
Granby	P.O. Box 56	Granby VT 05840	802-328-3611	No Fax
Grand Isle	9 Hyde Road	Grand Isle VT 05458	802-372-8830	No Fax
Granville	P.O. Box 66	Granville VT 05747	802-767-4403	No Fax
Greensboro	Box 115	Greensboro VT 05841	802-533-2911	No Fax
Groton	314 Scott Hwy	Groton VT 05046	802-584-3276	No Fax
Guildhall	P.O. Box 27	Guildhall VT 05905	802-676-3797	No Fax
Guilford	RR 3, Box 255	Brattleboro VT 05301	802-254-6857	802-257-5764
Halifax	P.O. Box 45	West Halifax VT 05358	802-368-7390	No Fax
Hancock	P.O. Box 100	Hancock VT 05748	802-767-3660	No Fax
Hardwick	P.O. Box 523	Hardwick VT 05843	802-472-5971	No Fax
Hartford	15 Bridge St	White River Jct. VT 05001	802-295-2785	No Fax
Hartland	P.O. Box 349	Hartland VT 05048	802-436-2444	802-436-2444
Highgate	P.O. Box 67	Highgate Center VT 05459	802-868-4697	No Fax
Hinesburg	P.O. Box 133	Hinesburg VT 05461	802-482-2281	802-482-2096
Holland	RR 1, Box 37	Holland, Derby Line VT 05830	802-895-4440	No Fax
Hubbardton	RR 1, Box 2828	Fair Haven VT 05743	802-273-2951	No Fax
Huntington	4930 Main Rd	Huntington VT 05462	802-434-2032	No Fax
Hyde Park	P.O. Box 98	Hyde Park VT 05655	802-888-2300	802-888-2113
Ira	RR #1, Box 3420	W. Rutland VT 05777	802-235-2745	No Fax

County	Address	City, State	Zip Code	Phone	Fax
VERMONT *continued*					
Irasburg	P.O. Box 51	Irasburg VT	05845	802-754-2242	No Fax
Isle La Motte	P.O. Box 250	Isle La Motte VT	05463	802-928-3434	802-928-3002
Jamaica	P.O. Box 173	Jamaica VT	05343	802-874-4681	No Fax
Jay	RFD #2, Box 136	Jay VT	05859	802-988-2996	No Fax
Jericho	P.O. Box 67	Jericho VT	05465	802-899-4936	802-899-4786
Johnson	P.O. Box 383	Johnson VT	05656	802-635-2611	802-635-9523
Kirby	RR #2, Box 102	Lyndonville VT	05851	802-626-9386	No Fax
Landgrove	Box 508	Londonderry VT	05148	802-824-3716	No Fax
Leicester	RR #2, Box 2117-1	Leicester VT	05733	802-247-5961	No Fax
Lemington	RR 1, Box 170	Canaan VT	05903	802-277-4814	No Fax
Lincoln	RD #1, Box 1830	Bristol VT	05443	802-453-2980	No Fax
Londonderry	P.O. Box 118	S. Londonderry VT	05155	802-824-3356	No Fax
Lowell	P.O. Box 7	Lowell VT	05847	802-744-6559	No Fax
Ludlow	P.O. Box 307	Ludlow VT	05149	802-228-3232	802-228-2813
Lunenburg	P.O. Box 54	Lunenburg VT	05906	802-892-5959	No Fax
Lyndon	P.O. Box 167	Lyndonville VT	05851	802-626-5785	No Fax
Maidstone	P.O. Box 118	Guildhall VT	05905	802-676-3210	No Fax
Manchester	P.O. Box 909	Manchester Center VT	05255	802-362-1315	802-362-1314
Marlboro	P.O. Box E	Marlboro VT	05344	802-254-2181	No Fax
Marshfield	P.O. Box 30	Marshfield VT	05658	802-426-3305	No Fax
Mendon	34 US, Rt. 4	Rutland VT	05701	802-775-1662	No Fax
Middlebury	94 Main St.	Middlebury VT	05753	802-388-4041	802-388-4364
Middlesex	RR 3, Box 4600	Montpelier VT	05602	802-223-5915	802-223-0569
Middletown Springs	P.O. Box 1197	Middletown Springs VT	05757	802-235-2220	No Fax
Milton	P.O. Box 18	Milton VT	05468	802-893-4111	802-893-1005
Monkton	RFD 1, Box 2015	N. Ferrisburg VT	05473	802-453-3800	No Fax
Montgomery	P.O. Box 356	Montgomery Center VT	05471	802-326-4719	No Fax
Montpelier	City Hall, 39 Main St	Montpelier VT	05602	802-223-9500	802-223-9519
Moretown	R.R. Box 1594	Moretown VT	05660	802-496-3645	NoFax
Morgan	P.O. Box 45	Morgan VT	05853	802-895-2927	No Fax
Morriston	P.O. Box 748	Morrisville VT	05661	802-888-6370	802-888-6375
Mount Holly	P.O. Box 248	Mount Holly VT	05758	802-259-2391	802-259-2391
Mount Tabor	P.O. Box 245	Mount Tabor VT	05739	802-293-5282	No Fax
Newark	RR #1, Box 50C	Newark VT	05871	802-467-3336	No Fax
Newbury	P.O. Box 126	Newbury VT	05051	802-866-5521	802-866-5301
Newfane	P.O. Box 36	Newfane VT	05345	802-365-7772	No Fax
New Haven	RD 1, Box 4	New Haven VT	05472	802-453-3516	No Fax
Newport City	74 Main St.	Newport VT	05855	802-334-2112	802-334-5632
Newport Town	P.O. Box 85	Newport Center VT	05857	802-334-6442	802-334-6442
North Hero	P.O. Box 38	North Hero VT	05474	802-372-6926	802-372-3806

County	Address	City, State	Zip Code	Phone	Fax

VERMONT *continued*

County	Address	City, State	Zip Code	Phone	Fax
Northfield	26 S. Main St	Northfield VT	05663	802-485-5421	802-485-8426
Norton	P.O. Box 148	Norton VT	05907	802-822-5513	No Fax
Norwich	P.O. Box 376	Norwich VT	05055	802-649-1419	802-649-0123
Orange	P.O. Box 233	E. Barre VT	05649	802-479-2673	No Fax
Orwell	P.O. Box 32	Orwell VT	05760	802-948-2032	No Fax
Panton	P.O. Box 174	Vergennes VT	05491	802-475-2333	No Fax
Pawlet	P.O. Box 128	Pawlet VT	05761	802-325-3309	802-325-6109
Peacham	P.O. Box 244	Peacham VT	05862	802-592-3218	No Fax
Peru	P.O. Box 127	Peru VT	05152	802-824-3065	No Fax
Pittsfield	P.O. Box 556	Pittsfield VT	05762	802-746-8170	No Fax
Pittsford	Plains Road	Pittsford VT	05763	802-483-2931	802-483-6612
Plainfield	P.O. Box 217	Plainfield VT	05667	802-454-8461	No Fax
Plymouth	HC 70, Box 39A	Plymouth VT	05056	802-672-3655	802-672-5466
Pomfret	P.O. Box 286	N. Pomfret VT	05053	802-457-3861	No Fax
Poultney	86-88 Main St	Poultney VT	05764	802-287-5761	802-287-5110
Pownal	P.O. Box 411	Pownal VT	05261	802-823-7757	802-823-0116
Proctor	Main St	Proctor VT	05765	802-459-3333	802-459-2356
Putney	P.O. Box 233	Putney VT	05346	802-387-5862	No Fax
Randolph	Drawer B	Randolph VT	05060	802-728-5682	No Fax
Reading	P.O. Box 72	Reading VT	05062	802-484-7250	No Fax
Readsboro	P.O. Box 246	Readsboro VT	05350	802-423-5405	802-423-5423
Richford	P.O. Box 236	Richford VT	05476	802-848-7751	802-848-7752
Richmond	P.O. Box 285	Richmond VT	05477	802-434-2221	802-434-5570
Ripton	Box 10	Ripton VT	05766	802-388-2266	No Fax
Rochester	P.O. Box 238	Rochester VT	05767	802-767-3631	No Fax
Rockingham	P.O. Box 339	Bellows Falls VT	05101	802-463-4336	802-463-1228
Roxbury	P.O. Box 53	Roxbury VT	05669	802-485-7840	802-485-7840
Royalton	P.O. Box 680	S. Royalton VT	05068	802-763-7207	
Rupert	Box 140	W. Rupert VT	05776	802-394-7728	No Fax
Rutland City	P.O. Box 969	Rutland VT	05702	802-773-1801	No Fax
Rutland Town	P.O. Box 225	Center Rutland VT	05736	802-773-2528	802-773-7295
Ryegate	P.O. Box 332	Ryegate VT	05042	802-584-3880	No Fax
St Albans City	P.O. Box 867	St. Albans VT	05478	802-524-1501	802-524-1505
St Albans Town	P.O. Box 37	St. Albans Bay VT	05481	802-524-2415	802-527-2833
St George	RD 2, Box 455	Williston VT	05495	802-482-2522	No Fax
St Johnsbury	34 Main St.	St. Johnsbury VT	05819	802-748-4331	802-748-1268
Salisbury	P.O. Box 66	Salisbury VT	05769	802-352-4228	802-352-4228
Sandgate	RR 1, Box 2466	Sandgate VT	05250	802-375-9075	
Searsburg	P.O. Box 157	Wilmington VT	05363	802-464-8081	No Fax
Shaftsbury	P.O. Box 409	Shaftsbury VT	05262	802-442-4038	802-442-4043

County	Address	City, State	Zip Code	Phone	Fax
VERMONT *continued*					
Sharon	P.O. Box 250	Sharon VT	05065	802-763-8268	No Fax
Sheffield	P.O. Box 165	Sheffield VT	05866	802-626-8862	No Fax
Shelburne	P.O. Box 88	Shelburne VT	05482	802-985-5116	802-985-9550
Sheldon	P.O. Box 66	Sheldon VT	05483	802-933-2524	No Fax
Sherburne	P.O. Box 429	Killington VT	05751	802-422-3243	802-422-3030
Shoreham	P.O. Box 11	Shoreham VT	05770	802-897-5841	No Fax
Shrewsbury	RR 1, Box 658	Cuttingsville VT	05738	802-775-5689	No Fax
S. Burlington	575 Dorset St	S. Burlington VT	05403	802-658-7952	No Fax
South Hero	P.O. Box 175	South Hero VT	05486	802-372-5552	No Fax
Springfield	96 Main St.	Springfield VT	05156	802-885-2104	No Fax
Stamford	RR #1, Box 718	Stamford VT	05352	802-694-1361	802-694-1636
Stannard	P.O. Box 94	Greensboro Bend VT	05842	802-533-2577	
Starksboro	P.O. Box 91	Starksboro VT	05487	802-453-2639	No Fax
Stockbridge	P.O. Box 39	Stockbridge VT	05772	802-234-9371	802-234-9371
Stowe	P.O. Box 248	Stowe VT	05672	802-253-6133	802-253-6137
Strafford	P.O. Box 27	Strafford VT	05072	802-765-4411	No Fax
Stratton	P.O. Box 166	W. Wardsboro VT	05360	802-896-6184	802-896-6630
Sudbury	RR 1, Box 1238	Sudbury VT	05733	802-623-7296	No Fax
Sunderland	P.O. Box 295	E. Arlington VT	05252	802-375-6106	No Fax
Sutton	P.O. Box 106	Sutton VT	05867	802-467-3377	802-467-8341
Swanton	P.O. Box 711	Swanton VT	05488	802-868-4421	No Fax
Thetford	P.O. Box 126	Thetford Center VT	05075	802-785-2922	802-785-2031
Tinmouth	RR 1, Box 551	Wallingford VT	05773	802-446-2498	No Fax
Topsham	RR 1	West Topsham VT	05086	802-439-5505	No Fax
Townshend	P.O. Box 223	Townshend VT	05353	802-365-7300	No Fax
Troy	Main St	North Troy VT	05859	802-988-2663	No Fax
Tunbridge	P.O. Box 6	Tunbridge VT	05077	802-889-5521	No Fax
Underhill	P.O. Box 32	Underhill Center VT	05490	802-899-4434	802-899-2137
Vergennes	P.O. Box 35	Vergennes VT	05491	802-877-2841	802-877-1155
Vernon	P.O. Box 116	Vernon VT	05354	802-257-0292	802-254-3561
Vershire	Rte 1, Box 66C	Vershire VT	05079	802-685-2227	802-685-2227
Victory	HCR 60, Box 511	N. Concord VT	05858	802-328-2400	No Fax
Waitsfield	RR 1, Box 390	Waitsfield VT	05673	802-496-2218	No Fax
Walden	RR #1, Box 57	W. Danville VT	05873	802-563-2220	No Fax
Wallingford	P.O. Box 327	Wallingford VT	05773	802-446-2336	No Fax
Waltham	RD #2, Box 2696	Vergennes VT	05491	802-877-3641	No Fax
Wardsboro	P.O. Box 48	Wardsboro VT	05355	802-896-6055	802-896-1000
Warren	P.O. Box 337	Warren VT	05674	802-496-2709	No Fax
Washington	Town Clerks Office	Washington VT	05675	802-883-2218	No Fax
Waterbury	51 S. Main St	Waterbury VT	05676	802-244-8447	802-244-1014

County	Address	City, State	Zip Code	Phone	Fax
VERMONT *continued*					
Waterford	P.O. Box 56	Lower Waterford VT	05848	802-748-2122	No Fax
Waterville	P.O. Box 102	Waterville VT	05492	802-644-5758	No Fax
Weathersfield	Drawer E	Ascutney VT	05030	802-674-2626	802-674-2117
Wells	P.O. Box 585	Wells VT	05774	802-645-0188	No Fax
West Fairlee	P.O. Box 615	W. Fairlee VT	05083	802-333-9696	No Fax
VIRGINIA					
Accomack County	P.O. Box 388	Accomac VA	23301	804-787-5700	804-787-2468
Albemarle County	401 McIntire Rd	Charlottesville VA	22902	804-296-5841	804-296-5800
Alexandria (Indep.)	2300 King St	Alexandria VA	22314	703-838-4550	703-838-6433
Alleghany County	P.O. Box 917	Covington VA	24426	540-965-1600	540-965-1606
Amelia County	P.O. Box A	Amelia VA	23002	804-561-3039	804-561-6039
Amherst County	P.O. Box 462	Amherst VA	24521	804-946-9321	No Fax
Appomattox County	P.O. Box 863	Appomattox VA	24522	804-352-2637	804-352-4214
Arlington County	2100 Clarendon Blvd #302	Arlington VA	22201	703-358-3120	703-358-3295
Augusta County	P.O. Box 590	Verona VA	24482	540-245-5610	540-245-5621
Bath County	P.O. Box 309	Warm Springs VA	24484	540-839-7221	540-839-7222
Bedford County	122 E. Main St #202	Bedford VA	24523	540-586-7601	540-586-0406
Bedford (Indep.)	215 E. Main St	Bedford VA	24523	540-586-7102	540-586-7198
Bland County	P.O. Box 510	Bland VA	24315	540-688-4622	540-688-4622
Botetourt County	1 W. Main St., Box 1	Fincastle VA	24090	540-473-8223	540-473-8207
Bristol (Indep.)	497 Cumberland St	Bristol VA	24201	540-466-2221	540-645-7345
Brunswick County	P.O. Box 399	Lawrenceville VA	23868	804-848-3107	804-848-0424
Buchanan County	P.O. Drawer 950	Grundy VA	24614	540-935-6501	540-935-4479
Buckingham County	P.O. Box 252	Buckinghan VA	23921	804-969-4242	804-969-1638
Buena Vista (Indep.)	2039 Sycamore Ave	Buena Vista VA	24416	540-261-6121	540-261-2142
Campbell County	P.O. Box 100	Rustburg VA	24588	804-332-5161	804-332-7872
Caroline County	P.O. Box 447	Bowling Green VA	22427	804-633-5380	804-633-4970
Carroll County	405-1 N. Main St	Hillsville VA	24343	540-728-3331	540-728-4938
Charles City County	P.O. Box 128	Charles City VA	23030	804-829-2401	804-829-5819
Charlotte County	P.O. Box 608	Charlotte Court House VA	23923	804-542-5117	804-542-5248
Charlottesville (Indep.)	501 E. Jefferson St	Charlottesville VA	22902	804-972-4004	804-972-4092
Chesapeake (Indep.)	306 Cedar Rd	Chesapeake VA	23322	757-382-6166	757-382-6507
Chesterfield County	P.O. Box 40	Chesterfield VA	23832	804-748-1211	804-796-1753
Clarke County	102 N. Church St	Berryville VA	22611	540-955-5100	540-955-4002
Clifton Forge (Indep.)	P.O. Box 631	Clifton Forge VA	24422	540-863-2501	540-863-2538
Colonial Heights (Indep)	1507 Boulevard	Colonial Heights VA	23834	804-520-9265	804-520-9338
Covington (Indep.)	158 N. Court Ave	Covington VA	24426	540-965-6300	540-965-6303
Craig County	P.O. Box 308	New Castle VA	24127	540-864-5010	540-864-6732
Culpeper County	302 N. Main St	Culpeper VA	22701	540-825-3035	540-825-1677

VIRGINIA *continued*

County	Address	City, State	Zip Code	Phone	Fax
Cumberland County	P.O. Box 110	Cumberland VA	23040	804-492-3625	804-492-9224
Danville (Indep.)	P.O. Box 3300	Danville VA	24543	804-799-5100	804-799-6549
Dickenson County	P.O. Box 1098	Clintwood VA	24228	540-926-1676	540-926-1649
Dinwiddie County	P.O. Drawer 70	Dinwiddie VA	23841	804-469-4500	804-469-4503
Emporia (Indep.)	P.O. Box 511	Emporia VA	23847	804-634-3332	804-634-0003
Essex County	P.O. Box 1079	Tappahannock VA	22560	804-443-4331	804-443-4157
Fairfax County	12000 Govt. Ctr. Pkwy., Ste. 552	Fairfax VA	22035	703-324-2531	703-324-3956
Fairfax (Indep.)	10455 Armstrong St	Fairfax VA	22030	703-385-7855	703-385-7811
Falls Church (Indep.)	300 Park Ave	Falls Church VA	22046	703-241-5014	703-241-5146
Fauquier County	40 Culpeper St	Warrenton VA	22186	540-347-8680	540-349-2331
Floyd County	P.O. Box 218	Floyd VA	24091	540-745-9300	540-745-9305
Fluvanna County	P.O. Box 299	Palmyra VA	22963	804-589-3138	804-589-4976
Franklin County	108 E. Court St	Rocky Mount VA	24151	540-483-3030	540-483-3035
Franklin (Indep.)	207 W. 2nd Ave	Franklin VA	23851	804-562-8504	804-562-7982
Frederick County	107 N. Kent St	Winchester VA	22601	540-665-5666	540-667-0370
Fredericksburg (Indep.)	P.O. Box 7447	Fredericksburg VA	22404	540-372-1010	540-372-1158
Galax (Indep.)	P.O. Box 1187	Galax VA	24333	540-236-5773	540-236-2889
Giles County	120 N. Main St	Pearisburg VA	24134	540-921-2525	540-921-1846
Gloucester County	P.O. Box 329	Gloucester VA	23061	804-693-4042	804-693-6004
Goochland County	P.O. Box 10	Goochland VA	23063	804-556-5300	804-556-4617
Grayson County	P.O. Box 217	Independence VA	24348	540-773-2471	540-773-3673
Greene County	P.O. Box 358	Stanardsville VA	22973	804-985-5201	804-985-3705
Greensville County	1750 E. Atlantic St	Emporia VA	23847	804-348-4205	804-348-4257
Halifax County	P.O. Box 786	Halifax VA	24558	804-476-3300	804-476-3384
Hampton (Indep.)	22 Lincoln St	Hampton VA	23669	804-727-6392	804-728-3037
Hanover County	P.O. Box 470	Hanover VA	23069	804-537-6005	804-537-6234
Harrisonburg (Indep.)	345 S. Main St	Harrisonburg VA	22801	540-434-6776	540-434-0634
Henrico County	P.O. Box 27032	Richmond VA	23273	804-672-4386	804-672-4162
Henry County	P.O. Box 7	Collinsville VA	24078	540-638-5311	540-638-7970
Highland County	P.O. Box 190	Monterey VA	24465	540-468-2447	540-468-3248
Hopewell (Indep.)	300 N. Main St	Hopewell VA	23860	804-541-2243	804-541-2248
Isle of Wight County	P.O. Box 80	Isle of Wight VA	23397	804-357-3191	804-357-9171
James City County	P.O. Box 8784	Williamsburg VA	23187	804-253-6605	804-253-6833
King and Queen County	P.O. Box 177	King and Queen Courthouse VA	23085	804-785-7955	804-785-5700
King George County	P.O. Box 169	King George VA	22485	540-775-9181	540-775-5248
King William County	P.O. Box 215	King William VA	23086	804-769-4927	804-769-4964
Lancaster County	P.O. Box 167	Lancaster VA	22503	804-462-7501	804-462-0031
Lee County	P.O. Box 367	Jonesville VA	24263	540-346-7714	540-346-7712
Lexington (Indep)	P.O. Box 922	Lexington VA	24450	540-463-7133	540-463-5310
Loudoun County	P.O. Box 7000	Leesburg VA	20177	540-777-0202	540-777-0325

County	Address	City, State	Zip Code	Phone	Fax
VIRGINIA *continued*					
Louisa County	P.O. Box 160	Louisa VA	23093	540-967-0401	540-967-3411
Lunenburg County	Courthouse Square	Lunenburg VA	23952	804-696-2142	804-696-1798
Lynchburg (Indep.)	P.O. Box 60	Lynchburg VA	24505	804-847-1400	804-845-4304
Madison County	P.O. Box 705	Madison VA	22727	540-948-6102	540-948-3843
Manassas Park (Indep)	1 Park Center Ct	Manassas Park VA	22111	703-335-8813	703-335-0053
Martinsville (Independ)	P.O. Box 1112	Martinsville VA	24114	540-656-5180	540-656-5280
Matthews County	P.O. Box 839	Mathews VA	23109	804-725-7172	804-725-7805
Mecklenburg County	P.O. Box 307	Boydton VA	23917	804-738-6191	804-738-6804
Middlesex County	P.O. Box 428	Saluda VA	23149	804-758-4330	804-758-0061
Montgomery County	P.O. Box 806	Christiansburg VA	24073	540-382-6954	540-382-6943
Nelson County	P.O. Box 336	Lovingston VA	22949	804-263-4873	804-263-4135
New Kent County	P.O. Box 50	New Kent VA	23124	804-966-9695	804-966-9370
Newport News (Indep.)	2400 Washington Ave	Newport News VA	23607	804-247-8411	804-247-2383
Norfolk (Indep.)	810 Union St	Norfold VA	23510	804-664-4242	804-664-4239
Northampton County	P.O. Box 66	Eastville VA	23347	804-678-0440	804-678-0483
Northumberland County	P.O. Box 129	Heathsville VA	22473	804-580-7666	804-580-4321
Norton (Indep.)	P.O. Box 618	Norton VA	24273	540-679-1160	540-679-3510
Nottoway County	P.O. Box 92	Nottoway VA	23955	804-645-8696	804-645-8667
Orange County	P.O. Box 111	Orange VA	22960	540-672-3313	540-672-1679
Page County	117 S. Court St	Luray VA	22835	540-743-4142	540-743-4533
Patrick County	P.O. Box 466	Stuart VA	24171	540-694-6094	540-694-2160
Petersburg (Indep.)	Rm. 202 City Hall	Petersburg VA	23803	804-733-2301	804-732-9212
Pittsylvania County	P.O. Box 426	Chatham VA	24531	804-432-2041	804-432-4606
Poquoson (Indep.)	830 Poquoson Ave	Poquoson VA	23662	804-868-3500	804-868-8477
Portsmouth (Indep.)	P.O. Box 820	Portsmouth VA	23705	804-393-8746	804-393-5378
Powhatan County	P.O. Box 219	Powhatan VA	23139	804-598-5611	804-598-7835
Prince Edward County	P.O. Box 382	Farmville VA	23901	804-392-8837	804-392-6683
Prince George County	P.O. Box 68	Prince George VA	23875	804-733-2600	804-733-2602
Prince William County	1 County Complex Crt	Prince William VA	22192	703-792-6600	703-792-7484
Pulaski County	143 3rd St N.W., Suite 1	Pulaski VA	24301	540-980-7705	540-980-7717
Radford (Indep.)	619 2nd St	Radford VA	24141	540-731-3603	540-731-3689
Rappahannock Country	P.O. Box 519	Washington VA	22747	540-675-3342	540-675-1230
Richmond County	P.O. Box 1000	..Warsaw VA	22572	804-333-3415	804-333-3408
Richmond (Indep.)	900 E. Broad St., Suite 201	Richmond VA	23219	804-780-7970	804-780-7987
Roanoke County	P.O. Box 29800	Roanoke VA	24018	540-772-2006	540-772-2193
Rockbridge County	150 S. Main St.	Lexington VA	24450	540-463-4361	540-463-5981
Rockingham County	P.O. Box 1252	Harrisonburg VA	22801	540-564-3000	540-434-7163
Russell County	P.O. Box 1208	Lebanon VA	24266	540-889-8000	540-889-8011
Salem (Indep.)	P.O. Box 869	Salem VA	24153	540-375-3016	540-375-3003
Scott County	112 Water St, Suite 1	Gate City VA	24251	540-386-6521	540-386-9198

County	Address	City, State	Zip Code	Phone	Fax
VIRGINIA *continued*					
Shenandoah County	P.O. Box 452	Woodstock VA	22664	540-459-6165	540-459-6168
Smyth County	P.O. Box 188	Marion VA	24354	540-783-3298	540-783-9314
South Boston (Indep.)	P.O. Box 417	South Boston VA	24592	804-572-3621	804-575-4275
Southampton County	P.O. Box 400	Courtland VA	23837	804-653-3015	804-653-0227
Spotsylvania County	P.O. Box 99	Spotsylvania VA	22553	540-582-7010	540-582-9308
Stafford County	P.O. Box 339	Stafford VA	22555	540-659-8603	540-659-7643
Staunton (Indep.)	P.O. Box 58	Staunton VA	24402	540-332-3800	540-332-3807
Suffolk (Indep.)	P.O. Box 1858	Suffolk VA	23439	804-925-6344	804-925-6386
Surry County	P.O. Box 65	Surry VA	23883	804-294-5271	804-294-5204
Sussex County	P.O. Box 1397	Sussex VA	23884	804-246-7000	804-246-6013
Tazewell County	315 School St, Box 2	Tazewell VA	24651	540-988-7541	540-988-4246
Virginia Beach (Indep.)	Municipal Ctr	Virginia Beach VA	23456	804-427-4242	804-427-4135
Warren County	P.O. Box 908	Front Royal VA	22630	540-636-4600	540-636-6066
Washington County	205 Academy Dr	Abingdon VA	24210	540-676-6202	540-676-6201
Waynesboro (Indep.)	P.O. Box 1028	Waynesboro VA	22980	540-942-6600	540-942-6671
Westmoreland County	P.O. Box 1000	Montross VA	22520	804-493-0132	804-493-0134
Williamsburg (Indep.)	401 Lafayette St	Williamsburg VA	23185	804-220-6100	804-220-6109
Winchester (Indep.)	5 N. Kent St	Winchester VA	22601	540-667-5770	540-722-1063
Wise County	P.O. Box 570	Wise VA	24293	540-328-2321	540-328-9780
Wythe County	345 S. Fourth St	Wytheville VA	24382	540-223-6020	540-223-6030
York County	P.O. Box 532	Yorktown VA	23690	804-890-3320	804-890-3315
WASHINGTON					
Adams County	210 W. Broadway Ave	Ritzville WA	99169	509-659-0090	509-659-0118
Asotin County	P.O. Box 250	Asotin WA	99402	509-243-2060	509-243-2005
Benton County	P.O. Box 190	Prosser WA	99350	509-786-5600	509-786-5625
Chelan County	350 Orondo	Wenatchee WA	98801	509-664-5215	509-664-5599
Clallam County	223 E. 4th St	Port Angeles WA	98362	360-417-2231	360-417-2495
Clark County	P.O. Box 5000	Vancouver WA	98666	360-699-2232	360-737-6058
Columbia County	341 E. Main St	Dayton WA	99328	509-382-4542	509-382-4830
Cowlitz County	207 4th Ave N.	Kelso WA	98626	360-577-3020	360-577-2323
Douglas County	213 S. Ranier	Waterville WA	98858	509-745-8537	509-745-8027
Ferry County	P.O. Box 498	Republic WA	99166	509-775-5229	509-775-2492
Franklin County	1016 N. 4th St.	Pasco WA	99301	509-545-3535	509-545-2243
Garfield County	P.O. Box 278	Pomeroy WA	99347	509-843-1391	509-843-1224
Grant County	P.O. Box 37	Ephrata WA	98823	509-754-2011	509-754-5638
Grays Harbor County	P.O. Box 350	Montesano WA	98563	360-249-3731	360-249-3783
Island County	P.O. Box 5000	Coupeville WA	98239	360-679-7354	360-679-7381
Jefferson County	P.O. Box 1220	Port Townsend WA	98368	360-385-9100	360-385-9382
King County	610 3rd Ave	Seattle WA	98104	206-684-5600	206-684-8705

County	Address	City, State	Zip Code	Phone	Fax
WASHINGTON *continued*					
Kitsap County	614 Division St	Port Orchard WA	98366	360-876-7146	360-895-3932
Kittitas County	205 W. 5th Ave	Ellensburg WA	98926	509-962-7508	509-962-7667
Klickitat County	205 S. Columbus Ave	Goldendale WA	98620	509-773-4612	509-773-6779
Lewis County	360 N.W. North St.	Chehalis WA	98532	360-748-9121	No Fax
Lincoln County	P.O. Box 366	Davenport WA	99122	509-725-3031	509-725-0820
Mason County	411 N. 5th St.	Shelton WA	98584	360-427-9670	No Fax
Okanogan County	P.O. Box 72	Okanogan WA	98840	509-422-7275	No Fax
Pacific County	300 Memorial Ave	South Bend WA	98586	360-875-9320	360-875-9321
Pend Oreille County	P.O. Box 5025	Newport WA	99156	509-447-4119	509-447-0595
Pierce County	930 Tacoma Ave	Tacoma WA	98402	206-591-7455	206-597-3428
San Juan County	350 Court St. #1	Friday Harbor WA	98250	360-378-2898	360-378-7208
Skagit County	700 S. 2nd, Rm 202.	Mount Vernon WA	98273	360-336-9300	360-336-9307
Skamania County	P.O. Box 790	Stevenson WA	98648	509-427-9431	509-427-7386
Snohomish County	3000 Rockefeller Ave	Everett WA	98201	206-388-3466	No Fax
Spokane County	W. 1116 Broadway Ave	Spokane WA	99260	509-456-2265	509-456-2274
Stevens County	215 S. Oak, Rm 214	Colville WA	99114	509-684-3751	509-684-8310
Thurston County	2000 Lakeridge Dr SW	Olympia WA	98502	360-786-5440	360-754-4104
Wahkiakum County	P.O. Box 586	Cathlamet WA	98612	360-795-8048	360-795-0342
Walla Walla County	P.O. Box 1506	Walla Walla WA	99362	509-527-3200	509-527-3235
Whatcom County	311 Grand Ave	Bellingham WA	98225	360-676-6777	360-676-7727
Whitman County	404 N. Main St	Colfax WA	99111	509-397-6200	509-397-6355
Yakima County	128 N. 2nd St	Yakima WA	98901	509-574-1500	509-574-1501
WEST VIRGINIA					
Barbour County	8 North Main St	Philippi WV	26416	304-457-2232	304-457-4952
Berkeley County	100 W. King St	Martinsburg WV	25401	304-264-1927	304-267-1794
Boone County	200 State St	Madison WV	25130	304-369-3925	304-369-3925
Braxton County	P.O. Box 486	Sutton WV	26601	304-765-2833	304-765-2093
Brooke County	632 Main	Wellsburg WV	26070	304-737-3661	304-737-3668
Cabell County	750 5th Ave., Rm. 108	Huntington WV	25701	304-526-8625	304-526-8632
Calhoun County	P.O. Box 230	Grantsville WV	26147	304-354-6725	304-354-6910
Clay County	P.O. Box 190	Clay WV	25043	304-587-4259	304-587-7329
Doddridge County	118 E. Court St	West Union WV	26456	304-873-2631	304-873-1840
Fayette County	100 North Court St.	Fayetteville WV	25840	304-574-1200	304-574-2796
Gilmer County	10 Howard St	Glenville WV	26351	304-462-7641	304-462-5134
Grant County	5 Highland Ave	Petersburg WV	26847	304-257-4550	304-257-2593
Greenbrier County	P.O. Box 506	Lewisburg WV	24901	304-647-6602	No Fax
Hampshire County	P.O. Box 806	Romney WV	26757	304-822-5112	304-822-4039
Hancock County	102 N. Court St.	New Cumberland WV	26047	304-564-3311	304-564-4059
Hardy County	204 Washington St., Rm. 111	Moorefield WV	26836	304-538-2929	304-538-6832

County	Address	City, State	Zip Code	Phone	Fax
WEST VIRGINIA *continued*					
Harrison County	301 W. Main St.	Clarksburg WV	26301	304-624-8611	304-624-8673
Jackson County	Court St.	Ripley WV	25271	304-372-2011	304-372-5259
Jefferson County	110 E. Washington	Charles Town WV	25414	304-725-9761	304-725-7916
Kanawha County	409 Virginia St E	Charleston WV	25301	304-357-0130	304-357-0585
Lewis County	P.O. Box 87	Weston WV	26452	304-269-8215	304-269-8202
Lincoln County	P.O. Box 497	Hamlin WV	25523	304-824-3336	304-824-7972
Logan County	300 Stratton St	Logan WV	25601	304-792-8600	304-792-8621
Marion County	211 Adams St	Fairmont WV	26554	304-367-5445	304-367-5374
Marshall County	600 7th St	Moundsville WV	26041	304-845-1220	304-845-5891
Mason County	200 6th St	Point Pleasant WV	25550	304-675-1997	304-675-2521
McDowell County	90 Wyoming St., Suite 109.	Welch WV	24801	304-436-8544	304-436-8599
Mercer County	P.O. Box 1716	Princeton WV	24740	304-487-8311	304-487-8351
Mineral County	150 Armstrong St	Keyser WV	26726	304-788-3924	304-788-4109
Mingo County	P.O. Box 1197	Williamson WV	25661	304-235-0330	304-235-0364
Monongalia County	243 High St	Morgantown WV	26505	304-291-7230	304-291-7233
Monroe County	P.O. Box 350	Union WV	24983	304-772-3096	304-772-5051
Morgan County	202 Fairfax St	Berkeley Springs WV	25411	304-258-8547	304-258-8630
Nicholas County	700 Main St.	Summersville WV	26651	304-872-3630	304-872-5424
Ohio County	1500 Chaplin St	Wheeling WV	26003	304-234-3656	304-234-3829
Pendleton County	P.O. Box 1167	Franklin WV	26807	304-358-2505	304-358-2473
Pleasants County	301 Court Ln.	Saint Marys WV	26170	304-684-7542	304-684-9315
Pocahontas County	900 10th Ave	Marlinton WV	24954	304-799-4549	304-799-6909
Preston County	101 W. Main St., Rm 201	Kingwood WV	26537	304-329-0070	304-329-0372
Putnam County	3389 Winfield Rd	Winfield WV	25213	304-586-0202	304-586-0200
Raleigh County	215 Main St.	Beckley WV	25801	304-255-9126	304-255-9352
Randolph County	P.O. Box 368	Elkins WV	26241	304-636-0543	304-636-5989
Ritchie County	115 E. Main St., Rm. 201	Harrisville WV	26362	304-643-2164	304-643-2962
Roane County	P.O. Box 69	Spencer WV	25276	304-927-2860	304-927-4165
Summers County	P.O. Box 97	Hinton WV	25951	304-466-7104	304-466-7128
Taylor County	P.O. Box 66	Grafton WV	26354	304-265-1401	304-265-3016
Tucker County	215 1st St	Parsons WV	26287	304-478-2414	304-478-4464
Tyler County	P.O. Box 66	Middlebourne WV	26149	304-758-2102	304-758-2126
Upshur County	40 W. Main St., Rm. 101	Buckhannon WV	26201	304-472-1068	304-472-1029
Wayne County	700 Hendricks St	Wayne WV	25570	304-272-6369	304-272-5318
Webster County	2 Court Sq. Rm. G1	Webster Springs WV	26288	304-847-2508	304-847-7671
Wetzel County	P.O. Box 156	New Martinsville WV	26155	304-455-8224	304-455-5256
Wirt County	P.O. Box 53	Elizabeth WV	26143	304-275-4271	No Fax
Wood County	P.O. Box 1474	Parkersburg WV	26101	304-424-1850	304-424-1864
Wyoming County	100 Main St.	Pineville WV	24874	304-732-8000	304-732-9659

County	Address	City, State	Zip Code	Phone	Fax
WISCONSIN					
Adams County	P.O. Box 278	Friendship WI	53934	608-339-4200	608-339-4514
Ashland County	201 W. Main St	Ashland WI	54806	715-682-7016	715-682-7919
Barron County	330 E. LaSalle Ave	Barron WI	54812	715-537-6210	715-537-6277
Bayfield County	117 E. 5th St	Washburn WI	54891	715-373-6119	715-373-6153
Brown County	305 E. Walnut St	Green Bay WI	54305	414-448-4470	No Fax
Buffalo County	407 2nd St	Alma WI	54610	608-685-6212	608-685-6213
Burnett County	7410 Country Rd, K #103	Siren WI	54872	715-349-2183	No Fax
Calumet County	206 Court St	Chilton WI	53014	414-849-2361	414-849-1469
Chippewa County	711 N. Bridge St	Chippewa Falls WI	54729	715-726-7994	715-726-7987
Clark County	517 Court St	Neillsville WI	54456	715-743-5162	715-743-5154
Columbia County	P.O. Box 177	Portage WI	53901	608-742-2191	608-742-9602
Crawford County	220 N Beaumont Rd	Prairie du Chien WI	53821	608-326-0219	608-326-0220
Dane County	210 M. L. King Jr. Blvd.	Madison WI	53709	608-266-4144	608-267-3110
Dodge County	127 E. Oak	Juneau WI	53039	414-386-3722	414-386-3902
Door County	421 Nebraska	Sturgeon Bay WI	54235	414-743-5511	414-746-2330
Douglas County	1313 Belknap St	Superior WI	54880	715-394-0350	715-394-3858
Dunn County	800 Wilson Ave	Menomonie WI	54751	715-232-1228	715-232-1324
Eau Claire County	721 Oxford Ave	Eau Claire WI	54703	715-839-4745	No Fax
Florence County	P.O. Box 410	Florence WI	54121	715-528-4252	No Fax
Fond du Lac County	P.O. Box 509	Fond du Lac WI	54936	414-929-3018	414-929-3293
Forest County	200 E. Madison St	Crandon WI	54520	715-478-3823	715-478-2430
Grant County	130 W. Maple St	Lancaster WI	53813	608-723-2727	608-723-7370
Green County	Courthouse	Monroe WI	53566	608-328-9439	608-328-2835
Green Lake County	492 Hill St	Green Lake WI	54941	414-294-4021	414-294-4009
Iowa County	222 N. Iowa St	Dodgeville WI	53533	608-935-5628	608-935-3024
Iron County	300 Taconite St	Hurley WI	54534	715-561-2945	715-561-2128
Jackson County	307 Main St	Black River Falls WI	54615	715-284-0204	715-284-0261
Jefferson County	320 S. Main St	Jefferson WI	53549	414-674-7235	No Fax
Juneau County	P.O. Box 100	Mauston WI	53948	608-847-9326	608-847-9369
Kenosha County	1010 56th St	Kenosha WI	53140	414-653-2444	414-653-2564
Kewaunee County	613 Dodge St	Kewaunee WI	54216	414-388-4410	414-388-4410
La Crosse County	400 4th St N	La Crosse WI	54601	608-785-9644	No Fax
Lafayette County	P.O. Box 170	Darlington WI	53530	608-776-4838	No Fax
Langlade County	800 Clermont St	Antigo WI	54409	715-627-6209	715-627-6303
Lincoln County	1110 E. Main St	Merrill WI	54452	715-536-0318	715-536-0360
Manitowoc County	P.O. Box 421	Manitowoc WI	54221	414-683-4012	414-683-4499
Marathon County	500 Forest St.	Wausau WI	54403	715-847-5214	715-848-9210
Marinetta County	P.O. Box 320	Marinette WI	54143	715-732-7406	715-732-7532
Marquette County	P.O. Box 236	Montello WI	53949	608-297-9132	608-297-7606
Menominee County	P.O. Box 279	Keshena WI	54135	715-799-3312	715-799-1322

County	Address	City, State	Zip Code	Phone	Fax
WISCONSIN *continued*					
Milwaukee County	901 N 9th St	Milwaukee WI	53233	414-278-4000	414-223-1257
Monroe County	P.O. Box 195	Sparta WI	54656	608-269-8714	No Fax
Oconto County	301 Washington St	Oconto WI	54153	414-834-6855	414-834-6867
Oneida County	P.O. Box 400	Rhinelander WI	54501	715-369-6150	715-369-6222
Outagamie County	410 S. Walnut St	Appleton WI	54911	414-832-5095	No Fax
Ozaukee County	P.O. Box 994	Port Washington WI	53074	414-284-9411	414-284-8100
Pepin County	P.O. Box 39	Durand WI	54736	715-672-8856	715-672-8677
Pierce County	P.O. Box 267	Ellsworth WI	54011	715-273-3531	715-273-6861
Polk County	P.O. Box 549	Balsam Lake WI	54810	715-485-9299	715-485-9275
Portage County	1516 Church St	Stevens Point WI	54481	715-346-1428	715-345-5361
Price County	Courthouse, Rm 108	Phillips WI	54555	715-339-2515	No Fax
Racine County	730 Wisconsin Ave	Racine WI	53403	414-636-3208	414-636-3851
Richland County	P.O. Box 337	Richland Center WI	53581	608-647-3011	No Fax
Rock County	51 S. Main	Janesville WI	53545	608-757-5650	No Fax
Rusk County	311 Miner Ave E	Ladysmith WI	54848	715-532-2139	715-532-2175
Saint Croix County	1101 Carmichael Rd	Hudson WI	54016	715-386-4652	715-381-4400
Sauk County	515 Oak St	Baraboo WI	53913	608-356-5581	608-355-3292
Sawyer County	P.O. Box 686	Hayward WI	54843	715-634-4867	No Fax
Shawano County	311 N Main St.	Shawano WI	54166	715-524-2129	715-524-5157
Sheboygan County	615 N 6th St	Sheboygan WI	53081	414-459-3023	414-459-4383
Taylor County	P.O. Box 403	Medford WI	54451	715-748-1483	715-748-1415
Trempealeau County	36245 Main St.	Whitehall WI	54773	715-538-2311	715-538-4210
Vernon County	P.O. Box 46	Viroqua WI	54665	608-637-3568	No Fax
Vilas County	P.O. Box 369	Eagle River WI	54521	715-479-3660	715-479-3605
Walworth County	P.O. Box 995	Elkhorn WI	53121	414-741-4233	414-741-4221
Washburn County	10 4th Ave	Shell Lake WI	54871	715-468-7421	715-468-7836
Washington County	P.O. Box 1986	West Bend WI	53095	414-335-4318	414-335-4490
Waukesha County	1320 Pewaukee Rd	Waukesha WI	53188	414-548-7589	No Fax
Waupaca County	P.O. Box 307	Waupaca WI	54981	715-258-6250	No Fax
Waushara County	P.O. Box 338	Wautoma WI	54982	414-787-0444	414-787-0425
Winnebago County	P.O. Box 2808	Oshkosh WI	54903	414-236-4882	414-236-4882
Wood County	P.O. Box 8095	Wisconsin Rapids WI	54495	715-421-8451	No Fax
WYOMING					
Albany County	County Courthouse	Laramie WY	82070	307-721-2541	307-721-2544
Big Horn County	P.O. Box 31	Basin WY	82410	307-568-2357	307-568-9375
Campbell County	500 S. Gillette Ave, Suite 220	Gillette WY	82716	307-682-7285	307-687-6455
Carbon County	P.O. Box 6	Rawlins WY	82301	307-328-2668	307-328-2669
Converse County	P.O. Drawer 990	Douglas WY	82633	307-358-2244	307-358-4065
Crook County	P.O. Box 37	Sundance WY	82729	307-283-1323	307-283-1091

County	Address	City, State	Zip Code	Phone	Fax
WYOMING *continued*					
Fremont County	450 N. 2nd St., Rm 220	Lander WY	82520	307-332-2405	307-332-1132
Goshen County	P.O. Box 160	Torrington WY	82240	307-532-4051	307-532-7375
Hot Springs County	415 Arapahoe St	Thermopolis WY	82443	307-864-3515	307-864-3333
Johnson County	76 N. Main St	Buffalo WY	82834	307-684-7272	307-684-2708
Laramie County	P.O. Box 608	Cheyenne WY	82003	307-633-4266	307-633-4240
Lincoln County	P.O. Box 670	Kemmerer WY	83101	307-877-9056	307-877-3101
Natrona County	P.O. Box 863	Casper WY	82602	307-235-9216	307-235-9367
Niobrara County	P.O. Box 420	Lusk WY	82225	307-334-2211	307-334-3013
Park County	1002 Sheridan	Cody WY	82414	307-587-2204	307-587-5549
Platte County	P.O. Box 728	Wheatland WY	82201	307-322-2315	307-322-9571
Sheridan County	224 S. Main St	Sheridan WY	82801	307-674-6822	307-674-2909
Sublette County	P.O. Box 250	Pinedale WY	82941	307-367-4372	307-367-6396
Sweetwater County	P.O. Box 730	Green River WY	82935	307-875-9360	307-872-6337
Teton County	P.O. Box 1727	Jackson WY	83001	307-733-4430	307-739-8681
Uinta County	P.O. Box 810	Evanston WY	82930	307-789-1780	307-783-0511
Washakie County	P.O. Box 260	Worland WY	82401	307-347-3131	307-347-9366
Weston County	1 W. Main St	Newcastle WY	82701	307-746-4744	307-746-9505

APPENDIX S5

State Income Tax

This Appendix consists of a suggested query letter to State Departments of Revenue or Taxation and an address and phone list of those departments.

Forty-three states and the District of Columbia—all states but Alaska, Florida, Nevada, South Dakota, Texas, Washington, and Wyoming—collect personal income taxes. Therefore, when searching for assets in the forty-three states, you need not rely solely on federal IRS tax returns. Before dealing with the IRS, try the states in which your target relative worked which have state income taxes. State tax returns generally contain copies of all or most of the federal income tax schedules and forms. (See Internal Revenue Service Appendix S19 for a list of those forms most important to your search.) A state return is usually easier and quicker to get than the corresponding federal tax return. Once you get a copy of the return, you may have trouble reading and understanding some of the forms; if so, consult a reputable CPA or tax accountant.

Don't overlook interviewing the particular bookkeeper or accountant who helped your relative prepare his or her tax returns. That preparer just might know quite a bit about your target's financial affairs. For technical reasons, or by design, some asset information may have not found its way onto any income tax form.

Most states keep old tax records for at least three years **from** the tax year deadline, a total of about 3.5 years. When approaching the state tax or revenue department, assume you can get what you want. If you don't, appeal to a supervisor. Remember you'll need a power of attorney, a death certificate, or a court order designating you as personal representative.

State tax returns are a substantial resource in finding hard–fact financial information on your relative. These returns may contain information on motor vehicles, IRAs, 401K plans, and various other possessions your relative owned. They should give you at least a rough idea of what assets you are looking for and an estimate of their magnitude.

If you feel your target relative was due a state income tax refund, contact the State Unclaimed Property Office in the state where the return was filed. (See State Unclaimed Property Appendix R1.)

There is a very real possibility of your relative (if disabled) or the estate being entitled to a refund of at least part of the income tax paid during his or her last working year. Using an example from the federal tax system, here is how that comes about. When your relative was employed, F.I.C.A. and federal income taxes were withheld from his or her salary or wages. But with death or disability coming before the end of the tax year, *too much* was withheld. It's a progressive tax system, remember, and so the tax on, say, $40,000 is considerably *more* than *twice* the tax on $20,000. The federal government will not initiate contact with the estate or attorney unless they believe *additional* taxes are owed. As the heir or the one holding power of attorney, it is up to you to pursue the matter of overpaid income taxes.

Here is a numerical example, based on your relative having an annual salary of $40,000 and one tax exemption.

	If Lived Full Year	If Lived Only Half Year
Actual income for tax year:	$40,000.00	$20,000.00
Correct monthly deduction (each of 12 months):	$694.50	$250.33
Tax withheld after 6 months:	$4167.00	$4167.00
Tax owed after 6 months:	$4167.00	$3004.00
Refund due after 6 months:	0	$1163.00

SUGGESTED LETTER TO THE DEPARTMENT OF TAXATION

Date

Your Name
Address
City/State/Zip
Day Phone
Nights/Weekend Phone
Fax

State Director
Department of Taxation
Address (see State Tax Appendix)

Re: Name
Social Security Number
Last Known Address
City/State/Zip
Tax ID# (if known)

Dear Director,

The above named person is deceased (incapacitated) and I am attempting to assemble his/her assets and economic history.

Please provide me with a copy of the last filed income tax return, with any amendments, of the person named above. I have included documentation that will allow you to provide me with the copies of the information requested. (See Enclosure)

Please contact me at the address/telephone number listed above if further information is needed in order to obtain the tax return requested.

Sincerely,

Signed

☛ If required, enclose one or more of the following with a self-addressed stamped envelope:

- proof of bloodline relationship
- power of attorney
- death certificate
- court order stating that you are executor or guardian
- signed letter of request by relative for whom information is requested

STATE INCOME TAX

ALABAMA
Dept. of Revenue
Income Tax Division
P.O. Box 327410
Montgomery, AL 36132-7410
Telephone: (334) 242-1000
Fax: (334) 242-0550

ALASKA
No state income tax.

ARIZONA
Arizona Dept. of Revenue
Taxpayer Assistance
P.O. Box 29086
Phoenix, AZ 85038-9086
Telephone: (602) 255-3381
Fax: (602) 542-4765

ARKANSAS
Dept. of Finance and Adminstration
Income Tax Division
P.O. Box 1272
Little Rock, AR 72203
ATTN: Taxpayer Assistance
Telephone: (501) 682-7751
Fax: (501) 682-1691

CALIFORNIA
State of California
Franchise Tax Board
P.O. Box 942867
Sacramento, CA 94267-0041
Fax: (916) 369-5340
Toll Free: (800) 852-5711

COLORADO
Taxpayer Services Division
Colorado Dept. of Revenue
1375 Sherman St. #186
Denver, CO 80261
Telephone: (303) 232-2416
Fax: (303) 866-3211

CONNECTICUT
Dept. of Revenue Services
Taxpayer Services Division
25 Sigourney St.
Hartford, CT 06106
Telephone: (203) 297-5962
Fax: (203) 297-5714

DELAWARE
Delaware Division of Revenue
Carvel State Office Bldg.
820 N. French St.
Wilmington, DE 19801
Telephone: (302) 577-3300
Fax: (302) 577-3689
Web Site:
http://www.state.de.us/govern/agencies/revenue/revenue.htm

FLORIDA
No state income tax.

GEORGIA
State of Georgia
Dept. of Revenue
270 Washington St. S.W., Room 213
Atlanta, GA 30334
Telephone: (404) 656-4188
Fax: (404) 651-9490

HAWAII
Dept. of Taxation
Taxpayer Service
830 Punchbowl St., Middle Court
P.O. Box 259
Honolulu, HI 96809
ATTN: Tom Peterson
Telephone: (808) 587-4242
Fax: No Fax
Toll Free: (800) 222-3229

IDAHO
State Tax Commission
800 Park Blvd., Plaza IV
Boise, ID 83722
Telephone: (208) 334-7660
Fax: (208) 334-7844

STATE INCOME TAX

ILLINOIS
Dept. of Revenue
101 W. Jefferson St.
Springfield, IL 62794
Telephone: (217) 785-2602
Fax: (217) 782-6337
Toll Free: (800) 732-8866

INDIANA
Dept. of Revenue
Tax Policy Division
100 N. Senate
ATTN: Room N105
Indianapolis, IN 46204-2253
Telephone: (317) 232-2240
Fax: No Fax

IOWA
Dept. of Revenue and Finance
Taxpayer Services Division and Information
Hoover State Office Bldg.
Des Moines, IA 50319
Telephone: (515) 281-3114
Fax: (515) 242-6040

KANSAS
Dept. of Revenue
Division of Taxation, Tax Assistant
Docking State Office Bldg.
915 S.W. Harrison St.
Topeka, KS 66625-0001
Telephone: (913) 296-0222
Fax: (913) 291-3614

KENTUCKY
Commonwealth of Kentucky
Revenue Cabinet
Taxpayer Ombudsman
P.O. Box 930
Station #15
Frankfort, KY 40602-0930
Telephone: (502) 564-7822
Fax: (502) 564-8296

LOUISIANA
State of Louisiana
Dept. of Revenue and Taxation
P.O. Box 201
Baton Rouge, LA 70821-0201
Telephone: (504) 925-7537
Fax: (504) 925-7641

MAINE
State of Maine
Income Tax Division
Bureau of Taxation
State House Station # 24
Augusta, ME 04333
Telephone: (207) 626-8475
Fax: (207) 287-4028

MARYLAND
State of Maryland
Comptroller of the Treasury
Income Tax Division
State Income Tax Bldg.
Annapolis, MD 21411
Telephone: (410) 974-3981
Fax: (410) 974-2967
and (410) 974-5808
Toll Free: (800) 638-2937

MASSACHUSETTS
Commonwealth of Massachusetts
Dept. of Revenue
Leverette Saltonstall Bldg.
100 Cambridge St.
Boston, MA 02204
Telephone: (617) 727-4545
Fax: (617) 626-4150
Toll Free: (800) 392-6089

MICHIGAN
Income Tax Division
Michigan Dept. of Treasury
Treasury Bldg.
Lansing, MI 48922
Telephone: (517) 373-3196
Fax: (517) 373-4023
Toll Free: (800) 487-7000

STATE INCOME TAX

MINNESOTA
Dept. of Revenue
Taxpayer Assistance
Mail Station 4453
St. Paul, MN 55146
Telephone: (612) 296-3781
Fax: (612) 297-7430

MISSISSIPPI
State Tax Commission
102 Woolfolk Bldg.
P.O. Box 1033
Jackson, MS 39215
Telephone: (601) 359-1105
Fax: (601) 359-6516

MISSOURI
Missouri Dept. of Revenue
Division of Taxation and Collection
P.O. Box 629
Jefferson City, MO 65505-0629
Telephone: (573) 751-3505
Fax: (573) 751-7273

MONTANA
Dept. of Revenue
Income and Misc. Tax Assistance
Capitol Station, Box 5805
Helena, MT 59620
Telephone: (406) 444-3674
or (406) 444-0291
Fax: (406) 444-6642

NEBRASKA
Dept. of Revenue
Taxpayer Assistance
P.O. Box 94818
Lincoln, NE 68509
Telephone: (402) 471-2971
Fax: (402) 471-5608
Toll Free: (800) 742-7474

NEVADA
No state income tax.

NEW HAMPSHIRE
Dept. of Revenue Administration
P.O. Box 457
Concord, NH 03302
Telephone: (603) 271-2318
Fax: (603) 271-6121

NEW JERSEY
State of New Jersey
Dept. of Revenue
Document Control Center
Trenton, NJ 08646
Telephone: (609) 588-2200
Fax: No Fax
Toll Free: (800) 323-4400 (in New Jersey)

NEW MEXICO
Taxation and Revenue Dept.
and Motor Vehicle Division
P.O. Box 630
Santa Fe, NM 87509-0630
Telephone: (505) 827-0700
Fax: (505) 827-0940

NEW YORK
Dept. of Taxation and Finance
Central Photocopy Unit
W.A. Harriman Campus
Albany, NY 12227
Telephone: (518) 457-7177
Fax: (518) 457-7427

NORTH CAROLINA
North Carolina Dept. of Revenue
Office Services Division
P.O. Box 25000
Raleigh, NC 27640
Telephone: (919) 733-4684
Fax: No Fax

NORTH DAKOTA
Office of the State Tax Commissioner
State Capitol
600 E. Boulevard Ave.
Bismarck, ND 58505-0599
Telephone: (701) 328-2770
or (701) 328-3450
Fax: (701) 328-3700

STATE INCOME TAX

OHIO
Dept. of Taxation
ATTN: Marga Santamaria
P.O. Box 2476
Columbus, OH 43266-0076
Telephone: (614) 846-6712
Fax: (614) 466-6401

OKLAHOMA
Oklahoma Tax Commission
Income Tax Division
Tax Assistant Division
Connors Bldg., 5th Floor
P.O. Box 53403
Oklahoma City, OK 73152-3160
Telephone: (405) 521-3403
Fax: (405) 521-2035

OREGON
Dept. of Revenue
955 Center St. N.E.
Revenue Bldg., Room 135
Salem, OR 97310
Telephone: (503) 945-8210
Fax: No Fax

PENNSYLVANIA
Pennsylvania Dept. of Revenue
Bureau of Administrative Services
Central Records Division
12th Floor, Strawberry Sq.
Harrisburg, PA 17128-1200
Telephone: (717) 787-3683
Fax: No Fax

RHODE ISLAND
Dept. of Administration
Division of Taxation
One Capitol Hill
Providence, RI 02908
Telephone: (401) 277-2905
Fax: (401) 277-6006

SOUTH CAROLINA
State of South Carolina
Dept. of Revenue and Taxation
301 Gervais St.
Columbia, SC 29201
Telephone: (803) 737-4766
Fax: (803) 737-4898

SOUTH DAKOTA
No state income tax.

TENNESSEE
Dept. of Revenue
Andrew Jackson State Office Bldg.
500 Deaderick St.
Nashville, TN 37242
Telephone: (615) 741-3580
Fax: (615) 532-6396

TEXAS
No state income tax.

UTAH
Tax Commission
Hever M. Wells Bldg.
210 N. 1950 W.
Salt Lake City, UT 84134
Telephone: (801) 297-2200
Fax: No Fax

VERMONT
State of Vermont
Dept. of Taxes
109 State St.
Montpelier, VT 05609-1401
Telephone: (802) 828-2865
Fax: No Fax

VIRGINIA
Tax Commission
Dept. of Taxation
P.O. Box 1115
Richmond, VA 23218-1115
Telephone: (804) 367-8031
Fax: (804) 367-0985

WASHINGTON
No state income tax.

STATE INCOME TAX

WEST VIRGINIA
Dept. of Tax and Revenue
Tax Division
P.O. Box 3784
Charleston, WV 25337-3784
Telephone: (304) 558-3333
Fax: (304) 558-3269

WISCONSIN
State of Wisconsin
Dept. of Revenue
Income, Sale and Excise Tax Division
Revenue Audit Bureau
P.O. Box 8903
Madison, WI 53708-8903
Telephone: (608) 266-2890
Fax: No Fax

WYOMING
No state income tax.

DISTRICT OF COLUMBIA
Dept. of Finance and Revenue
Taxpayer Assistance Division
441 4th St. N.W., Room 550N
Washington, DC 20001
Telephone: (202) 727-6104
or (202) 727-6120
Fax: (202) 727-9069

APPENDIX S6

Credit Reports

This appendix contains the addresses of three of the major U.S. companies which issue business and consumer credit reports. It could be helpful to obtain such reports on your deceased or impaired relative because it might contain such information as:

- Addresses dating back at least seven years
- Details of checking and savings accounts
- Details of loans applied for and/or received
- Buying patterns
- Real estate loan details (loan amounts, property addresses, etc.)
- Work and salary history, stock options received, etc.
- Other financial holdings (principle residences or vacation homes, vehicles, etc.)

Below are the national credit report agencies. Fees are also listed. Send name, addresses, Social Security number, year of birth, and mailing addresses for past five years.

TRW
Attn: N.C.A.C.
P.O. Box 2104
Allen, TX 75002-2104
Toll Free: (800) 682-7654
$8.00 fee

TRANSUNION
P.O. Box 390
Springfield, PA 19064
Telephone: (610) 690-4909
Toll Free: (800) 851-2674
$8.00 fee

EQUIFAX
P.O. Box 740241
Atlanta, GA 30374
Telephone: (404) 885-8000
$8.00 fee for copy of file
Free investigation over phone.

SUGGESTED LETTER TO RECEIVE A CREDIT REPORT

Date

Your Name
Address
State/City/Zip
Day Phone
Night/Weekend Phone
Fax

Credit Bureau
Address

Re: Full Name of Target
Current Address (dating back five years)
Date of Birth
Social Security Number
Spouse's Full Name

To Whom it may concern:

Please provide me with a copy of a credit report on the above named person. (Explain in detail your reason for seeking this information.)

I have included the proper fees and documentation that will allow you to provide me with copies of the information requested. (See Enclosure)

Please contact me at the address/telephone number listed above if further information is needed in order to obtain a copy of a credit report.

Sincerely,

Signed

☛ You may find resistance from the credit reporting agency, so use creativity by asking an established business to request the credit report for you.

APPENDIX S7

General Information Sources

The more specific the information you have, on the places and dates where your target relative resided or worked, the better. But you have to do the best you can with what you have.

This appendix contains the fifty states' General Information telephone numbers. Perhaps the helpful person on the other end of the line can point you towards specific state agencies (along with their addresses, telephone and fax numbers) to aid in your search. For states in which professional licensure is spread among many far–flung boards and commissions, these General Information numbers may get you started towards more specific search locales. Licensing boards are often staffed by persons of long tenure; perhaps one of them will recall having had contact with your relative.

We're edging here towards "long shots," but a few telephone calls cost little in comparison with the value of assets you might locate.

Your goal is to narrow your search to a small number of relevant state agencies and to a manageable number of cities or counties in which your relative might have lived. When you contact the State General Information operator give him or her as much information as you can (specific places, dates and occupations) without overwhelming them with too much extraneous detail.

STATE GOVERNMENT GENERAL INFORMATION

ALABAMA
(334) 242-8000

ALASKA
(907) 465-2111

ARIZONA
(602) 542-4900

ARKANSAS
(501) 682-3000

CALIFORNIA
(916) 322-9900

COLORADO
(303) 866-5000

CONNECTICUT
(203) 566-2211

DELAWARE
(302) 739-4000

FLORIDA
(904) 488-1234

GEORGIA
(404) 656-2000

HAWAII
(808) 586-2211

IDAHO
(208) 334-2411

ILLINOIS
(217) 782-2000

INDIANA
(317) 232-1000

IOWA
(515) 281-5011

KANSAS
(913) 296-0111

KENTUCKY
(502) 564-2500

LOUISIANA
(504) 342-6600

MAINE
(207) 582-9500

MARYLAND
(410) 974-3901

MASSACHUSETTS
(617) 727-7030

MICHIGAN
(517) 373-1837

MINNESOTA
(612) 296-6013

MISSISSIPPI
(601) 359-1000

MISSOURI
(314) 751-2000

MONTANA
(406) 444-2511

NEBRASKA
(402) 471-2311

NEVADA
(702) 687-5000

NEW HAMPSHIRE
(603) 271-1110

NEW JERSEY
(609) 292-2121

NEW MEXICO
(505) 827-8110

NEW YORK
(518) 474-2121

NORTH CAROLINA
(919) 733-1110

NORTH DAKOTA
(701) 328-2000

OHIO
(614) 466-2000

OKLAHOMA
(405) 521-2011

OREGON
(503) 378-3106

PENNSYLVANIA
(717) 787-2121

RHODE ISLAND
(401) 277-2000

SOUTH CAROLINA
(803) 734-1000

SOUTH DAKOTA
(605) 773-3011

TENNESSEE
(615) 741-3011

TEXAS
(512) 463-4630

UTAH
(801) 538-3000

VERMONT
(802) 828-1110

VIRGINIA
(804) 786-0000

WASHINGTON
(360) 753-5000

WEST VIRGINIA
(304) 558-3456

WISCONSIN
(608) 266-2211

WYOMING
(307) 777-7220 or
(307) 777-5910 or
(307) 777-7011

DISTRICT OF COLUMBIA
(202) 727-1000

APPENDIX S8

Accident Reports

Perhaps your target relative was fatally injured in an accident. If so, you would be wise to obtain a copy of the accident report.

This Appendix consists of the usual query letter along with identifying information for each of the 50 state and District of Columbia agencies which maintain accident records. If the accident took place five or more years ago (the agencies listed differ in how long these records are kept on their premises), you may be sent to search in the state archives (State Archives Appendix S17).

The accident report tells you who was held responsible for the accident, the dollar amount of fines imposed, the names of witnesses and accident investigators, and the names of the insurance companies involved.

Insurance companies commonly contest larger claims and so financial settlements can take years to become final. This is especially the case when no close relative or friend was available to press for settlement or when no lawyer was actively involved. Perhaps the cash award in your relative's favor (with the amount possibly indicated in the accident file) took place some years after the tragic event. If five or more years has elapsed, that money might have been turned over to the state's Unclaimed Property Office (see State Unclaimed Property Appendix R1).

SUGGESTED LETTER TO RECEIVE AN ACCIDENT REPORT

Date

Your Full Name
Address
City/State/Zip
Day Phone
Nights/Weekend Phone
Fax

Name of State Agency
Address (see Accident Report Appendix S8)

Re: Name
Social Security Number
Last Known Address
City/State/Zip

To whom it may concern:

I am in the process of reviewing the life of the person named above. Please check your files to see if you have a report of a **fatal** accident that happened on (date) at (specify: city, county, road, highway, Interstate, etc.) Please mail me a copy of the report. I have included documentation that will allow you to provide me with the copies of the information requested. (See Enclosure.)

Please contact me at the address/telephone number listed above if further information or fees are needed in order to obtain a copy of the accident report.

Sincerely,

Signed

☛ This is public information in most states.

ACCIDENT REPORTS

ALABAMA
State of Alabama
Dept. of Public Safety
Accident Reports
P.O. Box 1471
Montgomery, AL 36102-1471
Telephone: (334) 242-4371
Fax: No Fax

ALASKA
Dept. of Public Safety
F.A.R.S
P.O. Box 20020
Juneau, AK 99807
Telephone: (907) 465-4343
Fax: (907) 269-2107

ARIZONA
Traffic Records Section
2102 Encanto Blvd.
P.O. Box 6638
Phoenix, AZ 85005
Telephone: (602) 223-2000
Fax: No Fax

ARKANSAS
Arkansas State Police
Accident Records
P.O. Box 5901
Little Rock, AR 72215
Telephone: (501) 221-8236
Fax: No Fax

CALIFORNIA
Highway Patrol
Switrs Unit
2555 1st Ave.
Sacramento, CA 95818
Telephone: (916) 657-7154
Fax: (916) 657-8628

COLORADO
State of Colorado
Motor Vehicle Division
Driver Services
140 W. 6th Ave.
Denver, CO 80261
Telephone: (303) 205-5600
Fax: No Fax

CONNECTICUT
Reports and Records
P.O. Box 2794
Middletown, CT 06457-9294
Telephone: (203) 685-8250
Fax: No Fax

DELAWARE
Delaware State Police
Traffic Control Section
P.O. Box 430
Dover, DE 19903
Telephone: (302) 739-5933
Fax: (302) 739-5966

FLORIDA
Division of Administrative Services
Crash Records Section
2100 Mahan Drive
Tallahassee, FL 32308
Telephone: (904) 487-3535
Fax: (904) 488-2441

GEORGIA
Dept. of Public Safety
Accident Reporting Section
P.O. Box 1456
Atlanta, GA 30371
Telephone: (404) 624-7660
Fax: (404) 624-6706

HAWAII
State of Hawaii
Records Division HPD
801 S. Beretania St.
Honolulu, HI 96813
Telephone: (808) 529-3271
Fax: No Fax

IDAHO
Transportation Dept.
Highway Safety
P.O. Box 7129
Boise, ID 83707
Telephone: (208) 334-8110
Fax: (208) 334-3858

ACCIDENT REPORTS

ILLINOIS
Illinois State Police
Accident Reports Unit
500 Iles Park Pl.
Suite 200
Springfield, IL 62718
Telephone: (217) 785-0614
Fax: No Fax

INDIANA
Indiana State Police
Vehicle Crash Records
301 N. Indiana Goverment
Center N.
100 N. Senate Ave.
Indianapolis, IN 46204
Telephone: (317) 232-8286
Fax: No Fax

IOWA
Driver Services
Park Fair Mall-100 Euclid
P.O. Box 9204
Des Moines, IA 50306
Telephone: (515) 237-3070
Fax: (515) 237-3152

KANSAS
Kansas Highway Patrol
Attn. Office Records Assistance
122 S.W. 7th St.
Topeka, KS 66603
Telephone: (913) 296-6800
Fax: (913) 296-5956

KENTUCKY
Kentucky State Police
Criminal Records Dept.
1250 Louisville Rd.
Frankfort, KY 40601
Telephone: (502) 227-8718
Fax: (502) 227-8734

LOUISANA
Dept. of Public Safety/Corrections
Office of State Police
Traffic Records
P.O. Box 66614
Baton Rouge, LA 70896-6614
Telephone: (504) 925-6157
Fax: No Fax

MAINE
Maine State Police
Traffic Division
State House Station
Augusta, ME 04333
Telephone: (207) 287-3397
Fax: (207) 287-6248

MARYLAND
Central Accident Records Division
Maryland State Police Headquarters
1711 Belmont Ave.
Baltimore, MD 21244
Telephone: (410) 298-3390
Fax: (410) 298-3198

MASSACHUSETTS
Dept. of Public Safety
Accident Records
1135 Tremont
Boston, MA 02120
Telephone: (617) 351-9434
Fax: No Fax

MICHIGAN
Michigan State Police
Central Records Division
Freedom of Information Unit
7150 Harris Dr.
Lansing, MI 48913
Telephone: (517) 322-5509
Fax: (517) 322-0635

ACCIDENT REPORTS

MINNESOTA
Dept. of Public Safety
Accident Records
107 Transportation Bldg.
395 John Ireland Blvd.
St. Paul, MN 55155
Telephone: (612) 296-2045
Fax: (612) 297-5574

MISSISSIPPI
Dept. of Public Safety
Safety Responsibility Branch
P.O. Box 958
Jackson, MS 39205-0958
Telephone: (601) 987-1255
Fax: (601) 987-1419

MISSOURI
Missouri Highway Patrol
Traffic Division
P.O. Box 568
Jefferson City, MO 65102
Telephone: (573) 526-6113
Fax: (573) 751-9419

MONTANA
Montana Highway Patrol
Accident Records Bureau
2550 Prospect
Helena, MT 59620
Telephone: (406) 444-3278
Fax: (406) 444-4169

NEBRASKA
Dept. of Rd.
Accident Records
P.O. Box 94669
Lincoln, NE 68509
Telephone: (402) 479-4645
Fax: (402) 479-4325

NEVADA
Dept. of Motor Vehicles
and Public Safety
Records Section
555 Wright Way
Carson City, NV 89711-0250
Telephone: (702) 687-5505
Fax: (702) 687-6798

NEW HAMPSHIRE
Dept. of Safety
10 Hazen Dr.
Concord, NH 03305
Attn: Repro
Telephone: (603) 271-2128
Fax: No Fax

NEW JERSEY
Motor Vehicle Services
Fatal Accident Administration
CN 173
West Trenton, NJ 08666
Telephone: (609) 292-8018
Fax: (609) 633-7635

NEW MEXICO
Dept. of Public Safety
P.O. Box 1628
Santa Fe, NM 87504-1628
Attn: Records
Telephone: (505) 827-9181
Fax: (505) 827-3396

NEW YORK
State of New York
Division of Motor Vehicles
Public Service Bureau
Empire State Plaza
Albany, NY 12228
Telephone: (518) 474-0710
Fax: (518) 474-0718

NORTH CAROLINA
State of North Carolina
Collision Reports-DMV
1100 New Bern Ave.
Raleigh, NC 27697
Telephone: (919) 733-7250
Fax: (919) 733-9605

NORTH DAKOTA
Drivers License Division
608 E. Blvd.
Bismarck, ND 58505
Telephone: (701) 328-2000
Fax: (701) 328-2553

ACCIDENT REPORTS

OHIO
Ohio State Highway Patrol
Traffic Records
P.O. Box 7037
Columbus, OH 43205
Telephone: (614) 466-3536
Fax: (419) 756-2452

OKLAHOMA
Dept. of Public Safety
Accident Records
P.O. Box 11415
Oklahoma City, OK 73136-0415
Telephone: (405) 425-2196
Fax: (405) 425-2046

OREGON
Dept. of Motor Vehicles
Attn: Accident Records
1905 Lana Ave., N.E.
Salem, OR 97314
Telephone: (503) 945-5098
Fax: (503) 945-5294

PENNSYLVANIA
Center for Highway Safety
Pennsylvania State Police
Attn: Traffic Accident Unit
1800 Elmerton Ave.
Harrisburg, PA 17110
Telephone: (717) 783-5516
Fax: (717) 783-4384

RHODE ISLAND
Division of Safety and Responsibility
286 Main St.
Pawtucket, RI 02860
Telephone: (401) 277-2970
Fax: No Fax

SOUTH CAROLINA
Dept. of Public Safety
Financial Responsibility Office
Attn: Financial Responsibility
P.O. Box 100178
Columbia, SC 29207-31786
Telephone: (803) 251-2969
Fax: No Fax

SOUTH DAKOTA
Dept. of Transportation
Accident Records
118 W. Capitol
Pierre, SD 57501-9935
Telephone: (605) 773-3868
Fax: No Fax

TENNESSEE
Financial Responsibility Dept.
Tennessee Dept. of Safety
1150 Foster Ave.
P.O. Box 945
Nashville, TN 37249-1000
Telephone: (615) 741-3954
Fax: No Fax

TEXAS
Texas Dept. of Public Safety
Statistical Services
Attn: Accident Records
P.O. Box 15999
Austin, TX 78761-5999
Telephone: (512) 424-2600
Fax: (512) 465-2507

UTAH
Dept. of Public Safety
Drivers License Division
P.O. Box 30560
Salt Lake City, UT 84130-0560
Telephone: (801) 965-4437
Fax: No Fax

VERMONT
Accident/Records Unit
DMV
120 State St.
Montpelier, VT
Telephone: (802) 828-2050
Fax: No Fax

ACCIDENT REPORTS

VIRGINA
Records Management
Dept. of State Police
Attn: Information Request Workcenter
P.O. Box 27412
Richmond, VA 23260
Telephone: (804) 674-2026
Fax: (804) 674-2105

WASHINGTON
Washington State Patrol
Attn: Accident Records
P.O. Box 42628
Olympia, WA 98504-2628
Telephone: (206) 459-6420
Fax: No Fax

WASHINGTON, DC
Accidents Reports
Washington, DC
300 Indiana Ave. NW
Washington, DC 20001
Telephone: (202) 727-4357
Fax: No Fax

WEST VIRGINA
Division of Motor Vehicles
Driver Improvement Unit
Capitol Complex, Bldg. 3
Charleston, WV 25317
Telephone: (304) 558-3913
Fax: (304) 558-0037

WISCONSIN
DMV Traffic Accidents Section
Room 804
P.O. Box 7919
Madison, WI 53707-7919
Telephone: (608) 266-8753
Fax: (608) 267-0606

WYOMING
Accident Records Division
Dept. of Transportation
5300 Bishop Blvd.
P.O. Box 1708
Cheyenne, WY 82003
Telephone: (307) 777-4450
Fax: (307) 777-4772

APPENDIX S9

Motor Vehicle Departments

This Appendix contains the addresses, telephone numbers, and fax numbers of the 50 State Motor Vehicle Departments. You can obtain records of motor vehicles, all types of recreational vehicles, and any other on and off road vehicles. Be sure to make the inquiry in your relative's complete name, D/B/A (Doing Business As) names, or the names of closely held corporations. Vehicle records are not kept in the name of the corporate officer. These departments will be able to provide motor vehicle ownership histories dating back seven to fifteen years.

SUGGESTED LETTER TO STATE MOTOR VEHICLE DEPARTMENT

Date

Your Name
Address
City/State/Zip
Day Phone
Nights/Weekend Phone
Fax

State Motor Vehicle Department
Address (see Motor Vehicle Appendix)

Re: Name
Address
City/State/Zip
Social Security Number

To whom it may concern:

The above named person may have had a registered motor vehicle during the last ten (10) years in (state).

Please contact me at the address/telephone number listed above if further information is needed in order to obtain a copy of his/her vehicle registration.

Sincerely,

Signed

☛ Generally this is public information.

MOTOR VEHICLE DEPARTMENTS

ALABAMA

Alabama Dept. of Revenue
Motor Vehicle Division
1202 Gordon Persons Bldg.
50 N. Ripley St.
P.O. Box 327630
Montgomery, AL 36132-7630
Telephone: (334) 242-9102
Fax: (334) 242-4385
Special Information: Search requests may be made by phone or mail.
Materials needed: VIN, titles, and copy of death certificate (for proof of relation).

ALASKA

Research Division
2150 E. Dowling Rd.
Anchorage, AK 99507
Telephone: (907) 269-5559
Fax: (907) 333-8615
Special Information: Search requests may only be made by mail. There is a $5 fee per vehicle.
Materials needed: Type, year, make of vehicle, and name.

ARIZONA

Motor Vehicle Division
Records Unit
P.O. Box 2100, Mail Drop 504M
Phoenix, AZ 85001
Telephone: (602) 255-0072
Fax: No Fax
Special Information: Search request may only be made by mail. There is a fee of $3 per car.
Materials needed: Plate, VIN, and name.

ARKANSAS

Dept. of Motor Vehicles
P.O. Box 1272
Little Rock, AR 72203
Telephone: (501) 682-7000
Fax: (501) 682-7900
Special Information: Search request may only be made by mail. There is a $3 charge per car.
Materials needed: VIN.

CALIFORNIA

Headquarters Operation
Dept. of Motor Vehicles
Registrations Services Unit
P.O. Box 942869
Sacramento, CA 94269-0001
Telephone: (916) 657-6920
Fax: (916) 657-8144
Special Information: Search requests may be made by phone. Ask for report number 70 when writing in. In letter explain why you are looking for this information. There is a $5 charge per car.
Materials needed: License plate number.

COLORADO

Motor Vehicle Division
Traffic Records Section
140 W. 6th Ave., Room 103
Denver, CO 80204
Telephone: (303) 205-5613
Fax: No Fax
Special Information: Search requests must be made in writing. Information goes back no longer than 7 years. There is a $2.20 fee per vehicle.
Materials needed: Send in your own drivers license and family members along with any information you may hold on the vehicle.

CONNECTICUT

Motor Vehicles Dept.
Copy Records Unit
60 State St.
Wethersfield, CT 06161-0503
Telephone: (203) 566-3723
Fax: (203) 566-4862
Special Information: Call and request a form; the rest is done by mail. There is at least a $5 fee depending on request, number of vehicles and people.

MOTOR VEHICLE DEPARTMENTS

DELAWARE

Division of Motor Vehicles
P.O. Box 698
Dover, DE 19903
Attn. Correspondent Dept.
Telephone: (302) 739-3147
Fax: (302) 739-2602
Special Information: Search request may only be made by mail. There is a $4 fee per record.
Materials needed: VIN or serial number, person's name and Delaware address

FLORIDA

Motor Vehicle Division
Highway Safety & Motor Vehicle Dept.
Information Resource Service
Neil Kirkman Bldg., Room A-126
Tallahassee, FL 32399-0624
Telephone: (904) 488-3881
Fax: (904) 488-0149
Special Information: Search request may only be made by mail. Send computer printout. There is a 50¢ fee per name.
Materials needed: Exact name (first, middle, and last), city lived in (not necessary)

GEORGIA

Motor Vehicle Division
Attn: Research Section
P.O. Box 74081
Atlanta, GA 30374-0381
Telephone: (404) 362-6500
Fax: No Fax
Special Information: Search requests can be done by phone or mail. When writing in send a self addressed envelope. There is a $1 charge per search.
Materials needed: Name, I.D. number, and any information on the vehicle.

HAWAII

Division of Motor Vehicles
P.O. Box 30330
Honolulu, HI 96820
Telephone: (808) 532-4325
Fax: No Fax
Special Information: Search requests may be made by phone or mail. Mail is preferred.
State Privacy Act: Hawaii will not search for a car not specifically requested. Their state does not allow this.
Materials needed: The name of the person and the license number must be provided.

IDAHO

Idaho Transportation Dept.
Motor Vehicle Title Records
PO Box 34
Boise, ID 83781-0034
Telephone: (208) 334-8773
Fax: (208) 334-8658
Special Information: Search requests must be in writing. There is a $4 fee per vehicle record.
Materials needed: Make, model, and license number.

ILLINOIS

Secretary of State
Vehicle Ownership Division
Record Inquiry Section
Room 408 Howlett Bldg.
Springfield, IL 62756
Telephone: (217) 782-6854
Fax: (217) 542-0122
Special Information: Search requests may be made by phone, fax, or mail. First call and ask for a form to be sent to you. There is a charge of $4 per vehicle record. You must have your form completed before searching.

MOTOR VEHICLE DEPARTMENTS

INDIANA

Bureau of Motor Vehicles
Vehicle Records
Indiana Government Center North
100 N. Senate, Room N 404
Indianapolis, IN 46204
Telephone: (317) 233-6000
Fax: (317) 233-5131
Special Information: Search request may be made by mail only. There is a $4 charge per vehicle. 4 years prior is $8 per vehicle.
Materials needed: Registration, license number, type, title, make, vehicle I.D., and year.

IOWA

Dept. of Transportation
Office of Vehicle Registration
Records & Titles
Park Fair Mall
100 Euclid Ave.
Des Moines, IA 50306-9204
Telephone: (515) 237-3055
Fax: (515) 237-3181
Special Information: Search requests are only accepted when mailed. There is a charge of $2.70 per 15 minutes of time it takes to search, and a 10¢ charge per copy of record found. They bill you when they send the records.
Materials needed: Name and any other information that you may have. License number and VIN are helpful.

KANSAS

Dept. of Revenue
Division of Vehicle Titles &
Registration Bureau
Docking State Office Bldg.
915 S.W. Harrison
Topeka, KS 66626-0001
Telephone: (913) 296-3621
Fax: (913) 296-3852
Special Information: Search requests are accepted in writing. There is a fee of $3.50 if everything is current. If prior to 5 years then there is a $10 charge.
Materials needed: Year, make, I.D. number, and tag number are helpful, but a name is sufficient.

KENTUCKY

Division of Motor Vehicle
Licensing
P.O. Box 2014
Frankfort, KY 40601
Telephone: (502) 564-3298
Fax: (502) 564-2950
Special Information: Search requests can be done by mail only. They cannot search by name (state law). There is a $2 charge per vehicle.
Materials needed: VIN, make, and model.

LOUISIANA

Office of Motor Vehicles
P.O. Box 64886
Baton Rouge, LA 70896
Attn: Prestige Plate Unit
Telephone: (504) 925-6264
Fax: (504) 925-4738
Special Information: Search requests may be made in writing only. There is a $7.50 charge per vehicle. If there is more than one vehicle found for a person, the requester will be contacted for additional charge.
Materials needed: Year, vehicle I.D., make, model, name, DOB, and Social Security number.

MOTOR VEHICLE DEPARTMENTS

MAINE

Secretary of State
Division of Motor Vehicles
State House Station #29
Augusta, ME 04333
Telephone: (207) 287-3556
Fax: (207) 287-6304
Special Information: Search requests may only be written. There is a $5 charge per vehicle.
Materials needed: DOB, and name are necessary.

MARYLAND

Maryland Motor Vehicle Administration
6601 Ritchie Hwy., N.E.
Counter 206
Glen Burnie, MD 21062
Telephone: (410) 768-7508
Fax: (410) 768-7653
Special Information: Search requests are accepted in writing or in person. There is a $5 charge per vehicle non-certified, and a $10 charge for certified (court record).
Materials needed: Name, DOB, current address, VIN, title number, and tag number.

MASSACHUSETTS

Dept. of Motor Vehicles
1135 Tremont
Boston, MA 02120
Attn: Mail Listing
Telephone: (617) 351-4500
Fax: No Fax
Special Information: Search requests are accepted in writing only and with a check enclosed. There is a $5 charge per name and a $10 charge per document needed (if you need proof of registration).

MICHIGAN

Michigan Dept. of State
Record Look Up Unit
7064 Crowner Dr.
Lansing, MI 48918
Telephone: (517) 322-1624
Fax: (517) 322-1181
Special Information: Search requests are accepted in writing or by phone if a credit card is available. There is a charge per vehicle of $6.55 for a current record search. An additional $6.55 if multiple vehicles are found.
Materials needed: Name and address.

MINNESOTA

Motor Vehicle Records
Room 159 Transportation Bldg.
395 John Ireland Blvd.
St Paul, MN 55155
Telephone: (612) 296-6911
Fax: (612) 282-5512
Special Information: Search requests can be done by mail or in person. Information only dates back as far as 7 years. There is a $4.50 charge per vehicle, and $1.50 for supporting paperwork; also $1 additional charge for each certified copy.
Materials needed: Plate, VIN, title, name, and address

MISSISSIPPI

Mississippi State Tax Commission
P.O. Box 1140
Jackson, MS 39215
Telephone: (601) 359-1243
Fax: (601) 359-1255
Special Information: Search requests can only be done in writing. There is a $1 charge per vehicle. Certified copies need to be requested (same charge).
Materials needed: Name and city.

MOTOR VEHICLE DEPARTMENTS

MISSOURI

Dept. of Revenue
Motor Vehicle Bureau
P.O. Box 100
Jefferson City, MO 65105
Telephone: (573) 526-3669
Fax: No Fax

Special Information: Search requests can be done in writing. It takes about 4 to 6 weeks to process. There is a $4 charge per vehicle record.

Materials needed: Name is sufficient. You need to specify the exact information you want.

MONTANA

Dept. of Motor Vehicles
Title & Registration Bureau
1032 Buckskin Dr.
Deer Lodge, MT 59722
Telephone: (406) 846-6000 (press 2 at the prompt)
Fax: No Fax

Special Information: Search requests are done in writing. There is a $6 charge needed before the search begins.

Materials needed: At least name, make, and model.

NEBRASKA

Dept. of Motor Vehicles
301 Centennial Mall S.
P.O. Box 94789
Lincoln, NE 68509
Telephone: (402) 471-2281
Fax: (402) 471-3918

Special Information: Search requests are in writing or in person. There is a $1 charge per vehicle.

Materials needed: Name is sufficient information for search.

NEVADA

Dept. of Motor Vehicles
and Public Safety
Records Office
555 Wright Way
Carson City, NV 89711-0250
Telephone: (702) 687-5505
Fax: (702) 687-6798

Special Information: Search request are in writing. Call for an account packet. There is a $5 charge per vehicle. Packet cannot be mailed; it must be presented within 10 to 12 days.

NEW HAMPSHIRE

New Hampshire Dept. of Safety
Director of Motor Vehicles
10 Hazen Dr.
Concord, NH 03305
Telephone: (603) 271-2251
Fax: No Fax

Special Information: Search requests are done in writing. There is a $2 charge per search.

Materials needed: Plate number, name, DOB, (if no DOB and the name is common, contact the DMV.)

NEW JERSEY

Motor Vehicle Services
Certified Information
CN 403
Trenton, NJ 08666
Telephone: (609) 292-4570
Fax: (609) 292-4102

Special Information: Search requests are done in writing.

Materials needed: DOB, VIN, and full name.

MOTOR VEHICLE DEPARTMENTS

NEW MEXICO
Motor Vehicle Division
Vehicle Services Bureau
Attn: Research Drivers Services
P.O. Box 1028
Santa Fe, NM 87504
Telephone: (505) 827-2220
Fax: (505) 827-0395
Special Information: Search requests are written. There is no charge.
Materials needed: Name (include M.I.), DOB, and Social Security number

NEW YORK
New York Dept. of Motor Vehicles
Division of Data Preparation
Abstract Room 430
Empire State Plaza
Albany, NY 12228
Telephone: (518) 474-0695
Fax: No Fax
Special Information: Search requests are in writing. There is a $5 charge per car.
Materials needed: DOB, name, owner, VIN, plate number, blank check

NORTH CAROLINA
Dept. of Transportation
Division of Motor Vehicles
1100 New Bern Ave.
Raleigh, NC 27697-0001
Telephone: (919) 733-3025 (press 0)
Fax: (919) 733-6951
Special Information: Search requests are in writing. There is a $1 charge per search.
Materials needed: Name, type of vehicle, Social Security number, DOB, and what you want to know.

NORTH DAKOTA
Dept. of Transportation
Motor Vehicle Division
608 E. Boulevard Ave.
Bismarck, ND 58505
Telephone: (701) 328-2725
Fax: No Fax
Special Information: Search requests are done by mail. There is a $3 charge per vehicle.
Materials needed: Name exact (include M.I.), and address.

OHIO
Bureau of Motor Vehicles
Registration Division
P.O. Box 16520
Columbus, OH 43266-0020
Attn: Vehicle Records
Telephone: (614) 752-7500
Fax: No Fax
Special Information: Search requests are done by mail. There is a fee of $3.50.
Materials needed: Title, VIN, name or plate number. Include what information you are looking for and a name, address, and phone number where you can be reached.

OKLAHOMA
Oklahoma Tax Commission
Motor Vehicle Division
2501 N. Lincoln Blvd.
Oklahoma City, OK 73194
Telephone: (405) 521-3217
Fax: No Fax
Special Information: Search requests are done by mail. There is a fee of $1. Cannot search by name.
Materials needed: VIN and title

MOTOR VEHICLE DEPARTMENTS

OREGON

Dept. of Motor Vehicles
Attn: Record Services
1905 Lana Ave. N.E.
Salem, OR 97314
Telephone: (503) 945-5000
Fax: (503) 945-5425
Special Information: Search requests must be done in writing. There is a $4 charge per vehicle. One week turnaround time.
Materials needed: Name, address, and DOB

PENNSYLVANIA

PA Dept. of Transportation
Bureau of Drivers Licensing
P.O. Box 8690
Harrisburg, PA 17105
Telephone: (717) 787-2304
Fax: (717) 783-7974
Special Information: Search requests may only be written and need to be notarized. There is a $5 charge per car.
Materials needed: VIN, plate number, and name.

RHODE ISLAND

Division of Motor Vehicles
Registration Information Request
286 Main St.
Pawtucket, RI 02860
Telephone: (401) 277-2970
Special Information: Search requests may only be made in writing. There is a $10 charge per car.
Materials needed: Name and Social Security number.

SOUTH CAROLINA

Department of Motor Vehicles
c/o South Carolina Safety Dept.
5400 Broad River Rd.
Columbia, SC 29210
Telephone: (803) 251-2960
Fax: (803) 251-1577
Special Information: Search requests may only be made by mail. There is a $2 fee per car.
Materials needed: Name, DOB, Social Security number, car, and registration, if available.

SOUTH DAKOTA

Division of Motor Vehicles
118 W. Capitol Ave.
Pierre, SD 57501-2080
Telephone: (605) 773-3541
Fax: Not Listed
Special Information: Search requests may be made in writing only. There is a $2 charge per car.
Materials needed: Exact name and address.

TENNESSEE

Tennessee Dept. of Safety
Titling & Registration Division
44 Vantage Way Suite 160
Nashville, TN 37243-8050
Telephone: (615) 741-3101
Fax: (615) 360-1940
Special Information: Search requests are done by mail. The letter must be signed and notarized. There is a $1 charge per name.
Materials needed: VIN only, but name and address are helpful (especially with common names).

MOTOR VEHICLE DEPARTMENTS

TEXAS

Division of Motor Vehicles
Titles and Registration
8868 Research, Suite 108A
P.O. Box 2293
Austin, TX 78768-2293
Telephone: (512) 465-7445
Fax: (512) 476-8042
Special Information: Search requests may be made only by phone. There is no fee. They cannot search by name.
Materials needed: VIN is the only way they can search.

UTAH

Utah State Tax Commission
Division of Motor Vehicles
210 N. 1950 W.
Salt Lake City, UT 84134
Telephone: (801) 297-7780
Fax: (801) 297-8334
Special Information: Search requests may only be made by phone or mail. There is a $2 fee per car.
Materials needed: Name and any other information you may have.

VERMONT

Motor Vehicles Dept.
120 State St.
Montpelier, VT 05603
Telephone: (802) 828-2000
Fax: (802) 828-2170
Special Information: Search requests must be made by mail. There is a $4 fee per car.
Materials needed: VIN and plate number.

VIRGINIA

Commonwealth of Virginia
Dept. of Motor Vehicles
P.O. Box 27412
Richmond, VA 23269-0001
Telephone: (804) 367-0538
Fax: (804) 367-8891
Special Information: Search request must be written. There is a $5 fee per car.
Materials needed: Name, copy of death certificate. Explain exactly what you are looking for.

WASHINGTON

Licensing Services Manager
Dept. of Licensing Vehicle
Servicing Division
P.O. Box 2957, M/S: 48021
Olympia, WA 98507-2957
Telephone: (360) 902-3770
Fax: (206) 586-6703

WEST VIRGINIA

Division of Motor Vehicles
Capitol Complex, Bldg. 3
Records Division
Charleston, WV 25317
Telephone: (304) 558-3900
Fax: No Fax
Special Information: Search requests may be written as a formal request or you may call for format. There is a $5 fee per car (pay by check).
Materials needed: Name, DOB, and Social Security number. The more information the better.

WISCONSIN

Vehicle Records Information
Wisconsin Dept. of Transportation
4802 Sheboygan Ave. 53705
Madison, WI 53707-7911
Telephone: (608) 266-3666
Fax: (608) 267-6966
Special Information: Search request must be made in writing. $3 per vehicle.
Materials needed: VIN, name, plate, and title number. The more information the better.

MOTOR VEHICLE DEPARTMENTS

WYOMING

Laramie County Treasurer
P.O. Box 125
Cheyenne, WY 82003
Telephone: (307) 633-4232
Fax: (307) 633-4267
Special Information: Search requests may only be made by writing. There may be a charge depending on the request.
Materials needed: Send all information you may have on the person and your reason for requesting the information, along with proof of the right to obtain that information.

DISTRICT OF COLUMBIA

Transportation Systems Administration
Dept. of Public Works
301 C St. N.W., Room 1157, Window 1
Washington, DC 20001
Telephone: (202) 727-6680
Fax: (202) 724-4947
Special Information: Search requests may only be made in writing. There may be a fee depending on request.
Materials needed: Name, Social Security number, and VIN.

APPENDIX S10

Credit Card Reports

Records of your target relative's credit card purchases can tell you a great deal about his/her financial dealings. Remember to look for credit life or group life or accident insurance protection built into any credit card agreements your relative might have signed. You must provide documentation to prove your relationship to the person for whom you desire information.

This Appendix contains the sample query letter for you to use, along with the names, addresses, and telephone numbers of four of the major U.S. credit card companies.

AMERICAN EXPRESS
2423 E. Lincoln Dr.
Phoenix, AZ 85016
Telephone: (800) 544-2050
Fax: (602) 954-2158

MASTERCARD INTERNATIONAL
888 7th Ave.
New York, NY 10106
Telephone: (914) 249-4600
Fax: (212) 649-5033

DISCOVER CARD SERVICES
P. O. Box 29017
Phoenix, AZ 85038
Telephone: (800) 347-2683
Fax: No Fax

VISA INTERNATIONAL
3055 Clearview Way
San Mateo, CA 94402
Telephone: (800) 445-6500
Fax: (415) 378-4129

SUGGESTED LETTER TO OBTAIN CREDIT CARD HISTORY

Date

Your Full Name
Address
City/State/Zip
Day Phone
Nights/Weekend Phone
Fax

Credit Card Agency
Address (see page S10-1)

Re: Name
Address
Credit Card Account Number
Social Security Number
Zip Code of Residence

To whom it may concern:

I am requesting the credit card activity records of the person named above. (Specify time period, if known.) I am requesting this information because my relative has become incapacitated/passed away and I am attempting to reconstruct his/her financial history.

I have included documentation that will allow you to provide me with copies of the information requested. (See Enclosure)

Please contact me at the address/telephone number listed above if further information is needed in order to obtain this information. Also please provide me with information regarding possible group insurance or credit life insurance connected with this contract.

Sincerely,

Signed

☛ If required, enclose one or more of the following documents with a self-addressed stamped envelope:

- proof of bloodline relationship—birth certificate, etc.
- power of attorney
- death certificate
- court order naming you as the executor or guardian
- signed letter of request by relative for whom information is requested
- copy of will, if existing

APPENDIX S11

State Bank Regulators

This Appendix consists of a sample query letter and a directory of the 50 states and the District of Columbia State Bank Regulator agencies. These agencies keep records on every state–chartered bank as well as on federally–chartered ones within their borders. Some states have a separate office regulating savings and loan institutions and most states have a separate office regulating credit unions.

The state bank regulator *does not deal in individual account information* so they are not the ones to contact early in your search while you are first trying to locate your relative's possible bank accounts. The primary purpose of these bank regulator offices is to enforce state banking laws and regulations governing the business practices of banks within their jurisdiction.

There are at least three reasons why you might want to contact a state bank regulator:

- If the bank in which your relative once had an account failed or is no longer in business, the state banking office will be able to tell you which current bank is its successor. Remember, the FDIC does not forward such accounts to the State Unclaimed Property Office. Be persistent.
- If you suspect an unusual (unfair) banking practice during your search for assets, you may be able to receive help with your problem from the state bank regulator. Be ready to give the agency factual information both about the account and about your problem with the particular bank.
- You also may want to know whether state law provides for credit life insurance. If so, that could serve to pay off the balance of any loan your relative had at the time of his or her death.

SUGGESTED LETTER TO THE STATE BANK REGULATOR

Date

Your Full Name
Address
City/State/Zip
Day Phone
Nights/Weekend Phone
Fax

Name of Bank Regulator
Address (see State Banking Appendix)

Re: Name of Bank
Address
Name of Individual
Address
Social Security Number
Account Number
Type of Account

Dear Director,

I am seeking information regarding a bank account held in the name above.

According to my information this account has been [lost, moved to a new bank, insured by FDIC and removed from an insolvent bank, etc.] The bank officer I have spoken with is: ___________________.
His/her telephone number is: (_____) _______-___________.

Please contact me at the above address/telephone number if any further information is needed.

Sincerely,

Signed

☛ Not all of the above may apply to your question, so be as clear as possible in your letter.
This letter also applies to credit unions.
As required, enclose one or more of the following with a self-addressed stamped envelope:

- proof of bloodline relationship
- power of attorney
- court order stating you are the executor or guardian
- death certificate
- copy of will

STATE BANK REGULATORS

ALABAMA
State of Alabama
State Banking Dept.
101 S. Union St.
Montgomery, AL 36130-1201
Telephone: (334) 242-3452
Fax: (334) 242-3500

ALASKA
State of Alaska
Dept. of Commerce
Division of Banking, Securities and Corporations
P.O. Box 110807
Juneau, AK 99811-0807
Telephone: (907) 465-2521
Fax: (907) 465-2549

ARIZONA
State Banking Dept.
2910 N. 44th St., Suite 310
Phoenix, AZ 85018
Telephone: (602) 255-4421 Ext. 31
Fax: (602) 381-1225

ARKANSAS
Arkansas State Bank Dept.
323 Center St., Suite 500
Little Rock, AR 72201-2613
Telephone: (501) 324-9019
Fax: (501) 324-9028

CALIFORNIA
State of California
State Banking Dept.
801 Kay St., Suite 2124
Sacramento, CA 95814
Telephone: (916) 322-5966
Fax: (916) 322-5976
Toll Free: (800) 622-0620

COLORADO
State of Colorado
Dept. of Regulatory Agencies
Division of Banking
1560 Broadway, Suite 1175
Denver, CO 80202
Telephone: (303) 894-7575
Fax: (303) 894-7570

CONNECTICUT
Dept. of Banking
260 Constitution Plaza
Hartford, CT 06103
Telephone: (203) 240-8299
Fax: (203) 240-8178

DELAWARE
State of Delaware
Office of the State Bank Commissioner
555 E. Loockerman St., Suite 210
Dover, DE 19901
Telephone: (302) 739-4235
Fax: (302) 739-3609

FLORIDA
Financial Institutions
Division of Financial Investigations
Suite 2103, The Capitol
Tallahassee, FL 32399-0350
Telephone: (904) 488-5275
Fax: (904) 488-7060

GEORGIA
Dept. of Banking and Finance
2990 Brandywine Rd., Suite 200
Atlanta, GA 30341-5565
Telephone: (770) 986-1633
Fax: (770) 986-1654

HAWAII
State of Hawaii
Dept. of Commerce and Consumer Affairs
Division of Financial Institutions
P.O. Box 2054
Honolulu, HI 96813
1010 Richard St.
Honolulu, HI 96805
Telephone: (808) 586-2820
Fax: (808) 586-2818

IDAHO
State of Idaho
Dept. of Finance
P.O. Box 83720
Boise, ID 83720-0031
Telephone: (208) 334-3313
Fax: (208) 332-8099
or (208) 332-8098

STATE BANK REGULATORS

ILLINOIS
Commissioner of Banks and Trust Companies
310 S. Michigan Ave., Room 2130
Chicago, IL 60604
Telephone: (312) 793-7068
Fax: (312) 793-7097

INDIANA
Dept. of Financial Institutions
402 W. Washington St.
Room W-066
Indianapolis, IN 46204-2759
Telephone: (317) 232-3955
Fax: (317) 232-7655

IOWA
Iowa Division of Banking
200 E. Grand Ave., Suite 300
Des Moines, IA 50309
Telephone: (515) 281-4014
Fax: (515) 281-4862

KANSAS
Office of the State Bank Commissioner
700 Jackson, Suite 300
Topeka, KS 66603-3714
Telephone: (913) 296-2266
Fax: (913) 296-0168

KENTUCKY
Commonwealth of Kentucky
Dept. of Financial Institutions
477 Versailles Rd.
Frankfort, KY 40601
Telephone: (502) 573-3390
Fax: (502) 573-8787

LOUISIANA
State of Louisiana
Commissioner of Financial Institutions
P.O. Box 94095
Baton Rouge, LA 70804-9095
Telephone: (504) 925-4660
Fax: (504) 925-4548

MAINE
Dept. of Professional and Financial Regulation
Bureau of Banking
36 State House Station
Augusta, ME 04333
Telephone: (207) 624-8570
Fax: (207) 624-8590

MARYLAND
Dept. of Labor, Licensing and Regulation
State Bank Commissioner
Attn: Paul Keifer
501 St. Paul Place, 13th Floor
Baltimore, MD 21202-2272
Telephone: (410) 333-6808
Fax: (410) 333-0475

MASSACHUSETTS
Commonwealth of Massachusetts
Office of the Commissioner of Banks
Leverett Saltonstall Bldg., Room 2004
100 Cambridge St.
Boston, MA 02202
Telephone: (617) 727-3120,
press 2, then press 1
Fax: (617) 727-0607

MICHIGAN
Financial Institutions Bureau
333 S. Capitol, Suite A
Lansing, MI 48909
Telephone: (517) 373-6950
Fax: (517) 373-9475

MINNESOTA
State of Minnesota
Dept. of Commerce
State Banking Division
133 E. 7th St.
St. Paul, MN 55101
Telephone: (612) 296-2715
Fax: (612) 296-8591

STATE BANK REGULATORS

MISSISSIPPI
Dept. of Banking and Consumer Finance
State of Mississippi
304 Walter Sillers State Office Bldg.
550 High St.
Jackson, MS 39202
P.O. Drawer 23729
Jackson, MS 39225-3729
Telephone: (601) 359-1031
Fax: (601) 359-3557

MISSOURI
State of Missouri
Division of Finance
Truman State Office Bldg.
301 W. High St.
Jefferson City, MO 65101
Telephone: (573) 751-3242
Fax: (573) 751-9192

MONTANA
State of Montana
Dept. of Commerce
Commissioner of Financial Institutions
846 Front St.
P.O. Box 200546
Helena, MT 59620-0546
Telephone: (406) 444-2091
Fax: (406) 444-4186

NEBRASKA
State of Nebraska
Dept. of Banking and Finance
1200 "N" St., #311 The Atrium
P.O. Box 95006
Lincoln, NE 68509-5006
Telephone: (402) 471-2171
Fax: (402) 471-3062

NEVADA
State of Nevada
Financial Institutions Division
Dept. of Business and Industry
2501 E. Sahara, Suite 300
Las Vegas, NV 89104
Telephone: (702) 486-4120
Fax: (702) 486-4563

NEW HAMPSHIRE
State of New Hampshire
Banking Dept.
169 Manchester St.
Concord, NH 03301
Telephone: (603) 271-3561
Fax: (603) 271-1090

NEW JERSEY
State of New Jersey
Dept. of Banking
CN 040
Trenton, NJ 08625-0840
Telephone: (609) 292-1102
Fax: (609) 292-0050

NEW MEXICO
State of New Mexico
Regulation and Licensing Dept.
Financial Institutions Division
725 St. Michael's Dr.
P.O. Box 25101
Santa Fe, NM 87504
Telephone: (505) 827-7100
Fax: (505) 827-7107

NEW YORK
State of New York
Banking Dept.
Two Rector St.
New York, NY 10006
Telephone: (212) 618-6445
Fax: (212) 618-6440

NORTH CAROLINA
State of North Carolina
Banking Commission
702 Oberlin Rd., Suite 400
Raleigh, NC 27605
Telephone: (919) 733-3016
Fax: (919) 733-6918

STATE BANK REGULATORS

NORTH DAKOTA
State of North Dakota
Dept. of Banking and
Financial Institutions
2900 N. 19th St., Suite 3
Bismarck, ND 58501-5305
Telephone: (701) 328-9933
Fax: (701) 328-9955

OHIO
Ohio Dept. of Commerce
Division of Banks
77 S. High St., 21st Floor
Columbus, OH 43266-0549
Telephone: (614) 466-2932
Fax: (614) 466-5594

OKLAHOMA
State Banking Dept.
4545 N. Lincoln Blvd., Suite 1645
Oklahoma City, OK 73105
Telephone: (405) 521-2783
Fax: (405) 525-9701

OREGON
State of Oregon
Division of Financial and Corporate Securities
350 Winter St. N.E. # 410
Salem, OR 97310
Telephone: (503) 378-4140
Fax: (503) 378-4178

PENNSYLVANIA
Commonwealth of Pennsylvania
Dept. of Banking
333 Market St., 16th Floor
Harrisburg, PA 17101-2290
Telephone: (717) 787-1854
Fax: (717) 787-8773
Toll Free: (800)-PABANKS (in Pennsylvania only)

RHODE ISLAND
Division of Banking
Rhode Island Dept. of Business Regulation
233 Richmond St., #231
Providence, RI 02903-4231
Telephone: (401) 277-2405
Fax: (401) 331-9123

SOUTH CAROLINA
State Board of Financial Institutions
Calhoun Office Bldg.
1015 Sumter St., Room 309
Columbia, SC 29201
Telephone: (803) 734-2001
Fax: (803) 734-2013

SOUTH DAKOTA
Division of Banking
State Capitol
500 E. Capitol Ave.
Pierre, SD 57501-5070
Telephone: (605) 773-3421
Fax: (605) 773-5367

TENNESSEE
Dept. of Financial Institutions
Banking Division
John Sevier Bldg., 4th Floor
500 Charlotte Ave.
Nashville, TN 37243-0705
Telephone: (615) 741-6013
Fax: (615) 741-2883

TEXAS
Texas Dept. of Banking
2601 N. Lamar Blvd.
Austin, TX 78705-4294
Telephone: (512) 475-1300
Fax: (512) 475-1313

UTAH
State of Utah
Dept. of Financial Institutions
324 S. State St., Suite 201
P.O. Box 89
Salt Lake City, UT 84110-0089
Telephone: (801) 538-8830
Fax: (801) 538-8894

VERMONT
Dept. of Banking, Insurance and Securities
Banking Division
89 Main St.
Drawer 20
Montpelier, VT 05620-3101
Telephone: (802) 828-3307
Fax: (802) 828-3306

STATE BANK REGULATORS

VIRGINIA
State Corporation Commission
Bureau of Financial Institutions
1300 E. Main St., Suite 800
P.O. Box 640
Richmond, VA 23218-0640
Telephone: (804) 371-9657
Fax: (804) 371-9416
Toll Free: (800) 552-7945 (in Virginia only)

WASHINGTON
State of Washington
Dept. of Financial Institutions
Division of Banks
P.O. Box 41200
Olympia, WA 98504-1200
Telephone: (360) 902-8704
Fax: (360) 753-6070

WEST VIRGINIA
State of West Virginia
Division of Banking
Bldg. #3, Room 311
State Capitol Complex
1900 Kanawha Blvd. E.
Charleston, WV 25305-0240
Telephone: (304) 558-2294
Fax: (304) 558-0442

WISCONSIN
State of Wisconsin
Office of the Commissioner of Banking
101 E. Wilson St., 5th Floor
P.O. Box 7876
Madison, WI 53703-7876
Telephone: (608) 266-1621
Fax: (608) 267-6889

WYOMING
State of Wyoming
Dept. of Audit
Division of Banking
Herschler Bldg., 3 E.
Cheyenne, WY 82002
Telephone: (307) 777-7797
Fax: (307) 777-3555

DISTRICT OF COLUMBIA
Government of the District of Columbia
Office of Banking and Financial Institutions
717 14th St. N.W., 11th Floor
Washington, DC 20005
Telephone: (202) 727-1566
Fax: (202) 727-1588

APPENDIX S12

State Savings & Loan Regulators

For a sample query letter to a State Savings and Loan Regulatory Agency, modify the one given in the State Bank Regulators Appendix S11. This current Appendix consists of a directory of the Savings and Loan Regulatory Agencies in the eleven states that have them. In the other forty states the State Bank Regulator also regulates savings and loan institutions.

Thousands of accounts go unattended in these institutions. After (usually) five years of inactivity, the account balances are turned over to the State Unclaimed Property Office.

The case of insolvent savings and loans is somewhat different. Many of these had their accounts protected, up to $100,000, by the Federal Deposit Insurance Corporation. If you find that a savings and loan in which your target relative had an account did go under, the State Savings and Loan Regulator can give you information to help you contact the successor bank, or federal agency regional office, to inquire on the insured account balance.

As in the case of the State Bank Regulators, the Savings and Loan Regulators *keep no information on individual accounts*. Their business is to enforce the state's savings and loan statutes and regulations.

STATE SAVINGS AND LOANS REGULATORS

ALABAMA
See State Bank Regulators Appendix S11

ALASKA
See State Bank Regulators Appendix S11

ARIZONA
See State Bank Regulators Appendix S11

ARKANSAS
Securities Department
201 E. Markham St., 3rd Floor
Little Rock, AR 72201
Telephone: (501) 324-9260
Fax: (501) 324-9268

CALIFORNIA
Department of Savings and Loan
300 S. Spring St., Suite 16502
Los Angeles, CA 90013
Telephone: (213) 897-8242
Fax: (213) 897-8432

COLORADO
Division of Financial Services
Department of Regulatory Agencies
1560 Broadway, Suite 1520
Denver, CO 80202
Telephone: (303) 894-2336
Fax: (303) 894-7885

CONNECTICUT
See State Bank Regulators Appendix S11

DELAWARE
See State Bank Regulators Appendix S11

FLORIDA
See State Bank Regulators Appendix S11

GEORGIA
See State Bank Regulators Appendix S11

HAWAII
See State Bank Regulators Appendix S11

IDAHO
See State Bank Regulators Appendix S11

ILLINOIS
Office of Banks and Real Estate
500 E. Monroe, Suite 900
Springfield, IL 62701
Telephone: (217) 782-6181
Fax: (217) 784-5941

INDIANA
See State Bank Regulators Appendix S11

IOWA
See State Bank Regulators Appendix S11

KANSAS
See State Bank Regulators Appendix S11

KENTUCKY
See State Bank Regulators Appendix S11

LOUISIANA
See State Bank Regulators Appendix S11

MAINE
See State Bank Regulators Appendix S11

MARYLAND
See State Bank Regulators Appendix S11

MASSACHUSETTS
See State Bank Regulators Appendix S11

STATE SAVINGS AND LOANS REGULATORS

MICHIGAN
Savings and Loan Division
Department of Commerce
P.O. Box 30224
Lansing, MI 48909
Telephone: (517) 373-7213
Fax: (517) 335-1109

MINNESOTA
See State Bank Regulators Appendix S11

MISSISSIPPI
See State Bank Regulators Appendix S11

MISSOURI
Department of Economic Development
Division of Finance
301 W. High St.
P.O. Box 716
Jefferson City, MO 65102-0836
Telephone: (314) 751-4243
Fax: (314) 751-9192

MONTANA
See State Bank Regulators Appendix S11

NEBRASKA
See State Bank Regulators Appendix S11

NEVADA
See State Bank Regulators Appendix S11

NEW HAMPSHIRE
See State Bank Regulators Appendix S11

NEW JERSEY
See State Bank Regulators Appendix S11

NEW MEXICO
See State Bank Regulators Appendix S11

NEW YORK
See State Bank Regulators Appendix S11

NORTH CAROLINA
Savings Institutions Division
1110 Navaho Dr., Suite 301
Raleigh, NC 27609
Telephone: (919) 850-2888
Fax: (919) 850-2853

NORTH DAKOTA
See State Bank Regulators Appendix S11

OHIO
Financial Institutions
77 S. High St., 21st Floor
Columbus, OH 43266-0512
Telephone: (614) 466-3723
Fax: (614) 466-5594

OKLAHOMA
See State Bank Regulators Appendix S11

OREGON
See State Bank Regulators Appendix S11

PENNSYLVANIA
See State Bank Regulators Appendix S11

RHODE ISLAND
See State Bank Regulators Appendix S11

SOUTH CAROLINA
See State Bank Regulators Appendix S11

SOUTH DAKOTA
See State Bank Regulators Appendix S11

TENNESSEE
See State Bank Regulators Appendix S11

TEXAS
Savings and Loan Dept.
2601 N. Lamar Blvd., Suite 201
Austin, TX 78705
Telephone: (512) 475-1350
Fax: (512) 475-1360

STATE SAVINGS AND LOANS REGULATORS

UTAH
See State Bank Regulators Appendix S11

VERMONT
See State Bank Regulators Appendix S11

VIRGINA
See State Bank Regulators Appendix S11

WASHINGTON
See State Bank Regulators Appendix S11

WEST VIRGINIA
See State Bank Regulators Appendix S11

WISCONSIN
Department of Financial Institutions
Division of Savings Institutions
P.O. Box 8306
Madison, WI 53708-8306
Telephone: (608) 242-2180
Fax: (608) 242-2187

WYOMING
See State Bank Regulators Appendix S11

DISTRICT OF COLOMBIA
See State Bank Regulators Appendix S11

APPENDIX S13

National Credit Union Offices

For a sample query letter to one of these six offices, modify the letter in the State Bank Regulators Appendix S11. Any of the regional offices in this Appendix can give you information on what happened to the money in an insured account or in an insolvent credit union within their region. If there is a successor credit union, they will know its name and address. Remember, credit union accounts were insured up to $100,000, protecting those funds in case credit unions became insolvent and closed. If you or your relative failed to collect on an account such as this, you have every right, even now, to recover the account.

Many credit unions issued "shares" when they were formed; often a member's shares are listed separately from his savings or checking accounts. So when you inquire, be sure to ask about share accounts or possibly other types. Credit union procedures have generally been less formal than those of banks because the credit unions had fewer state and federal regulations they had to abide by.

NATIONAL CREDIT UNION ADMINISTRATION

REGION I (Albany)
National Credit Union Administration
9 Washington Sq.
Washington Ave. Extension
Albany, New York 12205
Telephone: (518) 464-4180
Fax: (518) 464-4195

Connecticut	New York
Maine	Rhode Island
Massachusetts	Vermont
New Hampshire	

REGION II (Capital)
National Credit Union Administration
1775 Duke St.
Alexandria, VA 22314
Telephone: (703) 518-6300
Fax: (703) 518-6319

Delaware	Pennsylvania
District of Columbia	Virginia
Maryland	West Virginia
New Jersey	

REGION III (Atlanta)
National Credit Union Administration
7000 Central Parkway, Suite 1600
Atlanta, Georgia 30328
Telephone: (770) 396-4042
Fax: (770) 698-8211

Alabama	Mississippi
Arkansas	North Carolina
Florida	Puerto Rico
Georgia	South Carolina
Kentucky	Tennessee
Louisiana	Virgin Islands

REGION IV (Chicago)
National Credit Union Administration
4225 Naperville Rd., Suite 125
Lisle, IL 60532-3658
Telephone: (708) 245-1000
Fax: (708) 245-1015

Illinois	Missouri
Indiana	Ohio
Michigan	Wisconsin

REGION V (Austin)
National Credit Union Administration
4807 Spicewood Springs Rd., Suite 5200
Austin, Texas 78759
Telephone: (512) 349-4500
Fax: (512) 349-4511

Arizona	North Dakota
Colorado	Oklahoma
Iowa	South Dakota
Kansas	Texas
Minnesota	Utah
Nebraska	Wyoming
New Mexico	

REGION VI (Pacific)
National Credit Union Administration
2300 Clayton Rd., Suite 1350
Concord, California 94520
Telephone: (510) 825-6125
Fax: (510) 486-3729

Alaska	Idaho
American Samoa	Montana
California	Nevada
Guam	Oregon
Hawaii	Washington

ASSET LIQUIDATION MANAGEMENT CENTER
President, ALMC
4807 Spicewood Springs Rd., Suite 5100
Austin, Texas 78759-8490
Telephone: (512) 795-0999
Fax: (512) 795-8244

APPENDIX S14

State Insurance Regulators

This Appendix includes two suggested query letters (one to the American Council of Life Insurance, the other to a State Insurance Commissioner), and a directory listing the 50 states and the District of Columbia State Insurance Regulatory Agencies.

There are two search issues regarding life insurance: (1) locating the policy about which you have incomplete knowledge, and (2) questioning the claim–honoring practices of the insurance company once you have located a copy of the policy your target relative had with them.

Lost Life Insurance Policies

Start the insurance portion of your asset search by writing down what you currently know about each insurance policy your relative had (or even *might* have had) in force at the time of his or her death or impairment. That will include such details as:

- Name of the insurance company
- Type policy (whole or term life, automobile, health, disability, homeowner's, etc.)
- Face amount or amounts of the policy
- Policy number
- Name, address and telephone number of the insurance agency which sold your relative the policy, or serviced it
- Name and telephone number of the insurance salesperson working for that agency
- Date of last known insurance premium payment by your relative (see canceled checks); and
- General status (in force, lapsed, borrowed against, etc.) of that policy at the time of death or impairment

Your next step is to confirm the existence or non–existence of each of these supposed policies and to get copies of any of them which might still hold obtainable assets. For life insurance, an early source of information is:

American Council of Life Insurance
1001 Pennsylvania Avenue, N.W.
Washington, DC 20004
Voice: (202) 624–2000
Consumer Help Line: (800) 942–4242.

The American Council of Life Insurance offers searches of the one hundred largest life insurance companies in the United States. **Their success rate is not very good**, however, because there are over 2100 life insurance companies in the country and they limit inquiries to a total of only 4000 per month. If you found a copy of the insurance policy among your target relative's effects but cannot locate the company, again the American Council may be able to get you the name of the "successor" company. Insurance companies are often sold, or merged with others, and names change. If you run into a dead end, contact the American Council of Life Insurance. There is no such thing as an insurance company disappearing after suffering a financial downturn; the distressed company is always bought by a more profitable successor company.

Then you may need the State Insurance Commissioner in the state where the insurance was in force to review what the insurance company has told you are the reasons they are not paying. The rapidly growing number of Alzheimer's patients is a considerable source of misplaced or forgotten life insurance policies. If your relative is afflicted with this disorder, be sure to inquire whether his or her policy contains a disability waiver of premium on that account. We hope that life insurance companies will soon start providing lists of their insured who have exceeded their actual life expectancy, a sort of insurance version of states' unclaimed property rolls.

Questionable Insurance Company Business Practices

Even if you locate the insurance company and obtain a copy of the policy, you may still have valid reasons to question their claim–honoring practices. Be especially wary of companies' claims of "statutes of limitations" or any vague or unsubstantiated reasons why your relative's heirs should not collect. Making sure insurance companies play "by the book" is the reason for existence of the state insurance regulatory office. If you have any doubts about the business practices or veracity of an insurance company, contact the appropriate state insurance regulator with all the details you can come up with. In casualty (non–life insurance) claims, such independent reports of those made by police, the fire marshal, or the state highway patrol may be obtained and forwarded to the State Insurance Regulator for review.

For specific information on unknown assets connected to your relative's having been injured in an automobile accident, see Accident Reports Appendix S8. For information on collecting insurance premium overpayments or health care overpayments, see Insurance Appendix R10.

SUGGESTED LETTER REQUESTING ASSISTANCE FROM STATE INSURANCE REGULATORS

Date

Your Name
Address
City/State/Zip
Day Phone
Nights/Weekend Phone
Fax

State Insurance Regulator
Address (see Insurance Regulators Appendix)

Re: Name
Address
Social Security Number
Insurance Carrier, Address/Telephone #
Agent's Name

Dear Insurance Commissioner,

I am writing to you because I am not satisfied that in the above individual's case all regulations were followed in the resolution of the insurance matter. Perhaps your office could assist me in this matter. The insurance involved:

- life insurance
- automobile insurance
- health insurance
- real estate insurance
- other (specify)

The facts as I know them are:

- Be brief and organized; use specific names not pronouns;
- State what you think should have been done that was not done.
- Attach copies of correspondence you have received from the referenced company.

Sincerely,

Signed

SUGGESTED LOST LIFE INSURANCE POLICY LETTER

Date

Your Name
Address
City/State/Zip
Day Phone
Nights/Weekend Phone
Fax

American Council of Life Insurance
1001 Pennsylvania Ave., N.W.
Washington, DC 20004
Telephone: (202) 624-2000

Re: Search Name
Address or Addresses
Social Security Number
Company Name (if known)
Agent Name
City where policy was purchased

To whom it may concern,

Please assist me in finding the life insurance policy for the above named. He/she is my (specify relationship). I am requesting this information because my relative has become incapacitated/passed away and I am attempting to reconstruct his/her financial history.

Please contact me at the address/telephone number above if you need any further information.

Sincerely,

Signed

☛ As required, enclose one or more of the following:

- power of attorney
- death certificate
- proof of bloodline relationship
- court order stating you are executor or guardian
- copy of will

STATE INSURANCE REGULATORS

ALABAMA
State of Alabama
Department of Insurance
135 S. Union St.
Montgomery, AL 36130-3351
Telephone: (334) 269-3550
Fax: (334) 240-3194

ALASKA
State of Alaska
Department of Commerce
and Economic Development
Division of Insurance
P.O. Box 110805
Juneau, AK 99811-0805
Telephone: (907) 465-2515
Fax: (907) 465-3422

ARIZONA
State of Arizona
Department of Insurance
2910 N. 44th St., Suite 210
Phoenix, AZ 85018
Telephone: (602) 912-8400
Fax: (602) 912-8404

ARKANSAS
Arkansas State Insurance Department
1200 W. 3rd St.
Little Rock, AR 72201
Telephone: (501) 371-2600
Fax: No Fax

CALIFORNIA
State of California
Department of Insurance
300 S. Spring St.
Los Angeles, CA 90013
Telephone: (213) 897-8921
Fax: (213) 736-4891

COLORADO
State of Colorado
Division of Insurance
Department of Regulatory Agencies
1560 Broadway, Suite 850
Denver, CO 80202
Telephone: (303) 894-7499
Fax: (303) 894-7455

CONNECTICUT
State of Connecticut
Department of Insurance
153 Market St., 11th Floor
P.O. Box 816
Hartford, CT 06142-0816
Telephone: (203) 297-3800
Fax: (203) 566-7410

DELAWARE
State of Delaware
Department of Insurance
P.O. Box 7007
Dover, DE 19903
Telephone: (302) 739-4251
Fax: (302) 739-5280

FLORIDA
Office of the Treasurer
Department of Insurance
200 E. Gaines St.
Tallahassee, FL 32399-0327
Telephone: (904) 922-3153
Fax: (904) 488-7061

GEORGIA
State of Georgia
Office of the Commissioner of Insurance
7th Floor, West Tower
2 M. L. King Jr. Dr., S.W.
Atlanta, GA 30334
Telephone: (404) 656-2070
Fax: (404) 657-8542

HAWAII
Department of Insurance
Insurance Division
250 S. King St., 5th Floor
P.O. Box 3614
Honolulu, HI 96811
Telephone: (808) 586-2790
Fax: (808) 586-2806

IDAHO
Idaho Department of Insurance
700 W. State St.
Boise, ID 83720-0043
Telephone: (208) 334-4250
Fax: (208) 334-4398

STATE INSURANCE REGULATORS

ILLINOIS
State of Illinois
Department of Insurance
320 W. Washington St.
Springfield, IL 62767
Telephone: (217) 782-4515
Fax: (217) 782-5020

INDIANA
Indiana Department of Insurance
311 W. Washington St., Suite 300
Indianapolis, IN 46204-2787
Telephone: (317) 232-2385
Fax: (317) 232-5251

IOWA
Iowa Insurance Division
Lucas State Office Bldg.
E. 12th & Grand
Des Moines, IA 50319
Telephone: (515) 281-5705
Fax: (515) 281-3059

KANSAS
Kansas Insurance Department
420 S.W. 9th St.
Topeka, KS 66612-1678
Telephone: (913) 296-3071
Fax: (913) 296-2283

KENTUCKY
Commonwealth of Kentucky
Department of Insurance
P.O. Box 517
Frankfort, KY 40602-0517
Telephone: (502) 564-3630
Fax: (502) 564-6090

LOUISIANA
State of Louisiana
Department of Insurance
P.O. Box 94214
Baton Rouge, LA 70804-9214
Telephone: (504) 342-5900
Fax: (504) 342-3078

MAINE
Department of Professional
and Financial Regulation
Bureau of Insurance
124 Northern Ave.
Gardiner, ME 04345
Telephone: (207) 624-8475
Fax: (207) 624-8599

MARYLAND
Maryland Insurance Administration
Insurance Division
501 St. Paul Place
Baltimore, MD 21202
Telephone: (410) 333-6300
Fax: (410) 333-6650

MASSACHUSETTS
Division of Insurance
470 Atlantic Ave.
Boston, MA 02110-2223
Telephone: (617) 521-7794
Fax: (617) 521-7772

MICHIGAN
State of Michigan
Department of Consumer
and Industry Services
Insurance Bureau
P.O. Box 30220
Lansing, MI 48909
Telephone: (517) 373-0240
Fax: (517) 335-4978

MINNESOTA
State of Minnesota
Department of Commerce
133 E. 7th St.
St. Paul, MN 55101
Telephone: (612) 296-4026
Fax: (612) 296-4328

MISSISSIPPI
Mississippi Insurance Department
1804 Walter Sillers Bldg.
P.O. Box 79
Jackson, MS 39205-0079
Telephone: (601) 359-3569
Fax: (601) 359-2474

STATE INSURANCE REGULATORS

MISSOURI
Department of Insurance
301 W. High St.
Truman Building
Jefferson City, MO 65101
Telephone: (573) 751-4126
Fax: (573) 751-1165

MONTANA
State of Montana
Insurance Division
Mitchell Building
P.O. Box 4009
Helena, MT 59604
Telephone: (406) 444-2040
Fax: (406) 444-3497

NEBRASKA
State of Nebraska
Department of Insurance
941 "O" St., Suite 400
Lincoln, NE 68508
Telephone: (402) 471-2201
Fax: (402) 471-4610

NEVADA
State of Nevada
Division of Insurance
Capitol Complex
1665 Hot Springs Rd., #152
Carson City, NV 89710
Telephone: (702) 687-4270
Fax: (702) 687-3937

NEW HAMPSHIRE
State of New Hampshire
Insurance Department
169 Manchester St.
Concord, NH 03301
Telephone: (603) 271-2261
Fax: (603) 271-1406

NEW JERSEY
State of New Jersey
Department of Insurance
Division of Enforcement and
Consumer Protection
CN 325
Trenton, NJ 08625
Telephone: (609) 633-7667
Fax: (609) 292-5865

NEW MEXICO
Department of Insurance
P.O. Drawer 1269
Santa Fe, NM 87504-1269
Telephone: (505) 827-4500
Fax: (505) 827-4734

NEW YORK
State of New York
Insurance Department
160 W. Broadway
New York, NY 10013
Telephone: (212) 602-0967
Fax: (212) 602-0437

NORTH CAROLINA
Department of Insurance
State of North Carolina
P.O. Box 26387
Raleigh, NC 27611
Telephone: (919) 733-7343
Fax: (919) 733-6495

NORTH DAKOTA
Department of Insurance
State of North Dakota
600 E. Boulevard
5th Floor State Capitol
Bismarck, ND 58505-0320
Telephone: (701) 328-2440
Fax: (701) 224-4880

OHIO
State of Ohio
Department of Insurance
2100 Stella Court
Columbus, OH 43215-1067
Telephone: (614) 644-2651
Fax: (614) 644-3743

STATE INSURANCE REGULATORS

OKLAHOMA
State of Oklahoma
Insurance Department
P.O. Box 53408
Oklahoma City, OK 73152-3408
Telephone: (405) 521-2828
Fax: (405) 521-6652

OREGON
Consumer Protection Section
Insurance Division
350 Winter St. N.E., Room 440-2
Salem, OR 97310
Telephone: (503) 378-4636
Fax: (503) 378-4351

PENNSYLVANIA
Commonwealth of Pennsylvania
Insurance Department
Strawberry Sq., Room 1311
Harrisburg, PA 17120
Telephone: (717) 787-2317
Fax: (717) 783-1059

RHODE ISLAND
State of Rhode Island
Insurance Division
233 Richmond St., Suite 233
Providence, RI 02903
Telephone: (401) 277-2223
Fax: (401) 751-4887

SOUTH CAROLINA
State of South Carolina
Department of Insurance
P.O. Box 100105
Columbia, SC 29202
Telephone: (803) 737-6117
Fax: (803) 737-6205

SOUTH DAKOTA
Department of Commerce and Regulation
Division of Insurance
500 E. Capitol
Pierre, SD 57501-5070
Telephone: (605) 773-3563
Fax: (605) 773-5369

TENNESSEE
State of Tennessee
Department of Commerce and Insurance
Policy Holders Service Section
500 James Robertson Pkwy.
Nashville, TN 37243-0574
Telephone: (615) 741-2218
Fax: (615) 532-2788
Toll Free: (800) 342-4029

TEXAS
Texas Department of Insurance
P.O. Box 149104
Austin, TX 78714-9104
Telephone: (512) 463-6169
Fax: (512) 475-2005

UTAH
State of Utah
Insurance Department
State Office Building, Room 3110
Salt Lake City, UT 84114
Telephone: (801) 538-3800
Fax: (801) 538-3829

VERMONT
Department of Banking, Insurance,
and Securities
89 Main St., Drawer 20
Montpelier, VT 05620-3101
Telephone: (802) 828-3301
Fax: (802) 828-3306

VIRGINIA
Commonwealth of Virginia
State Corporation Commission
Bureau of Insurance
P.O. Box 1157
Richmond, VA 23218
Telephone: (804) 371-9741
Fax: (804) 371-9511

STATE INSURANCE REGULATORS

WASHINGTON
State of Washington
Insurance Commissioner
Insurance Building
P.O. Box 40255
Olympia, WA 98504-0255
Telephone: (360) 753-7300
Fax: (360) 586-3535
Consumer Hot-Line: (800) 562-6900

WEST VIRGINIA
Insurance Commission
Consumer Service Division
P.O. Box 50540
Charleston, WV 25305-0540
Telephone: (304) 558-3386
Fax: (304) 558-0412

WISCONSIN
Office of the Commissioner of Insurance
121 E. Wilson St.
P.O. Box 7873
Madison, WI 53707-7873
Telephone: (608) 266-3585
Fax: (608) 266-9935

WYOMING
State of Wyoming
Insurance Department
Herschler Building
122 W. 25th St.
Cheyenne, WY 82002
Telephone: (307) 777-7401
Fax: (307) 777-5895

DISTRICT OF COLUMBIA
Insurance Administration
Consumer and Regulatory Affairs
441 4th St. N.W.
8th Floor N.
Washington, DC 20001
Telephone: (202) 727-8000
Fax: (202) 727-7940

APPENDIX S15

Professional Licensing

A surprisingly wide array of trades and professions require some sort of state license. If your target relative worked in one of those vocations you may be able to locate his or her file. In it you may find such information as a resume showing further personal history, academic records and transcripts, local addresses, trade status (e.g., apprentice, journeyman, or master), or membership in professional societies. On that last possibility, keep in mind that many of these professional groups sponsor group life insurance as well as other supplemental coverages.

A few states—as indicated in the contact list in this Appendix—don't have a central Professional Licensing Board. In those cases, contact the state's General Information Office listing in Appendix S7.

Here are the occupations which require licenses in most states.

Accountant
Anesthesiologist
Appraiser
Architect
Auctioneer
Audiologist
Barber
Boxer
Broker
Builder
Business Licenses
Commercial Driver
Community Planner
Contractor
Controlled Substances Counselor
Dental Hygienist
Dentist
Dietitian
Electrician
Employment Agency
Engineer (all types)
Environmental Health
Examination Services
Family Therapist
Forester
Funeral Director
Geologist
Guide/Outfitter
Hairdresser
Hearing Aid Dealer
Instructor
Interior Designer
Land Sales
Landscape Architect
Lawyer
Licensed Practical Nurse
Manager
Manicurist
Medical Corporation
Mortician
Nail Technician
Naturopath
Nurse
Nurse Aide Registry
Occupational Therapist
Optometrist
Paramedic
Pharmacist
Physical Assistant
Physical Therapist
Physician
Pilot
Plumber
Podiatrist
Polygraph Examiner
Private Alarm Contractor
Private Investigator
Professional Service Promoter
Psychologist
Referee
Registered Nurse
Roofer
Shop Owner
Shorthand Reporter
Social Worker
Speech Pathologist
Surveyor
Time Share
TV/Radio Technician
Vehicle Salesperson
Veterinarian

SUGGESTED LETTER TO A PROFESSIONAL LICENSING DEPARTMENT

Date

Your Name
Address
City/State/Zip
Day Phone
Nights/Weekend Phone
Fax

State Professional Licensing Office/Board
Address (see Professional Licensing Appendix)

Re: Name
Last Known Address
Social Security Number
Last Known Telephone Number

Dear Director:

I am requesting licensing information regarding the above person.

My purpose in requesting this information is that I am reconstructing this person's economic history. I understood he/she was employed as a (specify profession). Will you please check your records to see if this person is/was licensed in your state.

In the event you need additional information before you can release information to me, please contact me at the above address and telephone number.

Sincerely,

Signed

☛ This is public information.

PROFESSIONAL LICENSING

ALABAMA
See Preface

ALASKA
Division of Occupational Licensing Programs
Commerce and Economic Development Department
333 Willoughby Ave., 9th Floor
P.O. Box 110806
Juneau, AK 99811
Telephone: (907) 465-2534
Fax: (907) 465-2974

ARIZONA
See Preface

ARKANSAS
See Preface

CALIFORNIA
Department of Consumer Affairs
400 “R” St., Suite 3000
Sacramento, CA 95814
Telephone: (916) 445-4465
Fax: (916) 323-6639

COLORADO
Department of Regulatory Agencies
1560 Broadway, #1550
Denver, CO 80202
Telephone: (303) 894-7855
Fax: (303) 894-7885

CONNECTICUT
Consumer Protection
Professional, Occupational Licensing and Regulation
165 Capitol Ave.
Hartford, CT 06106
Telephone: (203) 566-1810
Fax: (203) 566-7630

DELAWARE
Department of Administrative Services
Division of Professional Regulation
Cannon Building, Suite 203
P.O. Box 1401
Dover, DE 19903
Telephone: (302) 739-4522
Fax: (302) 739-2711

FLORIDA
Florida Department of State
Division of Licensing
The Capitol, MS #4
Tallahassee, FL 32399-0250
Telephone: (904) 487-0482
Fax: (904) 488-2789

GEORGIA
State Examining Board
Office of the Secretary of State
166 Pryor St., S. W.
Atlanta, GA 30303
Telephone: (404) 656-3900
Fax: (404) 651-9532

HAWAII
Department of Commerce and Consumer Affairs
Division of Licensing and Regulation
P.O. Box 3469
Honolulu, HI 96801
Telephone: (808) 586-2850
Fax: (808) 586-2689

IDAHO
State of Idaho
Bureau of Occupational Licenses
Owyhee Plaza
1109 Main St., Suite 220
Boise, ID 83702-5642
Telephone: (208) 334-3233
Fax: (208) 334-3945

ILLINOIS
Department of Professional Regulation
320 W. Washington St., 3rd Floor
Springfield, IL 62786
Telephone: (217) 785-0800
Fax: (217) 782-7645

PROFESSIONAL LICENSING

INDIANA
Indiana Professional Licensing Agency
302 W. Washington St., Room E034
Indianapolis, IN 46204-2700
Telephone: (317) 232-2980
Fax: (317) 233-5559

IOWA
Professional Licensing
and Regulation Division
Department of Commerce
1918 S.E. Hulsizer
Ankeny, IA 50021
Telephone: (515) 281-4126
Fax: (515) 281-7411

KANSAS
See Preface

KENTUCKY
Division of Occupations and Professions
Berry Hill Annex
P.O. Box 456
Frankfort, KY 40602
Telephone: (502) 564-3296
Fax: (502) 564-4818

LOUISIANA
Department of Social Services
Licensing Bureau
P.O. Box 3078
Baton Rouge, LA 70821
Telephone: (504) 922-0015
Fax: (504) 922-0014

MAINE
Department of Professional
and Financial Regulation
Office of Licensing and Enforcement
State House Station # 35
Augusta, ME 04333
Telephone: (207) 624-8603
Fax: (207) 624-8637

MARYLAND
Department of Labor, Licensing
and Regulation
501 St. Paul Place
Baltimore, MD 21202
Telephone: (410) 333-6200
Fax: (410) 333-1229

MASSACHUSETTS
Division of Registration
Leverett Saltonstall Bldg., Government Center
100 Cambridge St., 15th Floor
Boston, MA 02202
Telephone: (617) 727-3074
Fax: (617) 727-2197

MICHIGAN
Department of Consumer
and Industry Services
Occupational and Professional Regulation
611 W. Ottawa St.
Lansing, MI 48933
Telephone: (517) 373-1870
Fax: (517) 335-6696

MINNESOTA
Licensing Unit
Department of Commerce
133 E. 7th
St. Paul, MN 55101
Telephone: (612) 296-4518
Fax: (612) 296-4328

MISSISSIPPI
See Preface

MISSOURI
Division of Professional Registration
P.O. Box 1335
3605 Missouri Blvd.
Jefferson City, MO 65102
Telephone: (314) 751-0293
Fax: (314) 751-4176

PROFESSIONAL LICENSING

MONTANA
Professional and Occupational Licensing Bureau
Department of Commerce
111 N. Jackson
P.O. Box 200513
Helena, MT 59620-0513
Telephone: (406) 444-3737
Fax: (406) 444-1667

NEBRASKA
Division of Professional and Occupational Licensure
P.O. Box 95007
Lincoln, NE 68509
Telephone: (402) 471-2115
Fax: (402) 471-3577

NEVADA
See Preface

NEW HAMPSHIRE
SOICC of New Hampshire
64 Old Suncook Rd.
Concord, NH 03301
Telephone: (603) 228-3349
Fax: (603) 228-3209
E-Mail: SOICCNHY

NEW JERSEY
Office of the Director
Division of Consumer Affairs
Department of Law and Public Safety
P.O. Box 45027
Newark, NJ 07101
Telephone: (201) 504-6320
Fax: (201) 648-3538

NEW MEXICO
Boards and Commissions
Regulations and Licensing Department
P.O. Box 25101
Santa Fe, NM 87504
Telephone: (505) 827-7004
Fax: (505) 827-7107

NEW YORK
Division of Professional Licensing Services
Cultural Education Center
Albany, NY 12230
Telephone: (518) 474-3817
Fax: (518) 473-0578

NORTH CAROLINA
See Preface

NORTH DAKOTA
Secretary of State
State of North Dakota
600 East Boulevard Ave.
Bismarck, ND 58505-0500
Telephone: (701) 328-2900
Fax: (701) 328-2992

OHIO
Department of Commerce
Division of Financial Institutions
77 S. High St., 20th Floor
Columbus, OH 43266-0546
Telephone: (614) 466-3636
Fax: No Fax

OKLAHOMA
See Preface

OREGON
See Preface

PENNSYLVANIA
Bureau of Professional and Occupational Affairs
Department of State
P.O. Box 2649
Harrisburg, PA 17105
Telephone: (717) 787-8503
Fax: (717) 787-7769

RHODE ISLAND
State of Rhode Island
Department of Health
Professional Regulation
3 Capitol Hill, Room 104
Providence, RI 02908
Telephone: (401) 277-2827
Fax: (401) 277-1272

PROFESSIONAL LICENSING

SOUTH CAROLINA
Department of Labor, Licensing
and Regulation
Landmark Center
3600 Forest Dr., Suite 200
P.O. Box 11329
Columbia, SC 29211-1329
Telephone: (803) 734-9600
Fax: (803) 734-4207

SOUTH DAKOTA
Department of Commerce and Regulations
Professional and Occupational Licensing
910 E. Sioux Ave.
Pierre, SD 57501
Telephone: (605) 773-3178
Fax: (605) 773-3018

TENNESSEE
Division of Regulatory Boards
500 James Robertson Parkway
2nd Floor Volunteer Plaza
Nashville, TN 37243-0572
Telephone: (615) 741-3449
Fax: (615) 741-6470

TEXAS
Department of Licensing and Regulation
Enforcement Division
P.O. Box 12157
Austin, TX 78711
Telephone: (512) 463-7352
Fax: (512) 463-1376

UTAH
Department of Commerce
Division of Occupational
and Professional Licensing
160 E. 3rd S.
P.O. Box 45805
Salt Lake City, UT 84145-0805
Telephone: (801) 530-6628
Fax: (801) 530-6738

VERMONT
Office of Professional Regulation
Office of the Secretary of State
109 State St.
Montpelier, VT 05609-1106
Telephone: (802) 828-2367
Fax: (802) 828-2496

VIRGINIA
Department of Professional
and Occupational Licensing
3600 West Broad St.
Richmond, VA 23230-4917
Telephone: (804) 367-8500
Fax: (804) 367-9537

WASHINGTON
Department of Licensing
1125 Washington St., S.E.
Olympia, WA 98507-8001
Telephone: (360) 902-3600
Fax: (360) 664-2550

WEST VIRGINIA
See Preface

WISCONSIN
Department of Regulation and Licensing
1400 E. Washington Ave.
P.O. Box 8935
Madison, WI 53708
Telephone: (608) 266-8609
Fax: (608) 267-0644

WYOMING
Professional Licensing Board
2020 Carey Ave, Suite 201
Cheyenne, WY 82002
Telephone: (307) 777-7788
Fax: (307) 777-3508

DISTRICT OF COLUMBIA
Occupational and Professional Licensing
614 "H" St., N.W.
Washington, DC 20001
Telephone: (202) 727-7480
Fax: (202) 727-7662

APPENDIX S16

Corporate Records

This Appendix furnishes you with the names, addresses, voice and fax telephone numbers of the 50 states and the District of Columbia offices which maintain records on corporations. Records are kept (usually for at least seven years) on both currently active corporations and on those which have wound up their affairs. Looking into these records may provide you information on corporate stock owned by your relative as well as names of persons he or she did business with.

SUGGESTED LETTER TO THE STATE CORPORATE DIVISION

Date

Your name
Address
City/State/Zip
Day Phone
Nights/Weekend Phone
Fax

State Office
Address (see State Corporate Division Appendix)

Re: Name and/or Corporate Name
Address
City/State/Zip
Social Security Number
Tax ID #

Dear Director,

I have reason to believe that the person named above owned a corporation registered in your state during (specific time period). Please check your records for a corporation listed by this name. (If you know the name of the corporation, you may ask for a copy of the Board of Directors and Officers.) Please check for D/B/A (Doing Business As) or trade names used by this person in conducting his/her business affairs.

Please contact me at the address/telephone number listed above if further information is needed in order to obtain the requested information.

Sincerely,

Signed

☛ Generally, this is public information.

CORPORATE RECORDS

ALABAMA
Secretary of State
Corporation Section
11 S. Union St., Suite 36104
P.O. Box 5616
Montgomery, AL 36103-5616
Telephone: (334) 242-5324
Fax: (334) 240-3138

ALASKA
Dept. of Commerce and
Economic Development
Attn. Corporate Section
P.O. Box 110808
Juneau, AK 99811
Telephone: (907) 465-2530
Fax: (907) 465-3257

ARIZONA
Corporation Commission
1300 W. Washington
Phoenix, AZ 85007
Telephone: (602) 542-3026
Fax: (602) 542-3414

ARKANSAS
Corporate Supervisor
058 State Capitol Bldg.
Little Rock, AR 72201
Telephone: (501) 682-3409
Fax: (501) 682-3437

CALIFORNIA
Corporate Division
Office of the Secretary of State
1500 11th St.
Sacramento, CA 95814
Telephone: (916) 657-5251
Fax: No Fax

COLORADO
Corporate Division
Dept. of State
1560 Broadway, Suite 200
Denver, CO 80202
Telephone: (303) 894-2251
Fax: (303) 894-2242

CONNECTICUT
Commercial Recording Division
Office of the Secretary of State
30 Trinity St.
Hartford, CT 06106
Telephone: (203) 566-2764
Fax: (203) 566-6192

DELAWARE
Corporation Division
Dept. of State
Townsend Bldg.
P.O. Box 898
Dover, DE 19903
Telephone: (302) 739-3073
Fax: (302) 739-3812

FLORIDA
Division of Corporations
Dept. of State
P.O. Box 6327
Tallahassee, FL 32314
Telephone: (904) 487-6000
Fax: (904) 487-6012

GEORGIA
Business Information and Service Division
Secretary of State's Office
2 M.L. King Jr. Dr. S.E., Suite 315 W. Tower
Atlanta, GA 30334-1530
Telephone: (404) 656-2817
Fax: (404) 651-9059

HAWAII
Dept. of Commerce and Consumer Affairs
P.O. Box 40
Honolulu, HI 96810
Telephone: (808) 586-2850
Fax: (808) 586-2733

IDAHO
Office of the Secretary of State
State Capitol
700 W. Jefferson, Room 203
Boise, ID 83720-0080
Telephone: (208) 334-2300
Fax: (208) 334-2282

CORPORATE RECORDS

ILLINOIS

Corporations Division
Dept. of the Secretary of State
Business Services
328 Howlett Bldg.
2nd and Edwards Sts.
Springfield, IL 62756
Telephone: (217) 782-7880
Fax: (217) 782-4528

INDIANA

Corporations Division
Office of the Secretary of State
302 W. Washington, Room E018
Indianapolis, IN 46204
Telephone: (317) 232-6576
Fax: (317) 233-3387

IOWA

Corporations Division
Office of the Secretary of State
E. 14th and Walnut Sts.
Hoover Bldg., 2nd Floor
Des Moines, IA 50319
Telephone: (515) 281-5204
Fax: (515) 242-5953

KANSAS

Secretary of State
Corporations Division
State Capitol Bldg.
300 S.W. 10th Ave., 2nd Floor
Topeka, KS 66612
Telephone: (913) 296-4564
Fax: (913) 296-4570

KENTUCKY

Kentucky Secretary of State
Corporation Records
P.O. Box 718
Frankfort, KY 40602-0718
Telephone: (502) 564-7330
Fax: (502) 564-4075

LOUISIANA

Commercial Division
Dept. of State
P.O. Box 94125
Baton Rouge, LA 70804-9125
Telephone: (504) 925-4704
Fax: (504) 925-4726

MAINE

Secretary of State
Corporations Division
State House Station # 101
Augusta, ME 04333
Telephone: (207) 287-4180
Fax: (207) 287-5874

MARYLAND

Dept. of Assessments and Taxation
301 W. Preston St., Room 809
Baltimore, MD 21201
Telephone: (410) 225-1184
Fax: (410) 333-7097
ON LINE: 800-463-6009 (in Maryland only)

MASSACHUSETTS

Corporations Division
Director of Corporation
One Ashburton Place, Room 1710
Boston, MA 02108
Telephone: (617) 727-2853
Fax: (617) 742-4538

MICHIGAN

Michigan Dept. of Consumer
and Industry Services
Corporations and Securities Bureau
P.O. Box 30054
Lansing, MI 48909-7554
Telephone: (517) 334-6206
Fax: No Fax

MINNESOTA

Corporations Division
Office of the Secretary of State
180 State Office Bldg.
100 Constitution Ave.
St. Paul, MN 55155-1299
Telephone: (612) 296-2803
Fax: (612) 215-0683

CORPORATE RECORDS

MISSISSIPPI
Corporations Division
Office of the Secretary of State
P.O. Box 136
Jackson, MS 39205
Telephone: (601) 359-1333
Fax: (601) 359-1607

MISSOURI
Corporations Division
Office of the Secretary of State
600 W. Main, Room 322
P.O. Box 778
Jefferson City, MO 65102
Telephone: (314) 751-3200
Fax: (314) 751-5841

MONTANA
Business Services Bureau
Office of Secretary of State
State Capitol, Room 225
Helena, MT 59620
Telephone: (406) 444-2034
Fax: (406) 444-3976

NEBRASKA
Dept. of State
Corporations Division
Suite 1301, Capitol Bldg.
Lincoln, NE 68509-4608
Telephone: (402) 471-2554
Fax: (402) 471-3666

NEVADA
Commercial Recordings
Office of the Secretary of State
Capitol Complex
Carson City, NV 89710
Telephone: (702) 687-5203
Fax: (702) 687-3471

NEW HAMPSHIRE
Corporations Division
Secretary of State
Room 204 State House
107 N. Main St.
Concord, NH 03301-4989
Telephone: (603) 271-3244
Fax: (603) 271-3247

NEW JERSEY
Division of Commercial Recording
Dept. of State
820 Bear Tavern Rd.
CN 308
Trenton, NJ 08625
Telephone: (609) 530-6412
Fax: (609) 530-6433

NEW MEXICO
Corporations Dept.
Corporations Commission
PERA Bldg., Room 418
Santa Fe, NM 87504
Telephone: (505) 827-4511
Fax: (505) 827-4387

NEW YORK
Dept. of State
Division of Corporations and State Records
Albany, NY 12231-0001
Telephone: (518) 473-2492
Fax: (518) 474-5173
Corp. Search: (900) TEL-CORP

NORTH CAROLINA
Dept. of Secretary of State
Corporations Division
300 N. Salisbury St.
Raleigh, NC 27603-5909
Telephone: (919) 733-4201
Fax: (919) 733-1837

NORTH DAKOTA
Corporations Division
Office of the Secretary of State
600 E. Boulevard Ave.
Bismarck, ND 58505-0500
Telephone: (701) 328-4284
Fax: (701) 328-2992

OHIO
Secretary of State
Corporate Division
30 E. Broad St., 14th Floor
Columbus, OH 43266-0418
Telephone: (614) 466-3910
Fax: (614) 466-2892

CORPORATE RECORDS

OKLAHOMA
Office of the Secretary of State
Corporations Division
101 State Capitol
Oklahoma City, OK 73105-4897
Telephone: (405) 521-3911
Fax: (405) 521-3771

OREGON
Corporation Division
Secretary of State
255 Capitol St., N.E., Suite 151
Salem, OR 97310
Telephone: (503) 986-2200
Fax: (503) 378-4381

PENNSYLVANIA
Corporation Bureau
Dept. of State
P.O. Box 87221
Harrisburg, PA 17105-8721
Telephone: (717) 787-1057
Fax: No Fax

RHODE ISLAND
Corporations Division
Office of the Secretary of State
100 N. Main St.
Providence, RI 02903
Telephone: (401) 277-3040
Fax: (401) 277-1309

SOUTH CAROLINA
Corporations Division
Secretary of State
Wade Hampton Bldg.
P.O. Box 11350
Columbia, SC 29211
Telephone: (803) 734-2170
Fax: (803) 734-2164

SOUTH DAKOTA
Secretary of State
Corporations/UCC Supervisor
500 E. Capitol, Suite 205
Pierre, SD 57501
Telephone: (605) 773-4845
Fax: (605) 773-4550

TENNESSEE
Division of Services
Office of the Secretary of State
James K. Polk Bldg., 18th Floor
505 Deaderick St.
Nashville, TN 37243-0306
Telephone: (615) 741-2286
Fax: (615) 741-7310

TEXAS
Corporate Division
Office of the Secretary of State
P.O. Box 13697
Austin, TX 78711-3697
Telephone: (512) 463-5555
Fax: (512) 463-5709
Copies/Certificates: (512) 463-5578

UTAH
State of Utah
Division of Corporations and Commercial Code
Heber M. Wells Bldg.
160 E. 300 S.
P.O. Box 146705
Salt Lake City, UT 84145-6705
Telephone: (801) 530-6024
Fax: (801) 530-6438

VERMONT
Office of the Secretary of State
Corporations Division
109 State St.
Montpelier, VT 05609-1104
Telephone: (802) 828-2386
Fax: (802) 828-2853

VIRGINIA
State Corporation Commission
1300 E. Main St.
Richmond, VA 23219
Telephone: (804) 371-9733
Fax: (804) 371-9133

CORPORATE RECORDS

WASHINGTON
Corporate Division
Office of the Secretary of State
505 E. Union, 2nd Floor
P.O. Box 40234
Olympia, WA 98504-0234
Telephone: (360) 753-7115
Fax: No Fax

WEST VIRGINIA
Corporations Division
Secretary of State
State Capitol, W. 139
Charleston, WV 25305
Telephone: (304) 558-8000
Fax: (304) 558-0900

WISCONSIN
Office of the Secretary of State
Corporations Division
P.O. Box 7846
Madison, WI 53707
Telephone: (608) 266-3590
Fax: (608) 267-6813

WYOMING
Corporations Division
Office of the Secretary of State
110 Capitol Bldg.
Cheyenne, WY 82002
Telephone: (307) 777-7311
Fax: (307) 777-5339

DISTRICT OF COLUMBIA
Corporations Divisions
Consumer and Regulatory Affairs
614 "H" St. N.W., Room 407
Washington, DC 20001
Telephone: (202) 727-7287
Fax: (202) 727-7083

APPENDIX S17

State Archives

As mentioned in Vital Records Appendix S3, early state records (often those compiled before 1950) are to be found in State Archives. You will be amazed at the information they retain—newspaper articles, recorded media (e.g., records, audio or video tape recordings), death notices, and much more. Most State Archive personnel love to dig into the past; you may find them surprisingly helpful and accommodating.

This appendix helps your search along by listing those 50 states and the District of Columbia repositories of archives along with their addresses, voice telephone and fax numbers.

SUGGESTED LETTER TO STATE ARCHIVES

Date

Your Full Name
Address
City/State/Zip
Day Phone
Nights/Weekend Phone
Fax

State Archives Office
Address (see State Archives Appendix)

Re: Name
Address
City/State/Zip
Social Security Number
Type of Employment

Dear Director,

Please search your files for records relating to the above named individual. (Explain your reason for asking for this information.)

Please contact me at the address/telephone number listed above if further information is needed in order to obtain a copy of this file.

Sincerely,

Signed

☛ This is public information.

STATE ARCHIVES

ALABAMA
Dept. of Archives and History
624 Washington Ave.
P.O. Box 300100
Montgomery, AL 36130-0100
Telephone: (334) 242-4361
Fax: (334) 240-3433

ALASKA
Dept. of Education
Division of Libraries, Archives, and Museums
Alaska State Library
P.O. Box 110571
Juneau, AK 99811-0571
Telephone: (907) 465-2910
Fax: (907) 465-2151

ARIZONA
State Archives Division
Dept. of Library, Archives and Public Records
1700 W Washington, Room 442
Phoenix, AZ 85007
Telephone: (602) 542-4159
Fax: (602) 542-4402

ARKANSAS
State Historian
History Commission
One Capitol Mall
Little Rock, AR 72201
Telephone: (501) 682-6900
Fax: No Fax

CALIFORNIA
State Archives
1020 "O" St.
Sacramento, CA 95814
Telephone: (916) 653-7715
Fax: (916) 653-7363

COLORADO
Archives and Public Records Division
Dept. of Administration
1313 Sherman St., Room 1B-20
Denver, CO 80203
Telephone: (303) 866-2055
Fax: (303) 866-2257

CONNECTICUT
State of Connecticut
Connecticut State Library
231 Capitol Ave.
Hartford, CT 06106
Telephone: (203) 566-3690
Fax: (203) 566-2133

DELAWARE
State of Delaware
Division of Historical and Cultural Affairs
Hall of Records
Dover, DE 19901
Telephone: (302) 739-5318
Fax: (302) 739-6711

FLORIDA
Bureau of Archives and Records Management
Division of Library and Information Services
500 S. Bronough St.
Tallahassee, FL 32399-0250
Telephone: (904) 487-2073
Fax: (904) 488-4894

GEORGIA
Dept. of Archives and History
330 Capitol Ave., S.E.
Atlanta, GA 30334
Telephone: (404) 656-2358
Fax: (404) 657-8427

HAWAII
State Archives
Dept. of Accounting and General Services
Iolani Palace Grounds
Honolulu, HI 96813
Telephone: (808) 586-0329
Fax: (808) 586-0330

IDAHO
State Historical Society
Library and Archives
450 N. 4th St.
Boise, ID 83702
Telephone: (208) 334-3356
Fax: (208) 334-3198

STATE ARCHIVES

ILLINOIS
State Archives and Records Division
Archives Building
Springfield, IL 62756
Telephone: (217) 782-4682
Fax: (217) 524-3930

INDIANA
Indiana State Archives and Historical Division
State Library Building, #117
140 N. Senate
Indianapolis, IN 46204
Telephone: (317) 232-3661
Fax: (317) 233-1085

IOWA
Historical Division
Dept. of Cultural Affairs
Capitol Complex
600 E. Locust St.
Des Moines, IA 50319
Telephone: (515) 281-5111
Fax: (515) 282-0502

KANSAS
Research Collections
State Historical Society
6425 S.W. 6th Ave.
Topeka, KA 66615
Telephone: (913) 272-8681
Fax: (913) 272-8682

KENTUCKY
Public Records Division
Dept. for Library and Archives
P.O. Box 537
Frankfort, KY 40602-0537
OR
300 Coffee Tree Road
Frankfort, KY 40601
Telephone: (502) 875-7000
Fax: (502) 564-5773

LOUISIANA
Archives Records Management
and History Office
P.O. Box 94125
Baton Rouge, LA 70804
Telephone: (504) 922-1200
Fax: (504) 922-0433

MAINE
Maine State Archives
Cultural Building
Station House 84
Augusta, ME 04333
Telephone: (207) 287-5795
Fax: (207) 287- 5739

MARYLAND
Maryland State Archives
Hall of Records
350 Rowe Blvd.
Annapolis, MD 21401
Telephone: (410) 974-3914/3916
Fax: (410) 974-3895

MASSACHUSETTS
Massachusetts Archives Division
220 Morrissey Blvd.
Boston, MA 02125
Telephone: (617) 727-2816
Fax: (617) 727-8730

MICHIGAN
Dept. of State
Bureau of History
717 W. Allegan
Lansing, MI 48918-1837
Telephone: (517) 373-1408
Fax: (517) 373-0851

MINNESOTA
State Archives Dept.
Minnesota Historical Society
345 Kellogg Blvd. W.
St. Paul, MN 55102
Telephone: (612) 297-4502
Fax: (612) 296-9961

STATE ARCHIVES

MISSISSIPPI
Mississippi Dept. of Archives and History
P.O. Box 571
Jackson, MS 39205-0571
Telephone: (601) 359-6850
Fax: (601) 359-6905

MISSOURI
Missouri State Archives
Office of the Secretary of State
600 W. Main
P.O. Box 778
Jefferson City, MO 65102
Telephone: (573) 751-3280
Fax: (573) 526-7333

MONTANA
Montana Historical Society
225 N. Roberts St.
Helena, MT 59620
Telephone: (406) 444-2681
Fax: (406) 444-2696

NEBRASKA
Library/Archives
Nebraska State Historical Society
P.O. Box 82554
Lincoln, NE 68501
Telephone: (402) 471-4771
Fax: (402) 471-3100

NEVADA
Nevada State Library and Archives
Division of Archives and Records
100 Stewart St.
Capitol Complex
Carson City, NV 89710
Telephone: (702) 687-5210
Fax: (702) 687-8330

NEW HAMPSHIRE
Records Management and Archives
71 S. Fruit St.
Concord, NH 03301-2140
Telephone: (603) 271-2236
Fax: (603) 271-2272

NEW JERSEY
New Jersey State Archives
185 W. State St., CN 307
Trenton, NJ 08625
Telephone: (609) 292-6260
Fax: (609) 396-2454

NEW MEXICO
State Records Center and Archives
404 Montezuma Ave.
Santa Fe, NM 87503
Telephone: (505) 827-7332
Fax: (505) 827-7331

NEW YORK
New York State Archives and
Records Administration
Room 11D40
Cultural Education Ctr.
Albany, NY 12230
Telephone: (518) 474-8955
Fax: (518) 473-9985

NORTH CAROLINA
Division of Archives and History
109 E. Jones St.
Raleigh, NC 27601-2807
Telephone: (919) 733-7305
Fax: (919) 733-8807

NORTH DAKOTA
State Historical Society of North Dakota
North Dakota Heritage Center
612 E. Boulevard Ave.
Bismarck, ND 58505-0830
Telephone: (701) 328-2667
Fax: (701) 328-3710

OHIO
Archives/Library Division
1982 Velma Ave.
Columbus, OH 43211-2497
Telephone: (614) 297-2510
Fax: (614) 297-2546

STATE ARCHIVES

OKLAHOMA
Oklahoma Dept. of Libraries
200 N.E. 18th St.
Oklahoma City, OK 73105
Telephone: (405) 521-2502
Fax: (405) 525-7804

OREGON
Archives Division
Office of the Secretary of State
800 Summer St. N.E.
Salem, OR 97310
Telephone: (503) 373-0701
Fax: (503) 373-0953

PENNSYLVANIA
Pennsylvania State Archives
P.O. Box 1026
Harrisburg, PA 17108-1026
Telephone: (717) 783-3281
Fax: (717) 787-4822

RHODE ISLAND
Rhode Island State Archives
Office of the Secretary of State
337 Westminister St.
Providence, RI 02903
Telephone: (401) 277-2353
Fax: (401) 277-3199

SOUTH CAROLINA
South Carolina Dept. of Archives and History
1430 Senate St.
P.O. Box 11669
Columbia, SC 29211-1669
Telephone: (803) 734-8577
Fax: (803) 734-8820

SOUTH DAKOTA
South Dakota State Archives
900 Governors Dr.
Pierre, SD 57501
Telephone: (605) 773-3804
Fax: (605) 773-6041

TENNESSEE
State Library and Archives
403 7th Ave. N.
Nashville, TN 37243-0312
Telephone: (615) 741-7996
Fax: (615) 741-6471

TEXAS
Texas State Archives
P.O. Box 12927
Austin, TX 78711
Telephone: (512) 463-5480
Fax: (512) 463-5436

UTAH
State Archives and Records Service
Archives Building, State Capitol
Salt Lake City, UT 84114
Telephone: (801) 538-3012
Fax: (801) 538-3354

VERMONT
Vermont State Archives
Office of the Secretary of State
26 Terrace St.
Montpelier, VT 05609-1103
Telephone: (802) 828-2308
Fax: (802) 828-2496

VIRGINIA
Library of Virginia
11th St. at Capitol Square
Richmond, VA 23219
Telephone: (804) 786-2332
Fax: (804) 786-5855

WASHINGTON
Washington State Archives
1120 Washington St. S.E.
P.O. Box 40238
Olympia, WA 98504-0238
Telephone: (360) 753-5485
Fax: (360) 664-8814

STATE ARCHIVES

WEST VIRGINIA
Archives and History Section
1900 Kanawha Blvd. E.
Cultural Center
Charleston, WV 25305-0300
Telephone: (304) 558-0220
Fax: (304) 558-2779

WISCONSIN
State Historical Society of Wisconsin
816 State St.
Madison, WI 53706
Telephone: (608) 264-6400
Fax: (608) 264-6404

WYOMING
Wyoming Dept. of Commerce
Cultural Resources Division
Archives
6101 Yellowstone Rd.
Cheyenne, WY 82002
Telephone: (307) 777-7826
Fax: (307) 777-7044

After Fall 1997:
Archives Records Management
and Micrograph Services
Barrett Building
Cheyenne, WY 82002
Telephone: (307) 777-7826
Fax: (307) 777-7044

DISTRICT OF COLUMBIA
District of Columbia Archives
1300 Naylor Ct., N.W.
Washington, DC 20001-4225
Telephone: (202) 727-2052
Fax: (202) 727-6076

APPENDIX S18

Women's Commissions

Over two–thirds of the 50 states and the District of Columbia have offices devoted specifically to aiding women with items of discrimination, the bureaucracy or with insensitive private companies. This Appendix consists of a sample complaint letter and a directory of those offices. If you are a woman and feel you are being given a runaround in your search for your relative's assets, don't hesitate to call or write the appropriate women's commission. They may be able to help.

SUGGESTED LETTER TO WOMEN'S COMMISSION

Date

Your Full Name
Address
City/State/Zip
Day Phone
Nights/Weekend Phone
Fax

Women's Commission
Address (see Women's Commissions Appendix)

Re: Name of Agency
Address
City/State/Zip

To whom it may concern,

I have been seeking information from various state agencies regarding the whereabouts of my relative's assets or my own. It has occurred to me that I am not getting the degree of cooperation I feel I deserve.

Enclosed please find a copy of my correspondence including the name of the person I have contacted. Would you please contact this agency on my behalf as (state reason you feel you are not getting cooperation).

Sincerely,

Signed

P.S. Enclosed is my self-addressed stamped envelope.

WOMENS COMMISSIONS

ALABAMA
No Women's Commission

ALASKA
No Women's Commission

ARIZONA
Governor's Office for Women
1700 W. Washington, Room 101-A
Phoenix, AZ 85007
Telephone: (602) 542-1755
Fax: (602) 542-5804
Toll Free: (800) 253-0883

ARKANSAS
No Women's Commission

CALIFORNIA
Commission on the Status of Women
1303 J St., Suite 400
Sacramento, CA 95814
Telephone: (916) 445-3173
Fax: (916) 322-9466

COLORADO
No Women's Commission

CONNECTICUT
Permanent Commission on the Status of Women
State of Connecticut
18-20 Trinity St.
Hartford, CT 06106
Telephone: (203) 240-8300
Fax: (203) 240-8314

DELAWARE
Delaware Commission for Women
Old Sears Bldg. 4425 N. Market
Wilmington, DE 19802
Telephone: (302) 761-8005
Fax: No Fax

FLORIDA
No Women's Commission

GEORGIA
Commission on Women
P.O. Box 38481
Atlanta, GA 30334
Telephone: (404) 657-2956
Fax: (404) 657-9260

HAWAII
Commission on the Status of Women
Office of the Lieutenant Governor
235 S. Beratenia St. #407
Honolulu, HI 96813
Telephone: (808) 586-5757
Fax: (808) 586-5756

IDAHO
Commission on Women's Programs
450 W. State St.
Boise, ID 83720
Telephone: (208) 334-4673
Fax: (208) 334-4646

ILLINOIS
Special Assistant For Women
Office of the Governor
Consumer Affairs
100 W. Randolph, Suite 16-100
Chicago, IL 60601
Telephone: (312) 814-2121
Fax: (312) 814-5512

INDIANA
No Women's Commission

IOWA
Commission on the Status of Women
Dept. of Human Rights
Lucas State Office Bldg.
Des Moines, IA 50319
Telephone: (515) 281-4461
Fax: (515) 242-6119
Toll Free: (800) 558-4427

KANSAS
No Women's Commission

WOMENS COMMISSIONS

KENTUCKY
Commission on Women
614A Shelby St.
Frankfort, KY 40601
Telephone: (502) 564-6643
Fax: (502) 564-2315

LOUISIANA
Office of Women's Services
Division of Administration
P.O. Box 94095
Baton Rouge, LA 70804-9095
Telephone: (504) 922-0960
Fax: (504) 922-0959

MAINE
No Women's Commission

MARYLAND
Maryland Commission for Women
311 W. Saratoga, Room 232
Baltimore, MD 21201
Telephone: (410) 767-7137
Fax: (410) 333-0079

MASSACHUSETTS
Executive Office
Office of the Governor
State House, Room 360
Boston, MA 02133
Telephone: (617) 727-9173
Fax: (617) 727-9723

MICHIGAN
Michigan Women's Commission
611 W. Ottawa St., 3rd Floor
Lansing, MI 48913
Telephone: (517) 373-2884
Fax: (517) 335-1649

MINNESOTA
Commission on the Economic Status of Women
85 State Office Bldg.
St. Paul, MN 55155
Telephone: (612) 296-8590
Fax: (612) 296-1321

MISSISSIPPI
No Women's Commission

MISSOURI
Missouri Council on Women's Economic Development
P.O. Box 1684
Jefferson City, MO 65102
Telephone: (314) 751-0810
Fax: (314) 751-8835

MONTANA
No Women's Commission

NEBRASKA
Commission on the Status of Women
P.O. Box 94985
Lincoln, NE 68509
Telephone: (402) 471-2039
Fax: (402) 471-5655

NEVADA
No Women's Commission

NEW HAMPSHIRE
Commission on the Status of Women
Room 334 State House Annex
Concord, NH 03301
Telephone: (603) 271-2660
Fax: (603) 271-2361

NEW JERSEY
New Jersey Dept. of Community Affairs
Division on Women
101 S. Broad St., CN 801
Trenton, NJ 08625-0801
Telephone: (609) 292-8840
Fax: (609) 633-6821

NEW MEXICO
Commission on the Status of Women
2401 12th St. N.W.
Albuquerque, NM 87104-2302
Telephone: (505) 841-8920
Fax: (505) 841-8926
Toll Free: (800) 432-9168

WOMENS COMMISSIONS

NEW YORK
Women's Division
Executive Chamber
633 3rd Ave. 38th Floor
New York, NY 10017
Telephone: (212) 681-4580
Fax: (212) 681-4643

NORTH CAROLINA
North Carolina Council for Women
526 N. Wilmington St.
Raleigh, NC 27604-1199
Telephone: (919) 733-2455
Fax: (919) 733-2464

NORTH DAKOTA
Commission on the Status of Women
North Dakota Economic Development and Finance
C/O Sheila Auch, Administrative Assistant
1833 E. Bismarck Expressway
Bismarck, ND 58504-6708
Telephone: (701) 328-5310

OHIO
Women's Division
Bureau of Employment Services
145 S. Front St., 6th Floor
Columbus, OH 43215
Telephone: (614) 466-4496
Fax: (614) 466-7912

OKLAHOMA
Intergovernmental Affairs
440 S. Houston St., Suite 304
Tulsa, OK, 74127
Telephone: (918) 581-2801
Fax: (918) 581-2835

OREGON
Commission for Women
PSU, Smith Center, Room M-315
P.O. Box 751
Portland, OR 97207
Telephone: (503) 725-5889
Fax: (503) 725-5889

PENNSYLVANIA
No Women's Commission

RHODE ISLAND
No Women's Commission

SOUTH CAROLINA
Commission on Women
2221 Devine St., Suite 408
Columbia, SC 29205
Telephone: (803) 734-9143
Fax: (803) 734-9109

SOUTH DAKOTA
No Women's Commission

TENNESSEE
No Women's Commission

TEXAS
Commission on Women
Office of the Governor
P.O. Box 12428
Austin, TX 78711
Telephone: (512) 463-1782
Fax: (512) 463-1849

UTAH
Commission on Women and Children
1160 State Office Bldg.
Salt Lake City, UT 84114
Telephone: (801) 538-1736
Fax: (801) 538-3027

VERMONT
Governor's Commission on the Status of Women
126 State St. Drawer 33
Montpelier, VT 05633-6801
Telephone: (802) 828-2851
Fax: (802) 828-2930

VIRGINIA
Status of Women
Mrs. Ann Marie Morgan
7407 Bark Ridge Rd.
Chesterfield, VA 23803
Telephone: No Phone
Fax: No Fax

WASHINGTON
No Women's Commission

WOMENS COMMISSIONS

WEST VIRGINIA
Women's Commission
Room 637, Capitol Complex
Charleston, WV 25305
Telephone: (304) 558-0070
Fax: (304) 558-3240

WISCONSIN
Women's Council
16 N. Carroll St., Suite 720
Madison, WI 53703
Telephone: (608) 266-2219
Fax: (608) 266-5046

WYOMING
No Women's Commission

DISTRICT OF COLUMBIA
Commission for Women
2000 14th St. N.W., 3rd Floor
Washington, DC 20009
Telephone: (202) 939-8083
Fax: (202) 939-8763

APPENDIX S19

Internal Revenue Service

This Appendix consists of addresses, voice telephone, and fax numbers of each of the four Regional Offices of the IRS. You may wish to request copies of each of the major personal income tax schedules and forms your target relative is likely to have filled out in his or her tax returns. These are:

Schedule or Form	Name of Form
▪ Schedule A	Itemized Deductions
▪ Schedule B	Interest and Dividend Income
▪ Schedule C	Profit or Loss From Business
▪ Schedule D	Capital Gains and Losses
▪ Schedule E	Supplemental Income and Loss
▪ Schedule F	Profit or Loss From Farming
▪ Schedule SE	Self–Employment Tax
▪ Form 2106	Employee Business Expenses
▪ Form 2119	Sale of Your Home
▪ Form 3903	Moving Expenses

Federal income tax Schedules D and E will provide particularly valuable information about your target relative's assets. Besides asking for his or her original return, don't forget to ask the IRS for any *amended* returns. For other tax return tips, see State Income Tax Appendix S5. If your relative paid too much federal income tax for his or her last year, you may be able to get a refund. See the example in State Income Tax Appendix S5 or consult a competent CPA or tax attorney.

REGIONAL OFFICES OF THE INTERNAL REVENUE SERVICE

NORTHEAST REGION
90 Church St.
Room 1128
New York, NY 10007
Telephone: (212) 264-7061
Fax: (212) 264-2996

SOUTHEAST REGION
401 W. Peachtree St. N.W.
Atlanta, GA 30365
Telphone: (404) 331-6048
Fax: (404) 331-0031

MIDSTATES REGION
4050 Alpha Rd.
Dallas, TX 75244
Telephone: (214) 308-7000
Fax: (214) 308-7008

WESTERN REGION
P.O. Box 420889
San Francisco, CA 94142
Telephone: (415) 556-3300
Fax: (415) 556-1112

SCHEDULES A&B (Form 1040)

Department of the Treasury
Internal Revenue Service (99)

Schedule A—Itemized Deductions

► Attach to Form 1040. ► See Instructions for Schedules A and B (Form 1040).

OMB No. 1545-0074

1995

Attachment Sequence No. **07**

Name(s) shown on Form 1040 | Your social security number

Medical and Dental Expenses		**Caution:** *Do not include expenses reimbursed or paid by others.*		
	1	Medical and dental expenses (see page A-1)	1	
	2	Enter amount from Form 1040, line 32. [2]		
	3	Multiply line 2 above by 7.5% (.075)	3	
	4	Subtract line 3 from line 1. If line 3 is more than line 1, enter -0-		4
Taxes You Paid (See page A-1.)	5	State and local income taxes	5	
	6	Real estate taxes (see page A-2)	6	
	7	Personal property taxes	7	
	8	Other taxes. List type and amount ►	8	
	9	Add lines 5 through 8		9
Interest You Paid (See page A-2.)	10	Home mortgage interest and points reported to you on Form 1098	10	
	11	Home mortgage interest not reported to you on Form 1098. If paid to the person from whom you bought the home, see page A-3 and show that person's name, identifying no., and address ►	11	
Note: Personal interest is not deductible.	12	Points not reported to you on Form 1098. See page A-3 for special rules	12	
	13	Investment interest. If required, attach Form 4952. (See page A-3.)	13	
	14	Add lines 10 through 13		14
Gifts to Charity If you made a gift and got a benefit for it, see page A-3.	15	Gifts by cash or check. If you made any gift of $250 or more, see page A-3	15	
	16	Other than by cash or check. If any gift of $250 or more, see page A-3. If over $500, you **MUST** attach Form 8283	16	
	17	Carryover from prior year	17	
	18	Add lines 15 through 17		18
Casualty and Theft Losses	19	Casualty or theft loss(es). Attach Form 4684. (See page A-4.)		19
Job Expenses and Most Other Miscellaneous Deductions (See page A-5 for expenses to deduct here.)	20	Unreimbursed employee expenses—job travel, union dues, job education, etc. If required, you **MUST** attach Form 2106 or 2106-EZ. (See page A-5.) ►	20	
	21	Tax preparation fees	21	
	22	Other expenses—investment, safe deposit box, etc. List type and amount ►	22	
	23	Add lines 20 through 22	23	
	24	Enter amount from Form 1040, line 32. [24]		
	25	Multiply line 24 above by 2% (.02)	25	
	26	Subtract line 25 from line 23. If line 25 is more than line 23, enter -0-		26
Other Miscellaneous Deductions	27	Other—from list on page A-5. List type and amount		27
Total Itemized Deductions	28	Is Form 1040, line 32, over $114,700 (over $57,350 if married filing separately)? **NO.** Your deduction is not limited. Add the amounts in the far right column for lines 4 through 27. Also, enter on Form 1040, line 34, the **larger** of this amount or your standard deduction. **YES.** Your deduction may be limited. See page A-5 for the amount to enter. ►		28

For Paperwork Reduction Act Notice, see Form 1040 instructions. PRINTED IN U.S.A. **Schedule A (Form 1040) 1995**

Schedules A&B (Form 1040) 1995 OMB No. 1545-0074 Page 2

Name(s) shown on Form 1040. | Your social security number

Schedule B—Interest and Dividend Income

Attachment Sequence No. 08

Part I Interest Income

(See pages 15 and B-1.)

Note: If you received a Form 1099-INT, Form 1099-OID, or substitute statement from a brokerage firm, list the firm's name as the payer and enter the total interest shown on that form.

Note: *If you had over $400 in taxable interest income, you must also complete Part III.*

			Amount
1	List name of payer. If any interest is from a seller-financed mortgage and the buyer used the property as a personal residence, see page B-1 and list this interest first. Also, show that buyer's social security number and address ▶	1	
2	Add the amounts on line 1	2	
3	Excludable interest on series EE U.S. savings bonds issued after 1989 from Form 8815, line 14. You MUST attach Form 8815 to Form 1040	3	
4	Subtract line 3 from line 2. Enter the result here and on Form 1040, line 8a ▶	4	

Part II Dividend Income

(See pages 15 and B-1.)

Note: If you received a Form 1099-DIV or substitute statement from a brokerage firm, list the firm's name as the payer and enter the total dividends shown on that form.

Note: *If you had over $400 in gross dividends and/or other distributions on stock, you must also complete Part III.*

			Amount
5	List name of payer. Include gross dividends and/or other distributions on stock here. Any capital gain distributions and nontaxable distributions will be deducted on lines 7 and 8 ▶	5	
6	Add the amounts on line 5	6	
7	Capital gain distributions. Enter here and on Schedule D* . [7]		
8	Nontaxable distributions. (See the inst. for Form 1040, line 9.) [8]		
9	Add lines 7 and 8	9	
10	Subtract line 9 from line 6. Enter the result here and on Form 1040, line 9 ▶	10	

**If you do not need Schedule D to report any other gains or losses, see the instructions for Form 1040, line 13, on page 16.*

Part III Foreign Accounts and Trusts

(See page B-2.)

If you had over $400 of interest or dividends **or** had a foreign account or were a grantor of, or a transferor to, a foreign trust, you must complete this part.	Yes	No
11a At any time during 1995, did you have an interest in or a signature or other authority over a financial account in a foreign country, such as a bank account, securities account, or other financial account? See page B-2 for exceptions and filing requirements for Form TD F 90-22.1		
b If "Yes," enter the name of the foreign country ▶		
12 Were you the grantor of, or transferor to, a foreign trust that existed during 1995, whether or not you have any beneficial interest in it? If "Yes," you may have to file Form 3520, 3520-A, or 926		

For Paperwork Reduction Act Notice, see Form 1040 instructions. PRINTED IN U.S.A. **Schedule B (Form 1040) 1995**

H831 1040-4

SCHEDULE C (Form 1040)

Department of the Treasury Internal Revenue Service (99)

Profit or Loss From Business

(Sole Proprietorship)

▶ **Partnerships, joint ventures, etc., must file Form 1065.**

▶ **Attach to Form 1040 or Form 1041.** ▶ **See Instructions for Schedule C (Form 1040).**

OMB No. 1545-0074

1995

Attachment Sequence No. **09**

Name of proprietor | **Social security number (SSN)**

A Principal business or profession, including product or service (see page C-1) | **B Enter principal business code** (see page C-6) ▶

C Business name. If no separate business name, leave blank. | **D Employer ID number (EIN), if any**

E Business address (including suite or room no.) ▶
City, town or post office, state, and ZIP code

F Accounting method: (1) ☐ Cash (2) ☐ Accrual (3) ☐ Other (specify) ▶

G Method(s) used to value closing inventory: (1) ☐ Cost (2) ☐ Lower of cost or market (3) ☐ Other (attach explanation) (4) ☐ Does not apply (if checked, skip line H) — Yes / No

H Was there any change in determining quantities, costs, or valuations between opening and closing inventory? If "Yes," attach explanation

I Did you "materially participate" in the operation of this business during 1995? If "No," see page C-2 for limit on losses

J If you started or acquired this business during 1995, check here ▶ ☐

Part I Income

1	Gross receipts or sales. **Caution:** *If this income was reported to you on Form W-2 and the "Statutory employee" box on that form was checked, see page C-2 and check here* ▶ ☐	1
2	Returns and allowances	2
3	Subtract line 2 from line 1	3
4	Cost of goods sold (from line 40 on page 2)	4
5	**Gross profit.** Subtract line 4 from line 3	5
6	Other income, including Federal and state gasoline or fuel tax credit or refund (see page C-2)	6
7	**Gross income.** Add lines 5 and 6 ▶	7

Part II Expenses. Enter expenses for business use of your home **only** on line 30.

8	Advertising	8	**19**	Pension and profit-sharing plans	19
9	Bad debts from sales or services (see page C-3)	9	**20**	Rent or lease (see page C-4):	
			a	Vehicles, machinery, and equipment	20a
10	Car and truck expenses (see page C-3)	10	b	Other business property	20b
			21	Repairs and maintenance	21
11	Commissions and fees	11	**22**	Supplies (not included in Part III)	22
12	Depletion	12	**23**	Taxes and licenses	23
13	Depreciation and section 179 expense deduction (not included in Part III) (see page C-3)	13	**24**	Travel, meals, and entertainment:	
			a	Travel	24a
14	Employee benefit programs (other than on line 19)	14	b	Meals and entertainment	
15	Insurance (other than health)	15	c	Enter 50% of line 24b subject to limitations (see page C-4)	
16	Interest:				
a	Mortgage (paid to banks, etc.)	16a	d	Subtract line 24c from line 24b	24d
b	Other	16b	**25**	Utilities	25
17	Legal and professional services	17	**26**	Wages (less employment credits)	26
18	Office expense	18	**27**	Other expenses (from line 46 on page 2)	27

28	**Total expenses** before expenses for business use of home. Add lines 8 through 27 in columns ▶	28
29	Tentative profit (loss). Subtract line 28 from line 7	29
30	Expenses for business use of your home. Attach **Form 8829**	30
31	**Net profit or (loss).** Subtract line 30 from line 29. • If a profit, enter on **Form 1040, line 12,** and ALSO on **Schedule SE, line 2** (statutory employees, see page C-5). Estates and trusts, enter on Form 1041, line 3. • If a loss, you MUST go on to line 32.	31

32 If you have a loss, check the box that describes your investment in this activity (see page C-5).

- If you checked 32a, enter the loss on **Form 1040, line 12,** and ALSO on **Schedule SE, line 2** (statutory employees, see page C-5). Estates and trusts, enter on Form 1041, line 3.
- If you checked 32b, you MUST attach **Form 6198.**

32a ☐ All investment is at risk.
32b ☐ Some investment is not at risk.

For Paperwork Reduction Act Notice, see Form 1040 instructions. PRINTED IN U.S.A. **Schedule C (Form 1040) 1995**

Schedule C (Form 1040) 1995 **Name** ______ **SSN**______ Page **2**

Part III Cost of Goods Sold (see page C-5)

33	Inventory at beginning of year. If different from last year's closing inventory, attach explanation	33	
34	Purchases less cost of items withdrawn for personal use	34	
35	Cost of labor. Do not include salary paid to yourself	35	
36	Materials and supplies	36	
37	Other costs	37	
38	Add lines 33 through 37	38	
39	Inventory at end of year	39	
40	**Cost of goods sold.** Subtract line 39 from line 38. Enter the result here and on page 1, line 4	40	

Part IV Information on Your Vehicle.

Complete this part **ONLY** if you are claiming car or truck expenses on line 10 and are not required to file Form 4562 for this business. See the instructions for line 13 on page C-3 to find out if you must file.

41 When did you place your vehicle in service for business purposes? (month, day, year) ▶ ....../....../......

42 Of the total number of miles you drove your vehicle during 1995, enter the number of miles you used your vehicle for:

a Business .... b Commuting .... c Other ....

43 Do you (or your spouse) have another vehicle available for personal use? ☐ Yes ☐ No

44 Was your vehicle available for use during off-duty hours? ☐ Yes ☐ No

45a Do you have evidence to support your deduction? ☐ Yes ☐ No

b If "Yes," is the evidence written? ☐ Yes ☐ No

Part V Other Expenses.

List below business expenses not included on lines 8–26 or line 30.

46 Total other expenses. Enter here and on page 1, line 27	46	

SCHEDULE D (Form 1040)

Department of the Treasury Internal Revenue Service (99)

Capital Gains and Losses

▶ Attach to Form 1040. ▶ See Instructions for Schedule D (Form 1040).

▶ Use lines 20 and 22 for more space to list transactions for lines 1 and 9.

OMB No. 1545-0074

1995

Attachment Sequence No. **12**

Name(s) shown on Form 1040 | Your social security number

Part I Short-Term Capital Gains and Losses—Assets Held One Year or Less

	(a) Description of property (Example: 100 sh. XYZ Co.)	**(b)** Date acquired (Mo., day, yr.)	**(c)** Date sold (Mo., day, yr.)	**(d)** Sales price (see page D-3)	**(e)** Cost or other basis (see page D-3)	**(f) LOSS** If (e) is more than (d), subtract (d) from (e)	**(g) GAIN** If (d) is more than (e), subtract (e) from (d)
1							
2	Enter your short-term totals, if any, from line 21 2						
3	**Total short-term sales price amounts.** Add column (d) of lines 1 and 2 . . . 3						
4	Short-term gain from Forms 2119 and 6252, and short-term gain or loss from Forms 4684, 6781, and 8824 4						
5	Net short-term gain or loss from partnerships, S corporations, estates, and trusts from Schedule(s) K-1 5						
6	Short-term capital loss carryover. Enter the amount, if any, from line 9 of your 1994 Capital Loss Carryover Worksheet 6						
7	Add lines 1 through 6 in columns (f) and (g) 7					( )	
8	**Net short-term capital gain or (loss).** Combine columns (f) and (g) of line 7 . . . . ▶ 8						

Part II Long-Term Capital Gains and Losses—Assets Held More Than One Year

	(a)	(b)	(c)	(d)	(e)	(f)	(g)
9							
10	Enter your long-term totals, if any, from 10						
11	**Total long-term sales pri e amounts.** Add column (d) of lines 9 and 10 . . . 11						
12	Gain from Form 4797; long-term gain from Forms 2119, 2439, and 6252; and long-term gain or loss from Forms 4684, 6781, and 8824 12						
13	Net long-term gain or loss from partnerships, S corporations, estates, and trusts from Schedule(s) K-1 13						
14	Capital gain distributions 14						
15	Long-term capital loss carryover. Enter the amount, if any, from line 14 of your 1994 Capital Loss Carryover Worksheet 15						
16	Add lines 9 through 15 in columns (f) and (g) 16					( )	
17	**Net long-term capital gain or (loss).** Combine columns (f) and (g) of line 16 . . . . ▶ 17						

Part III Summary of Parts I and II

18 Combine lines 8 and 17. If a loss, go to line 19. If a gain, enter the gain on Form 1040, line 13. **Note:** *If both lines 17 and 18 are gains, see the* ***Capital Gain Tax Worksheet*** *on page 24* . 18

19 If line 18 is a loss, enter here and as a (loss) on Form 1040, line 13, the **smaller** of these losses:

a The loss on line 18; **or**

b ($3,000) or, if married filing separately, ($1,500) . . . . 19 ( )

Note: *See the* ***Capital Loss Carryover Worksheet*** *on page D-3 if the loss on line 18 exceeds the loss on line 19* ***or*** *if Form 1040, line 35, is a loss.*

For Paperwork Reduction Act Notice, see Form 1040 instructions. Schedule D (Form 1040) 1995

Schedule D (Form 1040) 1995 Attachment Sequence No. 12 Page 2

Name(s) shown on Form 1040. Do not enter name and social security number if shown on other side. | Your social security number

Part IV **Short-Term Capital Gains and Losses—Assets Held One Year or Less** *(Continuation of Part I)*

	(a) Description of property (Example: 100 sh. XYZ Co.)	(b) Date acquired (Mo., day, yr.)	(c) Date sold (Mo., day, yr.)	(d) Sales price (see page D-3)	(e) Cost or other basis (see page D-3)	(f) LOSS If (e) is more than (d), subtract (d) from (e)	(g) GAIN If (d) is more than (e), subtract (e) from (d)
20							
21	Short-term totals. Add columns (d), (f), and (g) of line 20. Enter here and on line 2 .		21				

Part V **Long-Term Capital Gains and Losses—Assets Held More Than One Year** *(Continuation of Part II)*

	(a)	(b)	(c)	(d)	(e)	(f)	(g)
22							
23	Long-term totals. Add columns (d), (f), and (g) of line 22. Enter here and on line 10 .		23				

SCHEDULE E (Form 1040)

Department of the Treasury Internal Revenue Service (99)

Supplemental Income and Loss

(From rental real estate, royalties, partnerships, S corporations, estates, trusts, REMICs, etc.)

▶ Attach to Form 1040 or Form 1041. ▶ See Instructions for Schedule E (Form 1040).

OMB No. 1545-0074

1995

Attachment Sequence No. 13

Name(s) shown on return | Your social security number

Part I **Income or Loss From Rental Real Estate and Royalties** **Note:** *Report income and expenses from your business of renting personal property on* ***Schedule C*** *or* ***C-EZ*** *(see page E-1). Report farm rental income or loss from* ***Form 4835*** *on page 2, line 39.*

1	Show the kind and location of each **rental real estate property:**
A	
B	
C	

2 For each rental real estate property listed on line 1, did you or your family use it for personal purposes for more than the greater of 14 days or 10% of the total days rented at fair rental value during the tax year? (See page E-1.)

	Yes	No
A		
B		
C		

		Properties A	Properties B	Properties C		Totals (Add columns A, B, and C.)
Income:						
3 Rents received	3				3	
4 Royalties received	4				4	
Expenses:						
5 Advertising	5					
6 Auto and travel (see page E-2)	6					
7 Cleaning and maintenance	7					
8 Commissions	8					
9 Insurance	9					
10 Legal and other professional fees	10					
11 Management fees	11					
12 Mortgage interest paid to banks, etc. (see page E-2)	12				12	
13 Other interest	13					
14 Repairs	14					
15 Supplies	15					
16 Taxes	16					
17 Utilities	17					
18 Other (list) ▶	18					
19 Add lines 5 through 18	19				19	
20 Depreciation expense or depletion (see page E-2)	20				20	
21 Total expenses. Add lines 19 and 20	21					
22 Income or (loss) from rental real estate or royalty properties. Subtract line 21 from line 3 (rents) or line 4 (royalties). If the result is a (loss), see page E-2 to find out if you must file **Form 6198**	22					
23 Deductible rental real estate loss. **Caution:** *Your rental real estate loss on line 22 may be limited. See page E-3 to find out if you must file* ***Form 8582****. Real estate professionals must complete line 42 on page 2*	23	( )	( )	( )		

24 **Income.** Add positive amounts shown on line 22. **Do not** include any losses	24	
25 **Losses.** Add royalty losses from line 22 and rental real estate losses from line 23. Enter the total losses here	25	( )
26 Total rental real estate and royalty income or (loss). Combine lines 24 and 25. Enter the result here. If Parts II, III, IV, and line 39 on page 2 do not apply to you, also enter this amount on Form 1040, line 17. Otherwise, include this amount in the total on line 40 on page 2	26	

Schedule E (Form 1040) 1995 Attachment Sequence No. 13 Page 2

Name(s) shown on return. | Your social security number

Note: *If you report amounts from farming or fishing on Schedule E, you must enter your gross income from those activities on line 41 below. Real estate professionals must complete line 42 below.*

Part II Income or Loss From Partnerships and S Corporations

Note: *If you report a loss from an at-risk activity, you MUST check either column (e) or (f) of line 27 to describe your investment in the activity. See page E-4. If you check column (f), you must attach* **Form 6198.**

27	(a) Name	(b) Enter P for partnership; S for S corporation	(c) Check if foreign partnership	(d) Employer identification number	Investment At Risk? (e) All is at risk	(f) Some is not at risk
A						
B						
C						
D						
E						

	Passive Income and Loss		Nonpassive Income and Loss		
	(g) Passive loss allowed (attach Form 8582 if required)	(h) Passive income from Schedule K-1	(i) Nonpassive loss from Schedule K-1	(j) Section 179 expense deduction from Form 4562	(k) Nonpassive income from Schedule K-1
A					
B					
C					
D					
E					
28a Totals					
b Totals					

29 Add columns (h) and (k) of line 28a 29

30 Add columns (g), (i), and (j) of line 28b . . . . 30 ( )

31 Total partnership and S corporation income or (loss). Combine lines 29 and 30. Enter the result here and include in the total on line 40 below 31

Part III Income or Loss From Estates and Trusts

32	(a) Name	(b) Employer identification number
A		
B		

	Passive Income and Loss		Nonpassive Income and Loss	
	(c) Passive deduction or loss allowed (attach Form 8582 if required)	(d) Passive income from Schedule K-1	(e) Deduction or loss from Schedule K-1	(f) Other income from Schedule K-1
A				
B				
33a Totals				
b Totals				

34 Add columns (d) and (f) of line 33a 34

35 Add columns (c) and (e) of line 33b . . . . 35 ( )

36 Total estate and trust income or (loss). Combine lines 34 and 35. Enter the result here and include in the total on line 40 below 36

Part IV Income or Loss From Real Estate Mortgage Investment Conduits (REMICs)—Residual Holder

37 (a) Name	(b) Employer identification number	(c) Excess inclusion from Schedules Q, line 2c (see page E-4)	(d) Taxable income (net loss) from Schedules Q, line 1b	(e) Income from Schedules Q, line 3b

38 Combine columns (d) and (e) only. Enter the result here and include in the total on line 40 below 38

Part V Summary

39 Net farm rental income or (loss) from **Form 4835**. Also, complete line 41 below 39

40 TOTAL income or (loss). Combine lines 26, 31, 36, 38, and 39. Enter the result here and on Form 1040, line 17 ▶ 40

41 **Reconciliation of Farming and Fishing Income.** Enter your **gross** farming and fishing income reported on Form 4835, line 7; Schedule K-1 (Form 1065), line 15b; Schedule K-1 (Form 1120S), line 23; and Schedule K-1 (Form 1041), line 13 (see page E-4) 41

42 **Reconciliation for Real Estate Professionals.** If you were a real estate professional (see page E-3), enter the net income or (loss) you reported anywhere on Form 1040 from all rental real estate activities in which you materially participated under the passive activity loss rules . . 42

SCHEDULE F (Form 1040)
Department of the Treasury Internal Revenue Service (T)

Profit or Loss From Farming

▶ Attach to Form 1040, Form 1041, or Form 1065.
▶ See Instructions for Schedule F (Form 1040).

OMB No. 1545-0074
1995
Attachment Sequence No. 14

Name of proprietor | Social security number (SSN)

A Principal product. Describe in one or two words your principal crop or activity for the current tax year.

B Enter principal agricultural activity code (from page 2) ▶

C Accounting method: (1) ☐ Cash (2) ☐ Accrual

D Employer ID number (EIN), if any

E Did you "materially participate" in the operation of this business during 1995? If "No," see page F-2 for limit on passive losses. ☐ Yes ☐ No

Part I Farm Income—Cash Method. Complete Parts I and II (Accrual method taxpayers complete Parts II and III, and line 11 of Part I.)
Do not include sales of livestock held for draft, breeding, sport, or dairy purposes; report these sales on Form 4797.

1	Sales of livestock and other items you bought for resale	1	
2	Cost or other basis of livestock and other items reported on line 1	2	
3	Subtract line 2 from line 1		3
4	Sales of livestock, produce, grains, and other products you raised		4
5a	Total cooperative distributions (Form(s) 1099-PATR)	5a	5b Taxable amount — 5b
6a	Agricultural program payments (see page F-2)	6a	6b Taxable amount — 6b
7	Commodity Credit Corporation (CCC) loans (see page F-2):		
a	CCC loans reported under election		7a
b	CCC loans forfeited or repaid with certificates	7b	7c Taxable amount — 7c
8	Crop insurance proceeds and certain disaster payments (see page F-2):		
a	Amount received in 1995	8a	8b Taxable amount — 8b
c	If election to defer to 1996 is attached, check here ▶ ☐	8d Amount deferred from 1994	8d
9	Custom hire (machine work) income		9
10	Other income, including Federal and state gasoline or fuel tax credit or refund (see page F-3)		10
11	**Gross income.** Add amounts in the right column for lines 3 through 10. If accrual method taxpayer, enter the amount from page 2, line 51 ▶		11

Part II Farm Expenses—Cash and Accrual Method. Do not include personal or living expenses such as taxes, insurance, repairs, etc., on your home.

Line	Expense		Line	Expense	
12	Car and truck expenses (see page F-3—also attach **Form 4562**)	12	25	Pension and profit-sharing plans	25
13	Chemicals	13	26	Rent or lease (see page F-4):	
14	Conservation expenses. Attach **Form 8645**	14	a	Vehicles, machinery, and equipment	26a
15	Custom hire (machine work)	15	b	Other (land, animals, etc.)	26b
16	Depreciation and section 179 expense deduction not claimed elsewhere (see page F-4)	16	27	Repairs and maintenance	27
			28	Seeds and plants purchased	28
			29	Storage and warehousing	29
17	Employee benefit programs other than on line 25	17	30	Supplies purchased	30
			31	Taxes	31
18	Feed purchased	18	32	Utilities	32
19	Fertilizers and lime	19	33	Veterinary, breeding, and medicine	33
20	Freight and trucking	20	34	Other expenses (specify):	
21	Gasoline, fuel, and oil	21	a		34a
22	Insurance (other than health)	22	b		34b
23	Interest:		c		34c
a	Mortgage (paid to banks, etc.)	23a	d		34d
b	Other	23b	e		34e
24	Labor hired (less employment credits)	24	f		34f

35	**Total expenses.** Add lines 12 through 34f ▶	35
36	**Net farm profit or (loss).** Subtract line 35 from line 11. If a profit, enter on **Form 1040, line 18,** and ALSO on **Schedule SE, line 1.** If a loss, you MUST go on to line 37 (estates, trusts, and partnerships, see page F-5)	36
37	If you have a loss, you MUST check the box that describes your investment in this activity (see page F-5). If you checked 37a, enter the loss on **Form 1040, line 18,** and ALSO on **Schedule SE, line 1.** If you checked 37b, you MUST attach **Form 6198.**	37a ☐ All investment is at risk. 37b ☐ Some investment is not at risk.

For Paperwork Reduction Act Notice, see Form 1040 instructions. Cat. No. 11346H **Schedule F (Form 1040) 1995**

Schedule F (Form 1040) 1995 Page **2**

Part III **Farm Income—Accrual Method** (see page F-5)

Do not include sales of livestock held for draft, breeding, sport, or dairy purposes; report these sales on Form 4797 and do not include this livestock on line 46 below.

38	Sales of livestock, produce, grains, and other products during the year	**38**	
39a	Total cooperative distributions (Form(s) 1099-PATR) **39a** ____ **39b** Taxable amount	**39b**	
40a	Agricultural program payments **40a** ____ **40b** Taxable amount	**40b**	
41	Commodity Credit Corporation (CCC) loans:		
a	CCC loans reported under election	**41a**	
b	CCC loans forfeited or repaid with certificates **41b** ____ **41c** Taxable amount	**41c**	
42	Crop insurance proceeds	**42**	
43	Custom hire (machine work) income	**43**	
44	Other income, including Federal and state gasoline or fuel tax credit or refund	**44**	
45	Add amounts in the right column for lines 38 through 44	**45**	
46	Inventory of livestock, produce, grains, and other products at beginning of the year **46** ____		
47	Cost of livestock, produce, grains, and other products purchased during the year **47** ____		
48	Add lines 46 and 47 **48** ____		
49	Inventory of livestock, produce, grains, and other products at end of year **49** ____		
50	Cost of livestock, produce, grains, and other products sold. Subtract line 49 from line 48*	**50**	
51	**Gross income.** Subtract line 50 from line 45. Enter the result here and on page 1, line 11 ▶	**51**	

*If you use the unit-livestock-price method or the farm-price method of valuing inventory and the amount on line 49 is larger than the amount on line 48, subtract line 48 from line 49. Enter the result on line 50. Add lines 45 and 50. Enter the total on line 51.

Part IV **Principal Agricultural Activity Codes**

Caution: *File* ***Schedule C*** *(Form 1040), Profit or Loss From Business, or* ***Schedule C-EZ*** *(Form 1040), Net Profit From Business, instead of Schedule F if:*

- *Your principal source of income is from providing agricultural services such as soil preparation, veterinary, farm labor, horticultural, or management for a fee or on a contract basis, or*
- *You are engaged in the business of breeding, raising, and caring for dogs, cats, or other pet animals.*

Select one of the following codes and write the 3-digit number on page 1, line B:

120 **Field crop,** including grains and nongrains such as cotton, peanuts, feed corn, wheat, tobacco, Irish potatoes, etc.

160 **Vegetables and melons,** garden-type vegetables and melons, such as sweet corn, tomatoes, squash, etc.

170 **Fruit and tree nuts,** including grapes, berries, olives, etc.

180 **Ornamental floriculture and nursery products**

185 **Food crops grown under cover,** including hydroponic crops

211 **Beefcattle feedlots**

212 **Beefcattle,** except feedlots

215 **Hogs, sheep, and goats**

240 **Dairy**

250 **Poultry and eggs,** including chickens, ducks, pigeons, quail, etc.

260 **General livestock,** not specializing in any one livestock category

270 **Animal specialty,** including bees, fur-bearing animals, horses, snakes, etc.

280 **Animal aquaculture,** including fish, shellfish, mollusks, frogs, etc., produced within confined space

290 **Forest products,** including forest nurseries and seed gathering, extraction of pine gum, and gathering of forest products

300 **Agricultural production,** not specified

SCHEDULE SE (Form 1040)
Department of the Treasury
Internal Revenue Service (99)

Self-Employment Tax

▶ See Instructions for Schedule SE (Form 1040).
▶ Attach to Form 1040.

OMB No. 1545-0074
1995
Attachment Sequence No. **17**

Name of person with **self-employment** income (as shown on Form 1040)	Social security number of person with **self-employment** income ▶	

Who Must File Schedule SE

You must file Schedule SE if:

- You had net earnings from self-employment from **other than** church employee income (line 4 of Short Schedule SE or line 4c of Long Schedule SE) of $400 or more, **OR**
- You had church employee income of $108.28 or more. Income from services you performed as a minister or a member of a religious order **is not** church employee income. See page SE-1.

Note: *Even if you have a loss or a small amount of income from self-employment, it may be to your benefit to file Schedule SE and use either "optional method" in Part II of Long Schedule SE. See page SE-3.*

Exception. If your only self-employment income was from earnings as a minister, member of a religious order, or Christian Science practitioner **and** you filed Form 4361 and received IRS approval not to be taxed on those earnings, **do not** file Schedule SE. Instead, write "Exempt–Form 4361" on Form 1040, line 47.

May I Use Short Schedule SE or MUST I Use Long Schedule SE?

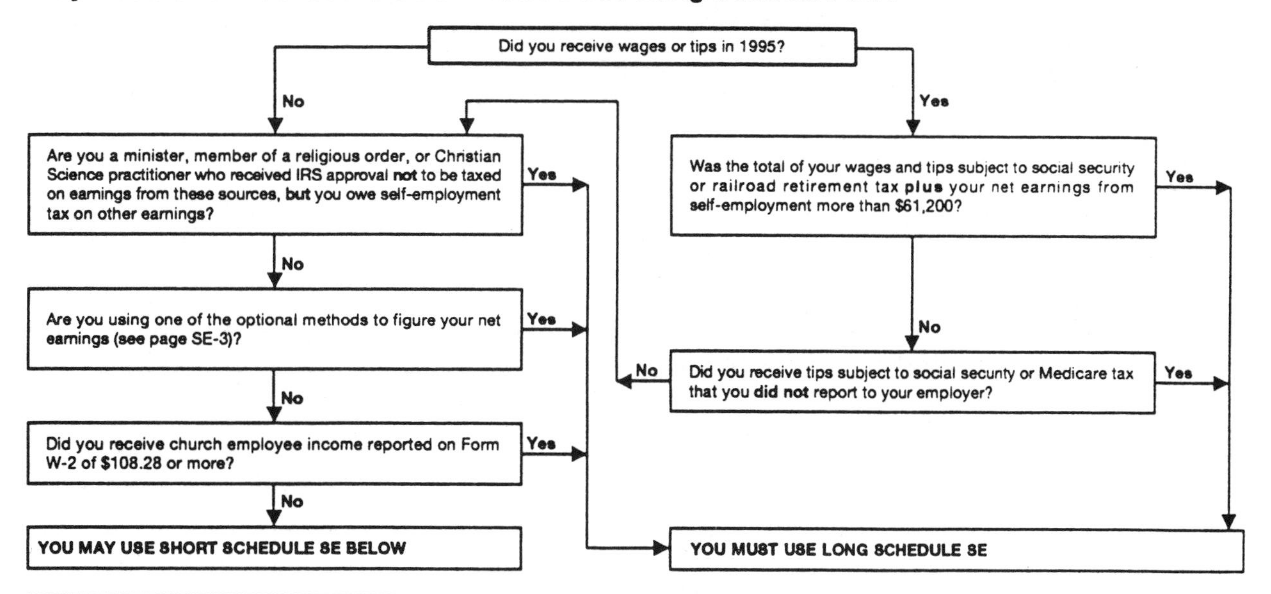

Section A—Short Schedule SE. Caution: *Read above to see if you can use Short Schedule SE.*

1	Net farm profit or (loss) from Schedule F, line 36, and farm partnerships, Schedule K-1 (Form 1065), line 15a	1	
2	Net profit or (loss) from Schedule C, line 31; Schedule C-EZ, line 3; and Schedule K-1 (Form 1065), line 15a (other than farming). Ministers and members of religious orders see page SE-1 for amounts to report on this line. See page SE-2 for other income to report	2	
3	Combine lines 1 and 2	3	
4	**Net earnings from self-employment.** Multiply line 3 by 92.35% (.9235). If less than $400, **do not** file this schedule; you do not owe self-employment tax ▶	4	
5	**Self-employment tax.** If the amount on line 4 is: • $61,200 or less, multiply line 4 by 15.3% (.153). Enter the result here and on **Form 1040, line 47.** • More than $61,200, multiply line 4 by 2.9% (.029). Then, add $7,588.80 to the result. Enter the total here and on **Form 1040, line 47.**	5	
6	**Deduction for one-half of self-employment tax.** Multiply line 5 by 50% (.5). Enter the result here and on **Form 1040, line 25** — 6		

Schedule SE (Form 1040) 1995 | Attachment Sequence No. 17 | Page 2

Name of person with **self-employment** income (as shown on Form 1040) | Social security number of person with **self-employment** income ▶

Section B — Long Schedule SE

Part I Self-Employment Tax

Note: If your only income subject to self-employment tax is **church employee income**, skip lines 1 through 4b. Enter -0- on line 4c and go to line 5a. Income from services you performed as a minister or a member of a religious order **is not** church employee income. See page SE-1.

A	If you are a minister, member of a religious order, or Christian Science Practitioner **and** you filed Form 4361, but you had $400 or more of **other** net earnings from self-employment, check here and continue with Part I ▶ ☐		
1	Net farm profit or (loss) from Schedule F, line 36, and farm partnerships, Schedule K-1 (Form 1065), line 15a. **Note:** Skip this line if you use the farm optional method. See page SE-3	1	
2	Net profit or (loss) from Schedule C, line 31; Schedule C-EZ, line 3; and Schedule K-1 (Form 1065), line 15a (other than farming). Ministers and members of religious orders see page SE-1 for amounts to report on this line. See page SE-2 for other income to report. **Note:** Skip this line if you use the nonfarm optional method. See page SE-3	2	
3	Combine lines 1 and 2.	3	
4a	If line 3 is more than zero, multiply line 3 by 92.35% (.9235). Otherwise, enter amount from line 3	4a	
b	If you elected one or both of the optional methods, enter the total of lines 15 and 17 here	4b	
c	Combine lines 4a and 4b. If less than $400, **do not** file this schedule; you do not owe self-employment tax. **Exception.** If less than $400 and you had **church employee income**, enter -0- and continue. ▶	4c	
5a	Enter your **church employee income** from Form W-2. **Caution:** See page SE-1 for definition of church employee income — 5a		
b	Multiply line 5a by 92.35% (.9235). If less than $100, enter -0-	5b	
6	**Net earnings from self-employment.** Add lines 4c and 5b	6	
7	Maximum amount of combined wages and self-employment earnings subject to social security tax or the 6.2% portion of the 7.65% railroad retirement (tier 1) tax for 1995	7	61,200
8a	Total social security wages and tips (total of boxes 3 and 7 on Form(s) W-2) and railroad retirement (tier 1) compensation — 8a		
b	Unreported tips subject to social security tax (from Form 4137, line 9) — 8b		
c	Add lines 8a and 8b	8c	
9	Subtract line 8c from line 7. If zero or less, enter -0- here and on line 10 and go to line 11 ▶	9	
10	Multiply the **smaller** of line 6 or line 9 by 12.4% (.124)	10	
11	Multiply line 6 by 2.9% (.029)	11	
12	**Self-employment tax.** Add lines 10 and 11. Enter here and on **Form 1040, line 47**	12	
13	**Deduction for one-half of self-employment tax.** Multiply line 12 by 50% (.5). Enter the result here and on **Form 1040, line 25** — 13		

Part II Optional Methods To Figure Net Earnings (See page SE-3).

Farm Optional Method. You may use this method **only** if:

- Your gross farm income[1] was not more than $2,400, **or**
- Your gross farm income[1] was more than $2,400 and your net farm profits[2] were less than $1,733.

14	Maximum income for optional methods	14	1,600
15	Enter the **smaller** of: two-thirds (2/3) of gross farm income[1] (not less than zero) **or** $1,600. Also, include this amount on line 4b above	15	

Nonfarm Optional Method. You may use this method **only** if:

- Your net nonfarm profits[3] were less than $1,733 and also less than 72.189% of your gross nonfarm income,[4] **and**
- You had net earnings from self-employment of at least $400 in 2 of the prior 3 years.

Caution: You may use this method no more than five times.

16	Subtract line 15 from line 14	16	
17	Enter the **smaller** of: two-thirds (2/3) of gross nonfarm income[4] (not less than zero) **or** the amount on line 16. Also, include this amount on line 4b above	17	

[1] From Schedule F, line 11, and Schedule K-1 (Form 1065), line 15b.
[2] From Schedule F, line 36, and Schedule K-1 (Form 1065), line 15a.
[3] From Schedule C, line 31; Schedule C-EZ, line 3; and Schedule K-1 (Form 1065), line 15a.
[4] From Schedule C, line 7; Schedule C-EZ, line 1; and Schedule K-1 (Form 1065), line 15c.

KBA **For Paperwork Reduction Act Notice, see Form 1040 Instructions.** **Schedule SE (Form 1040) 1995**

Form **2106**

Department of the Treasury
Internal Revenue Service (99)

Employee Business Expenses

▶ See separate instructions.

▶ Attach to Form 1040 or Form 1040-T.

OMB No. 1545-0139

1995

Attachment Sequence No. **54**

Your name	Social security number	Occupation in which expenses were incurred
	: :	

Part I **Employee Business Expenses and Reimbursements**

STEP 1 Enter Your Expenses		**Column A** Other Than Meals and Entertainment	**Column B** Meals and Entertainment
1 Vehicle expense from line 22 or line 29	1		
2 Parking fees, tolls, and transportation, including train, bus, etc., that **did not** involve overnight travel	2		
3 Travel expense while away from home overnight, including lodging, airplane, car rental, etc. **Do not** include meals and entertainment	3		
4 Business expenses not included on lines 1 through 3. **Do not** include meals and entertainment	4		
5 Meals and entertainment expenses (see instructions) . . .	5		
6 **Total expenses.** In Column A, add lines 1 through 4 and enter the result. In Column B, enter the amount from line 5	6		

Note: *If you were not reimbursed for any expenses in Step 1, skip line 7 and enter the amount from line 6 on line 8.*

STEP 2 Enter Amounts Your Employer Gave You for Expenses Listed in STEP 1			
7 Enter amounts your employer gave you that were **not** reported to you in box 1 of Form W-2. Include any amount reported under code "L" in box 13 of your Form W-2 (see instructions) . .	7		

STEP 3 Figure Expenses To Deduct on Schedule A (Form 1040) or Form 1040-T, Section B			
8 Subtract line 7 from line 6	8		
Note: *If **both columns** of line 8 are zero, **stop here.** If Column A is less than zero, report the amount as income on Form 1040, line 7, or Form 1040-T, line 1.*			
9 In Column A, enter the amount from line 8 (if zero or less, enter -0-). In Column B, multiply the amount on line 8 by 50% (.50) .	9		
10 Add the amounts on line 9 of both columns and enter the total here. **Also, enter the total on Schedule A (Form 1040), line 20, or Form 1040-T, Section B, line n.** (Qualified performing artists and individuals with disabilities, see the instructions for special rules on where to enter the total.) . . . . ▶		10	

For Paperwork Reduction Act Notice, see instructions. PRINTED IN U.S.A. Form **2106** (1995)

H831 1040-40

Form 2106 (1995) Name ______________________ SSN ______________ Page 2

Part II **Vehicle Expenses** (See instructions to find out which sections to complete.)

Section A.—General Information

			(a) Vehicle 1	(b) Vehicle 2
11	Enter the date vehicle was placed in service	11	/ /	/ /
12	Total miles vehicle was driven during 1995	12	miles	miles
13	Business miles included on line 12	13	miles	miles
14	Percent of business use. Divide line 13 by line 12	14	%	%
15	Average daily round trip commuting distance	15	miles	miles
16	Commuting miles included on line 12	16	miles	miles
17	Other personal miles. Add lines 13 and 16 and subtract the total from line 12	17	miles	miles

18 Do you (or your spouse) have another vehicle available for personal purposes? ☐ Yes ☐ No

19 If your employer provided you with a vehicle, is personal use during off-duty hours permitted? ☐ Yes ☐ No ☐ Not applicable

20 Do you have evidence to support your deduction? ☐ Yes ☐ No

21 If "Yes," is the evidence written? ☐ Yes ☐ No

Section B.—Standard Mileage Rate (Use this section only if you own the vehicle.)

22 Multiply line 13 by 30¢ (.30). Enter the result here and on line 1. (Rural mail carriers, see instructions.) 22

Section C.—Actual Expenses

			(a) Vehicle 1	(b) Vehicle 2
23	Gasoline, oil, repairs, vehicle insurance, etc.	23		
24a	Vehicle rentals	24a		
b	Inclusion amount (see instructions)	24b		
c	Subtract line 24b from line 24a	24c		
25	Value of employer-provided vehicle (applies only if 100% of annual lease value was included on Form W-2—see instructions)	25		
26	Add lines 23, 24c, and 25	26		
27	Multiply line 26 by the percentage on line 14	27		
28	Depreciation. Enter amount from line 38 below	28		
29	Add lines 27 and 28. Enter total here and on line 1	29		

Section D.—Depreciation of Vehicles (Use this section only if you own the vehicle.)

			(a) Vehicle 1	(b) Vehicle 2
30	Enter cost or other basis (see instructions)	30		
31	Enter amount of section 179 deduction (see instructions)	31		
32	Multiply line 30 by line 14 (see instructions if you elected the section 179 deduction)	32		
33	Enter depreciation method and percentage (see instructions)	33		
34	Multiply line 32 by the percentage on line 33 (see instructions)	34		
35	Add lines 31 and 34	35		
36	Enter the limitation amount from the table in the line 36 instructions	36		
37	Multiply line 36 by the percentage on line 14	37		
38	Enter the **smaller** of line 35 or line 37. Also, enter this amount on line 28 above	38		

Form **2119**

Department of the Treasury
Internal Revenue Service

Sale of Your Home

▶ Attach to Form 1040 for year of sale.

▶ See separate instructions. ▶ Please print or type.

OMB No. 1545-0072

1995

Attachment Sequence No. 20

Your first name and initial. If a joint return, also give spouse's name and initial. | Last name | Your social security number

Fill in Your Address Only If You Are Filing This Form by Itself and Not With Your Tax Return

Present address (no., street, and apt. no., rural route, or P.O. box no. if mail is not delivered to street address) | Spouse's social security number

City, town or post office, state, and ZIP code

Part I Gain on Sale

1 Date your former main home was sold (month, day, year) ▶ 1 / /

2 Have you bought or built a new main home? ☐ Yes ☐ No

3 If any part of either main home was ever rented out or used for business, check here ▶ ☐ and see page 3.

4	Selling price of home. Do not include personal property items you sold with your home	4	
5	Expense of sale (see page 3)	5	
6	Subtract line 5 from line 4	6	
7	Adjusted basis of home sold (see page 3)	7	
8	**Gain on sale.** Subtract line 7 from line 6	8	

Is line 8 more than zero?

Yes ⟶ If line 2 is "Yes," you **must** go to Part II or Part III, whichever applies. If line 2 is "No," go to line 9.

No ⟶ **Stop; see Loss on the Sale of Your Home** on page 1.

9 If you haven't replaced your home, do you plan to do so within the **replacement period** (see page 1)? ☐ Yes ☐ No

- If line 9 is "Yes," stop here, attach this form to your return, and see **Additional Filing Requirements** on page 1.
- If line 9 is "No," you **must** go to Part II or Part III, whichever applies.

Part II One-Time Exclusion of Gain for People Age 55 or Older—By completing this part, you are electing to take the one-time exclusion (see page 2). If you are not electing to take the exclusion, go to Part III now.

10 Who was age 55 or older on the date of sale? ☐ You ☐ Your spouse ☐ Both of you

11 Did the person who was 55 or older own and use the property as his or her main home for a total of at least 3 years of the 5-year period before the sale? See page 2 for exceptions. If "No," go to Part III now ☐ Yes ☐ No

12 At the time of sale, who owned the home? ☐ You ☐ Your spouse ☐ Both of you

13 Social security number of spouse at the time of sale if you had a different spouse from the one above. If you were not married at the time of sale, enter "None" ▶ 13

14 **Exclusion.** Enter the **smaller** of line 8 or $125,000 ($62,500 if married filing separate return). Then, go to line 15 — 14

Part III Adjusted Sales Price, Taxable Gain, and Adjusted Basis of New Home

15 If line 14 is blank, enter the amount from line 8. Otherwise, subtract line 14 from line 8 — 15

- If line 15 is zero, stop and attach this form to your return.
- If line 15 is more than zero and line 2 is "Yes," go to line 16 now.
- If you are reporting this sale on the installment method, stop and see page 4.
- All others, stop and **enter the amount from line 15 on Schedule D, col. (g), line 4 or line 12.**

16	Fixing-up expenses (see page 4 for time limits)	16	
17	If line 14 is blank, enter amount from line 16. Otherwise, add lines 14 and 16	17	
18	**Adjusted sales price.** Subtract line 17 from line 6	18	
19a	Date you moved into new home ▶ / / **b** Cost of new home (see page 4)	19b	
20	Subtract line 19b from line 18. If zero or less, enter -0-	20	
21	**Taxable gain.** Enter the **smaller** of line 15 or line 20	21	

- If line 21 is zero, go to line 22 and attach this form to your return.
- If you are reporting this sale on the installment method, see the line 15 instructions and go to line 22.
- All others, **enter the amount from line 21 on Schedule D, col. (g), line 4 or line 12,** and go to line 22.

22	Postponed gain. Subtract line 21 from line 15	22	
23	**Adjusted basis of new home.** Subtract line 22 from line 19b	23	

Sign Here Only If You Are Filing This Form by Itself and Not With Your Tax Return

Under penalties of perjury, I declare that I have examined this form, including attachments, and to the best of my knowledge and belief, it is true, correct, and complete.

Your signature — Date — Spouse's signature — Date

If a joint return, both must sign.

For Paperwork Reduction Act Notice, see separate instructions. Form **2119** (1995)

H831 1040-19 PRINTED IN U.S.A.

Form **3903**

Department of the Treasury
Internal Revenue Service

Moving Expenses

▶ Attach to Form 1040.

▶ See instructions.

OMB No. 1545-0062

1995

Attachment Sequence No. **62**

Name(s) shown on Form 1040 | **Your social security number**

Caution: *If you are a member of the armed forces, see the instructions before completing this form.*

1	Enter the number of miles from your **old home** to your **new workplace**	1	miles
2	Enter the number of miles from your **old home** to your **old workplace**	2	miles
3	Subtract line 2 from line 1. Enter the result but not less than zero	3	miles

Is line 3 at least 50 miles?

Yes ▶ Go to line 4. Also, see **Time Test** in the instructions.

No ▶ You **cannot** deduct your moving expenses. Do not complete the rest of this form.

4	Transportation and storage of household goods and personal effects	4	
5	Travel and lodging expenses of moving from your old home to your new home. **Do not** include meals	5	
6	Add lines 4 and 5	6	
7	Enter the total amount your employer paid for your move (including the value of services furnished in kind) that is **not** included in the wages box (box 1) of your W-2 form. This amount should be identified with code **P** in box 13 of your W-2 form	7	

Is line 6 more than line 7?

Yes ▶ Go to line 8.

No ▶ You **cannot** deduct your moving expenses. If line 6 is less than line 7, subtract line 6 from line 7 and include the result in income on Form 1040, line 7.

8	Subtract line 7 from line 6. Enter the result here and on Form 1040, line 24. This is your **moving expense deduction**	8	

For Paperwork Reduction Act Notice, see instructions.

H831 1040-30 PRINTED IN U.S.A.

Form **3903** (1995)

APPENDIX S20

Federal Archives

If your target relative was involved in federal employment, and especially if he or she worked overseas as a federal employee, you may find meaningful information by contacting:

National Archives and Records Administration
8th Street and Pennsylvania Avenue, N.W.
Washington, DC 20408
Voice: (202) 501–5525
Fax: (202) 208–6256.

The national archives are by no means limited to printed documents; broadcast media (radio and television tapes) are also included. Perhaps your relative was present at some historic event, or attended an important conference. Searching through these archives for items of family history is fascinating. You may uncover family achievements (and perhaps secrets) dating back to the Revolutionary War!

To help in your search you can modify the sample query letter in the State Archives Appendix S17.

APPENDIX S21

Passport Office

If your target relative lived abroad for extended periods while an American citizen, he or she had a United States passport. While passports can be obtained through any number of regional offices, you should conduct your search for foreign locales of your relative's residence through the main Washington D.C. office:

Passport Services
1425 "K" Street, N.W.
Washington, DC 20524
Voice: (202) 647–0518
Fax: (202) 647–5939.

Use the sample letter to contact that office. Once you have found *where* your relative lived while abroad, you may need to go on to attempt to discover any valuable foreign assets they may have accumulated or transferred while living there. Contact the American embassy or consulate office in that country to work out details on how to conduct your search there.

SUGGESTED LETTER FOR PASSPORT INFORMATION

Date

Your Full Name
Address
City/State/Zip
Day Phone
Nights/Weekend Phone
Fax

Washington DC Office
Passport Services
1425 "K" St. N.W.
Washington, DC 20524
Telephone: (202) 647-0518
Fax: (202) 647-5939

Re: Name
Last known address
Social Security Number
Type of Employment
Countries traveled to
Approximate dates of
foreign travel, if known

To whom it may concern:

I am requesting information regarding the above named person who is my (state relationship). I am requesting this information to accumulate a history of where this person might have lived, including overseas, and what assets they may have in another country.

I have included documentation that will allow you to provide me with copies of the information requested. (See Enclosure)

Please contact me at the address/telephone number listed above if further information is needed in order to obtain this information.

Sincerely,

Signed

☛ As required, enclose one or more of the following documents with a self-addressed stamped envelope. Don't be discouraged if you cannot provide the documents. Send the request with the information you have.

- proof of bloodline relationship—birth certificate, etc.
- power of attorney
- death certificate
- court order naming you as executor or guardian
- signed letter of request by relative for whom information is requested
- copy of will

APPENDIX S22

Freedom of Information Act Inquiries

In your search dealings with various officials and bureaucrats it's undoubtedly true that "you can catch more flies with honey than with vinegar." Still, there may come a time when you are faced with a particularly "reluctant" federal functionary and are driven to execute your rights under the Freedom of Information Act. This Appendix provides you with a sample query letter describing the records you want to access.

After receiving your FOIA request, most bureaucrats would rather comply with your request than spend an equivalent or larger amount of time explaining why it is that an American citizen has been forced to demand, through an Act of Congress, access to the public records kept by his own government. If the difficulty goes unresolved you may want to consult the office of your federal Representative or Senator.

SUGGESTED FORM LETTER IN REGARDS TO THE FREEDOM OF INFORMATION ACT

Date

Your Name
Address
City/State/Zip
Day Phone
Nights/Weekend Phone
Fax

Name and Address of Government Agency   Re: A Freedom of Information Request

Dear (general counsel or other designated official):

Pursuant to the Freedom of Information Act, 5 U.S.C. 552, I hereby request access to, or a copy of (describe the document), together with all appendices, annexes, or other materials attached to (document). If any expenses in excess of $_______ are incurred in connection with this request, please inform me in advance for my approval. (You may ask that any fees be waived if furnishing the information could be considered as "primarily benefitting the public.")

If you determine that some portions of the (document) are exempt from release, I request that you provide me with the remainder. I hereby reserve my right to appeal any such decisions.

If you do not grant this request within 10 working days, I will consider my request denied. If you should wish to discuss the matter, my telephone number is (____) _____ -_______.

Thank you in advance for your time and consideration.

Sincerely,

Signed

Resource Appendices

APPENDIX R1

State Unclaimed Property Offices

This Appendix is a large and valuable one to you in your asset search. Besides the usual query letter, it consists of a Checklist of types of assets most frequently lying unclaimed and a directory listing each state's unclaimed property agency with contact information. These state offices are very accessible and should be contacted early in your search. Unfortunately, 90% of the unclaimed assets will have not yet reached the Unclaimed Property Office, so certainly do not stop your search with this office.

A very important consideration, and one which may help you broaden your asset search, is the existence of "reciprocity agreements" among several of the states. Here's how reciprocity works.

Uncle John paid a $40 deposit to a Florida telephone company. He wrote the deposit check on his Massachusetts bank account. Also, he told the clerk in the Florida telephone company office that his permanent address was in Massachusetts. Some years later, Uncle John moved back to Massachusetts without reclaiming his telephone deposit. The Florida telephone company was unsuccessful in locating him to return his deposit, so after five years (the Florida abandonment period) the deposit was sent to the Florida Unclaimed Property Office. That office advertised Uncle John's unclaimed property, in accordance with Florida statute, but neither he nor his heirs claimed it.

Florida then forwarded the unclaimed $40 on to Massachusetts. Florida did this because: (1) Massachusetts was the last address for Uncle John known to them; and (2) Florida and Massachusetts are reciprocity states.

When Massachusetts advertised the existence of the unclaimed deposit, Uncle John's heirs were able to collect it.

Checklist of Property Most Frequently Turned Over to Unclaimed Offices

All property is stored in cash.

Account Balances

Checking Accounts
Savings Accounts
Matured Certificates of Deposit or Savings Certificates
Christmas Club Accounts
Money on deposit to secure funds
Security Deposits — Damage, clean up
Unidentified Deposits
Suspense Accounts
Any sum owing to a shareholder, certificate holder, member, bond holder, or other security holder, or participant such as:
- dividends
- interest
- principal payments
- equity payments
- profits
- other distributions

Escrows

Trusts, Investments & Escrow Accounts

Paying agent accounts
Unclaimed dividends
Funds held in a fiduciary capacity
Funds paid toward the purchase of share, or interest in a financial or business organization
Funds received for redemption of stocks and bonds
Stocks
Bonds
Any other certificates of ownership
Suspense liabilities

Official Checks

Certified checks
Cashier's checks
Registered checks
Treasurers checks
Drafts
Warrants
Money orders
Travelers checks (15 years from issue date)
Foreign exchange or currency
Any other official checks or exchange items

Miscellaneous Checks and Intangible Personal Property Held in the Ordinary Course of Business

Wages, payroll or salary
Commissions
Expense checks
Workmen's Compensation benefits
Pension checks
Credit checks or memos
Payments for goods and services
Customer overpayments such as credit card balances
Unidentified remittances
Unrefunded overcharges
Accounts payable
Credit balances — accounts receivable
Discounts due such as insurance premiums, dividends, etc.
Refunds such as rental deposits
Unredeemed gift certificates
Vendor checks
Mineral proceeds
Royalties
Unclaimed parimutuel tickets
Any other miscellaneous outstanding checks
Any checks that have been written off to income or surplus
Any other miscellaneous intangible personal property

Insurance

Amounts due and payable under terms of insurance policies
Claim payments
Drafts unpresented for payment (stale warrants)
Matured whole life, term or endowment insurance policies or annuity or supplementary contracts
Other amounts due under policy terms

continued on R1-3

Checklist of Property Most Frequently Turned Over to Unclaimed Offices

All property is stored in cash.

Utilities

Utility deposits
Membership fees
Refunds or rebates
Cooperative patronage accounts

Dissolutions

All property distributable in the course of voluntary or involuntary dissolution or liquidation which is unclaimed within one year after the date for final distribution is presumed abandoned.

Tangible Property

Contents of safe deposit boxes
Contents of any other safekeeping repository
Other tangible property

SUGGESTED LETTER TO THE UNCLAIMED PROPERTY OFFICE

Date

Your Full Name
Address
City/State/Zip
Day Phone
Nights/Weekend Phone
Fax

State Unclaimed Property Office
Address (see Unclaimed Property Appendix)

Re: Name
Address
Social Security Number
Date of Birth
Date of Death

To whom it may concern:

I am a relative or personal friend to a family searching for assets that remain in the ownership of the above name, and Social Security number. I am not a professional finder, and I will not require a fee agreement related to the property value.

Please search your records and if you find property attached to the above name, please provide me with the necessary forms your department requires to prove heirship and ownership.

Please let me know if you need any further information.

Sincerely,

Signed

☛ Check the Unclaimed Property Appendix for specific state privacy rules. This is public information in most states.

STATE UNCLAIMED PROPERTY OFFICES

ALABAMA

Agency: Unclaimed Property Section
Natural Resources and License Tax Division
P. O. Box 327580
Montgomery, AL 36132-7580

Telephone: (334) 242-9614

Fax: No Fax

Special Information:

- Search requests may be made by mail.
- Most property is considered abandoned after five (5) years.
- Property is held until claimed.
- Interest is not paid on unclaimed property.
- No estimate of total value of unclaimed property held by the state of Alabama.

STATE UNCLAIMED PROPERTY OFFICES

ALASKA

Agency:	Alaska Dept. of Revenue Unclaimed Property Section P. O. Box 110420 Juneau, AK 99811-0420
Telephone:	(907) 465-5886
Fax:	(907) 465-2375
Web Site:	http://www.revenue.state.ak.us/iea/ieunprop.htm (name search only)

Special Information:

- Search requests may be made in person, by phone, fax, or by mail.
- Most property is considered abandoned after five (5) years.
- Property is held until claimed.
- Interest is paid only if the account was bearing interest at the time it was received by the Unclaimed Property Office, not to exceed 10 years.
- There is over $9 million in unclaimed property in the state of Alaska.

STATE UNCLAIMED PROPERTY OFFICES

ARIZONA

Agency:

Arizona Dept. of Revenue
Comptroller's Section/ Unclaimed Property
1600 W. Monroe
Phoenix, AZ 85007

Telephone: (602) 542-4643

Fax: No Fax

Special Information:

- Search requests may be made in person, by mail or by phone.
- Most property is considered abandoned after five (5) years.
- Property is held until claimed.
- Interest is paid only if the account was bearing interest before being turned over to the Unclaimed Property Office.
- No estimate of total value of unclaimed property in the state of Arizona.

STATE UNCLAIMED PROPERTY OFFICES

ARKANSAS

Agency: Arkansas State Auditor
Unclaimed Property Division
103 W. Capitol, Suite 805
Little Rock, AR 72201

Telephone: (501) 324-9670

Fax: (501) 324-9676

Toll Free: (800) 252-4648

Special Information:

- Search requests may be made in person, by phone, fax, or by mail.
- Most property is considered abandoned after seven (7) years.
- Property is held until claimed.
- Interest is paid only if the account was bearing interest at the time it was turned over to the Unclaimed Property Division. Interest not paid after claimed.
- No estimate of total value of unclaimed property held by the state of Arkansas.

STATE UNCLAIMED PROPERTY OFFICES

CALIFORNIA

Agency: State Controller's Office
Unclaimed Property Division
Attn: Research Unit
P. O. Box 94285
Sacramento, CA 94250-5873

Telephone: (916) 445-8318
(916) 323-2827 (Outside of California)

Fax: No Fax

Toll Free: (800) 992-4647 (Inside of California)

Web Site: http://www.sco.gov (name search only)

Special Information:

- Search requests may be made in person, by phone or by mail.
- Most property is considered abandoned after three (3) years.
- Property is held until claimed.
- Interest on unclaimed property is paid at a maximum rate of 5% if the account was bearing interest when received by the Unclaimed Property Division.
- There is over $6 billion in unclaimed property in the state of California.
- California is a reciprocity state.

STATE UNCLAIMED PROPERTY OFFICES

COLORADO

Agency:	Colorado Unclaimed Property 1560 Broadway, Suite 630 Denver, CO 80202
Telephone:	(303) 894-2443
Fax:	No Fax
Toll Free:	(800) 825-2111

Special Information:

- Search requests may be made in person, by phone, or by mail.
- Most unclaimed property is considered abandoned after five (5) years.
- Property is held until claimed.
- Interest is paid on accounts only if the property was bearing interest before it was turned over to the Unclaimed Property Office.
- There is over $80 million in unclaimed property held by the state of Colorado.

STATE UNCLAIMED PROPERTY OFFICES

CONNECTICUT

Agency:	Unclaimed Property Division 55 Elm St. Hartford, CT 06106
Telephone:	(203) 566-5516
Fax:	No Fax
Toll Free:	(800) 833-7318
Web Site:	http://www.state.ct.us/ott/ (name search only)
Special Information:	▪ Search requests may be made in person, by phone, or by mail. ▪ Most property is considered abandoned after five (5) years. ▪ Property is held until claimed. ▪ Interest is paid on bank accounts at 4% on accounts that were bearing interest when received by the Unclaimed Property Division. ▪ There is over $250 million in unclaimed property held by the state of Connecticut, over $24 million in just one year.

STATE UNCLAIMED PROPERTY OFFICES

DELAWARE

Agency:	Delaware State Escheater 300 Indiana Ave. N.W., Room 5008 or P. O. Box 8931 Wilmington, DE 19899
Telephone:	(302) 577-3349
Fax:	(302) 577-3106
Special Information:	▪ Search requests may be made by mail. ▪ Most property is considered abandoned after five (5) years. ▪ Property is held until claimed. ▪ Interest is not paid on unclaimed property. ▪ No estimate of total value of unclaimed property held by the state of Delaware.

STATE UNCLAIMED PROPERTY OFFICES

FLORIDA

Agency:	Office of Comptroller Florida Dept. of Banking and Finance Abandoned Property Section The State Capitol Bldg. Tallahassee, FL 32399-0350
Telephone:	(904) 487-0510
Fax:	(904) 922-6014
Toll Free:	(800) 848-3792 (Only in Florida)
Web Site:	http://www.dbf.state.fl.us/index.html (name search only)

Special Information:

- Search requests may be made in person, by phone, fax, or by mail.
- Most property is considered abandoned after five (5) years.
- Property is held until claimed.
- Interest is not paid on unclaimed property.
- There is over $500 million in unclaimed property in the state of Florida.
- Florida is a reciprocity state.

STATE UNCLAIMED PROPERTY OFFICES

GEORGIA

Agency: Georgia Dept. of Revenue
Property Tax Division
Unclaimed Property Section
270 Washington St. S.W., Room 404
Atlanta, GA 30334

Telephone: (404) 656-4244

Fax: No Fax

Special Information:

- Search requests may be made in person, by phone, or by mail.
- Most property is considered abandoned after five (5) years.
- Property is held until claimed.
- Interest is not paid on unclaimed property.
- There is over $160 million in unclaimed property in the state of Georgia.

STATE UNCLAIMED PROPERTY OFFICES

HAWAII

Agency:

Unclaimed Property Branch
Financial Administration Division
Dept. of Budget and Finance
P. O. Box 150
Honolulu, HI 96810

Telephone: (808) 586-1589

Fax: (808) 586-1583

Special Information:

- Search request may be made by phone, fax, or by mail.
- Most property is considered abandoned after five (5) years.
- Property is held until claimed.
- Interest is not paid on unclaimed property.
- There is over $40 million in unclaimed property in the state of Hawaii.

STATE UNCLAIMED PROPERTY OFFICES

IDAHO

Agency:	Idaho State Tax Commission Unclaimed Property Section 800 Park Blvd., Plaza W. or P. O. Box 36 800 Park Blvd., Plaza IV Boise, ID 83722-2240
Telephone:	(208) 334-7596
Fax:	(208) 334-7655

Special Information:

- Search request may be made in person, by phone, fax, or by mail.
- Most property is considered abandoned after one (1) to fifteen (15) years.
- Most property is held until claimed.
- Interest is paid at 5% for a maximum of 10 years if the property was earning interest before it was remitted to the state.
- There is approximately $19 million in unclaimed property held by the state of Idaho.
- Idaho is a reciprocity state.

STATE UNCLAIMED PROPERTY OFFICES

ILLINOIS

Agency: State of Illinois
Unclaimed Property Division
500 Iles Park Place or
P. O. Box 19495
Springfield, IL 62794-9495

Telephone: (217) 785-6992

Fax: (217) 785-6999

Special Information:

- Search requests may be made by mail or fax.
- Most property is considered abandoned after five (5) years.
- Property is held until claimed.
- Interest is not paid on unclaimed accounts.
- No estimate of total value of unclaimed property held by the state of Illinois.
- Illinois is a reciprocity state.

NAME
ADDRESS
RELATIONSHIP
DATES

STATE UNCLAIMED PROPERTY OFFICES

INDIANA

Agency:	Office of Attorney General Unclaimed Property Division Indiana Government Center South, 5th Floor 402 W. Washington St. Indianapolis, IN 46204
Telephone:	(317) 232-6348
Fax:	(317) 323-7979
Toll Free:	(800) 447-5598
Web Site:	http://ideanet.doe.state.in.us/htmls/ag.html (name search only)

Special Information:

- Search requests may be made in person, by phone, or on-line.
- Most property is considered abandoned after seven (7) years.
- Interest is not paid on unclaimed property.
- There is a 25 year statute of limitations on claims beginning after the property has been turned over to the Unclaimed Property Division.
- There are approximately 200,000 names of persons believed to be owners of unclaimed property in the state of Indiana. The Unclaimed Property Division in Indiana currently holds almost $40 million in money and property.

STATE UNCLAIMED PROPERTY OFFICES

IOWA

Agency:	Office of Treasurer State of Iowa Hoover Bldg. 1305 E. Wanut Des Moines, IA 50319
Telephone:	(515) 281-5368 (must be transferred to Unclaimed Property Office)
Fax:	No Fax
Web Site:	http://www.state.ia.us/government/treasurer (name search only)
Special Information:	▪ Search requests may be made in person, by phone, or by mail. ▪ Most property is considered abandoned after three (3) years. ▪ Property is held until claimed. ▪ Interest is not paid on unclaimed property. ▪ No estimate of total value of unclaimed property held by the state of Iowa.

STATE UNCLAIMED PROPERTY OFFICES

KANSAS

Agency:	Kansas State Treasurer Unclaimed Property Division 900 S.W. Jackson, Suite 201 Topeka, KS 66612-1235
Telephone:	(913) 296-4165
Fax:	No Fax
Toll Free:	(800) 432-0386 (only in Kansas)
Web Site:	http://www.ink.org/public/uncl_prop/index.html (name search only)
Special Information:	▪ Search requests may be made by phone. ▪ Most property is considered abandoned after five (5) years. ▪ Interest is paid on abandoned property bearing interest at the time it was turned over to the Unclaimed Property Dept. ▪ Property is held until claimed. ▪ There is approximately $50 million in unclaimed property in the state of Kansas.

STATE UNCLAIMED PROPERTY OFFICES

KENTUCKY

Agency: Attn: Abandoned Property
Kentucky State Treasury
Capitol Annex, Suite 183
Frankport, KY 40611

Telephone: (502) 564-4722

Fax: No Fax

Special Information:

- Search requests may be made by phone or mail.
- Most property is considered abandoned after seven (7) years.
- Property is held until claimed.
- Interest is not paid on unclaimed property.
- There is over $40 million in unclaimed property held by thestate of Kentucky.

STATE UNCLAIMED PROPERTY OFFICES

LOUISIANA

Agency: State of Louisiana
Dept. of Revenue and Taxation
Unclaimed Property Section
P. O. Box 91010
Baton Rouge, LA 70821-9010

Telephone: (504) 925-7407

Fax: (504) 925-7494

Web Site: http://wwww.rev.state.la.us (name search only)

Special Information:

- Search requests may be made by phone, fax, or by mail.
- Most property is considered abandoned after five (5) years.
- Property is held until claimed.
- Interest is not paid on accounts bearing interest when they are turned over to the Unclaimed Property Section.
- There is over $3.9 million in unclaimed property in the state of Louisiana.

STATE UNCLAIMED PROPERTY OFFICES

MAINE

Agency: State of Maine
Treasury Dept.
Abandoned Property Dept.
State House Station
Augusta, ME 04333

Telephone: (207) 287-6668

Fax: No Fax

Special Information:

- Search requests must be made by mail.
- Most property is considered abandoned after five (5) years.
- Property is held until claimed.
- Interest is paid on accounts bearing interest when it was turned over to the Abandoned Property Dept.
- There is $25 million in unclaimed property held by the state of Maine.

STATE UNCLAIMED PROPERTY OFFICES

MARYLAND

Agency:	State of Maryland Comptroller of the Treasury Unclaimed Property Section 301 W. Preston St. Baltimore, MD 21201-2385
Telephone:	(410) 225-1705
Fax:	(410) 333-7150
Web Site:	http://sailor.lib.md.us/md.comptroller/money.html (name search only)
Special Information:	▪ Search requests may be made in person, by phone, fax, or by mail. ▪ Most property is considered abandoned after five (5) years. ▪ Property is held until claimed. ▪ Interest is paid at 5% on most accounts for a maximum of five (5) years only on accounts bearing interest at the time of being turned over to the Abandoned Property Division. ▪ The State Comptroller's Office has records on approximately 160,000 accounts, dating back to the 1960's. These accounts are worth about $68 million, and more money is turned over to the Unclaimed Property Section each year.

STATE UNCLAIMED PROPERTY OFFICES

MASSACHUSETTS

Agency: The Commonwealth of Massachusetts
Treasury Dept.
Abandoned Property Division
One Ashburton Place 12th Floor
Boston, MA 02108

Telephone: (617) 367-0400

Fax: (617) 248-3944

Web Site: http://www.magnet.state.ma.us/treasury (search address list only)
or
http://www.magnet.state.ma.us/dor/rfndlist.html
(state tax refund list)

Special Information:

- Search requests may be made only by mail.
- Most property is considered abandoned after three (3) years.
- Property is held until claimed.
- Interest is paid at 5% if the account is bearing interest when it was turned over to the Abandoned Property Division.
- No estimate of total value of unclaimed property held by the state of Massachusetts.
- Massachusetts is a reciprocity state.

STATE UNCLAIMED PROPERTY OFFICES

MICHIGAN

Agency: State of Michigan
Dept. of Treasury
Abandoned and Unclaimed Property Division
Lansing, MI 48922

Telephone: (517) 335-4327

Fax: No Fax

Special Information:

- Search requests may be made in person, by phone, or by mail.
- Most property is considered abandoned after two (2) to five (5) years.
- Interest is not paid on unclaimed property.
- Property is held until claimed.
- There is approximately $300 million in unclaimed property held by the state of Michigan.

STATE UNCLAIMED PROPERTY OFFICES

MINNESOTA

Agency: Minnesota Dept. of Commerce
Unclaimed Property Section
133 E. 7th St.
St. Paul, MN 55101

Telephone: (612) 296-2568

Fax: No Fax

Special Information:

- Search requests may be made in person, by phone, or by mail.
- Most property is considered abandoned after three (3) years.
- Property is held until claimed.
- Interest is not paid on unclaimed property.
- There is approximately $70 million in unclaimed property held by the state of Minnesota.
- Minnesota is a reciprocity state.

STATE UNCLAIMED PROPERTY OFFICES

MISSISSIPPI

Agency:

State Treasurer's Office
Unclaimed Property Division
Room 404, Sillers State Office Bldg.
or
P.O. Box 138
Jackson, MS 39205

Telephone: (601) 359-3600

Fax: (601) 359-2001

Special Information:

- Search requests may be made in person, by phone, fax, or by mail.
- Most property is considered abandoned after five (5) years.
- Property is held until claimed.
- Interest is paid only if the account was bearing interest at the time it was turned over to the Unclaimed Property Division.
- There is approximately $3 million in unclaimed property held by the state of Mississippi.

STATE UNCLAIMED PROPERTY OFFICES

MISSOURI

Agency: State of Missouri
Office of State Treasurer
Unclaimed Property Section
P.O. Box 1004
Jefferson City, Missouri 65102

Telephone: (314) 751-0840

Fax: (314) 526-6027

Web Site: http://www.ecodev.state.mo.us/treasure/unclprop.html
(name search only)

Special Information:

- Search requests may be made only in writing.
- Most property is considered abandoned after seven (7) years.
- Property is held until claimed.
- Interest is paid for up to seven (7) years if the account was bearing interest at the time it was turned over to the Unclaimed Property Division.
- There is over $86 million in unclaimed property held by the state of Missouri.
- Missouri is a reciprocity state.

STATE UNCLAIMED PROPERTY OFFICES

MONTANA

Agency: Montana Dept. of Revenue
Abandoned Property Section
Income and Miscellaneous Tax Division
P.O. Box 5805 Mitchell Bldg.
Helena, MT 59620

Telephone: (406) 444-2425

Fax: (406) 444-1505

Special Information:

- Search requests may be made in person, by phone, fax: or by mail.
- Most property is considered abandoned after five (5) years.
- Property is held until claimed.
- Interest is not paid on unclaimed property.
- There is approximately $12 million in unclaimed property held by the state of Montana.

STATE UNCLAIMED PROPERTY OFFICES

NEBRASKA

Agency:	State of Nebraska Unclaimed Property Division Office of State Treasurer Room 2003, Capitol Bldg or P.O. Box 94788 Lincoln, NE 68509-4788
Telephone:	(402) 471-2455
Fax:	(402) 471-4390
Special Information:	▪ Search requests may be made in person, by phone, fax, or by mail. ▪ Most property is considered abandoned after five (5) years. ▪ Property is held until claimed. ▪ Interest is not paid on unclaimed property. ▪ An estimated $25 million in unclaimed property is held by the State of Nebraska. ▪ Nebraska is a reciprocity state.

STATE UNCLAIMED PROPERTY OFFICES

NEVADA

Agency:	State of Nevada Dept. of Commerce Unclaimed Property Division 2501 E. Sahara Suite 304 State Mailroom Las Vegas, NV 89104
Telephone:	(702) 486-4140
Fax:	(702) 486-4177
Toll Free:	(800) 521-0019 (only in Nevada)
Special Information:	▪ Search requests may be made in person, by phone, fax, or by mail. ▪ Most property is considered abandoned after five (5) years. ▪ Property is held until claimed. ▪ Interest is not paid on unclaimed property. ▪ The state of Nevada is holding approximately $25 million in unclaimed property. ▪ Nevada is a reciprocity state.

STATE UNCLAIMED PROPERTY OFFICES

NEW HAMPSHIRE

Agency:	New Hampshire Treasury Dept. Division of Abandoned Property 25 Capitol St. Room 205, State House Annex Concord, NH 03301
Telephone:	(603) 271-2619
Fax:	(603) 271-3922
Special Information:	▪ Search requests may be made in person, by phone, fax, or by mail. ▪ Most property is considered abandoned after five (5) years. ▪ Property is held for 24 months by the state and may then be claimed by request to the governor and council. ▪ Interest is not paid on unclaimed property. ▪ No estimate of total value of unclaimed property held by the state of New Hampshire.

STATE UNCLAIMED PROPERTY OFFICES

NEW JERSEY

Agency:	New Jersey Dept. of Treasury Unclaimed Property Division CN-287 Trenton, NJ 08646-0214
Telephone:	(609) 292-9200
Fax:	No Fax

Special Information:

- Search requests can only be made in writing.
- Most property is considered abandoned after five (5) to ten (10) years.
- Property is held until claimed.
- Interest is paid if the account was bearing interest at the time it was turned over to the Unclaimed Property Division.
- No estimate of total value of unclaimed property held by the state of New Jersey.

STATE UNCLAIMED PROPERTY OFFICES

NEW MEXICO

Agency:	State of New Mexico Taxation and Revenue Dept. Unclaimed Property Division P.O. Box 25123 Sante Fe, NM 87504-5123
Telephone:	(505) 827-0822
Fax:	(505) 827-0940
Special Information:	▪ Search requests may be made by phone, fax, or by mail. ▪ Most property is considered abandoned after five (5) years. ▪ Property is held until claimed. ▪ Interest is not paid on unclaimed property. ▪ No estimate of total value of property held by the state of New Mexico.

STATE UNCLAIMED PROPERTY OFFICES

NEW YORK

Agency:	New York State Comptroller c/o Office of Unclaimed Funds A.E. Smith Office Bldg. Albany, NY 12236
Telephone:	(518) 474-4044
Fax:	No Fax
Toll Free:	(800)221-9311 (Only in New York)
Web Site:	http://www.ocs.state.ny.us/ (name search only)
Special Information:	▪ Search requests may be made in person, or preferably by mail. ▪ Most property is considered abandoned after two (2) to five (5) years. ▪ Property is held until claimed. ▪ Interest is paid on accounts only if the account was bearing interest at the time it was turned over to the Office of Unclaimed Funds. ▪ There is an estimated $4 billion in unclaimed property held by the state of New York. ▪ The list contains 6,000,000 names of people who appear to be entitled to these unclaimed funds.

STATE UNCLAIMED PROPERTY OFFICES

NORTH CAROLINA

Agency: Dept. of State Treasurer
Administrative Services Division
Escheat and Unclaimed Property Program
325 N. Salisbury St.
Raleigh, NC 27603-1385

Telephone: (919) 733-6876

Fax: (919) 715-0229

Web Site: http://www.treasurer.state.nc.us/treasurer (name search only)

Special Information:

- Search requests may be made in person, by phone, fax, or by mail.
- Most property is considered abandoned after five (5) years.
- Property is held until claimed.
- Interest is not paid on unclaimed property.
- There is over $150 million in unclaimed property held by the state of North Carolina.
- North Carolina is a reciprocity state.

STATE UNCLAIMED PROPERTY OFFICES

NORTH DAKOTA

Agency:	Unclaimed Property Division State Land Dept. 918 E. Divide, Suite 410 or P.O. Box 5523 Bismarck, ND 58502-5523
Telephone:	(701) 328-2805
Fax:	(701) 328-3650
Special Information:	■ Search requests may be made in person, by phone, fax, or by mail. ■ Most property is considered abandoned after five (5) years. ■ Property is held until claimed. ■ Interest is not paid in unclaimed property. ■ There are approximately 10,000 accounts worth over $8 million held by the state of North Dakota. ■ North Dakota is a reciprocity state.

STATE UNCLAIMED PROPERTY OFFICES

OHIO

Agency:	Ohio Dept. of Commerce Division of Unclaimed Funds 77 S. High St., 20th Floor Columbus, OH 43266-0545
Telephone:	(614) 466-4433
Fax:	(614) 752-5078
Special Information:	▪ Search requests may be made in person, by phone, by fax, or by mail. ▪ Most property is considered abandoned after five (5) years. ▪ Most property is held until claimed. ▪ Interest is not paid on unclaimed property. ▪ There is approximately $125 million in unclaimed property held by the state of Ohio.

STATE UNCLAIMED PROPERTY OFFICES

OKLAHOMA

Agency:	Oklahoma Tax Commission Unclaimed Property Section Attn: Don Wadel 3017 N. Stiles, 2nd Floor P.O. Box 53248 Oklahoma City, OK 73152-3248
Telephone:	(405) 521-4271
Fax:	(405) 521-2146
Toll Free:	(800) 522-8165 (only in Oklahoma)

Special Information:

- Search requests may be made in person, by phone, by fax, or by mail.
- Most property is considered abandoned after five (5) years.
- Property is held until claimed.
- Interest is not paid on unclaimed property.
- There is approximately $80 million in unclaimed property held by the state of Oklahoma.

STATE UNCLAIMED PROPERTY OFFICES

OREGON

Agency: Unclaimed Property and Estates Section
Division of State Lands
775 Summer St. N.E.
Salem, OR 97310

Telephone: (503) 378-3805 ext. 291

Fax: No Fax

Special Information:

- Search requests may be made in person or by mail.
- Most property is considered abandoned property after five (5) years.
- Property is held until claimed.
- Interest is not paid on abandoned property.
- No estimate of total value of property held by the state of Oregon.

STATE UNCLAIMED PROPERTY OFFICES

PENNSYLVANIA

Agency:	Pennsylvania State Treasurer Office of Unclaimed Property P.O. Box 1837 Harrisburg, PA 17105-1837
Telephone:	(717) 772-2722
Fax:	(717) 787-9079
Toll Free:	(800) 222-2046
Web Site:	http://libertynet.org/~patreas (name search only)

Special Information:

- Search requests may be made in person, by phone, fax, or by mail.
- Most property is considered abandoned after seven (7) years.
- Property is held until claimed.
- Interest is not paid on unclaimed property.
- No estimate of total value of unclaimed property held by the state of Pennsylvania.

STATE UNCLAIMED PROPERTY OFFICES

RHODE ISLAND

Agency: State of Rhode Island and Providence Plantations
Treasury Dept.
Unclaimed Property Division
P.O. Box 1435
Providence, RI 02901-1435

Telephone: (401) 277-6505

Fax: (401) 277-2212

Web Site: http://www.state.ri.us/treas/moneylst.html (name search only)

Special Information:

- Search requests may be made in person, by phone, fax, or by mail.
- Most property is considered abandoned after three (3) years.
- Property is held until claimed.
- Interest on unclaimed property is paid at 2.25% only if the account was bearing interest at the time it was turned over to the Unclaimed Property Division.
- No estimate of total value of unclaimed property held by the state of Rhode Island.
- Rhode Island is a reciprocity state.

STATE UNCLAIMED PROPERTY OFFICES

SOUTH CAROLINA

Agency: South Carolina State Tax Commission
Columbia Mills Bldg.
301 Gervais St.
P.O. Box 125
Columbia, SC 29214

Telephone: (803) 737-4771

Fax: No Fax

Special Information:

- Search requests may be made by phone or by mail.
- Most property is considered abandoned after five (5) years.
- Property is held until claimed.
- Interest is paid on unclaimed property if the account was bearing interest when it was turned over to the Tax Commission after June 30th, 1988.
- There is over $50 million in unclaimed property held by the state of South Carolina.

STATE UNCLAIMED PROPERTY OFFICES

SOUTH DAKOTA

Agency: State of South Dakota
Office of the Treasurer
State Capitol
500 E. Capitol Ave.
Pierre, South Dakota 57501

Telephone: (605) 773-3378

Fax: No Fax

Web Site: http://www.state.sd.us/state/executive/treasurer/prop.html (name search only)

Special Information:

- Search requests may be made by phone or by mail.
- Most property is considered abandoned after five (5) years and one (1) year for utilities, wages, and government entities.
- Property is held until claimed.
- Interest is not paid on unclaimed property.
- There is over $8 million in unclaimed property held by the state of South Dakota.

STATE UNCLAIMED PROPERTY OFFICES

TENNESSEE

Agency:	Treasury Dept. Division of Unclaimed Property Andrew Jackson State Office Bldg., 9th Floor Nashville, TN 37243-0242
Telephone:	(615) 741-6499
Fax:	(615) 532-4979

Special Information:

- Search requests may be made in person, by phone, fax, or by mail
- Most property is considered abandoned after two (2) to five (5) years.
- Property is held until claimed.
- Interest is paid if the account was bearing interest at the time it was turned over to the Unclaimed Property Division.
- There is approximately $60 million in unclaimed property held by the state of Tennessee.

STATE UNCLAIMED PROPERTY OFFICES

TEXAS

Agency:	Texas State Treasurer Unclaimed Property Division 200 E. 10 St., 6th Floor Attn: Public Outreach P.O. Box 12019 Austin, TX 78711-2019
Telephone:	(512) 463-3120
Fax:	(512) 463-1362
Toll Free:	(800) 321-2274 (in Texas only)
Special Information:	▪ Search requests may be made in person, by phone, or by mail. ▪ Most property is considered abandoned after three (3) years. ▪ Property is held until claimed. ▪ Interest is not paid on unclaimed property. ▪ No estimate of value of property held by the state of Texas.

STATE UNCLAIMED PROPERTY OFFICES

UTAH

Agency: Unclaimed Property Division
341 So. Main St., 5th Floor
Salt Lake City, UT 84111

Telephone: (801) 533-4101

Fax: No Fax

Web Site: http://www.treasurer.state.ut.us (name search only)

Special Information:

- Search requests may be made in person, phone, or by mail.
- Most property is considered abandoned after five (5) years.
- Property is held until claimed.
- Interest is paid only if the account was bearing interest when it was turned over to the Unclaimed Property Division.
- No estimate of total value of property held by the state of Utah.

STATE UNCLAIMED PROPERTY OFFICES

VERMONT

Agency:	State of Vermont Abandoned Property Division 133 State St. Montpelier, VT 05633-6200
Telephone:	(802) 828-2407
Fax:	(802) 828-2772
Toll Free:	(800) 642-3191 (only in Vermont)
Special Information:	▪ Search requests may be made by phone or by mail. ▪ Most property is considered to be abandoned after five (5) years. ▪ Interest is not paid on unclaimed property. ▪ Property is held until claimed. ▪ There is over $5 million in unclaimed property held by the state of Vermont.

STATE UNCLAIMED PROPERTY OFFICES

VIRGINIA

Agency:	Commonwealth of Virginia Dept. of Treasury Division of Unclaimed Property P.O. Box 2478 Richmond, VA 23218
Telephone:	(804) 225-2393
Fax:	(804) 786-4653
Toll Free:	(800) 468-1088 (only in Virginia)
Special Information:	▪ Search request may be made by mail. ▪ Most property is considered abandoned after five (5) years. ▪ Property is held until claimed. ▪ Interest is paid on unclaimed property if the account was bearing interest when it was turned over to the Division of Unclaimed Property. ▪ No estimate of total value of unclaimed property held by the state of Virginia. ▪ Virginia is a reciprocity state.

STATE UNCLAIMED PROPERTY OFFICES

WASHINGTON

Agency: State of Washington
Dept. of Revenue
Dept. of Unclaimed Property
P.O. Box 448
Olympia, WA 98504-7450

Telephone: (360) 586-2736

Fax: (360) 586-2163

Toll Free: (800) 435-2429 (only in Washington)

Web Site: http://www.wa.gov/dor/ucp.html (name search only)

Special Information:

- Search requests may be made in person, by phone, fax, by mail, or by using WIN machines.
- Most property is considered abandoned after five (5) years.
- Property is held until claimed.
- Interest is paid only if the account was bearing interest when it was turned over to the Dept. of Unclaimed Property.
- No estimate of total value of property held by the state of Washington.
- Washington is a reciprocity state.

STATE UNCLAIMED PROPERTY OFFICES

WEST VIRGINIA

Agency:	State of West Virginia Office of State Treasurer Division of Unclaimed Property State Capitol Charleston, WV 25305-0860
Telephone:	(304) 343-4000 ext. 297
Fax:	(304) 346-6602
Toll Free:	(800) 422-7498 (only in West Virginia)
Special Information:	▪ Search requests may be made in person, by phone, fax, or by mail. ▪ Most property is considered abandoned after five (5) years. ▪ Property is held until claimed. ▪ Interest is not paid on unclaimed property. ▪ The state of West Virginia is holding close to $1 million in unclaimed property.

STATE UNCLAIMED PROPERTY OFFICES

WISCONSIN

Agency:	State Treasurer of Wisconsin Unclaimed Property Section 101 E. Wilson, Floor 5 P.O. Box 2114 Madison, WI 53701-2114
Telephone:	(608) 267-7977
Fax:	(608) 266-2647
Web Site:	http://bayer.state.wi.us/agencies/ost (name search only)

Special Information:

- Search requests may be made by mail.
- Most property is considered abandoned after five (5) years.
- Property is held until claimed.
- Interest is paid only if the account was bearing interest when it was turned over to the Unclaimed Property Section.
- There is over $50 million in unclaimed property held by the state of Wisconsin.
- Wisconsin is a reciprocity state.

STATE UNCLAIMED PROPERTY OFFICES

WYOMING

Agency:	Wyoming State Treasurer Unclaimed Property Division 1st W. Herschler Bldg. 122 W. 25th St. Cheyenne, WY 82002
Telephone:	(307) 777-5590
Fax:	(307) 777-5430
Web Site:	Gopher://159.238.200.34/11/wgor/eb/sot (name search only)
Special Information:	▪ Search requests may be made by mail. ▪ Most property is considered abandoned after five (5) years. ▪ Property is held until claimed. ▪ Interest is not paid on unclaimed property. ▪ There is approximately $6.5 million in unclaimed property held by the state of Wyoming.

APPENDIX R2

State Public Employee and Teacher Retirement Programs

Each state has a Public Employee and Teacher Retirement Program. You may be surprised what this Appendix turns up in the way of your target relative's unknown assets. Besides the sample query letter, it consists of a Checklist of state and educational agencies which might be covered and a directory listing each of the fifty–one states' retirement program offices along with contact information.

Most of these State Employee and Teacher Retirement Programs were started in the mid–1930's and their coverage may be quite broad. Besides ordinary state civil servants and teachers, some programs include local police officers, firemen, elected officials, judges, even members of the National Guard. Contributions to the retirement fund are made by the employee and the employer (government entity or school district) on a matching basis. For example 5% of the employee's gross wages might be contributed by each. In that case, a total of 10% of the employee's gross wages, totaled over the years, form the principle. These retirement funds are interest–bearing *up to the present time* (not just during your relative's employment); hence the interest involved may be a very sizeable amount indeed.

A person's being *vested* in their state's retirement program ensures that both their contributions and their employer's contributions to the fund are frozen in the employee's account name and Social Security number until he or she reaches retirement age. Most public retirement programs provide for a lump sum payment to the employee or to his estate after he has become vested. Even if the employee or ex–employee dies before retirement age, that one-time payment may be *very substantial.*

When completing an employment history on your deceased relative, be sure not to overlook *short term* public employment. This might include a few months or a year of employment while waiting to be called up for the Selective Service draft or while attending college. In most cases, military service counts as employment time towards becoming vested in the retirement program.

As for most retirement programs, it is the responsibility of the former public employee's or teacher's heirs or estate to notify the retirement plan of his/her death. It is also true in most retirement programs that if a person dies prematurely it is the responsibility of the heirs to notify the plan of his/her death. It's quite unlikely any action towards distributing assets will be automatically taken if your relative dies in a state other than that of the retirement program. It's up to you and the other heirs to notify any possible retirement program of your relative's death.

SUGGESTED LETTER TO A PUBLIC EMPLOYEE OR TEACHER RETIREMENT PROGRAM

Date

Your Name
Address
City/State/Zip
Day Phone
Nights/Weekend Phone
Fax

State Retirement Program
Address (see Public Employee and
Teacher Retirement Appendix)

Re: Full Name
Address (in state where employed)
Social Security Number
Agency of Employment (if known)

Dear Director,

I am requesting that your agency search for an account in the name of the person listed above. This information is sought in order to reconstruct the life assets of my (state relationship) since this person has (become incapacitated, passed away, etc.).

I have enclosed proper documentation in order to receive this information. (See Enclosure) Please contact me at the above address if further information is needed.

Sincerely,

Signed

☛ As required, enclose one or more of the following with a self-addressed stamped envelope:

- proof of bloodline relationship
- power of attorney
- court order stating you are the executor or guardian
- death certificate
- copy of will

Employment that could be covered by Public Retirement Programs

Association of School Boards

Compensation Insurance Authority

Council on Arts and Humanities

High School Activities Association

State Lottery

State Fair

State Hospital

Student Loan Program

Water Resources and Power Development Authority

Department of Administration

Department of Agriculture

Department of Corrections

Department of Education

Department of Health

Department of Human Resources

Department of Institutions

Department of Labor and Employment

Department of Law

Department of Local Affairs

Department of Military Affairs

Department of Natural Resources

Department of Personnel

Department of Public Safety

Department of Regulatory Agencies

Department of Revenue

Department of Social Services

Department of State

Department of Transportation

Department of Treasury

Fire and Police Pension Association

General Assembly

Joint Budget Committee

Judicial Department

Legislative Council

Office of the District Attorneys

Office of the Governor

Office of Legislative Legal Services

Office of Lieutenant Governor

Regional Center

Special District Association

State Auditor's Office

State Historical Society

Institutes of Higher Education –College and Universities

Public Hospitals

Library Staff

PUBLIC EMPLOYEE AND TEACHER RETIREMENT PROGRAMS

ALABAMA

System:	Employees' Retirement System of Alabama 135 S. Union St. Montgomery, AL 36130-2150
Telephone:	(334) 832-4140
Fax:	(334) 240-3032
Years to become vested:	10 years
Membership:	Total Membership: 84,856 Active: 66,431 Inactive: 5,019 = 6% of membership Retired (receiving benefits): 17,925
Value of Inactive Accounts:	Unknown
Special Provisions:	Vested accounts grow at 8.5% yearly.

ALABAMA

System:	Teachers' Retirement Systems of Alabama 135 S. Union St. P.O. Box 302150 Montgomery, AL 36130-2150
Telephone:	(334) 832-4140
Fax:	(334) 240-3032
Years to become vested:	10 years
Membership:	Total Membership: 148,521 Active: 111,900 Inactive: 10,000 = 7% of membership Retired (receiving benefits): 31,841
Value of Inactive Accounts:	Unknown
Special Provisions:	Vested accounts grow at 8.25% yearly.

PUBLIC EMPLOYEE AND TEACHER RETIREMENT PROGRAMS

ALASKA

System:	Public Employee Retirement System Dept. of Administration Division of Retirement and Benefits P.O. Box 110203 Juneau, AK 99811-0203
Telephone:	(907) 465-4460
Fax:	(907) 465-3086
Years to become vested:	5 years
Membership:	Total Membership: 52,485 Active: 35,214 Inactive: 7,629 Vested Inactive: 3,249 projected monthly benefit = $582 Nonvested Inactive: 4,380 average account balance = $2,251 Retired (receiving benefits): 9,242
Value of Inactive Accounts:	$9,859,380
Special Provisions:	The average value of an inactive account is $1,292. Vested accounts accumulate interest at 4.5% annually.

ALASKA

System:	Teachers' Retirement System Dept. of Administration Division of Retirement and Benefits P.O. Box 110203 Juneau, AK 99811-0203
Telephone:	(907) 465-4460
Fax:	(907) 465-3086
Years to become vested:	8 years
Membership:	Total Membership: 6,859 Active: 2,200 Inactive: 1,767 Vested Inactive: 710 projected monthly benefit $1,087 Nonvested Inactive: 1,057 average account balance $10,411 Retired (receiving benefits): 3,602
Value of Inactive Accounts:	$11,004,427
Special Provisions:	The average value of an inactive account is $6,227.

PUBLIC EMPLOYEE AND TEACHER RETIREMENT PROGRAMS

ARIZONA

System:	Arizona State Retirement System 3300 N. Central Ave. P.O. Box 33910 Phoenix, AZ 85067-3910
Telephone:	(602) 240-2027
Fax:	(602) 266-4082
Toll Free:	(800) 621-3778 in Arizona
Years to become vested:	5 years
Membership:	Total Membership: 208,726 Active: 160,000 apprx. Inactive: 23,110 = 11% of membership Retired (receiving benefits): 40,000 apprx.

PUBLIC EMPLOYEE AND TEACHER RETIREMENT PROGRAMS

ARKANSAS

System:	Arkansas Public Employee Public Employee Retirement System One Capitol Mall, 2nd Floor Little Rock, AR 72201-1015
Telephone:	(501) 682-7812
Fax:	No Fax
Years to become vested:	10 years
Membership:	Total Membership: 69,241 Active: 42,000 Inactive: Not Available Vested Inactive: 2,441 Retired (receiving benefits): 12,800 apprx.
Value of Inactive Accounts:	Unknown

ARKANSAS

System:	Arkansas Teachers' Retirement Teacher Retirement System State of Arkansas Little Rock, AR 72201
Telephone:	(501) 682-1517
Fax:	(501) 682-2663
Years to become vested:	10 years
Membership:	Total Membership: 127,862 Active: 71,244 Inactive: 42,618 Vested Inactive: 991 Non-vested Inactive: 68,236 Retired (receiving benefits): 14,000 apprx.
Value of Inactive Accounts:	Unknown

PUBLIC EMPLOYEE AND TEACHER RETIREMENT PROGRAMS

CALIFORNIA

System:	California Public Employees Retirement P.O. Box 942701 Sacramento, CA 94229-2701
Telephone:	(916) 326-3829
Fax:	(916) 326-3410
Years to become vested:	5 years
Membership:	Total Membership: 688,125 Active: 200,950 Inactive: 78,939 = 11% of membership Inactive Vested: Unknown
Value of Inactive Accounts:	Unknown

CALIFORNIA

System:	California Teacher Retirement 7667 Folsom Blvd. P.O. Box 15275 Sacramento, CA 95826-0275
Telephone:	(916) 229-3870
Fax:	(916) 229-3704
Toll Free:	(800) 228-5453
Years to become vested:	5 years
Membership:	Total Membership: 500,000 Active: 327,513 Inactive: 54,159 Retired (receiving benefits): 130,576
Special Provisions:	There is $921,000,000 held by inactive accounts accruing 5.5% interest. The average value of an inactive account is $18,095.

PUBLIC EMPLOYEE AND TEACHER RETIREMENT PROGRAMS

COLORADO

System:	Public Employees Retirement Association 1300 Logan St. Denver, CO 80203
Telephone:	(303) 832-9550
Fax:	(303) 863-3825
Years to become vested:	60 months
Membership:	Total Membership: 214,000 Active: 141,000 Inactive: 33,000 Vested Inactive: 3,600 Nonvested Inactive: 29,400 = 14% of membership Retired (receiving benefits): 40,073
Value of Inactive Accounts:	$11,000,000 (After five years Dormant accounts are sent to Colorado Abandoned Property.)
Special Provisions:	The average value of an inactive account is $333. The statistics above are for both Public Employees and Teachers.

PUBLIC EMPLOYEE AND TEACHER RETIREMENT PROGRAMS

CONNECTICUT

System:	Connecticut Public Employees Retirement Division Office of the Comptroller 55 Elm St. Hartford, CT 06106
Telephone:	(203) 566-5639
Fax:	(203) 566-3071
Years to become vested:	10 years
Membership:	Total Membership: 79,936 Inactive: 4,065 Nonvested Inactive: 3,405 = 4% of membership Vested Inactive: 660
Value of Inactive Accounts:	$8,696,727
Special Provisions:	Accounts accrue interest at 5% per annum. The average value of an inactive account is $2,139.

CONNECTICUT

System:	Connecticut Teacher Retirement State Teachers Retirement Board 165 Capitol Ave. Hartford, CT 06106
Telephone:	(203) 241-8404
Fax:	(203) 566-3240
Years to become vested:	10 years
Membership:	Total Membership: 46,384 Active: 39,258 Inactive: 7,126 Vested Inactive: 3,400 Nonvested Inactive: 6,726 = 15% of membership
Value of Inactive Accounts:	Unknown

PUBLIC EMPLOYEE AND TEACHER RETIREMENT PROGRAMS

DELAWARE

System:	Pension Office Office of the State Personnel Thomas Collins Bldg. Dover, DE 19903
Telephone:	(302) 739-4208
Fax:	(302) 739-6129
Toll Free:	(800) 722-7300
Years to become vested:	5 years
Membership:	Total Membership: 41,502 Active: 27,390 Inactive: 599 Vested Inactive: 415 Nonvested Inactive: 184 = .04% of membership Retired (receiving benefits): 13,153
Value of Inactive Accounts:	$100,000
Special Provisions:	Teachers are included in this retirement program. The average value of an inactive account is $167.

PUBLIC EMPLOYEE AND TEACHER RETIREMENT PROGRAMS

FLORIDA

System:	Division of Retirement Cedars Executive Center, Bldg. C 2639 N. Monroe St. Tallahassee, FL 32399-1560
Telephone:	(904) 488-5541
Fax:	(904) 488-5290
Years to become vested:	10 years
Membership:	Total Membership: 1,173,625 Active: 586,625 Inactive: Not Available Vested Active: 244,604 Nonvested Active: 342,021 Vested Inactive: 22,392 Retired (receiving benefits): 125,021
Value of Nonvested Benefits:	$3,912,901,000
Special Provisions:	Teachers are included in this retirement program. The average value of a nonvested account is $9,185.

PUBLIC EMPLOYEE AND TEACHER RETIREMENT PROGRAMS

GEORGIA

System: Georgia Public Retirement
Employees Retirement System
Two Northside 75, Suite 300
Atlanta, GA 30318

Telephone: (404) 352-6400

Fax: (404) 352-6431

Years to become vested: 10 years

Membership: Total Membership: 125,850
Active: 83,324
Inactive: 24,925
Nonvested Inactive: 41,082 = 32% of membership
Retired (receiving benefits): 19,770

Value of Inactive Accounts: Unknown

GEORGIA

System: Georgia Teachers Retirement System
Suite 400
Two Northside 75 N.W.
Atlanta, GA 30318-7901

Telephone: (404) 352-6500

Fax: (404) 352-6536

Years to become vested: 10 years

Membership: Total Membership: 156,293
Inactive: 62,464
Vested Inactive: 220
Non-vested: 93,739

Special Provisions: Interest is paid on inactive accounts for the first 12 months.

PUBLIC EMPLOYEE AND TEACHER RETIREMENT PROGRAMS

HAWAII

System:	Employee's Retirement System Dept. of Budget and Finance 201 Merchant St. # 1400 Honolulu, HI 96813
Telephone:	(808) 586-1700
Fax:	(808) 586-1677
Years to become vested:	10 year non-contributory plan
Membership:	Total Membership: 86,057 Active: 58,498 Vested Inactive: 2,189 Nonvested Inactive: Unknown Retired (receiving benefits): 25,360
Value of Inactive Accounts:	Unknown
Special Provisions:	All state retirement systems are included in these statistics.

PUBLIC EMPLOYEE AND TEACHER RETIREMENT PROGRAMS

IDAHO

System:	Public Employee Retirement System of Idaho P.O. Box 83720 Boise, ID 83720-0078
Telephone:	(208) 334-3365
Fax:	(208) 334-4026
Years to become vested:	5 years
Membership:	Total Membership: 77,283 Active: 55,811 Inactive: 6,468 Nonvested Inactive: 3,151 = 4% of membership Vested Inactive: 3,317 Retired (receiving benefits): 19,272
Value of Inactive Accounts:	$80,000,000
Special Provisions:	The average value of an inactive account is $12,368.

PUBLIC EMPLOYEE AND TEACHER RETIREMENT PROGRAMS

ILLINOIS

System:	Illinois Public Employee Retirement S.R.S. P.O. Box 19255 Springfield, IL 62794-9255
Telephone:	(217) 785-7444
Fax:	(217) 785-7019
Years to become vested:	8 years
Membership:	Total Membership: 101,234 Active: 78,796 Inactive: 22,438 Vested Inactive: 2,652 Nonvested Inactive: 19,761 = 20% of membership Retired (receiving benefits): 39,104
Value of Inactive Accounts:	$264,075,696
Special Provisions:	The average value of an inactive account is $11,782.

ILLINOIS

System:	Illinois Teacher Retirement Teachers Retirement System P.O. Box 19253 Springfield, IL 62794-9253
Telephone:	(217) 753-0311
Fax:	(217) 787-2269
Years to become vested:	10 years
Membership:	Total Membership: 199,996 Active: 108,520 Inactive: 38,736 Vested Inactive: Unknown Non-Vested Inactive: Unknown Retired (receiving benefits): 52,740
Value of Inactive Accounts:	Unknown
Special Provisions:	Unknown

PUBLIC EMPLOYEE AND TEACHER RETIREMENT PROGRAMS

INDIANA

System:	Indiana Public Employee Retirement Fund Harrison Bldg. Suite 800 143 W. Market St. Indianapolis, IN 46204
Telephone:	(317) 233-4162
Fax:	(317) 232-1614
Years to become vested:	10 years
Membership:	Total Membership: 180,000 Active: 138,788 Inactive: 51,212 Vested Inactive: 4,500 Non-vested Inactive: 20,000 = 11% of membership
Value of Inactive Accounts:	$5,980,000
Special Provisions:	The average value of an inactive account is $244. Inactive non-vested accounts accrue interest at 7.75% per annum.

INDIANA

System:	Indiana Teacher Retirement Teacher's Retirement Fund 150 W. Market St. Suite 300 Indianapolis, IN 46204-2809
Telephone:	(317) 232-3869
Fax:	(317) 232-3882
Years to become vested:	10 years
Membership:	Total Membership: 133,653 Active: 43,770 Non-Vested: 19,603 = 6.82% of membership Inactive: 30,000 Vested Inactive: 1,899
Value of Inactive Accounts:	$16,000,000
Special Provisions:	The average value of an inactive account is $533.

PUBLIC EMPLOYEE AND TEACHER RETIREMENT PROGRAMS

IOWA

System:	Iowa Public Employees Retirement System Dept. of Personnel 600 E. Court Ave. Des Moines, IA 50306
Telephone:	(515) 281-0039
Fax:	(515) 281-0053
Years to become vested:	4 years
Membership:	Total Membership: 150,000 approx. Active: 134,485 approx. Inactive: 51,436 approx. Non-Vested Inactive: 29,308 Vested Inactive: 22,128 Retired (receiving benefits): 51,436
Value of Inactive Accounts:	$122,387,088
Special Provisions:	Teachers are included in the public retirement system. The average value of an inactive account is $2,379. Refunds due and unpaid to nonvested accounts is $4,192,147.

PUBLIC EMPLOYEE AND TEACHER RETIREMENT PROGRAMS

KANSAS

System:	Public Employee Retirement System Capitol Tower, 2nd Floor 400 S.W. 8th Topeka, KS 66603
Telephone:	(913) 296-6666
Fax:	(913) 296-2422
Toll Free	(800) 228-0366
Years to become vested:	9½ years
Membership:	Total Membership: 200,000 Active: 132,904 Inactive: 12,474 Non-Vested Inactive: 9,474 = 5% of membership Vested Inactive: 3,000 Retired (receiving benefits): 45,000
Value of Inactive Accounts:	Unknown
Special Provisions:	Teachers and public retirement systems are included in the statistics above. Inactive nonvested accounts accrue interest for five (5) years.

PUBLIC EMPLOYEE AND TEACHER RETIREMENT PROGRAMS

KENTUCKY

System:	Kentucky Public Employees Retirement System Parimeter Park W. 1260 Louisville Rd. Frankfort, KY 40601
Telephone:	(502) 564-4646
Fax:	(502) 564-5656
Years to become vested:	60 months or 1 month if 65 or older
Membership:	Total Membership: 188,982 Active: 121,426 Inactive: 30,392 Vested Inactive: 11,021 Retired (receiving benefits): 37,164
Value of Inactive Accounts:	$173,383,500
Special Provisions:	The average value of an inactive account is $6,731. The above statistics are a combination of three retirement systems.

KENTUCKY

System:	Kentucky Teacher Retirement System 479 Versailles Rd. Frankfort, KY 40601
Telephone:	(502) 573-3266
Fax:	(502) 573-6695
Years to become vested:	5 years
Membership:	Total Membership: 77,670 Active: 55,000 Vested Inactive: 2,289 Non-vested Inactive: 1,629 = 3% of membership Retired (receiving benefits): 22,670
Value of Inactive Accounts:	Unknown

PUBLIC EMPLOYEE AND TEACHER RETIREMENT PROGRAMS

LOUISIANA

System:	Louisiana State Employee Retirement System P.O. Box 44213 Baton Rouge, LA 70804
Telephone:	(504) 922-0600
Fax:	(504) 922-0614
Years to become vested:	10 years
Membership:	Total Membership: 115,090 Inactive: 20,769 Vested Inactive: 600 Nonvested Inactive: 20,169 = 18% of membership
Value of Inactive Accounts:	Unknown
Special Provisions:	Interest is not paid on inactive accounts.

LOUISIANA

System:	Teacher Retirement System of Louisiana P.O. Box 94123 Capitol Station Baton Rouge, LA 70804-9123
Telephone:	(504) 925-6446
Fax:	(504) 925-6366
Years to become vested:	10 years
Membership:	Total Membership: 131,032 Inactive: 10,071 Vested Inactive: 371 Nonvested Inactive: 9,754 = 10% of membership Retired (receiving benefits): 37,952
Value of Inactive Accounts:	Unknown

PUBLIC EMPLOYEE AND TEACHER RETIREMENT PROGRAMS

MAINE

System:	Maine State Retirement System 46 State House Station Augusta, ME 04333-0043
Telephone:	(207) 287-3461
Fax:	(207) 287-1032
Years to become vested:	10 years
Membership:	Total Membership: 130,558 Active: 50,000 Inactive: 40,279 = 46% of membership Nonvested Inactive: 39,300
Value of Inactive Accounts:	Unknown
Special Provisions:	Public and Teachers retirements are combined. Interest is paid on Inactive nonvested accounts for five (5) years.

PUBLIC EMPLOYEE AND TEACHER RETIREMENT PROGRAMS

MARYLAND

System:	State Retirement Agency Retirement and Pension Systems 301 W. Preston St. Room 701 Baltimore, MD 21201-2363
Telephone:	(410) 225-4051
Fax:	(410) 333-7550
Toll Free:	(800) 492-5909
Years to become vested:	5 years
Membership:	Total Membership: 249,460 Active: 170,000 Inactive: 20,915 Vested Inactive: 6,931 Nonvested Inactive: 13,984 = 18% of membership Retired (receiving benefits): 64,954
Employer Finance Nonvested:	$369,951,220
Special Provisions:	Public and Teachers retirements are included in this retirement system.

PUBLIC EMPLOYEE AND TEACHER RETIREMENT PROGRAMS

MASSACHUSETTS

System:	Massachusetts Public Retirement State Board of Retirement Office of the Treasurer 1 Ashburton Place Boston, MA 02108
Telephone:	(617) 367-7770
Fax:	(617) 723-1438
Years to become vested:	10 years
Membership:	Total Membership: 176,032 Active: 82,476 Vested Inactive: 50,000 Nonvested Inactive: 43,556
Value of Inactive Accounts:	Unknown

MASSACHUSETTS

System:	Massachusetts Teacher Retirement Treasure and Receiver General 1 Ashburton Place Boston, MA 02108
Telephone:	(617) 367-6900
Fax:	(617) 248-0372
Years to become vested:	10 years
Membership:	Total Membership: 176,032 Active: 82,476 Inactive: 50,000 Nonvested Inactive: 43,556 Vested Inactive: 50,000
Value of Inactive Accounts:	Unknown

PUBLIC EMPLOYEE AND TEACHER RETIREMENT PROGRAMS

MICHIGAN

System:	Bureau of Retirement Systems Dept. of Management and Budget General Office Bldg., Third Floor Wing A P.O. Box 30171 Lansing, MI 48909
Telephone:	(517) 322-6275
Fax:	(517) 322-5190
Years to become vested:	5, 8 or 10 years
Membership:	Total Membership: 418,569 Active: 65,133 Inactive: 138,528 Vested Inactive: 19,431 Non-vested Inactive: 119,097 = 28% of membership Retired (receiving benefits): 30,562
Value of Inactive Accounts:	Unknown

MICHIGAN

System:	Michigan Public School Employee Retirement System P.O. Box 30026 Lansing, MI 48909
Telephone:	(517) 322-6236
Fax:	(517) 322-6145
Years to become vested:	10 years
Membership:	Total Membership: 294,911 Active: Unknown Inactive: 13,988 Non-Vested: 178,969 Retired (receiving benefits): 103,151
Value of Inactive Accounts:	$811,613,427

PUBLIC EMPLOYEE AND TEACHER RETIREMENT PROGRAMS

MINNESOTA

System	Minnesota State Retirement System 175 W. Lafayette Frontage Rd., Suite 300 St. Paul, MN 55107
Telephone:	(612) 296-2761
Fax:	(612) 297-5238
Years to become vested:	3 years
Membership:	Total Membership: 70,000 Active: 53,752 Inactive: 14,012 Retired (receiving benefits): 12,899
Value of Inactive Accounts:	$2,387,000
Special Provision:	The average value of an inactive account is $287.

MINNESOTA

System:	Teachers Retirement Association Galary Bldg., Suite 500 17 W. Exchange St. St. Paul MN 55102
Telephone:	(612) 296-2409
Fax:	(612) 297-5999
Years to become vested:	3 years
Membership:	Total Membership: 115,000 approx. Active: 70,000 approx. Inactive: 20,000 approx. Vested Inactive: 6,297 Non-Vested Inactive: 14,012 = 16% of membership Retired (receiving benefits): 25,000 approx.
Value of Inactive Accounts:	Unknown

PUBLIC EMPLOYEE AND TEACHER RETIREMENT PROGRAMS

MISSISSIPPI

System:	Public Employees Retirement System 429 Mississippi St. Jackson, MS 39201
Telephone:	(601) 359-3589
Fax:	(601) 359-2285
Years to become vested:	4 years
Membership:	Total Membership: 230,089 Active: 135,117 Inactive: 57,085 Inactive Nonvested: 48,734 = 21% of membership Vested Inactive 8,351 Retired (receiving benefits) 37,887
Value of Inactive Accounts:	$63,338,987
Special Provisions:	Teachers and Public Retirement are combined. The average value of an inactive account is $1,110.

PUBLIC EMPLOYEE AND TEACHER RETIREMENT PROGRAMS

MISSOURI

System:	Missouri State Employees Retirement System 906 Leslie Blvd. P.O. Box 209 Jefferson City, MO 65102
Telephone:	(314) 751-2342
Fax:	(314) 751-7182
Years to become vested:	5 years
Membership:	Total Membership: 69,492 Vested Inactive: 7,484
Value of Inactive Accounts:	Unknown
Special Provisions:	In this program the employer makes the entire contribution and therefore the employee has no benefits prior to being vested.

MISSOURI

System:	Public School Retirement Division 701 W. Main St. P.O. Box 268 Jefferson City, MO 65102
Telephone:	(314) 634-5290
Fax:	(314) 634-7934
Toll Free:	(800) 392-6848
Years to become vested:	5 years
Membership:	Total Membership: 62,046 Active: 57,711 Inactive: Not Available Nonvested Inactive: Not Available
Value of Inactive Accounts:	Unknown
Special Provisions:	In this program the employer makes the entire contribution and therefore the employee has no benefits prior to being vested.

PUBLIC EMPLOYEE AND TEACHER RETIREMENT PROGRAMS

MONTANA

System:	Public Employees Retirement System Dept. of Administrations 1712 9th Ave. P.O. Box 200131 Helena, MT 59620-0131
Telephone:	(406) 444-3154
Fax:	(406) 444-5428
Years to become vested:	5 years
Membership:	Total Membership: 29,268 Active: 20,590 Inactive: 8,678 Inactive Nonvested: 6,013 = 13% of membership Retired (receiving benefits): 14,187
Value of Inactive Accounts:	Unknown

MONTANA

System:	Teacher's Retirement Division Dept. of Administration 1500 E. 6th Ave. Helena, MT 59601
Telephone:	(406) 444-3134
Fax:	(406) 444-2641
Years to become vested:	5 years
Membership:	Total Membership: 33,129 Active: 18,062 Inactive: 7,331 Inactive Nonvested: 4,204 = 14% of membership Retired (receiving benefits): 7,736
Value of Inactive Accounts:	$11,442,901
Special Provisions:	The average value of an inactive account is $2,712.

PUBLIC EMPLOYEE AND TEACHER RETIREMENT PROGRAMS

NEBRASKA

System:	Public Employees Retirement System P.O. Box 94816 Lincoln, NE 68509
Telephone:	(402) 471-2053
Fax:	(402) 471-9493
Toll Free:	(800) 245-5712
Years to become vested:	5 to 10 years with the exception of judges, who are vested immediately.
Membership:	Total Membership: 80,663 Active: 53,752 Inactive: 14,012 Retired (receiving benefits): 12,899
Value of Inactive Accounts:	$60,336,829

PUBLIC EMPLOYEE AND TEACHER RETIREMENT PROGRAMS

NEVADA

System:	Public Employees Retirement System 693 W. Nye Ln. Carson City, NV 89703
Telephone:	(702) 687-4208
Fax:	(702) 687-5131
Toll Free:	(800) 992-0990 ext. 4200 in Nevada
Years to become vested:	5 years
Membership:	Total Membership: 101,423 Active: 67,965 Inactive: 46,028 Vested Inactive: 2,227 Nonvested Inactive: 39,700 = 38.1% of membership
Value of Inactive Accounts:	Unknown

NEVADA

System:	Public Employee Retirement System 693 W. Nye Ln. Carson City, NV 89703
Telephone:	(702) 687-4208
Fax:	(702) 687-5131
Years to become vested:	5 years
Membership:	Total Membership: 67,000 Active: 61,420 Inactive: 41,927 Vested Inactive: 2,227 Retired (receiving benefits): Unknown
Value of Inactive Accounts:	Unknown

PUBLIC EMPLOYEE AND TEACHER RETIREMENT PROGRAMS

NEW HAMPSHIRE

System:	New Hampshire Retirement System 4 Chennel Drive Concord, NH 03301-8509
Telephone:	(603) 271-3351
Fax:	(603) 271-6806
Years to become vested:	10 years
Membership:	Total Membership: 56,000 Active: 44,000 Inactive: Not Available Retired (receiving benefits): 12,000
Value of Inactive Accounts:	Unknown
Special Provisions:	Teachers are included in the New Hampshire Retirement System.

PUBLIC EMPLOYEE AND TEACHER RETIREMENT PROGRAMS

NEW JERSEY

System:	Division of Pensions and Benefits 1 State St. Sq., CN 295 Trenton, NJ 08625-0295
Telephone:	(609) 292-3463
Fax:	(609) 633-9591
Years to become vested:	10 years
Membership:	Total Membership: 1,000,000 approx. Active: 500,000 approx. Inactive: 250,000 approx. Retired (receiving benefits): 250,000 approx.
Value of Inactive Accounts:	Unknown
Special Provisions:	Teachers are included in the New Jersey Division of Pensions.

PUBLIC EMPLOYEE AND TEACHER RETIREMENT PROGRAMS

NEW MEXICO

System:	Public Employees' Retirement Board PERA Bldg. P.O. Box 2123 Santa Fe, NM 87504
Telephone:	(505) 827-4700
Fax:	(505) 827-4670
Toll Free:	(800) 342-3422
Years to become vested:	5 years
Membership:	Total Membership: 63,650 Active: 50,470 Inactive: Not Available Retired (receiving benefits): 13,185
Value of Inactive Accounts:	Unknown

NEW MEXICO

System:	Educational Retirement Board P.O. Box 26129 Santa Fe, NM 87502
Telephone:	(505) 827-8030
Fax:	(505) 989-7738
Years to become vested:	5 years
Membership:	Total Membership: 85,000 Active: 54,000 Inactive: 14,000 Retired (receiving benefits): 17,000
Value of Inactive Accounts:	Unknown

PUBLIC EMPLOYEE AND TEACHER RETIREMENT PROGRAMS

NEW YORK

System:	New York Public Retirement System A.E. Smith Bldg., 6th Floor Albany, NY 12244
Telephone:	(518) 474-7736
Fax:	(518) 473-9104
Years to become vested:	10 years
Membership:	Total Membership: 605,544 Tier 1: 103,738 Tier 2: 74,523 Tier 3: 126,817 Tier 4: 300,466

NEW YORK

System:	New York State Teachers' Retirement System 10 Corporate Woods Dr. Albany, NY 12211-2395
Telephone:	(518) 447-2666
Fax:	(518) 447-2630
Years to become vested:	10 years
Membership:	Total Membership: 196,000 Active: 187,166 Nonvested Inactive: 80,867 = 43% of membership Vested Inactive: 5,207 Retired (receiving benefits): 86,000
Value of Inactive Accounts:	Unknown

PUBLIC EMPLOYEE AND TEACHER RETIREMENT PROGRAMS

NORTH CAROLINA

System:	Retirement Benefits 325 N. Salisbury St. Raleigh, NC 27603
Telephone:	(919) 733-4191
Fax:	(919) 733-9586
Years to become vested:	5 years
Membership:	Total Membership: 421,771 Active: 367,771 Inactive: 53,000 Vested Inactive: 21,200 Nonvested Inactive: 31,800 Retired (receiving benefits): Unknown
Value of Inactive Accounts:	$297,000,000
Special Provisions:	There are five retirement systems included in the above figures.

PUBLIC EMPLOYEE AND TEACHER RETIREMENT PROGRAMS

NORTH DAKOTA

System:	Public Employee Retirement System P.O. Box 1214 Bismarck, ND 58502
Telephone:	(701) 328-3900
Fax:	(701) 328-3920
Years to become vested:	5 years
Membership:	Total Membership: 21,000 Active: 16,569 Inactive: 1,125 Vested Inactive: 96 Non-Vested Inactive: 1,029 = 16% of membership
Value of Inactive Accounts:	Unknown

NORTH DAKOTA

System:	Teachers' Fund for Retirement P.O. Box 7100 Bismarck, ND 58507
Telephone:	(701) 328-9885
Fax:	(701) 328-9897
Years to become vested:	5 years
Membership:	Total Membership: 15,315 Active: 9,663 Vested Inactive: 1,219 Nonvested Inactive: 239 = 63% of membership Retired (receiving benefits): 4,433
Value of Inactive Accounts:	$4,039,736
Special Provisions:	The average value of an account is $3,504.

PUBLIC EMPLOYEE AND TEACHER RETIREMENT PROGRAMS

OHIO

System:	Public Employees Retirement System 227 E. Town St. Columbus, OH 43266
Telephone:	(614) 466-2822
Fax:	(614) 644-5024
Years to become vested:	5 years
Membership:	Total Membership: 444,205 Active: 347,937 Inactive: 96,268 = 5% of membership Retired (receiving benefits): 109,973
Value of Inactive Accounts:	Unknown
Special Provision:	Interest is paid on inactive accounts.

OHIO

System:	State Teachers Retirement System of Ohio 275 E. Broad. St. Columbus, OH 43215
Telephone:	(614) 227-4090
Fax:	(614) 227-5216
Years to become vested:	5 years
Membership:	Total Membership: 300,000 Active: 105,000 Inactive: 17,000 Nonvested Inactive: 88,000 = 4% of membership Retired (receiving benefits): 76,000
Value of Inactive Accounts:	Unknown
Special Provisions:	Interest is paid on inactive accounts.

PUBLIC EMPLOYEE AND TEACHER RETIREMENT PROGRAMS

OKLAHOMA

System: Oklahoma Public Employees Retirement System
Jim Thorpe Bldg. Room 580
Oklahoma City, OK 73105

Telephone: (405) 521-2381

Fax: (405) 521-6592

Years to become vested: 8 years

Membership: Total Membership: 53,594
Active: 43,987
Inactive: 3,563
Vested Inactive: 2,046
Retired (receiving benefits): 16,044

Value of Inactive Accounts: Unknown

OKLAHOMA

System: Oklahoma Teachers Retirement System
2801 N. Lincoln Blvd.
Oklahoma City, OK 73105
or
P.O. Box 53524
Oklahoma City, OK 73152

Telephone: (405) 521-2387

Fax: (405) 521-3810

Years to become vested: 10 years

Membership: Total Membership: 115,000 approx.
Active: 79,044
Inactive: 9,115
Vested Inactive: 2,467
Retired (receiving benefits): 29,007

Value of Inactive Accounts: Unknown

PUBLIC EMPLOYEE AND TEACHER RETIREMENT PROGRAMS

OREGON

System:	Public Employees Retirement System 200 S.W. Market St. Suite 700 P.O. Box 73 Portland, OR 97207
Telephone:	(503) 229-5824
Fax:	(503) 222-5502
Years to become vested:	5 years
Membership:	Total Membership: 160,000 Active: 111,173 Inactive: 70,000 Retired (receiving benefits): 60,000
Value of Inactive Accounts:	Unknown

PUBLIC EMPLOYEE AND TEACHER RETIREMENT PROGRAMS

PENNSYLVANIA

System:	Pennsylvania State Employees Retirement 30 N. 3rd St. Harrisburg, PA 17101
Telephone:	(717) 787-6780
Fax:	(717) 772-3741
Years to become vested:	10 years
Membership:	Total Membership: 193,841 Active: 112,637 Inactive: 4,300 Retired (receiving benefits): 81,204
Value of Inactive Accounts:	Unknown

PENNSYLVANIA

System:	Pennsylvania School Employees Retirement 5 N. 5th St. P.O. Box 125 Harrisburg, PA 17108
Telephone:	(717) 787-8540
Fax:	(717) 772-5372
Years to become vested:	10 years
Membership:	Total Membership: 315,000 Active: 200,000 Inactive: 36,500 Vested Inactive: 4,800 Nonvested Inactive: 31,700 = 9.5% of membership Retired (receiving benefits): 115,000
Value of Inactive Accounts:	Unknown

PUBLIC EMPLOYEE AND TEACHER RETIREMENT PROGRAMS

RHODE ISLAND

System:	Rhode Island Retirement Division 40 Fountain St. Providence, RI 02903
Telephone:	(401) 277-2203
Fax:	(401) 277-2430
Years to become vested:	10 years
Membership:	Total Membership: 48,500 Active: 30,000 Inactive: Not Available Retired (receiving benefits): 17,500
Value of Inactive Accounts:	Unknown
Special Provision:	Teachers are included in the Rhode Island Retirement Division.

PUBLIC EMPLOYEE AND TEACHER RETIREMENT PROGRAMS

SOUTH CAROLINA

System:	Retirement System P.O. Box 11960 Columbia, SC 29211
Telephone:	(803) 737-6800
Fax:	(803) 737-6947
Toll Free:	(800) 868-9002
Years to become vested:	5 years
Membership:	Total Membership: 207,371 Active: 190,000 Inactive: 101,000 Retired (receiving benefits): 356,924
Value of Inactive Accounts:	Unknown
Special Provisions:	$4,800,000,000 is obligated to retirees and inactive-vested members.

PUBLIC EMPLOYEE AND TEACHER RETIREMENT PROGRAMS

SOUTH DAKOTA

System:	South Dakota Retirement System Dept. of Labor 216 E. Capitol Ave. Pierre, SD 57501
Telephone:	(605) 773-3731
Fax:	(605) 773-3949
Years to become vested:	5 years
Membership:	Total Membership: 48,245 Inactive: 4,185 Vested Inactive: 2,202 Nonvested Inactive: 1,983 = 4% of membership Retired (receiving benefits): Not Available
Value of Inactive Accounts:	Unknown
Special Provisions:	Teachers are included in the South Dakota Retirement System.

PUBLIC EMPLOYEE AND TEACHER RETIREMENT PROGRAMS

TENNESSEE

System:	Tennessee Consolidate Retirement System Dept. of Treasury 10th Floor 1329 Andrew Jackson Bldg. Nashville, TN 37243
Telephone:	(615) 741-7063
Fax:	(615) 532-8725
Years to become vested:	5 years
Membership:	Total Membership: 231,687 Active: 160,000 Inactive: Not Available Vested Inactive: 8,276 Retired (receiving benefits): 60,000
Value of Inactive Accounts:	Unknown

PUBLIC EMPLOYEE AND TEACHER RETIREMENT PROGRAMS

TEXAS

System:	Employees Retirement System Capitol Station P.O. Box 13207 Austin, TX 78711-3207
Telephone:	(512) 476-6431
Fax:	(512) 867-3438
Years to become vested:	5 years
Membership:	Total Membership: 218,357 Active: 161,786 Inactive: 21,212 Vested Inactive: 1,583 Nonvested Inactive: 14,586 = 8% of membership Retired (receiving benefits): 35,359
Value of Inactive Accounts:	$65,685,966
Special Provisions:	The average value of an inactive account is $4,062.

TEXAS

System:	Teachers Retirement System 1000 Red River St. Austin, TX 78701-2698
Telephone:	(512) 397-6480
Fax:	(512) 370-0585
Toll Free:	(800) 223-8778
Years to become vested:	5 years, minimum age for a retiring employee after being vested to collect is 55.
Membership:	Total Membership: 732,000 Active: 600,000 Inactive: Not Available Retired (receiving benefits): 132,000
Value of Inactive Accounts:	Unknown

PUBLIC EMPLOYEE AND TEACHER RETIREMENT PROGRAMS

UTAH

System:	State Retirement Office 540 E. 200 S. Salt Lake City, UT 84102
Telephone:	(801) 366-7700
Fax:	(801) 366-7705
Toll Free:	(800) 365-8772
Years to become vested:	4 to 10 years
Membership:	Total Membership: 131,000 Active: 109,000 Inactive: Not Available Retired (receiving benefits): 22,000
Special Provisions:	Years need to become vested depend on the retirement system in which enrolled.

PUBLIC EMPLOYEE AND TEACHER RETIREMENT PROGRAMS

VERMONT

System:	Retirement Services 133 State St. Montpelier, VT 05633
Telephone:	(802) 828-2305
Fax:	(802) 828-5182
Years to become vested:	5 to 10 years
Membership:	Total Membership: 24,478 Active: 20,452 Inactive: 4,026 Vested Inactive: 823 Nonvested Inactive: 3,203 = 7.64% of membership Retired (receiving benefits): 6,004
Value of Inactive Accounts:	$132,776,072
Special Provisions:	Inactive accounts accrue interest at 5% per annum. The average value of an inactive nonvested account is $32,980.

VERMONT System:	 Teachers Retirement Retirement Services 133 State St. Montpelier, VT 05633
Telephone:	(802) 828-2305 Fax (802) 828-5182
Years to become vested:	10 years
Membership:	Total Membership: 21,107 Active: 12,124 Inactive: 8,983 Vested Inactive: 475 Nonvested Inactive: 792 = 10.9% of membership Retired (receiving benefits): 2,799
Value of Inactive Accounts:	Unknown

PUBLIC EMPLOYEE AND TEACHER RETIREMENT PROGRAMS

VIRGINIA

System:	Virginia Retirement System Field Services Section 1200 E. Main St. P.O. Box 3-X Richmond, VA 23218-0905
Telephone:	(804) 786-3831
Fax:	(804) 371-0613
Toll Free:	(800) 533-4458 in Virginia
Years to become vested:	5 years
Membership:	Total Membership: 340,397 Active: 262,297 Inactive: 78,100
Value of Inactive Accounts:	Unknown
Special Provisions:	Public and Teachers Retirement are combined into this system.

PUBLIC EMPLOYEE AND TEACHER RETIREMENT PROGRAMS

WASHINGTON

System:	Dept. of Retirement 1025 E. Union St. M/S: EF-11 P.O. Box 48380 Olympia, WA 98504-8380
Telephone:	(360) 709-4700
Fax:	(360) 753-3166
Years to become vested:	5 years
Membership:	Total Membership: 248,939 Active: 160,325 Inactive: 88,277 Retired (receiving benefits): 99,070
Value of Inactive Accounts:	Unknown
Special Provisions:	Inactive accounts continue to accrue interest until claimed. The figures above are the results of six different retirement systems.

WASHINGTON

System:	Teachers Retirement System 1025 E. Union St. P.O. Box 48380 Olympia, WA 98504-8380
Telephone:	(360) 709-4700
Fax:	(360) 753-3166
Years to become vested:	5 years
Membership:	Total Membership: 80,171 Active: 52,781 Inactive: 3,883 Retired (receiving benefits): 23,507
Value of Inactive Accounts:	$2,328,000,000
Special Provisions:	Inactive accounts continue to accrue interest until claimed. The figures above are the results of six different retirement systems.

PUBLIC EMPLOYEE AND TEACHER RETIREMENT PROGRAMS

WEST VIRGINIA

System:	State of West Virginia Consolidated Public Retirement Board Capitol Complex, Bldg. 5, Room 1000 Charleston, WV 25305-0720
Telephone:	(304) 558-3570
Fax:	(304) 558-6337
Toll Free:	(800) 642-8509
Years to become vested:	5 years
Membership:	Total Membership: 66,040 Active: 38,792 Inactive: 5,060 Vested Inactive: 2,286 Nonvested Inactive: 2,774 = 23.8% of membership Retired (receiving benefits): 21,514
Value of Inactive Accounts:	$39,449,433
Special Provisions:	Teachers are included in the public retirement system. The average value of an inactive account is $7,750.

PUBLIC EMPLOYEE AND TEACHER RETIREMENT PROGRAMS

WISCONSIN

System:	Dept. of Employee Trust Funds 201 E. Washington Ave. P.O. Box 7931 Madison, WI 53707
Telephone:	(608) 266-3285
Fax:	(608) 267-4549
Years to become vested:	5 years
Membership:	Total Membership: 370,000 Active: 225,000 Inactive: 62,000 Retired (receiving benefits): Unknown
Value of Inactive Accounts:	Unknown

PUBLIC EMPLOYEE AND TEACHER RETIREMENT PROGRAMS

WYOMING

System:	Retirement System Board Division Administration Herschler Bldg. 1st Floor E. Cheyenne, WY 82002
Telephone:	(307) 777-7691
Fax:	(307) 777-5995
Years to become vested:	4 years or 48 contributions
Membership:	Total Membership: 60,500 Active: 32,000 Inactive: 16,000 Vested Inactive: 2,958 Nonvested Inactive: 7,542 = 6% of membership Retired (receiving benefits): 12,500
Value of Inactive Accounts:	$39,000,000
Special Provisions:	Teachers are included in the Public Employee Retirement System.

PUBLIC EMPLOYEE AND TEACHER RETIREMENT PROGRAMS

DISTRICT OF COLUMBIA

System:	D.C. Retirement Board 1400 L St., N.W., Suite 300 Washington, DC 20005
Telephone:	(202) 535-1271
Fax:	(202) 535-1414
Years to become vested:	5 years
Membership:	Total Membership: 21,500 Active: Not Available Inactive: Not Available Retired (receiving benefits): Not Available
Value of Inactive Accounts:	Unknown
Special Provisions:	Teachers are included in the D.C. Retirement Board.

APPENDIX R3

Federal Home Loan Mortgage Guarantors

There are two federal programs which insure mortgages: Federal Housing Authority (FHA) and Housing and Urban Development (HUD). These home loan guaranty agencies were started during the 1940's, '50's and '60's. This Appendix provides you with a sample query letter and contact information for HUD's central Washington DC office and the ten regional offices.

If your target relative purchased his or her home with a government–insured loan, the lender collected the mortgage insurance premium for the entire loan term (25 to 40 years) out of the original proceeds of the mortgage, ***at its inception***. If your relative sold the house before the loan term had expired (with the loan subsequently being paid off), then the original borrower (your relative), or the estate, is entitled to a refund of the unused portion of the original insurance premium. In fact, very few of these loans reach full maturity before being paid off; a substantial pool of unknowing persons are due refunds on their home loan insurance. You may find you are in this pool. Remember, this money does not go out of existence!

If your target is in this situation, gather together necessary documentation on the house involved, and the history of your relative's financial dealings concerning it, and contact the appropriate HUD regional office about the possibility of a loan insurance premium refund. The loan servicing office—the office to which monthly loan payments were made—can provide you with the loan number.

SUGGESTED LETTER TO REGIONAL HUD OFFICE

Date

Your Name
Address
City/State/Zip
Day Phone
Nights/Weekend Phone
Fax

Department of Housing and Urban Development
Region _____ (see Federal Home Loan Mortgage
Guarantors Appendix)

Re: (Account number)

To whom it may concern:

I was the borrower named in the above account number.

That loan was originally scheduled for a term of (25/30/35) years. However that home was sold, and the original insured mortgage was paid off, *before the full term of the loan.*

I would like to receive a rebate on the unused portion of my mortgage insurance premium. Please send me appropriate forms and advise me how to go about getting the correct refund.

Sincerely,

Signed

P.S. Enclosed is my self-addressed stamped envelope.

HUD & FHA

Department of Housing and Urban Development
451 7th St. S.W.
P.O. Box 44372
Washington, DC 20410
Telephone: (202) 401-0388
Fax: (202) 708-0299
Toll Free: (800) 669-9777

Region 1
New England Area
10 Causeway St., Room 375
Boston, MA 02222
Telephone: (617) 565-5234
Fax: (617) 565-6558

Region 2
26 Federal Plaza, Room 3541
New York, NY 10278
Telephone: (212) 264-6500
Fax: (212) 264-0236

Region 3
Wanamaker Bldg.
110 Pennsylvania Sq. E.
Philadelphia, PA 19107
HUD Telephone: (215) 656-0503
HUD Fax: (215) 656-3427
FHA Telephone: (215) 656-0656
FHA Fax: (215) 656-3449

Region 4
75 Spring St. S.W., Room 600
Atlanta, GA 30303
Telephone: (404) 331-5136
Fax: (404) 730-2365

Region 5
77 W. Jackson Blvd., Room 2200
Chicago, IL 60604
Telephone: (312) 353-5680
Fax: (312) 886-2729

Region 6
1600 Throckmorton St.
Fort Worth, TX 76102
Telephone: (817) 885-5401
Fax: (817) 885-5629

Region 7
400 State Ave. Professional Bldg.
Kansas City, KS 66101
Telephone: (913) 551-6838
Fax: (913) 551-5416

Region 8
633 17th St.
1st Interstate Tower N.
Denver, CO 80202
Telephone: (303) 672-5258
Fax: (303) 844-2475
Toll Free: (800) 697-6967
(Support Center D.C.)

Region 9
450 Golden Gate Ave., 9th Floor
San Francisco, CA 94102
Telephone: (415) 436-6550
Fax: (415) 436-6510

Region 10
909 First Ave., Suite 190
Seattle, WA 98104-1000
Telephone: (206) 220-5205
Fax: (206) 220-5206

APPENDIX R4

Railroad Unions

Everyone who has been employed by a railroad has belonged to a railroad union. Depending on the work performed, they would be required to join the related union. Originally there were 16 unions and now there are 14.

If you don't know the local union address where your target lived while employed, use the suggested form letter and the appropriate national headquarters address in this Appendix. You may get a pleasant surprise regarding various benefits available through their union!

If the railroad union your relative belonged to has been terminated, then check with the U.S. Railroad Retirement Board (Appendix R7) for the name of the correct successor union and contact information.

RAILROAD UNIONS

Amalgamated Transit Union
President
5025 Wisconsin Ave. N.W.
Washington, DC 20016
Telephone: (202) 537-1645
Fax: (202) 244-7824

American Railway Supervisors Association
(merged into Brotherhood of Railway Carmen)

American Train Dispatchers Association
President
1401 S. Harlem Ave.
Berwyn, IL 60402
Telephone: (708) 795-5656
Fax: (708) 795-0832

Brotherhood of Maintenance of Way Employees
President
26555 Evergreen Rd., Suite 200
Southfield, MI 48076-4225
Telephone: (810) 948-1010
Fax: (810) 948-7150

Brotherhood of Railroad Signalmen
President
601 Golf Rd., Box U
Mount Prospect, IL 60056
Telephone: (847) 439-3732
Fax: (847) 439-3743

Brotherhood of Railway Carmen of U.S. & Canada
(see American Railway Supervisors Assoc.)

International Association of Mechanics & Aerospace Workers
President
9000 Machinists Place
Upper Marlboro, MD 20772-2687
Telephone: (301) 967-4500
Fax: (301) 967-4590

International Brotherhood of Boilermakers & Blacksmiths
President
753 State Ave.
565 Newbrotherhood Bldg.
Kansas City, KS 66101
Telephone: (913) 371-2640
Fax: (913) 281-8102

International Brotherhood of Electrical Workers
President
1125 15th, N.W.
Washington, DC 20005
Telephone: (202) 833-7000
Fax: (202) 467-6316

International Conference of Firemen & Oilers
President
1100 Circle 75 Parkway N.W.
Suite 350
Atlanta, GA 30339
Telephone: (770) 933-9104
Fax: (770) 933-0361

Joint Council Dining Car Employees
President
1130 S. Wabash Ave., #405
Chicago, IL 60605-2305
Telephone: (312) 427-4373
Fax: (312) 427-2108

National Marine Engineers Benefit Association of U.S.
1150 17th St. N. W., Suite 700
Washington, DC 20036
Telephone: (202) 466-7060
Fax: (202) 872-0912

National Transportation Supervisors Association
President
6 Wendy Lane
E. Northport, NY 11731
Terminated

RAILROAD UNIONS

Railway Labor Executives Association
President
400 N. Capitol St., N.W.
Suite 850
Washington, DC 20001
Telephone: (202) 737-1541
Fax: (202) 783-3107

Sheet Metal Workers' International Association
President
1750 New York Ave., N.W.
Washington, DC 20006
Telephone: (202) 783-5880
Fax: (202) 662-0894

Transportation Communications Union
President
3 Research Place
Rockville, MD 20850
Telephone: (301) 948-4910
Fax: (301) 948-1872

United Railway Supervisors Association
President
1204 S. 12th St.
Altoona, PA 16602
Terminated

United Transportation Union
President
14600 Detroit Ave.
Cleveland, OH 44107
Telephone: (216) 228-9400 ext. 262
Fax: (216) 228-5755

APPENDIX R5

Non–Railroad Unions

For railroad unions, see Railroad Unions Appendix R4. If you discover that your relative held long–term membership in any other kind of union, you should make some vigorous inquiries about his/her membership status. There are at least three reasons for this:

- Almost all union members have group life insurance policies with the premiums paid by their employers. When a new union contract is successfully negotiated, the face amount of this life insurance policy generally increases. This has happened many times since 1935.
- Many unions have their own retirement plans so check to see if all benefits have been paid to the union member's family. Be sure to ask for a complete copy of the member's benefit file. This is your right.
- Unions may be helpful in your search for work–related benefits waiting to be discovered.

Once you've identified your target's trade, contact the appropriate local union (usually listed in the local telephone book) with your relative's name, Social Security number, and probable union membership dates. Ask for a copy of his or her pension file.

John Evans belonged to the Brotherhood of Electrical Workers for seventeen years. He died suddenly at age 57. Over these seventeen years with several employers, John contributed, along with those employers, to three different retirement benefit packages. At the time of his death, John was estranged from his wife and daughter. Because communications with his heirs had broken down, four years elapsed between John's death and the discovery by his heirs of a retirement account and of the proceeds from two life insurance contracts. The retirement benefits continue to increase in value to this day because his widow is still alive.

APPENDIX R6

Pension Benefit Guaranty Corporation

The Pension Benefit Guaranty Corporation (PBGC) protects the retirement incomes of more than 41 million American workers—one of every three working persons—in about 67,000 defined benefit pension plans. A defined benefit plan provides a specified monthly benefit at retirement, often based on a combination of salary and years of service. *Many companies have gone out of business so people assume that their retirement is gone as well ...* ***not so****. In many cases, their retirement is taken over and paid by this federal agency.*

PBGC is currently anticipating they will pay pension benefits to 392,000 individuals. At the present time 182,000 individuals receive retirement benefits and 210,000 will receive retirement benefits when they reach retirement age in their specific plan.

PBGC currently is responsible for 2,094 terminated retirement plans. Over the past two years there has been a 20% increase in the people receiving benefits and a 10% increase in the number of plans being covered. During 1995, PBGC paid 763 million dollars to eligible retirees.

If you or your target relative worked for a company that went out of business, you should contact the office listed below to see if they are or were covered by PBGC:

Technical Assistance Division
Pension Benefit Guaranty Corporation
1200 K Street, N.W.
Washington, DC 20005
(800) 400-7242 (Technical Division).

APPENDIX R7

U.S. Railroad Retirement Board

This Appendix will provide you with the local railroad office handling the entire retirement account for any railroad employee. The railroad employees are indexed by Social Security numbers.

Once an employee is vested by having 10 years of service, including military service, then there will be a retirement account which may include a lump sum benefit if your target died prior to full life expectancy. In 1992, the average lump sum payment was $4,200. So pay attention and be persistent.

SUGGESTED RAILROAD RETIREMENT LETTER

Date

Your Name
Address
City/State/Zip
Day Phone
Nights/Weekend Phone
Fax

Railroad Retirement
Address (see U.S. Railroad Retirement Board Appendix R7)

Re: Name
Address
Social Security Number
Estimated years of Railroad Employment

Dear Director,

I am requesting information regarding the above person. According to the records I have reconstructed, he/she was employed by the (name of railroad) during this time (specify time period). The purpose of my inquiry is to reconstruct the assets of my (state relationship).

I have enclosed documentation that will enable you to give me this information. (See Enclosure)

Please contact me if you need any additional information before you may release the requested information.

Sincerely,

Signed

☛ Enclose as much documentation as possible along with a self-addressed stamped envelope:

- proof of bloodline relationship (birth certificate or marriage license)
- court order stating you are executor or guardian
- death certificate
- copy of will
- power of attorney

Offices of the U.S. Railroad Retirement Board

Headquarters
844 North Rush Street
Chicago, IL 60611-2092

Office of Legislative Affairs
1310 G Street, NW Suite 500
Washington, DC 20005-3004

Regional Offices and Regional Directors

Region 1	101 Marietta St., Ste. 2304	Atlanta, GA 30323-3001	Patricia Lawson	404/331-2691
Region 2	1421 Cherry St., Ste. 670	Philadelphia, PA 19102-1413	Richard D. Baird	215/656-6947
Region 3	1301 Clay St., Ste. 390N	Oakland, CA 94612-5227	Louis E. Austin	510/637-2982

Where Full and Part-Time Service is Provided

STATE	ZIP CODE	CITY	ADDRESS	REP	TELEPHONE
Alabama	35203-1126	Birmingham	Medical Forum Bldg, Rm. 426, 950 22nd St. North	Michael A. Core	205/731-0019
Arkansas	72211-4113	Little Rock	1200 Cherry Brook Drive, Suite 500	Ruby Bland	501/324-5241
Arizona	85002-3206	Phoenix	USPO Fed. Bldg., Room 221, 522 N. Central, P.O. Box 13206	Gale Bowman	602/379-4841
California	94612-5220	Oakland	Oakland Fed Bld., Ste. 392N, 1301 Clay St.	Thomas Hamm	510/637-2973
California	95821-4909	Sacramento	2985 Fulton Ave.	Daniel L. Williams	916/979-2055
California	91790-2726	West Covina	Building B, Ste. 360, 1515 W. Cameron Ave.	David J. Coughlan	818/814-8844
Colorado	80201-8869	Denver	177 Custom House, 20th and Stout Sts., P.O. Box 8869	Jacqueline R. Redden	303/844-4311
Connecticut	06511-5865	New Haven	414 Chapel St., Rm. 203	Vacant	203/773-2044
DC	20005-3004	Washington	1310 G St. NW, Ste. 520	Michael McCool	202/272-7707
Florida	33301-1946	Ft. Lauderdale	Fed Bldg, Rm. 407, 299 E. Broward Blvd.	Vacant	954/356-7372
Florida	32202-4412	Jacksonville	Bennett Fed Bldg, Rm. 315, 400 West Bay St., Box 35026	Henry G. Crowe	904/232-2546
Florida	33602-3953	Tampa	Fed Annex Bldg, Rm. 100, 501 Polk St.	Virginia W. Earl	813/228-2695
Georgia	30323-3001	Atlanta	101 Marietta St., Ste. 2306	Lyndon J. Lang	404/331-2841
Georgia	31412-8728	Savannah	Fed Comp Bldg No 2, Rm. B-105, 125 Barnard St., P.O. Box 8728	Katharine L. Ketenheim	912/652-4267
Illinois	60611-2092	Chicago	844 N. Rush St., Rm. 112	Robert J. Eggert	312/751-4500
Illinois	62525-1308	Decatur	132 S. Water St., Ste. 517, P.O. Box 1308	James L. McFadden	217/423-9747
Illinois	60434-0457	Joliet	101 N. Joliet St., P.O. Box 457	Michael A. Vidmar	815/740-2101
Illinois	61265-1367	Moline	Heritage Place, Ste. 517, 1515 5th Ave.	Gerald L. Stebbins	309/764-0028
Indiana	46802-3435	Fort Wayne	Fed. Bldg, Rm. 3161, 1300 S. Harrison St.	Shawn L. Stiver	219/423-1361
Indiana	46204-3530	Indianapolis	The Meridian Centre, Ste. 303, 50 S. Meridian	Robert Braltman	317/226-6111
Iowa	50309-2182	Des Moines	Fed. Bldg, Rm. 921, 210 Walnut St.	Carol Laird	515/284-4344
Kansas	67202-1802	Wichita	Market Centre, Rm. 125, 155 N. Market St.	William O. Johnson	316/269-7161
Kentucky	40201-3705	Louisville	Theatre Bldg, Ste. 301, 629 S. 4th Ave., P.O. Box 3705	Gene Gulhan	502/582-5208
Louisiana	70130-3394	New Orleans	501 Magazine St., Rm. 1045	Pamela Meyer	504/589-2597
Louisiana	71105-5216	Shreveport	1724 E. 70th St., Rm. C.	Leonard Parrish	318/676-3022

Offices of the U.S. Railroad Retirement Board

Where Full and Part-Time Service is Provided

STATE	ZIP CODE	CITY	ADDRESS	REP	TELEPHONE
Maine	04101-4157	Portland	Court Square Bldg, Rm. 210, 66 Pearl St.	Doreen Morrill	207/780-3542
Maryland	21201-2803	Baltimore	300 W. Pratt Bldg, Rm. 260, 300 W. Pratt St.	Casey N. Gresey	410/962-2550
Massachusetts	02208-2448	Boston	121 High St., Rm. 301, P.O. Box 2448	Raymond P. Fecteau	617/424-5790
Michigan	48226-2596	Detroit	McNamara Fed Bldg., Ste 1990, 477 W. Michigan Ave.	Michael A. Jansen	313/226-6221
Minnesota	55802-1392	Duluth	Fed Bldg, Rm. 125, 515 W. First St.	Ron Ellefson	218/720-5301
Minnesota	55101-1631	St. Paul	First Trust Center, Ste. 195, 180 E. 5th St.	Brian P. Running	612/290-3491
Mississippi	39269-1099	Jackson	McCoy Fed Bldg, Rm. 1003, 100 W. Capitol St.	Claude White	601/965-4229
Missouri	64106-2882	Kansas City	Fed Bldg, Rm. 258, 601 E. 12th St.	Daniel H. Hauser	816/426-5884
Missouri	63103-2818	St. Louis	Young Fed Bldg, Rm. 1213, 1222 Spruce St.	David Grogg	314/539-6220
Montana	59103-1351	Billings	GSA Office Tower, Rm. 101, 2900 4th Ave. N, P.O. Box 1351	Judith R. Bell	406/247-7375
Nebraska	68101-1415	Omaha	Fed Office Bldg, Rm. 1011, 106 S. 15th, P.O. Box 1415	Lawrence Zwart	402/221-4641
New Jersey	07102-2518	Newark	Rodino Fed. Bldg, Rm. 1435B, 970 Broad St.	Meredith L. Rogers	201/645-3990
New Mexico	87108-1520	Albuquerque	300 San Mateo NE, Rm. 401	Barbara E. Aylalan	505/262-6405
New York	12201-0529	Albany	O'Brien Fed. Bldg, Rm. 264, Clinton Ave. & Pearl St., P.O. Box 529	Daniel M. Layton	518/431-4004
New York	14202-2394	Buffalo	Dulsid Fed. Bldg, Rm. 1106, 111 W. Huron St.	Philip C. Dissek	716/551-4141
New York	11590-5119	Westbury	1400 Old Country Road, Ste. 204	Marle Baran	516/334-5940
New York	10278-0105	New York	Fed Bldg, Rm. 3404, 26 Federal Plaza	Rose I. Jonas	212/264-9820
No. Carolina	28205-6903	Charlotte	Mart Ofc Bldg, Rm. AA-405, 800 Briar Creek Rd.	Barry J. Hoffman	704/344-6118
No. Dakota	58107-0383	Fargo	USPO Bldg, Rm. 343, 657 2nd Ave. N., P.O. Box 383	John J. Ceterski	701/239-5117
Ohio	45202-4439	Cincinnati	CBLD Center, Rm. 201, 36 E. 7th St.	Jeffrey F. Szabo	513/684-3188
Ohio	44199-2093	Cleveland	Celebrezze Fed. Bldg, Rm. 907, 1240 E. 9th St.	Kevin B. McCrone	216/522-4053
Ohio	43215-3003	Columbus	131 North High St., Rm. 630	Shirley M. Berrier	614/469-5562
Ohio	43604-1593	Toledo	Fed Bldg, Rm. 321, 234 Summit St.	Sharon Wisniewski	419/259-7442
Ohio	44503-1423	Youngtown	Federal Forum, Rm. M-11-B, 20 Federal Plaza West	Ronald M. Kuzma	330/746-6338
Oklahoma	73102-3426	Oklahoma City	215 McGee Ave., Rm. 130	Dorotha Cezar	405/2314771
Oregon	97204-2807	Portland	Green-Wyatt Fed Bldg, Rm. 377, 1220 SW 3rd Ave.	Judy Oxborrow	503/326-2143
Pennsylvania	16603-0990	Altoona	615 Howard Ave., Rm. 209, P.O. Box 990	Roger Templeton	814/946-3601
Pennsylvania	17108-1697	Harrisburg	Fed Bldg, Rm. 504, 228 Walnut St., P.O. Box 11697	Joan M. Fields	717/782-4490
Pennsylvania	19102-1493	Philadelphia	1421 Cherry St., Ste. 660	Edward M. Chochrek	215/656-6993
Pennsylvania	15222-1311	Pittsburgh	Kossman Bldg, Rm. 1130, 100 Forbes Ave.	Michael L. Bauer	412/644-2696

Offices of the U.S. Railroad Retirement Board

Where Full and Part-Time Service is Provided

STATE	ZIP CODE	CITY	ADDRESS	REP	TELEPHONE
Pennsylvania	18508-1121	Scranton	Sinlawa Plaza II, Route #6, 717 Scranton Carbondale Hwy	Robert C. Ralston	717/346-5774
Tennessee	37902-2543	Knoxville	Duncan Fed Bldg, Rm. 126, 710 Locust St.	Sheila P. Gary	615/545-4500
Tennessee	38103-1884	Memphis	Davis Fed Bldg, Rm. 109, 167 N. Main St.	Judith M. Welch	901/544-3274
Tennessee	37228-1813	Nashville	233 Cumberland Bend, Ste. 206	Suzanne Givan	615/736-5131
Texas	76102-0420	Fort Worth	819 Taylor St., Rm. 10G02, P.O. Box 17420	Barbara Gettman	817/334-2638
Texas	77002-8051	Houston	Leland Fed Bldg, Ste. 845, 1919 Smith	Margie M. Grimes	713/209-3045
Utah	84138-1102	Salt Lake City	125 S. State St., Rm. 1205	Frank Kurek	801/524-5725
Virginia	23219-2313	Richmond	Ste 232, 704 E. Franklin St.	David P. Griffith	804/771-2997
Virginia	23510-1811	Norfolk	Fed Bldg, Rm. 616, 200 Granby Mall	Andronike K. Seamans	804/441-3335
Virginia	24002-0270	Roanoke	First Cambell Sq., Suite 460, 210 1st St. SW, P.O. Box 270	Fred E. Way	540/857-2335
Washington	98004-5901	Bellevue	Pacific First Plaza, Ste. 201, 155 108th Ave. NE	Virgie Seaton	206/553-5483
Washington	99201-1081	Spokane	US Courthouse, Rm. 492, W. 920 Riverside Ave.	Nancy M. Hand	509/353-2795
West Virginia	25721-2153	Huntington	New Fed Bldg, Rm. 112, 640 4th Ave., P.O. Box 2153	William M. Stevens	304/529-5561
Wisconsin	53203-2211	Milwaukee	Reuss Plaza, Ste. 1300, 310 W. Wisconsin Ave.	Thomas P. Hammersley	414/297-3961

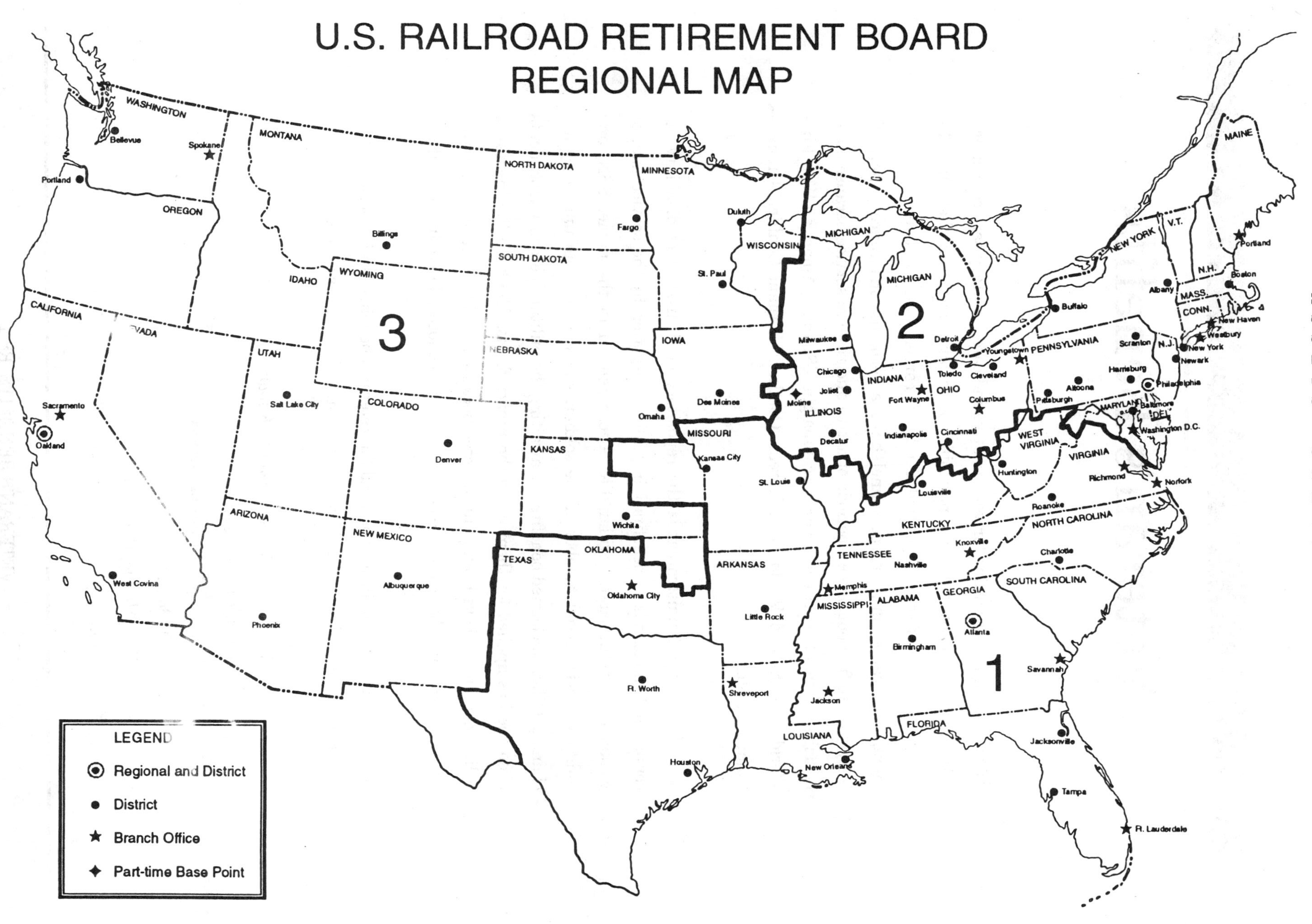
U.S. RAILROAD RETIREMENT BOARD
REGIONAL MAP
LEGEND
Regional and District
District
Branch Office
Part-time Base Point
1
2
3
WASHINGTON
Bellevue
Spokane
Portland
OREGON
MONTANA
Billings
IDAHO
WYOMING
CALIFORNIA
Sacramento
Oakland
West Covina
UTAH
Salt Lake City
COLORADO
Denver
ARIZONA
Phoenix
NEW MEXICO
Albuquerque
NORTH DAKOTA
Fargo
SOUTH DAKOTA
NEBRASKA
Omaha
KANSAS
Wichita
OKLAHOMA
Oklahoma City
TEXAS
Ft. Worth
Houston
MINNESOTA
Duluth
St. Paul
IOWA
Des Moines
MISSOURI
Kansas City
St. Louis
ARKANSAS
Little Rock
Shreveport
LOUISIANA
New Orleans
WISCONSIN
Milwaukee
MICHIGAN
MICHIGAN
Detroit
ILLINOIS
Chicago
Joliet
Moline
Decatur
INDIANA
Fort Wayne
Indianapolis
OHIO
Toledo
Cleveland
Columbus
Cincinnati
Youngstown
PENNSYLVANIA
Pittsburgh
Altoona
Harrisburg
Scranton
Philadelphia
NEW YORK
Buffalo
Albany
New York
Newark
N.J.
V.T.
N.H.
MAINE
Portland
MASS.
Boston
CONN.
New Haven
Westbury
MARYLAND
Baltimore
DEL.
Washington D.C.
WEST VIRGINIA
Huntington
VIRGINIA
Richmond
Roanoke
Norfolk
KENTUCKY
Louisville
NORTH CAROLINA
Charlotte
TENNESSEE
Knoxville
Nashville
Memphis
SOUTH CAROLINA
GEORGIA
Atlanta
Savannah
ALABAMA
Birmingham
MISSISSIPPI
Jackson
FLORIDA
Jacksonville
Tampa
Ft. Lauderdale

APPENDIX R8

Veteran's Benefits

If the search target outline for your relative indicates military service, you will certainly want to investigate the possibility of unclaimed veteran's benefits. This is especially true if your target had a military career spanning twenty years or more; most career military personnel have a term life insurance policy. It's important to find out precise periods of active and reserve service because many benefits are tied to particular wars or campaigns—Spanish–American War, First World War, Second World War, Korean Conflict, Vietnam Conflict, Grenada Campaign, etc.

The Veteran's Administration is the repository of thousands of disability accounts and thousands of benefits lying fallow, forgotten by the service man or woman who returned to civilian life. These remain in the name, SSN, and military service serial number of the soldier, sailor, or airman until they are claimed. Other unclaimed benefits are awaiting the military person's dependents if no one has applied for them using the *proper forms.* The term life insurance policy mentioned above is often uncollected because a valid death certificate was never presented to the insurance carrier who may be located in a distant state.

If your target has significant potential for veteran's benefits (and especially if he or she has a disability) you may want to buy the following very useful book:

What Every Veteran Should Know
Patrick L. Murphy, Director
Veterans Information Service
P.O. Box 111
East Moline, IL 61244
$10.

There are two military insurance programs you should be aware of: (1) Servicemen's Group Life Insurance (SGLI) covers active duty personnel (2)Veteran's Group Life Insurance covers those who have gotten out of the service. Over three million current or former servicemen and women are covered by policies in these programs. Prudential Company of America participates in both programs, so if you have specific questions regarding your target, you should contact them:

Prudential Company of America
Servicemen's Group Life Insurance
OSGLI
213 Washington Street
Newark, NJ 07102–2999
Voice: (800) 419–1473
Fax: (201) 643–8723

It is this author's hope that over time our concerted efforts will help make the Veteran's Administration more responsive, proactive, and user friendly in dealing with its constituency.

Veterans who are computer literate take note:
http://www.fedworld.gov/veteran.htm is an extremely well-organized "home page." Someone in the federal service, or their contractor, really had his or her head on straight in its design. This home page is very logically put together, easy to navigate in and a real pleasure to peruse. Click on *Department of Veterans Affairs*, then *Benefits, Veterans Benefits*. In this section *Pension* and *Life Insurance* (featuring Serviceman's Group Life Insurance and Veteran's Group Life Insurance) may be of interest. On the same level as *Veterans Benefits* there is also *Benefits for Survivors*.

The Internet is all too often a jumble of disorganized, if interesting, information. This valuable collection of information is what the Internet should be. And it should speed up your search for hidden assets a great deal if your target relative was ever in the military.

APPENDIX R9

Cooperatives

More than 47,000 cooperatives—"co–ops"—have been established over the past sixty years and millions of Americans have been members of them. These institutions were started by the federal government, mostly in the 1930's and mostly to help small farmers survive. Some cooperatives were established to cheaply buy supplies the farmer needed; others, to sell the goods the farmer produced. There are fuel cooperatives, tobacco cooperatives, electrical, telephone, etc.

If your target relative was ever involved in agriculture or food distribution, or lived in a rural setting, you should make a special effort to find out what cooperatives were operating in his or her area at that time and to see whether your target had a patronage or capital account with one or more of those cooperatives. These capital credit accounts amount to between 10% and 15% of every purchase the member made. If they traded with the cooperative for say twenty years, that could have accumulated to a sizeable sum! This was only one aspect of cooperative membership benefits; there were others. If your target was in such an organization and had such an account, it still exists under his or her name or Social Security number. The policy of most cooperatives is to pay out the capital account in a lump sum, to the estate, upon proof of the member's death.

We can't possibly list these 47,000 past and present cooperatives. Contact the appropriate county agent (in the counties in which your relative lived or worked) for a list of cooperatives to which he or she might possibly have belonged. Ask for the name, specific purpose, address, and telephone number of each such cooperative. Here is some further information on two of the main players in this unknown asset possibility.

Rural Electrical Cooperatives

Federal legislation in the mid–1930's provided for rural electrification. Low–cost loans paid for construction and maintenance of the electrical transmission facilities. Immense public works projects built the giant dams to house the generators. In most cases each person or family who paid for electricity through one of these cooperatives was given a "patronage capital account." Into that account went ten percent of their monthly payment, designated a benefit to be paid at death to their heirs.

The current value of all these patronage capital accounts amounts to some $55 million. This amounts to around $500 per cooperative member that is payable, in total, upon the death of that member. There are wrinkles. Some cooperatives' boards of directors allowed members to withdraw some portion of their accounts while the members were still alive. If there has been no contact between the electric co–op and your relative for more than five years, disposition of the money in his or her account has gone according to applicable state law.

Start your search with the county agent. Then use our suggested form letter.

Rural Telephone Cooperatives

These utility cooperatives are very much like their electrical counterparts. They serve to provide telephone service to rural American homes and there are currently about 5.5 million members of about 280 telephone cooperatives in forty–three states.

Normally about 15% of the monthly telephone bill goes into the patronage account. There is currently a total of $420 million in combined patronage capital and stock. Since only about 30% of the telephone systems operate as cooperatives, the ratepayer may have stock instead of a patronage capital account. Still, the average patronage account amounts to about $500, about the same as in the case of the electrical cooperatives.

To check on the status of your relative's membership in a rural telephone cooperative, contact the appropriate county extension agent and give him or her both your identifying information (name, address, telephone numbers) and that of your target relative, including SSN.

SUGGESTED LETTER TO A COOPERATIVE

Date

Your Full Name
Address
City/State/Zip
Day Phone
Night/Weekend Phone
Fax

Name of Cooperative
Address (see Cooperative Appendix)

Re: Name
Social Security Number
Last Known Address
City/State/Zip
Date of Death

To whom it may concern:

Please provide me with patronage account balances on the account named above. It is my understanding he/she paid for Electrical/Telephone (or other cooperatives) service at your cooperative from (year)____ to (year)____.

I would be happy to provide you with a certified copy of a death certificate and proof of my relationship if needed. Please contact me at the address/telephone number listed above if further information or fees are needed in order to obtain a copy of the patronage account.

Sincerely,

Signed

☛ As required, enclose one or more of the following with a self-addressed stamped envelope:

- proof of bloodline relationship
- power of attorney
- court order stating you are the executor or guardian
- death certificate
- copy of will

APPENDIX R10

Insurance

This Appendix provides you with tips on where your relative's unclaimed assets may reside within various kinds of insurance policies, policies containing some of the most substantial assets to be found in estates. While many heirs look only for paid–up life insurance policies, assets are often to be found in other types. Here are the major types and what to look for.

Life Insurance

Even lapsed life insurance policies should be investigated. There may have been a "waiver of premium," a provision for automatic payment of the premium in the event of debilitating illness. Unfortunately, and especially in the case of term life insurance policies (for which there is no cash value), records of such policies have been known to "mysteriously" disappear from the computer records of the insurance company. Then your best bet is to establish the status and provisions of your relative's policy, at the time of his or her death, by interviewing the responsible insurance agent.

In case your relative borrowed against the value of the whole life policy at some time, and never paid back that loan, the actual death benefit will be less than the policy face amount. In the same stack of papers with life insurance policies also be on the lookout for *annuities*. These too have policies and also have some sort of report which should have been mailed to your relative at least annually. This report will give the value of the annuity at that time, and give you clues as to what might still remain.

Automobile Insurance

If your relative was killed in an automobile accident, or seriously injured in one during the last ten years of his or her life, there is a possibility of entitlement to automobile insurance benefits. Investigations and negotiations following serious accidents often take years and your injured relative may have been in no condition to keep up with the turns and twists of the legal system. As heir, you must make it your business to get to the bottom of any such accident.

Start by getting the accident report (see Accident Reports Appendix S8). From it you should be able to determine if any of the following pertain:

- If your relative's car was financed, a credit life insurance policy would pay off the car loan in the event of death.
- If insurance claims are still pending, your relative's estate may ultimately be a beneficiary of any liability judgement regarding injury, death, or property damage.
- One or another of the insurance companies involved may pay the estate the full value of your target relative's wrecked car.
- Your relative's estate may be entitled to a refund on the unused portion of the automobile insurance premium.

Health Insurance

As recounted in Chapter 2, bereavement is a difficult time to plow through hospital and medical bills, and corresponding insurance claims, to try to make sense of them. But it's your obligation to accomplish this onerous chore sooner rather than later. There are two main circumstances you should be on the lookout for.

If your relative was ill for some extended time, it is highly possible that physician and hospital bills were paid from his or her checking account *prior to submission of those bills to the insurance company*. As heir, you have every right to put in a claim on behalf of the estate and to receive back whatever portion of those medical expenses the insurance company should have covered.

You should also check to see whether the hospital might have been overpaid. Occasionally the same bill is paid by *both* the patient and the insurance company. Medical insurance billing practices and procedures are very complicated; double payment happens fairly often. And the amounts involved can be formidable. Not at all an asset to ignore.

Homeowner's Insurance

Sometimes unscrupulous persons steal items from the household of the terminally ill or recently deceased owner. Servants are by no means the only possible suspects; often "respectable" friends, relatives, and professionals take this opportunity to fill their pockets—or the beds of their pickups. You should carefully examine your relative's homeowner's policy to see if there is an itemized list of household goods—especially the smaller valuable and easy to steal items such as jewelry—or some other record of holdings. If you don't find such a list, ask the insurance agent responsible; he/she may have it. When you have found or reconstructed such a list of possessions, match it with the inventory of objects actually found. Then submit a claim for the missing items.

It might happen that your ill or debilitated relative was not able to maintain and safeguard his or her property against such hazards as wind, water damage, or fire. By the same token, that elderly or bedridden relative was in no position to submit a claim for reimbursement of those losses. You now have to do this for the estate. Request the necessary forms. In any case in which you need clarification on statutes of limitations, or any interpretation of coverage, don't hesitate to contact the state insurance commissioner (see State Insurance Regulators Appendix S14). You are especially vulnerable to insurance companies' interpretations of their policies when you are from out of state, far removed from the scene. Don't be put off by small obstacles.

GLOSSARY

Nothing I have written should be regarded as a legal definition. To see what the law has to say on the meanings of these terms, consult a legal dictionary or an attorney.

Actuarial Tables. Statistical tables of life expectancy put together by the insurance industry to compute insurance risk and premiums. These tables determine the cost of life insurance.

Adoptive Records. Legal records (always executed by a court of law) altering parental ties.

Annuity. An investment made by a retirement system or insurance company from which one receives fixed payments for a lifetime or for a set number of years.

Beneficiary. Person designated by formal contract to receive cash benefits from a life insurance policy, retirement account, or residual lump sum benefit.

Birth Certificate. A legal recorded document verifying name, birth date, sex, place of birth, and parents' names.

Bloodline. The direct line of descent established by birth rather than by marriage.

Cooperatives. User-financed and often user-operated businesses that were created beginning in 1935 to increase buying power, provide new services and control costs of services usually to rural residences and businesses. Examples are Rural Electric and Telephone Co-ops.

Death Benefits. Money paid to a deceased person's stipulated beneficiary or estate.

Death Certificate. A legal document confirming death by name, location, Social Security number, and circumstances surrounding the death. It is witnessed and signed by a legally authorized county official.

Disability Waiver of Premium. A rider on a life insurance policy providing that the insurer forego premium payments in the event the insured is shown to be disabled (therefore unable to earn income). With this rider, the life insurance remains in force. Usually this rider requires an additional premium.

Divorce Decree. A legal record of dissolution of a marriage as determined by the county court administration.

Double Indemnity Life Insurance. A rider on life insurance calling for payment of twice the face amount of the policy upon proof of accidental death of the insured.

Estate. All of one's possessions, including all real property and debts, left at death.

Group Life Insurance. Insurance (usually term insurance) purchased by a group of persons (such as union members), often at reduced individual rates.

Heir. One who inherits or is entitled by law or by terms of a will to inherit the estate of another.

Individual Retirement Account (IRA). A deferred tax savings account set up by the individual through a stockbroker, banker, or financial institution. It is up to the individual to keep records on this type investment.

Interest Accrual. Money paid on principal at a specified rate of interest.

Keogh Plan. A tax-deferred savings plan designed for self-employed individuals.

Lapsed Life Insurance Policies. Insurance policies which are no longer in force due to non-payment of premiums while the insured is still alive. (Premiums are not required after death!)

GLOSSARY

Lump Sum Death Benefit. A final payment paid out of remaining retirement funds, usually paid upon proof of death of the member. This benefit often comes into play when the fund member has not lived to retirement age or has not reached life expectancy age.

Marriage License. A legal document establishing marriage between a man and a woman. The document includes their full names (including the woman's maiden name), ages, location of wedding, witnesses to the event. It is recorded in the county where the marriage took place.

Ordinary Life Insurance. This is the most expensive form of life insurance. Payment of premiums allows cash value to build up.

Patronage Accounts. Accounts set up by cooperatives for all, or a certain class, of their members (patrons). Credits to these patronage accounts are often determined as a percentage (often 10% or 15%) of the members' purchases. Upon proof of the death of a member, most coops pay that member's estate the total balance of his patronage account held over twenty years.

Pension. Money set aside through contributions made by an employee or employer, or both, during the employee's working years. This money usually increases in value according to the investment success of the pension plan. This money is distributed according to the plan's rules, usually going to ex-employees over a designated retirement age.

Personal Representative. The person designated to conduct the legal and financial business of an estate.

Statute of Limitations. A statute setting a time limit beyond which an asset cannot be recovered from a public or private holder.

Term Life Insurance. Life insurance valid for a specified number of years (the term). This is generally the least expensive life insurance and has no cash value.

Undistributed Annuity Balance. Residual value in an annuity left after the death of the payee. As specified in the annuity contract, the balance is paid to a named beneficiary.

Vestment. A fixed right, granted to an employee under a pension plan, which entitles that person to retirement benefits according to the specific retirement program and its rules. Once vestment is attained, all pension plan contributions are frozen until retirement age is reached.

Will. A legal instrument stating how a person wishes his/her possessions to be distributed to named individuals or charities upon his/her death.

About the author:

DAVID FOLSOM WILL HELP YOU TAP INTO UNCLAIMED MONEY WORTH BILLIONS!!

David Folsom is a pioneer in leading people to lost money they never even knew existed. Many of his friends and readers have collected thousands of dollars from their deceased relatives' pension funds, insurance policies, etc. By monitoring their assets searches, as well as from his own experience, Dave is constantly developing improved strategies and techniques to help Americans across the country discover lost or forgotten assets to which they are entitled. His expertise will help you simplify and systematize your assets search to make it as productive as possible.

Dave's efforts have been the rave of such talk shows as "The Oprah Winfrey Show" and "Smart Money"; he has also appeared on NBC and CNBC. He is one of this country's foremost experts in inheritance and unclaimed assets discovery.

ORDER FORM

PHONE ORDERS

TOLL FREE
800 286-5669

MAIL ORDERS

TWO DOT PRESS
P.O. BOX 21868
BILLINGS, MT 59104

Please send me:

QUANTITY | AMOUNT

____ Book(s): *Assets Unknown: How to Find Money You Didn't Know You Had,* 2nd Edition
$28.45 (U.S. funds only, includes U.S. shipping) $______

____ Booklet(s): *How To Find Money You Didn't Know You Had!*
Condensation of the book *Assets Unknown*
$11.95 (U.S. funds only, includes U.S. shipping) $______

TOTAL $______

PAYMENT METHOD

☐ Check (*make check payable to* TWO DOT PRESS)

Credit Card:

☐ VISA ☐ MasterCard ☐ DISCOVER ☐ AMERICAN EXPRESS

Card number ______________________ Expires __________

Name on card ______________________

______________________ NAME (please print or type)

______________________ AREA CODE + PHONE NUMBER

______________________ MAILING ADDRESS

____

______________________ CITY, STATE, ZIP CODE

______________________ SIGNATURE

__________ DATE